Al Frank's
New Prudent Speculator

Al Frank's
New Prudent Speculator

The Master of Value Investing Shows You How to Pick Winning Stocks

Al Frank

McGraw-Hill

New York   San Francisco   Washington, D.C.   Auckland   Bogotá
Caracas   Lisbon   London   Madrid   Mexico City   Milan
Montreal   New Delhi   San Juan   Singapore
Sydney   Tokyo   Toronto

This publication is designed to provide accurate and
authoritative information in regard to the subject matter
covered. It is sold with the understanding that neither the
author or the publisher is engaged in rendering legal, accounting,
or other professional service. If legal advice or other expert
assistance is required, the services of a competent professional
person should be sought.

*From a Declaration of Principles jointly adopted by a Committee
of the American Bar Association and a Committee of Publishers.*

Dust jacket photograph by *Judith Gordon*

McGraw-Hill

A Division of The *McGraw·Hill* Companies

Library of Congress Cataloging-in-Publication Data

Frank, Al.
    Al Frank's new prudent speculator: the master of value investing
shows you how to pick winning stocks/Al Frank.—Rev. ed.
      p. cm.
    Includes index.
    ISBN 1–55738–873–3
    1. Stocks. 2. Investments. 3. Speculation.   I. Frank, Al..
Prudent speculator. II. Title.
HG4661.F69   1996
332.64'5—dc20
                                        95–23360

Printed in the United States of America
5 6 7 8 9 0 BS 2 1 0 9 8

This book is dedicated to Victoria Baldwin,
my wife, best friend, and life partner, and
John Buckingham, my business partner.
Without their encouragement, support, and direct involvement,
I could not have written this book.

Contents

Preface

Information is not knowledge and knowledge is not wisdom. Information requires interpretation and integration with our belief and knowledge systems to become knowledge. Thereafter, wisdom requires critical thinking and considerations perhaps beyond logic, coupled with prudent action carefully reviewed over many years.

When I wrote *The Prudent Speculator: Al Frank on Investing* six years ago, I had 12 years of "professional" experience, plus a few more as an amateur. I thought I understood most of the important things to know about speculating with stocks and the stock market. Happily, I was fortunate to see early on that the concept of value, however ambiguous, was a valid notion and an operationally definable guide. The cliché "Buy low, sell high" is a verity—a great truth—even if it leads to the question of what is low and what is high.

Curiously, experience and practice have shown that determining high and low stock prices, although a critical component, is perhaps the least difficult aspect of successful profitability in the stock market. I was convinced of this six years ago, and I am even more convinced of it today. True, conditions change, and the absolute numbers of today are quite different from those of even a few years ago. For instance, 1,000 advancing issues on the New York Stock Exchange on any given day was a big deal when there were only 2,000 or fewer issues listed. At present, with over 3,200 issues listed, we see days with both 1,000 advancing and 1,000 declining issues on the same day.

I believe the philosopher Hegel said that changes in quantity can result in changes of quality. Changes in temperature can convert water from a solid (ice) to a liquid to a gas (vapor). In the case of the stock market, the tremendous expansions of the NYSE, Nasdaq (over-the-counter market), and mutual funds, the great changes in the increased numbers of people, issues, funds, and dollars have made qualitative changes to investing or speculating. We can cope with these changes, at least intellectually, by thinking mainly in terms of percentages and ratios, rather than actual numbers (nominal figures).

The two-to-one advances to declines of several years ago, perhaps 1,000 to 500 issues—an indication of good breadth and market strength—today might be 1,500 to 750 and a few years from now perhaps 2,000 to 1,000. While the numbers change easily, the ratios and relationships are rarely altered. Six years ago, a net 1,000 advances to declines (1,300 advances, 300 declines), might today look like 1,700 advances to 700 declines. Instead of worrying about the absolute numbers, we might content ourselves with recognizing that when 50 percent or more of the stocks trading were advancing or declining, the market was exhibiting strength or weakness, respectively.

A widely used danger signal is when more than 40 new 52-week lows occur during a few trading days. I believe this indicator was developed when it represented 2 percent or so of the stocks traded. Today, I believe 60 new lows are needed to represent the same proportion as several years ago. Rather than try to remember the proper number, remember the percentage, namely, 2 percent, so that six years from now, when 4,000 to 5,000 issues are listed on the NYSE, we will be on alert if 80 to 100 or more new lows are reported daily.

Although mutual funds were a factor six years ago, they are a very much bigger factor today. They are growing by leaps and bounds. For some of the startling statistics, see Chapter 10. Mutual funds come under the rubric institutional trading and have created a monster—some say a bubble, that will one day burst and cause havoc in the financial markets—but so far seem to have given somewhat greater stability (less volatility) to the stock markets. An expected flood of mutual fund redemptions failed to occur in the Crash of '87 or the Selloff of '90. The past four years without a 10 percent correction in most major averages might be attributed to the investment actions of mutual funds as fueled by the increasing mutual fund shareholders and money.

Another far-reaching change was the imposing by the NYSE of programmed-trading collars after a 50- and 100-point move in the Dow Jones Industrial Average, which has reduced extreme volatility and made the market seem safer. Coupled with similar restrictions in the Chicago futures markets, the risks of market meltdowns have been reduced.

At press time there is a raging debate about the possibility of a "new era" in the stock market. Historians and technicians point out that we currently see the lowest dividend ratio in the history of the stock market, below 2.5 percent. Based mainly on this criterion, but augmented with other apparent technical and historical excesses, bearish prognosticators have been predicting a severe market decline for the past few years. A "normal" four to seven percent decline may happen anytime.

Sooner or later a selloff of 20 percent or more certainly will happen, but it may well take another 12 to 18 months to transpire.

When a Crash seems imminent, we expect to have become defensive in reducing both our margin leverage and positions, and probably will hedge the remaining portfolio of core, still-undervalued holdings, with OEX put options. We also expect not to make the imprudent choices of 1987 and 1990. Much of my experience and many improvements are included in this revised, updated book.

My middle-age has been made pleasant and comfortable through my generally prudent speculating in the stock market. May you do as well.

—Al Frank

Acknowledgments

My speculative investment strategies are derived from the ideas and practices of too many people to mention, even if I could remember their names. Some of the more prominent individuals and sources are noted in the text pages. I do not claim many (if any) original or creative thoughts for this book. I do assert a reasonably consistent synthesis of other people's commentary and my real-time experiences in the field.

I keyed in several revisions of the manuscript, much aided by the proofreading and suggestions of Vicki Baldwin, who is a fine writer. I was particularly helped by the knowledge and expertise of John Buckingham, whose emendations and challenges toward greater clarity led to several improvements in the text and examples.

Compliments go to Michael Ryder, the text editor, who made a great many wonderfully positive changes in "polishing" and tightening the text. It was a pleasure to work with Michael and see so much overwriting reduced, resulting in a big improvement in clarity and readability.

The dust jacket photograph was made by Judith Gordon.

Even with all this help and improvement, there are undoubtedly gaffes for which I must take responsibility. I would be pleased to receive any comments or suggestions and can be reached at (505) 983-0412 or P.O. Box 8970, Santa Fe, NM 87504–8970.

Introduction

Dreamed of Rewards

The stock market may not bring you undreamed-of rewards, but if you are willing to get rich slowly, it is the place to make or maintain your fortune. Few enterprises bring the large systematic returns of a successful business. Real estate, though it has been the source of many fortunes, often begins with substantial equity employed over long periods of time. With the proper approach, attention, and long-term application, the stock market can hold its own with this and other traditional methods of making money on a grand scale. It is said that no other passive investment returns as much profit on average as the stock market. Happily, you don't need much money to start, and after a brief, initial study, successful stock investing can be done with a part-time commitment of only a few hours a week.

You can start your stock portfolio with a few hundred dollars, and build it by making additional contributions and utilizing the gains from market appreciation. True, at this rudimentary level it takes a long time to build substantial equity, but most people either have a long time or can start with more than a few hundred dollars. I am amazed when people in their 50s or 60s, in good health, tell me that they are too old to undertake a three- to five-year stock program, especially as their statistical life expectancies offer 20 to 30 years of future financial needs.

Let time work for you. As shown in Table I–1, if you begin with $2,000, add $2,000 a year for 19 more years, and accomplish a 15 percent after-tax (or tax-sheltered) compounded annual return, your $40,000 cash contribution would

Table I-1. After-tax Plus $2,000 per Year Compounded Growth (starting with $2,000, plus adding $2,000 annually and compounding at various rates)

Year	At 12%	Value	At 15%	Value	At 18%	Value	At 20%	Value	At 25%	Value
0		2,000		2,000		2,000	2,000	2,000		2,000
1	240	4,240	300	4,300	360	4,360	400	4,400	500	4,500
2	509	6,749	645	6,945	785	7,145	880	7,280	1,125	7,625
3	810	9,559	1,042	9,987	1,286	10,431	1,456	10,736	1,906	11,531
4	1,147	12,706	1,498	13,485	1,878	14,308	2,147	14,883	2,883	16,414
5	1,525	16,230	2,023	17,507	2,576	18,884	2,977	19,860	4,104	22,518
6	1,948	20,178	2,626	22,134	3,399	24,283	3,972	25,832	5,629	30,147
7	2,421	24,599	3,320	27,454	4,371	30,654	5,166	32,998	7,537	39,684
8	2,952	29,551	4,118	33,572	5,518	38,172	6,600	41,598	9,921	51,605
9	3,546	35,097	5,036	40,607	6,871	47,043	8,320	51,917	12,901	66,506
10	4,212	41,309	6,091	48,699	8,468	57,510	10,383	64,301	16,626	85,132
11	4,957	48,266	7,305	58,003	10,352	69,862	12,860	79,161	21,283	108,415
12	5,792	56,058	8,701	68,704	12,575	84,437	15,832	96,993	27,104	137,519
13	6,727	64,785	10,306	81,009	15,199	101,636	19,399	118,392	34,380	173,899
14	7,774	74,559	12,151	95,161	18,294	121,931	23,678	144,070	43,475	219,374
15	8,947	85,507	14,274	111,435	21,947	145,878	28,814	174,884	54,843	276,217
16	10,261	97,767	16,715	130,150	26,258	174,136	34,977	211,861	69,054	347,271
17	11,732	111,499	19,523	151,673	31,344	207,481	42,372	256,233	86,818	436,089
18	13,380	126,879	22,751	176,424	37,347	246,827	51,247	309,480	109,022	547,112
19	15,226	144,105	26,464	204,887	44,429	293,256	61,896	373,376	136,778	685,889
20	17,293	163,397	30,733	237,620	52,786	348,042	74,675	450,051	171,472	859,362
21	19,608	185,005	35,643	275,263	62,648	412,690	90,010	542,061	214,840	1,076,202
22	22,201	209,206	41,289	318,553	74,284	488,974	108,412	652,474	269,051	1,347,253
23	25,105	236,310	47,783	368,336	88,015	578,989	130,495	784,968	336,813	1,686,066
24	28,357	266,668	55,250	425,586	104,218	685,207	156,994	943,962	421,516	2,109,582
25	32,000	300,668	63,838	491,424	123,337	810,544	188,792	1,134,755	527,396	2,638,978

become $237,620 in 20 years. That portfolio would appreciate $35,643 in its 21st year, and thereafter could provide increasing growth or income for many years.

If you average a greater than 15 percent after-tax compounded annual return—which is likely if you take more risk by using leverage (in a margined account)—you receive a greater total return. Just improving from 15 percent to 18 percent compounded annually for 20 years increases total equity to $348,042—a 56 percent greater total return. Even more delicious is a 20 percent compounded return, resulting in an equity of $450,051—more than twice that of a 15 percent compounding. An almost undreamed-of return of 25 percent compounded annual gain would lead to $859,362 after 20 years. At this level, your portfolio could appreciate $214,840 in the 20th year alone, probably enough for most of us to live on, even given the endemic inflation built into our economy. Even if $200,000 only bought one-third as much in 20 years as it does now, it would be a nice financial cushion for the future.

My Background

Although my experience in the stock market is probably not unique, it is certainly out of the ordinary. None of my parents or extended family owned stocks, nor did I until I was 38 years old. I did not work for a bank or brokerage house, and did not take finance courses in college. I happened upon the stock market due to a general interest in the world and because my Ph.D. sponsor was an active market player. Like so many people, I believed "the market" was only for "richies," not for a working-class stiff like myself. Until I was almost 50 years old I never earned more than $25,000 a year, first as a printer and small printshop owner, then as a teacher and assistant professor. The stock market changed all that.

I began investing in stocks late in 1968 by buying an occasional position with the few hundred dollars I'd managed to accumulate. By 1977, my interest in the market had increased enough for me to become a "professional" by registering as an Investment Adviser, managing small sums for a few friends and acquaintances, and by publishing a newsletter called *The Pinchpenny Speculator*. At the time, my career orientation was toward higher education, and I thought of my newsletter as an educational publication, as indicated by its original subtitle, "A Fortnightly Epistle on Investing." The letter began as a journal of my experiences, mistakes, lesssons, and decisions. It still is. The first letters were typed on a manual typewriter, with 100 copies made at a local copier shop.

As my expertise and income increased, I obtained an electric typewriter. I learned COBOL computer programming in night classes at Santa Monica College, and generated computer analyses at school and at timesharing companies. After three years, I changed the newsletter's name to *The Prudent Speculator*, because too many people were confusing the former title with "penny stocks," an investment niche I eschew.

My investment advising was a part-time avocation for several years, until I was discovered by *The Hulbert Financial Digest* (*HFD*). In 1983, T*he Prudent Speculator* (*TPS*) was determined to be the best-performing newsletter of those monitored by *HFD* for each of the four quarters and for the year overall. Unsolicited publicity and subscriptions poured in to my residence, and life hasn't been the same since.

My Investment Credentials

TPS Portfolio, a so-called model portfolio representing my actual *margined* portfolio returned 117.74 percent for 1983, quite exceptional for a common-stock portfolio that didn't use market timing, high-flying options, or futures trading. Many would say that using margin—borrowed funds collateralized by stocks owned—was pretty high flying, but I have always believed leverage is a reasonable "businessperson's" technique, when used prudently. I explain this belief in detail in Chapter 5, "The Myths and Magic of Margin."

Far more important than any one year's results is the exceptional long-term performance of TPS Portfolio, especially before the Crash of '87, but even after that event, including the traumatic losses incurred in 1990. For its first six years, beginning with $8,006 in cash (equity) value and some $16,200 worth of stocks, my actual TPS Portfolio was able to appreciate 1,379 percent, which works out to a 45.48 percent annualized rate of return from March 11, 1977 through December 31, 1983. For the first 10 years (40 quarters) of TPS Portfolio, audited figures show a 44.0 percent annual return, from April 1, 1977 through March 31, 1987.

For 18.25 years TPS Portfolio managed a total net gain (accounting for trading commissions, margin expenses, dividends, but not taxes) of 4,322.20 percent, which is 22.92 percent compounded annually, including the carnage wrought by the Crash of '87 and the even worse decline of 1990. A replication of TPS Portfolio's audited performance report conducted by Deloitte Touche and "attested" to by Corby & Corby is displayed in Table I–2.

Hindsight and reflection show in detail Table I–2 that I "might have" avoided much of the damage suffered in those meltdowns and selloffs (see Chapter 6, "The Crash of '87 and the Selloff of '90"). Even having suffered through October–November of '87 and July–October of '90, TPS Portfolio still was able to outperform the major averages for over 15 years to be the second best-performing newsletter of those followed by *The Hulbert Financial Digest* since its inception.

As the justly required performance disclaimer says, past performance is no guarantee of future performance, and recommendations may not become profitable or equal past performance.

Table I-2. TPS Portfolio: Audited Investment Performance

Year	Actual Margined TPS[1]	Hypothetical Unmargined TPS[2]	S&P 500[3]
1977[4]	+70.28%	+34.48%	−0.91%
1978	+25.00%	+19.17%	+ 6.56%
1979	+63.46%	+33.81%	+18.44%
1980	+15.69%	+16.99%	+32.42%
1981	−0.74%	+17.28%	−4.91%
1982	+58.54%	+28.46%	+21.41%
1983	+117.74%	+45.44%	+22.51%
1984	−12.71%	+ 2.14%	+ 6.27%
1985	+50.72%	+23.41%	+32.16%
1986	+46.46%	+21.84%	+18.47%
1987	−55.65%	−23.78%	+ 5.23%
1988	+50.16%	+26.34%	+16.81%
1989	+20.69%	+16.76%	+31.49%
1990	−60.62%	−24.23%	−3.17%
1991	+69.58%	+31.03%	+30.55%
1992	+62.25%	+27.65%	+ 7.67%
1993	+41.00%	+20.17%	+ 9.99%
1994	−12.91%	−2.73%	−1.54%
1995–1st 6 mos.	+32.08%	+23.93%	+14.30% (est.)

Annualized Rates of Return for the 18.25-year Period [4]

+22.92%[1]	+16.95%[2]	+14.48%[3] (est.)

[1] Al Frank's actual margined portfolio (also known as TPS Portfolio); includes the effects of dividend income, margin interest, sales, purchases, cash additions, and withdrawals in computing the time-weighted percentage change in equity, compounded quarterly.

[2] Al Frank's hypothetical cash portfolio, calculated as if TPS Portfolio was never margined; includes market gains and losses, but not trading expenses or dividend income in computing the time-weighted change in market value, compounded quarterly.

[3] Source: *Stocks, Bonds, Bills, and Inflation 1994 Yearbook*, Chicago, IL: Ibbotson Associates, "Large Company Stocks: Total Returns."

[4] TPS Portfolio figures are for April 1977 through year-end, or nine months, as are S&P 500 total return figures.

I have modified my approach to better compensate for the kinds of risks present in the summers of '87 and '90 and to avoid suffering the repetition of similar events. We closely monitor margin levels going into both overbought and overvalued markets such as occurred during August–September 1987 and July–October 1990. I feel some confidence in the long-range record of prudent speculating, even while keeping in mind its recent big stumbles and the potential for future devastating short-term declines.

Can a Successful Strategy Be Communicated?

With this book I intend to encourage thoughtfulness and challenge assumptions, which should result in clarifying what you "know" but have not systematically applied. Such stimulation could lay the groundwork for further inquiry and action. I have worked hard to present accurate information that you can integrate into the matrix of your personal knowledge.

We will examine subtle, often commonplace errors or misleading ideas which are just *clichés* and slogans. We will challenge questionable dogma, false statements, and errors of reasoning that give rise to dubious assertions and unexamined half-truths. In these pages I am sharing valid, meaningful, and useful formulations. A good book on investing must involve psychology and semantics because, until we understand ourselves and our terms, we are unlikely to understand or consistently do well in the stock market.

Semantics Is More Than Just Wordplay

Right off, let us agree to a stipulated definition that all so-called investing in common stocks is a form of *speculation*. I believe it is important at the outset, throughout the pages of this book, and indeed in our everyday thinking about the stock market, to be aware and admit that when we trade stocks or buy them for their long-term potential, we are speculators. This is in keeping with classical definitions of that word and its cognates.

Consider the following entries in *The Random House College Dictionary* (Revised Edition, 1980, page 1262):

> **speculate** 1. to engage in thought or reflection; meditate. 2. to indulge in conjectural thought. 3. to engage in any business transaction involving considerable risk for the chance of large gains.

> **speculation** 1. the contemplation or consideration of some subject. 2. a single instance or process of consideration. 3. a conclusion or opinion reached by such contemplation. 4. conjectural consideration

of a matter; conjecture or surmise. 5. engagement in business transactions involving considerable risk for the chance of large gains.

speculative 1. pertaining to or of the nature of speculation, contemplation, conjecture, or abstract reasoning. . . . 4. of the nature of or
involving commercial or financial speculation.

speculator 1. a person who is engaged in commercial or financial
speculation.

I submit that when we trade stocks we undertake a "business transaction
involving considerable risk for the chance of large gains." Otherwise we would put
our money into Treasury bills. Furthermore, the whole process of systematic and
prudent stock speculation involves thought, reflection, contemplation, conjecture,
surmise, and abstract reasoning. Why then is the word "speculator" anathema to so
many who find the word "investor" comfortable and satisfying? Because "invest"
and "investment" carry connotations of gains and goods without great risks. Note
how the same dictionary (page 702) defines these terms:

invest 1. to put (money) to use, by purchase or expenditure, in something offering profitable returns, esp. interest or income. 2. to spend;
to invest large sums in books. 3. to use, give, or devote (time, talent,
etc.) as to achieve something; *he invested a lot of time in trying to
help retarded children*. 4. to furnish with power, authority, rank, etc.

investment 1. the investing of money or capital for profitable returns.
2. a particular instance or mode of investing money. 3. money or capital invested. 4. a property or right in which a person invests. 5. a
devoting, using, or giving of time, talent, emotional energy, etc., as to
achieve something.

Nowhere in any of the definitions of "invest" or "investment" do the words
chance, risk, or large gains occur. Investing is defined as both good and safe
because it offers "profitable returns"; it offers "to achieve something." Perhaps we
can trace the distrust of terms like "speculate" to their roots, which include to see
(e.g., spectacles) and to look out (visually and mentally contemplating the distance
and thereby the future)? Perception and conjecture are notoriously deceiving. The
impression is reinforced when we consider the comfortable connotation and psy-
chic association with clothes—a vest or vestment—that is the root of the word
"investment."

But there is no investment—let alone stock market transaction—that does not
carry with it chance and risk, and few stocks are bought without the thought of
gain—mostly "large gains." Even allegedly safe "investments" carry several con-

siderable risks. In early 1989 many "very safe" Triple A-rated bonds (e.g., RJR Nabisco) lost some 20 percent of their market price in a few days after the announcement of a proposed leveraged buyout. During 1994, 30-year U.S. Treasury bonds declined some 7.77 percent (including their initial high interest yields) in total return as their market values dropped when interest rates were pushed up by the Federal Reserve.

We know that common stocks can vary in price several percent on any given day, and over the course of a year some will more than double in market price while others will lose a great portion or even all of their previous market price. We also know that real estate is not immune from serious depreciation and loss, due to overbuilding, changes in neighborhoods, or economic downturns. Between 1990 and 1994, much of southern California real estate declined 20 percent or more in market price.

It irritates me so much to see advertising, couched in the most dignified words and euphemisms, encouraging "investing" in the most risky of financial instruments, such as commodities, limited partnerships, derivatives, or collectibles. After years of trying to get people to admit they were speculators, I have persuaded only a reluctant few and turned off many who did not want to think of themselves as speculators or what they did with stocks as speculating. Still, I will keep advocating this semantic honesty because it is so important to recognize that critical difference, which will help our outlook, thinking, and strategies.

"A speculator is a man who observes the future and acts before it occurs," according to Bernard Baruch, as quoted by *tomorrow's stocks* (P.O. Box 14111, Scottsdale, AZ 85267). While I like the stature of Baruch and love this quote, I'm not sure how we can observe the future before it occurs. But I do think we can anticipate many probable events and speculate on their likelihood, based upon historical precedents and current conditions.

Is This Approach for You?

There are many excellent books available on stock speculating (even if their authors insist they are investing), but there is not—nor will there ever likely be—a definitive, all-satisfying book. Most stock market participants are too different in their experiences, outlooks, and personalities to render any one approach appropriate for all.

My approach is a relatively simple system that has worked well for me for over 18 years of public practice. Because of the overall success of the method, many will find it appealing, yet few likely will pursue it completely, not because it is difficult, but because of preconceptions and attachments to other, conditioned beliefs.

However, even those of you who decide the complete approach is not your cup of tea may pick up many useful ideas with which to modify and improve your current speculative practices. All theoretical concepts presented herein are grounded in practice, and most of my speculative activities have a theoretical basis. There is always the danger that some of my rationales are rationalizations. Still, rationalizations can be examined and are thus more productive than assertions without foundation at all.

Four Cardinal Principles

Here is my gameplan. I buy undervalued stocks to be held until they are fully valued and then sold. If you think I've just said I buy low and sell high, that is very close to the main idea and you are almost correct. Alas, sometimes an undervalued stock becomes fully valued at a price lower than its original cost due to its corporation's problems, at which time I find myself having bought high and selling low. Occasional and even systematic losses are inescapable and an ordinary part of the overall process. Generally, losses are well overcome by gains over time.

Our speculative method has four essential components. Each is clear on its own but is interrelated with the other three. The first is stock *selection*, arguably the easiest part of the system. Stock analysis, monitoring, and selection are usually the most time-consuming chores for prudent speculators. Stock analysis requires systematic updating and review but, depending upon how many stocks you would want to follow and how sophisticated a computer system you employ, could probably be handled in two to five hours a week. It need not require daily involvement. Stock selection and valuation is reviewed in Chapters 2 and 9.

Stock selection is where some "Summer Speculators" get off the bandwagon. It sometimes takes years for an undervalued stock to become fully valued. A cheap stock often becomes cheaper before its fundamental (corporate) value is recognized years later in the stock market. This waiting game most often works in our favor. By the time many of our selected out-of-favor stocks do become recognized and priced fairly, their corporations have grown even more valuable, so that our initial estimated values or gains are substantially exceeded. Thus, *patience* becomes one of the four cardinal characteristics of prudent speculating. Patience is a doubled-edged skill, useful both in waiting for a good opportunity to come along and in holding the position for its optimum gain. Evidence of the historical value of patience is detailed throughout this book.

Here is a complication that frequently frustrates stock buyers. Common stocks—which represent equity ownership of corporations and "should" reflect the value of those corporations—often have a life of their own in the dynamics of the stock market. Stock prices are influenced by many noncorporate events, such as the general economic cycle, interest and inflation rates, the money supply, rumors, Federal Reserve policy, and overall faith in the government. Stock markets can become enthusiastically overbought and thereafter are likely to sell off in a pessimistic correction. Likewise, stock markets become oversold and thereafter are likely to rally. Markets also become overvalued and likely to decline, or undervalued and are likely to advance. Each of these conditions can apply to short-, intermediate-, or long-term periods, requiring appropriate strategies and responses. Our third principle, *risk management*, based on both corporate and market-wide considerations, is dealt with in Chapter 4.

Diversification is a fourth principle and is an integral part of portfolio management reviewed in Chapter 3. Several studies have shown that sufficient stock and industry diversification, as well as time diversification, can reduce many of the risks involved in speculation. Effective stock-portfolio management balances stock and time diversification, long-term market timing, dollar cost averaging, risk management, and individual needs affecting one's cash flow.

Summarizing my fourfold approach is the acronym PASADARM, which stands for *P*atience *A*nd *S*election *A*nd *D*iversification *A*nd *R*isk *M*anagement. Those *Ands* are logically conjunctive, meaning that all elements are tied together and work together. To question which is more important—for example, selection or diversification?—is to miss the point. Sufficient diversification is a safety measure intended to counter the effect of those carefully selected stocks that unexpectedly go sour. Risk management coordinates each of the three essentials, as well as considering overbought or oversold and overvalued or undervalued markets.

Technical Analysis versus Fundamental Analysis

There are two principal schools of speculating, with many variations of each school and some overlap of principles. I am essentially in the school of fundamental analysis for stock selection, and study the school of technical analysis for market timing. In a desert-island scenario where we are only allowed one or the other, I would have to choose fundamental analysis for corporation (stock) selection. After the stocks' price fluctuations in the fickle market run their volatile and erratic courses, the growing value of corporations will sooner or later be recognized in stock-market transactions and higher prices.

But we do not live on a desert island, and we can integrate both fundamental and technical methodologies. Interestingly enough, market-timing indications—generally ascribed to technical analysis—can be achieved in large measure by keeping track of fundamental valuations. As stock and market valuations become too high on average—historically and in relation to other criteria such as interest rates—selloff signals are generated. This is brought out in detail in Chapter 6 on the Crash of '87.

Luck Favors the Well Prepared

I have often been lucky in the stock market. That is, I have had some terrible luck and some wonderful luck. So many people approach investing with an adversarial attitude, as if "the market" is out there to entice them, frustrate them, and ultimately do them in. Of course "the market" is indifferent; it has no will, intention, or agenda. Personifying or reifying the market—attributing to it human characteristics—is a great way to play mind games on yourself. I have long felt, and experience has borne this out, that I had as much chance or more of enjoying good luck as suffering bad luck, especially if I attempted to understand much of what was ongoing, did my homework, and applied my gameplan systematically.

An ancient book of Chinese wisdom, the *Tao Teh King* by Lao Tzu tells us that it is not wise to go to extremes. How true that advice is in the stock market. On the other hand, it is wise to flow with nature and events, accepting them and adjusting to them. "Never fight the Fed (the Federal Reserve's interest rate and monetary policies) or the tape (the action of stock price trading)" is a Taoist-like idea, and sage advice. If you can develop that middle way, and include sufficient preparation, much good fortune will likely follow from your efforts. You don't have to be a genius or a certified public accountant, but neither can you just throw the proverbial darts, rely on blind luck, or count on tips from seemingly successful friends.

The information and suggestions in this book provide you with guidelines, ideas, and examples that will lead to handsome gains in the stock market. Of course, I am still studying and learning, frequently amused at how many things I don't know, but aware that an encyclopedic knowledge might be counterproductive. I have a manageable strategy that works and ain't broke, so I'm not particularly trying to fix it. Still, any speculative stock-market methodology can be improved, adjusted, and modified, especially as the nature of the investment world changes over time.

The past few years have seen an explosion of new "derivative instruments" (e.g., new future contracts, indexes, and options on indexes), changed regulations, dominance by institutional trading, and the internationalization of markets. Still, "the fundamental things apply, as time goes by." Buy low and sell high, and do it before the others!

1

Premises and Principles

Given the multitude of information, possibilities, published "successful" methods, and strategies for speculating with stocks, how is one to choose? The problem is especially vexing as apparently successful strategists dismiss their competitors' methods as being seriously flawed or completely missing the point. It is difficult to apply any of the numerous and conflicting systems when the skills involved seem to require a graduate degree in mathematics, accounting, or psychology.

As a first step to a method for investing, ask yourself: "Does this stock market method and strategy generally make sense to me?" Then determine, "Has this speculative approach actually made superior profits investing real money in the stock market over a multiyear period?" That a so-called expert puts his own money where his mouth is can be an acid test. I could hardly believe my ears the first time I heard a famous newsletter writer intone that he did not buy the stocks he recommended because owning them might color his thinking and distort his objectivity.

It's very easy for a newsletter editor or market commentator to say, "Sell all stocks!" on the basis that the market looks dangerous and we can always buy them back later. Using that strategy, a prudent speculator would have to: (1) pay two extra brokerage commissions—getting out now and back in later—(2) create income tax consequences; and (3) decide when to buy, often at higher prices than were received from bailing out. There are only a few newsletter writers and advisors who do buy stocks from the lists of stocks they recommend, as I do.

As anyone knows who has traded a system on paper and then traded that system in the marketplace, there is quite a difference in the outcome, usually to the detriment of the actual investment versus the theoretical. If you understand a system's basics and you know it has worked for a meaningful 10 years or longer, you're more likely to profit from it than from other alternatives no matter how scholarly or entertaining.

In March 1977, I began publishing my stock advisory newsletter *The Prudent Speculator* (originally titled *The Pinchpenny Speculator*), displaying my portfolio at the time with $16,200 in stocks and $8,007 in equity. This portfolio, referred to as TPS Portfolio, has from the start been used as a real-time, actual "model" portfolio and is referred to throughout this book. Its history is reviewed in Chapter 7. The details include the results of my selections, strategies, and decisions, for both winners and losers, in good times and bad, not only as "the record," but also as the actual results of the premises and principles I follow as well as mistakes made.

As of June 30, 1995, CPA audited and attestation statements of TPS Portfolio's performance show a 22.92 percent compounded annual total return—including the difficult losses endured during the Crash of '87 and the Selloff of '90—for the 18.25 years since April 1, 1977. That compounded annual return is based on TPS Portfolio being heavily margined for the entire period. A hypothetical rendering of TPS Portfolio as a nonmargined account (that is, as if all transactions were for cash) results in an annualized rate of market appreciation of 16.95 percent, not including dividends, reinvestments from proceeds, or trading costs.

One condition that permitted me to gain those returns and become successful was that I started speculating in relative ignorance. I began with few if any preconceptions, and quickly found a personally compatible approach that was manageable, comprehensible, and worked consistently. No matter how intelligent and effective a system might be, it probably will not succeed for you unless you understand it, believe in it, and are able to practice it systematically and with consistency, especially in the face of panics and short-term losses.

Belief Is the Ground of Speculation

Before first writing this book six years ago, I used to think that patience was the most important quality of a successful speculator. Without minimizing the essential ingredient of patience, I have come to realize that *belief* may be the most important characteristic for success in long-term, consistent, speculation. If we do not believe in what we are doing, how can we find the patience and perseverance to carry on when the process is tedious, subject to mistakes and pitfalls, and when we cannot even avoid numerous, individual losses?

Speculation is not a religion, but faith is surely the individual's basis for participating in a system that attempts to anticipate future prospects according to present perceptions and past experiences. We do not need miracles to believe in the rewards of effective stock speculation. Historical precedents and statistical probability are sufficient. Happily, there is incontrovertible evidence that common stocks on average provide the greatest return on equity of any kind of investment over long periods of time. Our first order of business, then, is to briefly study the history of stock price performance over the past six decades and in doing so, convince ourselves that the past is prologue to the future, albeit with unknown fluctuations along the way (see Table 1–1).

A Small Set of Simple Ideas

Many people have been conditioned to believe that investing is an esoteric and highly skilled enterprise. Obviously, those who get paid to invest for others act as if they had irreplaceable training, high I.Q., insights, and nonpublic information that gives them an advantage over the average wage earner. Little could be further from the truth. Successful investing involves only a handful or two of considerations that are available to anyone with a 6th-grade education. You probably know most of them already. In this chapter we will review some of the basics so that you will see how ordinary is speculating. Ordinary English words such as: compounding, price, value, worth, patience, diversification, market timing, performance, and margin leverage form an important part of the jargon of the market.

The Miracle of Compounding

Although I wrote that we do not need miracles, there is a miracle associated with speculation—the miracle of compounding. Many have commented upon the fan-

Table 1–1. 69-Year Returns of Financial Instruments and Inflation

$1 Invested Year-End 1925 through Year-End 1994

Category of Investment	12/31/94 Value	Compounded Rate
Small Company Stocks	$2,842.77	12.2%
S&P 500 Total Return	810.54	10.2
Long-Term Corporate Bonds	38.01	5.4
Long-Term Government Bonds	25.86	4.8
Intermediate Government Bonds	30.84	5.1
U.S. Treasury Bills	12.19	3.7
Inflation	8.35	3.1

Source: Adapted from Ibbotson Associates, *Stocks, Bonds, Bills, and Inflation 1995 Yearbook (SBBI)*, Chicago, IL: Ibbotson Associates, Inc., 1995.

tastic results of the consistent compounded annual growth of money or businesses. Warren Buffett, probably the greatest stock speculator in history, claimed in early 1986 that if you had invested $10,000 in the partnership he started in 1956, and maintained that investment through the years by moving on to Berkshire Hathaway after the partnership was disbanded in 1969, you would have $15 million some 32 years later, a superlative return indeed.

Few of us would have had the money, or the temperament to leave an investment untouched for over three decades, without wanting to use some or all of it for "emergencies," or perceived necessities. Ravages upon most long-appreciated funds might also have been visited by Uncle Sam taxing annual realized gains (although with Buffett's practice of no dividends, tax consequences are postponed until shares are sold). Still, imagine setting up a trust fund of $10,000 at your child's birth and having it become worth $15 million 32 years later. Heck, how about seeing it grow to $867,000 after 20 years (using the same compounded rate), a nest egg for college and a capital start in adult life?

As truly handsome and exceptional as Mr. Buffett's record is, in actuality it is "only" 25.68 percent compounded annually. Table 1–2 is a brief compounded annual growth table to show how patience and perseverance could lead to independent wealth at various levels of performance. While these figures refer to the growth of an initial $100, you can compare beginning with $10,000 by just adding two zeros to the totals shown. For example, where an initial $100 becomes $146,977 after 40 years compounding at 20 percent per year, an initial $10,000 would become $14,697,700 if left to accumulate and compound for four decades, and if not diminished by taxes or other expenses.

To be fair, investors outside Buffett's partnership, merely holding Berkshire Hathaway common shares likely would incur trading commissions and income taxes along the way. These ongoing expenses might be less than we imagine, given very long-term holding periods during which commissions are minimized and taxes are not incurred until a position is sold. It is also possible to keep much of your capital compounding in tax-deferred programs such as pension, IRA, 401(k) or Keogh accounts, and to minimize commissions through discount brokers.

Clearly, the miracle of compounding becomes greater with the passing years. This is an often overlooked but very important truth. For instance, a healthy 15 percent annualized rate of return (after costs and taxes) for 20 years becomes $1,636.70 per $100 initial equity. Contrast that 1,536.70 percent gain with the next 20 years, after which the total return becomes a 26,686 percent gain of the initial $100 amount. While the first 20 years would bring $1,536.70 per $100 originally invested, the second 20 years would bring some $26,686.

Table 1-2. Compound Annual Growth per Initial $100

Year	10%	12.5%	15%	17.5%	20%	22.5%	25%
1	110	113	115	119	120	123	125
2	121	127	132	138	144	150	156
3	133	142	152	162	173	184	195
4	146	160	175	191	207	225	244
5	161	180	201	224	249	276	305
6	177	203	231	263	299	338	382
7	195	228	266	309	358	414	477
8	214	256	306	363	430	507	596
9	236	289	352	427	516	621	745
10	259	325	405	502	619	761	931
11	285	365	465	589	743	932	1,164
12	314	411	535	693	892	1,142	1,455
13	345	462	615	814	1,070	1,399	1,819
14	380	520	708	956	1,284	1,714	2,274
15	418	585	814	1,124	1,541	2,099	2,842
16	460	658	936	1,320	1,849	2,571	3,553
17	505	741	1,076	1,551	2,219	3,150	4,441
18	556	833	1,238	1,823	2,662	3,859	5,551
19	612	937	1,423	2,142	3,195	4,727	6,939
20	673	1,055	1,637	2,516	3,834	5,791	8,674
21	740	1,186	1,882	2,957	4,601	7,094	10,842
22	814	1,335	2,165	3,474	5,521	8,690	13,553
23	895	1,501	2,489	4,082	6,625	10,645	16,941
24	985	1,689	2,863	4,796	7,950	13,040	21,176
25	1,084	1,900	3,292	5,636	9,540	15,974	26,470
26	1,192	2,138	3,786	6,622	11,448	19,568	33,087
27	1,311	2,405	4,354	7,781	13,737	23,970	41,359
28	1,442	2,706	5,007	9,142	16,485	29,364	51,699
29	1,586	3,044	5,758	10,742	19,781	35,971	64,624
30	1,745	3,424	6,621	12,622	23,738	44,064	80,779
31	1,919	3,852	7,614	14,831	28,485	53,978	100,974
32	2,111	4,334	8,757	17,427	34,182	66,123	126,218
33	2,323	4,876	10,070	20,476	41,019	81,001	157,772
34	2,555	5,485	11,581	24,060	49,222	99,226	197,215
35	2,810	6,171	13,318	28,270	59,067	121,552	246,519
36	3,091	6,942	15,315	33,217	70,880	148,902	308,149
37	3,400	7,810	17,613	39,030	85,056	182,404	385,186
38	3,740	8,786	20,254	45,861	102,068	223,445	481,483
39	4,115	9,884	23,293	53,886	122,481	273,721	601,853
40	4,526	11,120	26,786	63,316	146,977	335,308	752,316

Keep It Simple, Stupid (KISS)

KISS is an amusing acronym, particularly applicable to speculating with stocks. Being simple, in the best sense of that word, is one of the hardest things to do. Many believe that if a subject or a practice is too easy, it must not be very valuable. We may be conditioned to believe the popular adage, "No pain, no gain." In reality, pain may more often be counterproductive, destructive, and defeating than beneficial. Others may tend to complicate the process of speculating with psychological attitudes, perhaps feeling guilty for receiving such handsome rewards for so little effort. Some people undoubtedly lose in the stock market in a subconscious effort to punish themselves, like compulsive or addicted gamblers. In such cases, one could easily believe that being simple was being stupid.

For developing and maintaining simplicity in stock speculation, as well as in life, I recommend the *Tao Teh King* by Lao Tzu, a book worth reading time and again. There are many translations of this brief, 84-verse book of "the way," which represents the fourth century B.C. philosophy of Chinese taoism. Of many excellent translations, I am partial to the one "Interpreted as Nature and Intelligence" by Archie J. Bahm [Albuquerque, NM: World Books, 1986].

In verse 9 we are told, "Going to extremes is never best . . . The way to success is this: having achieved your goal, be satisfied not to go further. For this is the way Nature operates." Fabulous advice for the successful speculator, both for daily decisions to take reasonable profits, and for mitigating dramatic dangers such as market crashes. As with so many seminal works, the more often I read the *Tao Teh King*, the more I see applicable wisdom in its description of the intelligent person conforming to nature's ways. Other translations offer more poetic language and different emphases, but I have found Bahm's rendering very clear, helpful, and satisfying.

Descriptions and Realities

The opening lines of the *Tao Teh King* (in Bahm's translation) are:

> Nature can never be completely described, for such a description of Nature would have to duplicate Nature.
>
> No name can fully express what it represents.

Words cannot express or describe completely what they are meant to represent. We name things or ideas, and try to infuse them with sufficient meaning to communicate and instruct. Be alert, however, to the partial nature of description and to the manifold ineffable details a concept may contain. So we begin with a few basic premises and principles—value, price, and worth—and hope they are communicatively adequate.

Value

Value is a meaningful, measurable, and manageable idea that can be quantified and used to determine potential gains or losses in the prices of stocks. Value is a basic, nonradical, fundamentalist tenet. We can analyze within certain limits the probable value of a corporation, and then compare that estimated value per share of its common stock to its current market price. Chapters 2 and 3 review some of the basic measures commonly used to arrive at such estimates.

The importance of the premise of value is that, since a share of stock represents a unit of ownership (equity) of a corporation, it is not just a piece of paper traded on some exchange, but a claim on the physical and intangible assets of the corporation. A good analogy is to compare estimating the value of a corporation with estimating the value of a house or small business. While estimates of properties may vary significantly, the value of a house or business property is nevertheless "real" and permits the borrowing of money (a mortgage or line of credit) against such estimated value.

There are several types of value. Some analysts value a stock (corporation) in terms of its potential future earnings' (or dividends') stream. Where earnings are the principal consideration, earnings discount models may be developed and computed in an effort to estimate the present value based upon future earnings. One can also value a corporation strictly in terms of its assets, or merely on the basis of the dividends it pays and is likely to pay over some future period. Some evaluations are based on all of these or other criteria. Some of the many criteria of value are reviewed in Chapters 2 and 3.

Valuing corporations is my cornerstone of speculation. It is vital to understand this concept. We do not analyze stocks, we analyze corporations; we do not buy stocks, we buy corporations, at least small fractions of them. While we might like to buy whole corporations, or major portions of them if we could, we must content ourselves with a few hundred or thousand shares of our selected corporations.

Warren Buffett has made many interesting, informative, and sage statements about speculating in corporations. He found it amazing that either a person gets the idea of value immediately or seems never to accept it completely. The idea that a company may be trading at a fraction of its clearly recognized value as a going concern, in terms of the market price of its common shares, seems so obvious. Yet, great numbers of market players could care less about the values of corporations in which they dabble through trading their shares. They tend to concentrate merely on the likelihood of a market or a stock going up or down because of its recent price and volume of trading action.

"Occasionally, sensational businesses are given away," said Buffett, on Adam Smith's "Money World" (6/20/88), citing the example of one of his core holdings.

"In the mid '70s, the whole Washington Post Company was selling for $80 million at a time when the properties were worth not less than $400 million. The price was there for all to see." How does it happen that a great corporation can sell for only 20 percent of its appraised value? Buffett's explanation: "People just didn't feel very enthusiastic about the world then."[1]

Price

You may think that *price* and *worth* are synonymous with value. These three should always be distinguished from one another, for only at rare moments are they functionally equivalent, representing the same dollar amount. The price of a stock refers to the dollar amount at which it is trading or has traded at a particular time (bought or sold), often at a market day's close. Rarely is the fluctuating price of a stock the same as its corporation's value. Like a pendulum, the price of a stock swings from one side (undervalued) through a fair value range to the other side (overvalued), being most of the time out of sync with the stock's analyzed value.

The erroneous notion that the current price of a stock is what it should be because of the actions of the market's rational and informed participants is known as the efficient market hypothesis. An extension of this misguided notion is that there is no way to outperform the market's average except by taking additional risk. Because of the wide fluctuation of a stock's price, and the price action of the stock market over long periods of time, I have come to believe that the market is generally inefficient, that it seldom fairly represents the fundamental values of the underlying corporations it represents.

Worth

Worth is the third important description of a dollar amount associated with a corporation's stock. For a variety of reasons, a stock's objectively estimated fundamental value may not be the same as its worth to a shareholder. For example, I may determine that a stock's fundamental value approximates $30 per share, while its current price is $25, but I would want to sell it at its current price because I am concerned that the market in general is about to suffer a severe selloff. In such a case, I would rather capture the $25 than take the chance of waiting for the fair value of $30. In this case, worth is less than value but equal to price.

In another example, I might find a stock valued at $30 trading for $33. I may determine that, given the current conditions of the economy, the inflation/interest rate balance, and a strongly uptrending stock in a rising market, I will take the

---

[1] From *Outstanding Investor Digest*, Henry Emerson, ed., (32 West 40th Street, New York, NY 10018), p. 11.

"reasonable" chance of holding the stock for $35 or more. For a modicum of prudence and protection, perhaps I would apply trailing stop-loss limits (explained in Chapter 3). In this case, the stock's worth (to me) is greater than its market price, which is greater than its estimated value.

You might think it is a mere matter of semantics when I say that a stock may be worth more to me than its fair or fundamental value. You may say, if it's worth holding for $35 per share, isn't that the stock's considered value? Shouldn't the stock's value include considerations such as price momentum or the trend of the market? No, I don't think so. I believe it is very important to distinguish between a stock's estimated fundamental value and its context-dependent worth, which is the price I might find acceptable for buying or selling that stock (for either more or less than its fundamental value) due to additional considerations. And, just as the fundamental value changes with changing corporate conditions, so a stock's worth would change with changing personal and market conditions.

There may be other nonspeculative considerations, such as taxes, which determine a stock's worth to be different than its value for its owner. Without getting too tricky or sophisticated, take the case of a stock that reaches its fair value near the end of the year. If I sell the stock before year-end, I will have to pay taxes on its gains by the following April 15. However, if I wait a few days to sell, I won't have to pay taxes until the following year, thus having the use of those taxes for almost 12 additional months. Say profits would be $10,000 and taxes would amount to about $4,000 (adding state taxes). If money costs 10 percent annually, in this example one could save $400 in equivalent interest if I sell after December 31, so the stock's worth to me is at least $400 more than its fundamental value. Other examples could include the costs and gains associated with hedged positions, more about which can be found in Chapter 8.

A corollary to the premise of value is that sooner or later "value will out." Unfortunately, fundamental value is not always realized, no matter how long a stock is held. Some corporations go bankrupt in such a manner that the market price of their stock is always undervalued until the final blow. Other corporations are merged or bought out at prices below their fair values. Happily, many corporations are bought out at prices well above their fair values and those are the cases where one corporation is worth more to the acquiring entity than the target's fundamental value would indicate. Such worth may be found in the fit and synergy that a buyout is intended to produce, or in some hidden or intangible assets not readily calculable in normally determining fundamental value.

My experience is that 25 percent of the stocks I have carefully selected fail to make any profit, let alone reach their original estimated fair values. A few have lost 100 percent of their purchase price, but many have lost lesser amounts, almost breaking even. The saving grace is that 75 percent of selected stocks have traded above their original cost prices, with many trading well above their original valuations. *It is important to understand that a corporation's fundamental value is not a static concept nor a one-time estimate.* It changes whenever there is a significant alteration in a corporation's financials—balance sheet and earnings statement—or whenever it seems appropriate to attribute higher or lower valuation ratios because of growth rates, trends, interest rates, the general market level, or even a new invention or product.

Patience and the 50 Percent Principle

A big part of our strategy is to be patient while waiting for the fundamental value of a corporation to be recognized in its stock's price—the much maligned buy-and-hold technique. *Under ideal conditions, the sell level is when the stock's price equals its fundamental value, which equals its worth.* An alternative and more common sell level is when worth incorporates value with perceived corporate and market conditions; for example, when a stock's value is affected by a change in interest rates.

Falling interest rates are generally positive for so-called interest sensitive stocks such as banks, savings and loans, and mortgage companies. During the first five months of '95, Federal National Mortgage (symbol FNM, Fannie Mae to its shareholders) advanced from $72.875 per share to $100 per share, a gain of 37 percent, as the 30-year Treasury bond dropped from 8.0 percent to 6.5 percent. In fact, the second-best performing stock industry group after technology was the savings and loans category during this period.

Another aspect of this strategy is waiting for a corporation's stock to trade at 50 percent or less than its fundamental value before buying. This 50 percent undervalued level is arbitrary but not capricious. Under certain circumstances it might be too rigid. However, in keeping to such a policy, we maintain our commitment not to overpay for a stock. This discipline diminishes downside risk and therefore creates the likelihood of relatively greater upside potential. As I've said and will repeat throughout this book, theory doesn't always work in reality, but ours has worked often enough to produce very lucrative long-term gains with stocks. (See our long-term performance in Figure I–2.)

An example of a stock that became sufficiently undervalued to recommend is IBM. I recall that in 1987 one of our portfolio managers recommended the sale of IBM at $145 per share to a new client who had some shares in her portfolio. Fundamental analysis told us that IBM was not worth its current price and would not likely be much of a money maker in the foreseeable future, and this client's smallish portfolio was overweighted with IBM. Our client was incensed that we could recommend the sale of IBM, perhaps the greatest corporation in the world in her eyes at that time. I've no idea of what happened to that client or her IBM shares, as she quit based upon our outrageous suggestion. I know that for the first 16 years of our money management program we never recommended nor bought IBM. Finally, IBM traded down to $47 per share in 1994, at which time our analysis suggested it was undervalued by 50 percent and would likely trade for $95 per share or more in the next three to five years. We thus purchased several hundred shares for several clients. At this writing, about a year later, IBM has traded at over $110 per share, but our current goal price is $130 per share.

The 50 percent undervalued buy principle sometimes blocks us from acquiring stocks of excellent corporations which, in time, have great market price appreciations. Following the philosophical principle of "rule utilitarianism" and systematic consistency has served us well, and because of that we can argue in favor of maintaining such guidelines. Rule utilitarianism is the philosophical assertion that more is gained from the utility of always following sound rules than in breaking them, even though that sometimes seems unnecessary. Stopping at red stop lights at three o'clock in the morning (even when no cops or cars are seen nearby) to maintain a continuing safety factor is an example of rule utilitarianism.

The Need for Diversification

Maintaining our analytic methodology, portfolio strategy, and steadfast patience even though some of our stocks or the market in general takes a tumble are practical applications of rule utilitarianism. When you believe in your system, in the long-term, advancing nature of undervalued stocks and the market on average, then you are able to hold an undervalued stock through its recurring downward fluctuations in market price, even through a 50 percent or more decline in price. In this regard, Buffett has pointed out that, "You ignore that possibility at your own peril. In the history of almost every major company in this country, it has happened. You shouldn't own common stocks if a decrease in their value by 50 percent would cause you to feel stress."[2]

Even with careful selection, as previously mentioned, stocks do not always work out as anticipated. In fact, in a given 12-month period, 40 percent or more of my carefully selected stocks may be short-term "losers." Many of these short-term losers turn around in two or three years and become handsome winners. This means that, in addition to having patience, I want to be widely diversified with many different stocks from several industries in my portfolio. I want to have at least 25 and preferably 35 or more stocks in 15 to 17 different industries in a portfolio, so that when 5 or 10 stocks underperform, that result is offset by the good

---

[2] *Outstanding Investor Digest*, p. 9.

performance of the 15 or 25 others. Actual examples of these statistics and mechanics are detailed in Chapter 7.

The Intervening Stock Market

Speculating with common stocks is somewhat complicated in that stocks trade on various stock exchanges and the over-the-counter market. We can think of "the stock market" (of course, there are many stock markets, and many categories of stocks within each) as an institution which has developed characteristics and dynamics of its own, often independent of the stocks and corporations it represents.

I share Warren Buffett's attitude that we could just as well do without the daily trading markets as far as our approach to stocks is concerned. That is, we could buy the stocks we want today, and if the market ceased trading for years (or we went away on a very long vacation), we could return in a few years to enjoy the fruits of our corporations' growth and profits.

Still, we do know that markets have fluctuating periods of advancing and declining cycles. Markets become overvalued from time to time and thereafter decline, after which they become undervalued and subsequently advance. Markets alternate: they become overbought, and thereafter selloff, after which they become oversold—which lays the foundation for the next rally. These swings from over-bought and overvalued to oversold and undervalued are not neat, nor are the turn-ing points easily predictable, if at all. Market movements are further complicated by the nature of short-term, intermediate-term, and long-term "trends," which sometimes yield conflicting current readings.

One could simply ignore market swings, as have many great investors. Consider Peter Lynch, formerly of Fidelity Magellan Fund fame, but still an active investor. He says he attempts always to be fully invested, trading stocks for their long-term and short-term potential regardless of alleged market states or condi-tions, which he asserts with becoming modesty and honesty that he is not smart enough to predict. The importance of Lynch's humility and strategy is backed up by his record. Over the 10-year span of the '80s, the Fidelity Magellan Fund he managed at that time had gained a total return of 1,169.79 percent, the best long-term performance among thousands of mutual funds.[3]

Market Timing

Other students of investing have displayed historical indexes to show how much better off one would be avoiding the market's great, periodic, and cyclic declines, thereafter becoming aggressively invested during the market's great, periodic, and

---

[3] Source: Lipper Analytical Services, Inc., as published in *Barron's*, May 5, 1989.

cyclic advances. Once again, theoretical hindsight proves superior to real-time decisions. The attempt to avoid declines and catch advances is called market timing. Market-timing approaches and techniques are legion.

Some market timers time the markets for intraday movements of options and futures contracts, while others are short-term profit-scalping timers, who consider a day or two sufficient exposure. Still others concentrate on the intermediate term of a few weeks to several months, perhaps concentrating upon telephone switching between equity mutual funds and money market funds when certain technical indicators "give signals." Many market participants are unaware that they are influenced by market gossip and faulty analysis, even though they decide from time to time to "get out" merely because of all the pessimism abroad. Some of us may be long-term timers, dealing with multiyear periods by adjusting our participation (speculation) levels or by augmenting existing positions with shorter-term insurance-hedging instruments, as reviewed in Chapter 8.

Among students of the stock market, a great debate rages about market timing, including whether it can be done effectively for more than one or two lucky guesses, and is productive for the average speculator to dabble in at all. As usual with stock market debates, there are extreme and rigid positions for the main camps, while some individuals embrace a common sense, pragmatic compromise that attempts to use effective ideas from the opposing extremes.

We should like to avoid most of the great market declines, such as 1929–32, 1973–74, September–November 1987, and July–October 1990. On the other hand, all of these severe declines set the stage for excellent market advances, which allowed the buy-and-hold (and averaging down) speculator a good chance to recover significantly in the bounce-back reactions. Recall that even in the Crash of '29, there was a 50 percent comeback rally early in 1930. Then, when a great many market players had given up by '32, there was a huge 127 percent rally from February 1933 through February 1934. Again, in the depths of the depression, the Dow Jones Industrial Average managed a 127 percent gain in 32 months, from July 1934 into March 1937.

In the summer of 1995, we see that the market had completely recovered from the Crash of '87 and its Meltdown Monday (October 19), closing DJIA of 1738.74. The DJIA had moved above its pre-Crash, all-time closing high on August 25, 1987 of 2722.42 to 4736.29 on July 17, 1995, an advance of 2013.87 points (73.97 percent), not counting dividends that account for some 50 percent of the total return of blue-chip stocks.

How neat it would have been to have enjoyed most of the 43.6 percent Dow Jones Industrial Average (DJIA) gain registered between December 31, 1986 (1895.95) and the high at August 25, 1987 (2722.42), and yet thereafter to have avoided most of the 36.1 percent DJIA selloff through October 19. How wonderful to have recognized the market's massive oversoldness and relative undervaluation at the close of trading on Monday (October 19) or after the opening on Tuesday (October 20) and to have returned to the market in time to catch most of the DJIA's 72.52 percent rise over the next 33 months.

A similar example of short-term market plunge and recovery can be seen in the selloff of '90, which was especially deep for small-company stocks. From the all-time DJIA high of 2997.75 on July 16, 1990, the DJIA declined to 2365.10 on October 11, 1990, a sharp drop of 632.65 points (21.10) percent in less than three months. Fortunately, by January 31, 1994, the DJIA had recovered to another all-time high of 3978.36, advancing 1613.26 points (68.21 percent), not counting dividends.

The rollercoaster ride continued in 1994. After trading for much of the year in a range of less than 10 percent below its high of January 31, 1994, the DJIA had a minor selloff in November, before stabilizing and having a traditional, if anemic, year-end rally which carried through to many all-time new highs by July 1995.

Whatever the market dynamics and our abilities to adjust to them, it seems clear that coping with major market moves should be considered, even if we can never catch all of their advancing trends or avoid all of their declining trends. Then too, individual stocks and industry groups often run counter to the major trend in either direction, complicating the simplistic notion that merely timing the trends of certain major averages and indexes such as the DJIA or the S&P 500 will always be likewise reflected in our portfolios of undervalued stocks.

Nevertheless, we want to be aggressive in undervalued and oversold markets, and defensive in overvalued and overbought markets. In between, we can pursue an optimistic policy based upon the historic upward bias to the market, especially augmented with good stock selection. The parameters for determining market undervaluations and overvaluations, as well as overbought and oversold criteria, are reviewed in Chapter 4.

Performance, Dollars and Percentages

Although price, value, and worth are expressed in dollars and cents (if awkwardly in eighths, sixteenths, thirty-seconds, etc.), performance is expressed in percentages and those are the numbers on which to concentrate. If Berkshire Hathaway common shares close up $50 for the day in mid-1995, that is in truth something less than a 1/4 of 1 percent advance, as the stock (at that time) traded around $22,000 per share. By the way, in late 1989, Berkshire Hathaway was trading around $8,100 per share. But if a $2 stock advances a mere 1/8 (12.5 cents) for the day, it then has appreciated over 6 percent. If we owned 10 shares of Berkshire Hathaway ($220,000 market value), they would have increased $500 in market value. A $220,000 position in a $2 stock up 1/8 would have increased $27,500 in market price. It's the percentages that matter and tell the story, especially as portfolios are priced in terms of total market value.

Unfortunately, percentages can easily be used to mislead the unwary. For example, if a portfolio increases in price at 15 percent per year compounded it will double in a little less than five years (see Table 1–1). The thumbnail computation for compounding is called the Rule of 72, divide the annual percentage into 72 to see how long it would take to double at that rate. For example, a 10 percent annual growth rate would take about 7.2 years to double the value of the asset.

Some unscrupulous (or ignorant) investment advisors could present misleading performance figures that sound correct. For example, a compounded annualized rate of return of 15 percent for five years provides a 201.14 percent increase— a 101.14 percent gain. If you divide 101.14 percent by five (years), you might think you gained an annual return of 20.23 percent compounded per year instead of the actual 15 percent compounded annual return. The five-year "average return" would be 20.23 percent per year, but not compounded annually. A 20 percent compounded annual gain for five years becomes 148.8 percent in five years, not 101.14 percent!

Certain common sense or intuitive perceptions imply that a low-priced or a small-market-capitalization stock can advance faster and farther than a high-priced stock or a large-market-capitalization stock. *Market capitalization is the total dollar amount obtained by multiplying the number of shares outstanding times the price per share of a stock.* If a corporation has one million shares outstanding, trading at $5 per share, its market "cap" is $5 million.

There are elements of statistical probability in these intuitive notions about potential corporate growth and price appreciation, discussed at length in Chapter 2. It certainly seems easier for a corporation with $50 million in sales to grow faster than IBM with its $50+ billion in sales. For IBM to grow 10 percent a year, it has to create the equivalent of another $5 billion corporation; for a $50 million corporation to grow 20 percent, it only has to gain another $10 million in sales.

Intuitively, it seems easier for a stock to advance from $5 to $10 than from $50 to $100. But such intuitions can be wrong. Fundamental analysis can show that the $50 stock is undervalued and represents far more proportional worth than the overvalued (perhaps worthless) $5 stock, and thus is far more likely to double in market price despite its higher current price. *Again, we are interested in the percentages involved rather than dollar amounts.* We will not be misled by stock splits, where one share of an $80 stock becomes two shares of a $40 stock, causing no change in the stock's fundamental valuation (with all financial numbers halved to account for the split). But we will notice that a $2 advance on each of our new shares of the $40 stock, represents a 5 percent gain on the split shares, while a $2 advance would only have been a 2.5 percent gain if the stock had not been split and was trading at $80 per share.

Margin, Leverage, and Pyramiding

The subject of margin perhaps involves the greatest number of preconceptions and misconceptions of any term or subject involving stock speculation. *Margin refers to the practice of borrowing money against the market value of a stock or stock portfolio.* This is a somewhat complicated subject, reviewed in detail in Chapter 5, "The Myths and Magic of Margin." It is important to understand just what margin is, what can be done with it, what pitfalls to avoid, and how to protect oneself against abusing it and suffering the consequences.

Many people think that the stock market is risky enough to begin with, and certainly no place to use borrowed funds for "investing," let alone speculating. Attitudes range from those who never borrow money (and certainly not for buying things they don't need) to those who used (actually overused) margin and were wiped out in 1929 or thereafter. If the use and effects of margin are approached rationally, employing it need not be more dangerous than buying a house. Most people mortgage (borrow against the house's equity) 75 to 80 percent or more of the house's appraised market value in order to acquire it. This is like leveraging a corporation, using the corporation's value to borrow against, in order to pay most of the cash portion of the purchase.

Obviously, one can overpay for a house and take out too large a mortgage for one's income which sometimes becomes an overwhelming burden, especially in an economic downturn. Under such circumstances, one could lose the house and the improvements and down payment that went with it. Because some people are foolish or unfortunate is no reason to avoid taking a prudent mortgage. Where would modern business be without short-term borrowed funds to buy inventory and meet fluctuating cash flow, and long-term borrowing to build or upgrade plants and purchase modern equipment for anticipated growth and improved returns on equity? Just as a thoughtful and prudent "businessperson's risk" is made in home buying or business expansion, so borrowing can be an effective tool for enhancing total return of an undervalued, diversified, long-term stock portfolio.

The flexibility gained through the use of margin allows an investor to buy additional stocks without using additional cash or selling currently held positions. Suppose I have an unmargined portfolio of 20 stocks—positions against which I can borrow money from my broker—with a market value of $100,000, and I believe that all the stocks I own are very attractive (undervalued). I do not want to sell any of my current positions, but I have found some other similarly undervalued stocks that I would like to buy. If market conditions seem propitious, by using the loan value or borrowing power of my portfolio, I could borrow up to $50,000 in cash, which would allow me to buy up to another $100,000 of stocks. This would leave me owing the broker $100,000 and still be in possession of my $100,000 equity. I would then be on 50 percent "margin," owning 50 percent of the market value of my portfolio and owing (a debit balance of) the other 50 percent. I would have $200,000 worth of stocks working for (or against) me. That much is clear.

Well, maybe not so clear to those who have never contemplated the concept. Some people confuse *margin* with *leverage*. Margin is the cash component, the amount one must put up to buy stocks "on margin," and thereafter it becomes one's equity of cash value ownership proportion (margin percentage) of the portfolio. Leverage is merely the other side of the equation. At 50 percent margined I would be 100 percent leveraged, that is, I would have 100 percent more stock than my equity, than an unmargined portfolio of the same equity value. If through market value decline, my equity (margin) falls to 40 percent, then I would be 150 percent leverage, (60 percent loan / 40 percent equity = 150 leverage).

Now suppose my $200,000 margined portfolio gains 10 percent in market price during the next few months, but all the stocks it contains remain undervalued. Again, I find more great-looking, analyzed bargains. With that 10 percent portfolio gain ($20,000), I can buy another $20,000 worth of stock by borrowing 50 percent of the gain, which created a new $10,000 loan value, or $20,000 worth of buying power, without putting up additional cash. I can "pyramid" my unrealized profits, which is to say, put them to work for me without cashing out some still undervalued positions (and without creating tax consequences).

Am I at greater risk after buying the additional $20,000 worth of stocks than I was before the 10 percent market gain? Not significantly, because even after I buy the additional stock I am still in a 50 percent margined position. That is, my equity ($110,000) coupled with my loan (of $110,000) controls $220,000 worth of stock. But look at the effect—I'm now controlling $220,000 worth of stock based upon my initial $100,000 of equity. If the portfolio continues to advance, I can continue to add stocks, based on increased borrowing or purchasing power.

Of course, if the portfolio declines, the losses of original capital are magnified in proportion to the percentage the portfolio is margined and pyramided. In this example, a 10 percent market price loss on a $220,000 portfolio would represent a 22 percent loss of original equity. It's not a free ride.

Because I have not emphasized the very real risks of stock investing and the increased danger of doing so with margin does not mean that these risks don't exist or that I am oblivious to them. For now, try to keep an open mind about the subject of margin, to be reviewed and explained in several additional commentaries later in this book.

Summary

Perhaps the most important characteristics of a successful stock speculator are belief and patience. If one understands the upward long-term bias of the stock market and has the patience to wait for bargains, and thereafter the patience hold them for their fair values—a process that can take many years—the likelihood of handsome gains is great.

Stocks are measured in terms of their current price, their corporations' current and future estimated values, and their worth to the individual speculator based upon market, economic, tax, and other considerations. We want to buy stocks when they are bargains, when their market prices are at least 50 percent below their estimated present or near future fundamental values. We want to sell stocks when they are fairly valued. Sometimes we will take less than full value if we are concerned about a serious marketwide decline. Sometimes we will hold out for a premium above fair valuation if stock and market trends and conditions appear propitious.

I cannot emphasize too strongly that this process requires tremendous patience, both in waiting for undervalued stocks, but even more so in holding onto stocks for their fair valuations. It is important to keep the basics clearly in mind and to be consistent and systematic in our methodology. Many of our stocks will fail to reach anticipated values or even profitability, while many will go on to outperform our most liberal estimates. Because some of the best-looking stocks will become losers, it is important to maintain a widely diversified portfolio. In such a portfolio, the winning stocks tend to gain much more than the losing stocks lose, resulting in a positive long-term average appreciation. Growth and value are usually long-term propositions. Although there will be periods of disappointment, the overall average gains will likely provide handsome returns.

We select stocks based on their corporations' fundamentals, and we purchase them based on their market undervaluation in order to profit by selling them at or above full valuation. But we also consider the condition of the stock market in general. The stock market can be overvalued and overbought, and thus likely to decline; or undervalued and oversold, and thus likely to advance. Obviously, the stock market can be some combination of these criteria, so that our purchase or sale of stocks will be affected by our determinations of the stock market's condition and the significant likelihood of its advancing, declining, or maintaining a trading range. Still, we are buying corporations' stocks for their potential, which is usually far more important that so-called market timing.

After the strategies of stock selection, portfolio management, and market timing are well understood, total returns can be enhanced through the prudent use of margin borrowing funds against the market value of portfolios in order to buy additional undervalued stocks, increase diversification, and take advantage of bargains in propitious markets. Not many speculators or professionals really understand all the technicalities of margined portfolios, especially the underlying rational premises. We think we have a good handle on the technique, as reviewed in Chapter 5.

2

Fundamental Corporate Analysis

I can't decide whether thoughtful philosophers would make good stock marketeers, or successful investors and speculators would make good philosophers. For example, an important subject in philosophy is the problem of appearance versus reality. Common sense or a bit of reflection tells us that what we see, hear, or otherwise sense does not necessarily correspond to underlying or ultimate realities. We see individual stock prices jump up one day and drop down the next. We see the stock market do the same, and every day there are reasons given for what has happened. It's not that many of these reasons are untrue or miss the point entirely; it's just that they are neither necessary nor sufficient to create the effects ascribed to them (they are not causal). Market analysis that goes beyond the basic precept that the market advances because there are more buyers than sellers is often wrong or misleading.

Many stock market participants act like lemmings crowding this way or that, periodically rushing euphorically into a near market top or, in panic, out of a near market bottom. These behaviors are stimulated by an emphasis on superficial appearances at the expense of significant underlying realities. Perhaps the worst single offending and misleading area is stock price. If the price is going up, that's good; if it's going down, that's bad. While this fluctuation or effect sometimes represents a strong underlying reality, often it doesn't. A stock's price is many times the temporary result of the lemminglike rush into or out of the stock for reasons that are independent of its, the market's, and the economy's underlying realities. One major reality often masked by a stock's price appearance (market action) is the fundamental value and growth of the corporation represented by the stock. If we can cut through the daily weather of stormy and sunny days to recognize the

21

long-term climate of seasons and growth, we will obtain a much better understanding of what is actually going on and what is likely to happen in the future.

Cutting through the short-term ephemera is what a speculator attempts to do in looking out for the long-term probability of future events. The person who thinks as a speculator is a step ahead on the road to reality in recognizing the futility of guessing, estimating, or analyzing the outcomes of financial commitments. The speculator invests, but with a greater understanding and appreciation for the risks, seeable and unforeseeable.

The Reality of Corporate Value and Growth

Fundamental analysis is really *corporation analysis*, but of course it is usually called *stock analysis*. In that semantic shift from stocks to corporations lies the root of much erroneous thinking among investors. Just as our outlooks and strategies are colored by our emphasis on the word *stock*—we say we deal in stocks and we are in the *stock market*—so too what passes for fundamental corporate analysis may be overwhelmed and distorted by constantly referring to *stock analysis*.

One of the complications of investing is that stocks have a life of their own for long periods of time. Because they are traded in markets and on exchanges, stocks have certain characteristics that are often independent of the corporations they represent. It is this pieces-of-paper and stock-market-dynamics independence that makes it doubly difficult to avoid mixing analysis of corporations with analysis of stocks as objects in the market. After all, when working with stocks, who among us thinks we are buying corporations? And how many would really care how well a company is managed if we had a way to pick stocks that almost always gained 20 to 25 percent or more a year?

Ironically, it is by evaluating *businesses* that we stand the best chance of finding stocks that may appreciate 20 percent to 25 percent a year, at least over a multiyear period. I have often been called a good stock picker, but actually I pick corporations.

One of the major themes of this book is that *prudent stock investors deal in corporations*. We are first and foremost prudent corporation speculators, who inspect present worth and future growth probabilities. We buy, hold, and sell common stocks because they represent equity positions in corporations—we buy, hold and sell very small ownership percentages of corporations. In that sense we literally buy into and sell out of the equivalent of limited partnerships, with most of their benefits and without many of the hassles (such as restricted entry and illiquid exit) limited partnerships involve.

A parallel to the corporation versus stock relationship may be seen in our thinking about health. We can concentrate on the causes of good health or illness or we can focus on their symptoms. That is, we can think of a stock's price as a symptom of the corporation's perceived health or illness. *Symptom management* is an important area in medicine yet the basis of a cure lies in understanding the causes of a disease, not merely in focusing on its symptoms. So, too, the basis of speculating in common stocks lies in concentrating on the "health" and prognoses for corporations rather than on the apparent and often misleading symptomatic, temporary price fluctuations of their stocks.

Since the stock market has a dynamic of its own, often independent of corporate reality, we could practice some effective stock management if we could keep in mind that we deal in corporations; we are in the corporation market. Our focus and effectiveness would then probably improve immensely.

Technical analysis of stocks, on the other hand, tends to deal only with stocks, especially their quantities of shares traded and their market price changes. You will not find much, if any, technical analysis of stocks in this book. You will find some technical market analysis, which is almost independent of individual stock criteria. While I believe there are some successful technicians who can ride the stock-market trends and scalp some profits, I also believe their successes are generally inferior to those of effective stock fundamentalists. A prudent speculator buys value and growth—undervalued healthy corporations and unappreciated rapidly growing corporations—the shares of which reflect their values in increased market prices over the years.

I believe there are far more pure fundamentalists than pure technicians, although I imagine some technicians would dispute that observation. Technicians are proud of their basic premise, sometimes overweeningly so, that all they need to see is the trending price/volume action of a stock on a chart to determine if it is a buy, sell, or hold.

Technicians and fundamentalists alike need not know, care, nor remember what a corporation does, but the fundamentalist's decisions are based on such staples as its balance sheets and income statements, its position *vis à vis* macroeconomic movements, or even impending or actual buyout announcements. On some occasions I've seen technical analysts strongly recommend a stock at its buyout price because they did not pay attention to fundamental news. Their charts merely showed the price rise on high volume, which automatically triggered a buy signal.

Many technicians also attend to corporate fundamentals, monetary conditions, interest-rate levels, and economic policy. Some fundamentalists also pay heed to technical indicators of specific stocks, if not individual stocks, then the market in general or its subsets. I do not want to divert our attention on fruitless debates about the pros and cons of each approach. I still believe it is worthwhile for students of stock speculation—by which I always mean corporate speculation—to become aware of major investment approaches to see if one or another (or a specific aspect in an otherwise incomprehensible or unwieldy system) has insights for our eclectic approach. When doctrinaire technicians claim that all they need to know about a corporation is already reflected in the price/volume action of its stock, I believe they overstate their case. They are flirting dangerously with fallacious after-the-fact reasoning (*post hoc, ergo propter hoc*).

Down-and-Dirty Analysis May Be Good Enough

Fundamental corporate analysis, as practiced by professionals who have a vested interest in erudition and esoteric expertise, can be an exceedingly complex, time-consuming enterprise. Just think of all the accounting and auditing that goes on in a major corporation. Add to that the many projections made by the corporation's marketing department and the efforts by management for cost control and efficiencies in manufacture and distribution.

Not only might we want to know the past contributions of research and development projects, we might also want to be aware of current and anticipated funding, as well as the possibility of any gangbuster products in the pipeline. However, there is great danger of information overload, of missing the forest by being preoccupied with the trees. There is also the problem that we are projecting or reinforcing uncertain future events on unrepeatable or questionable past events.

There are wonderful stories about clever company analysts counting the cars in the parking lot, visiting plants and offices at night (to see if extra shifts are working), and keeping tabs with the corporation's printers to see if orders for shipping cartons are on the increase. There are few if any stories about how such clever observations have sometimes proved misleading. If the corporation was on double shift, rapidly building up inventory and storing the excess at its retail outlets in all those cartons it ordered, while its sales were decreasing significantly, you would not recognize this by inspecting the plant, carton-maker, and shipping dock, but you could notice inventory buildups and slower sales gains by reviewing the corporation's quarterly and annual financials (accounting statements).

On the other hand, I love the story told by Bernard Baruch in his autobiography, *My Own Story*, about sending an agent to check out a railroad in the Midwest. The agent walked along the tracks and noticed that a lot of coal was lying around the tracks. He wired back that the railroad was doing good business, on the observation that their coal cars were filled to overflowing as evidenced by the spilt coal. Another investor interested in the railroad had a detailed and handsome research report compiled and published, which required a few months of investigation and analysis. By then, Baruch had done his buying and was happy to sell out with a big gain after the good news was quantified and distributed.

The Super Seven Selectors or the Big Three?

You needn't be a certified public accountant or an industrial spy at the loading docks in order to find undervalued stocks (which is to say corporations), trading for less than their fair, intrinsic, or fundamental value (take your pick) in terms of their stock market prices. You can actually discover undervalued companies by checking out only three of the most fundamental measures of a corporation's value; or you may investigate further by including another four ratios. All these valuation figures are published, public information readily available for anyone to inspect. It's simple and above board, though perhaps a little boring compared to all the tales of insider information, corporate raiders, or market-maker manipulations one hears so much about.

In preparing this chapter, I questioned if three criteria would be sufficient for effective stock picking, or if I needed at least five, or perhaps seven (at least for alliteration and luck), or even several more. I've wondered how much information and how many nuances there are that I might be taking for granted. There is a tradeoff between methods that are oversimplified and ones that are overwhelming. I am also concerned that, after 26 years of studying corporations and the stock market, I have gained a number of intuitions and attitudes that are completely foreign to many people reading this book, and which I have perhaps glossed over.

The "big three" fundamental criteria are *price/earnings*, *price/revenues*, and *price/book value* ratios. With these alone, I think we could find all the undervalued stocks we could use. Of course, we would want to work out criterion levels and a gestalt relationship (how the whole represents its parts) among the ratios. For instance, if the book value and revenues were deeply discounted—very cheap in relation to the stock's price—we might not be very concerned about the current price/earnings ratio. Further, we might look at the five- to seven-year trends of these ratios as support for their probable continuation over the next few years.

From another point of view—and I hope this doesn't frustrate or confuse you—the big three could be *price/cash flow*, *return on equity*, and *market capitalization*. I think if one were limited to only three criteria, there would be a strong likelihood of finding all the undervalued stocks we could use with these three criteria substituting for those mentioned above, with similar caveats and considerations. As this and the next chapter unfold, I hope you'll see why I believe such minimalist analytic criteria are sufficient for effective stock picking.

I honestly believe that one would do better speculating with a modicum of information than with too much. Also, one would do well to explore intuition and nonanalytical powers, so genuinely discussed in Bennett W. Goodspeed's *The Tao-*

Jones Averages, wherein Taoism and right-brain thinking are reviewed in hopes of moving toward a whole-brained approach to life as well as investing. Remember, information alone is not knowledge, and knowledge by itself is not wisdom. Wisdom is not necessarily an outcome of reviewing information and gaining knowledge; it is an integration and distillation, which often involves going beyond what passes for information and factual knowledge to include intuition.

For my part, I have tried to latch onto the "big picture" statistical assumptions and outcomes. Since I do not believe that we can have certain knowledge of the future—perhaps such an admission is a first small step toward wisdom—it doesn't bother me that stock market outcomes are uncertain and often unpredictable, at least with great precision.

So many people have told me they do not like investing in stocks and the stock market because they have so little control over events and outcomes. Often, these same people crow about how great real estate is because of its tangibility and accessibility. They have convinced themselves they have economic control with real estate. After all, it's real (tangible), isn't it? In the past several years, talk to any number of midwestern farmers, Texans, Californians or New Englanders about how much control they have (or had) over their real estate. The illusion of real-state control versus the reality of unexpected trends in interest rates and bond prices should be recognized by all readers seeking to comprehend the speculative but long-term beneficial nature of investing.

Since I believe that I operate in an economic system that will continue pretty much in its present form, I expect past patterns will likely be repeated in a similar if imprecise manner in the future. Thus, if the stock market has advanced—managed a total return of 10.2 to 12.2 percent per annum on average—for over 69 years, I suppose that it will continue to do so for an appreciable while longer. I take it that this positive-sum game in stocks is a reflection of the positive-sum earnings of their corporations over the years.

Along the road to investment success, there may be any number of variations; the big picture is made up of many little images. There are periods when some kinds of corporations fare better than others, only later to be eclipsed themselves. If I can find a sufficient number of diversified, undervalued companies, while avoiding fully valued or overvalued businesses, perhaps I can capture twice the gains of the historical averages. Perhaps I can also find techniques to anticipate patterns of corporate growth and regression, as well as predictive indications of market manias and depressions (and thus better historical averages) by minimizing exposure to long-term market declines and maximizing participation in long-term market advances.

At any rate, I believe it is good common sense to go with the flow, to find economic values that are underpriced in the marketplace. By persevering in this quest, albeit with many corporate stumbles and market misfortunes, we should be able to enjoy the fruits of our analytic and intuitive skills.

In this chapter I will review seven criteria for picking an undervalued corporation, even though you might want to settle on only three of these, as previously noted. If several of these fundamental financial criteria indicate significant to serious undervaluedness, the stock under analysis is a bargain and likely to outperform the general market over the next three to five years. I must admit that I haven't run a study on all the stocks I recommended over the past 18 years that were mainly considered in terms of these criteria, because the number of permutations is too great to find a single, neat formula. In many cases, one must make a judgment call when some criteria are screamingly undervalued and others are not. Rarely is a corporation's stock perfectly undervalued by each and every measure.

Not necessarily in order of importance—because different fundamentals are more important for some corporations than for others—the seven selection criteria I will concentrate on are:

1. Price to earnings (P/E).
2. Price to sales or revenues (P/R).
3. Price to book value (P/BV).
4. Price to cash flow (P/CF).
5. Return on equity or net worth (ROE).
6. Market capitalization (market cap).
7. Return on assets (ROA).

You may be shocked or disappointed not to see *dividend yield, current ratio, debt to equity,* or *price to net working capital,* among other widely followed criteria, listed above. These and other ratios, fundamentals, and considerations will be reviewed in Chapter 9. For now, let us agree to have a "willing suspension of disbelief" that the Super Seven Selectors are sufficient (if not all necessary) for superior stock selection.

What we are doing is called *screening*. We review many corporations' financials, looking for those configurations that meet our basic criteria. If we find too many stocks meeting one set of fundamentals, say P/E 10 or less, price per share less than two times book value per share, and revenues per share equal to or less than price per share, we can raise one or more of our criteria. The next pass-through might select stocks at P/E 9 or less, 1.5 times book value or less, or 0.75 or less revenues to price. These passes can be made in a relatively short time, after which individual stocks can be inspected for additional, available fundamental information.

Essentially, this initial filtering of the undervalued wheat from its fairly or overvalued chaff usually provides us with too great a selection of bargain stocks.

However, from this first "harvest" we may obtain 100 or more candidates, which are then analyzed further for superior total configurations of these or other criteria. We also test further for dubious or undesirable characteristics, usually found by perusing quarterly and annual reports as well as checking out trends and projections, or perhaps just noticing high debt ratios.

The Importance of P/E

The price/earnings ratio (P/E) is probably the most quoted fundamental indicator. Some analysts downgrade the practice of relying on current (most recently reported) earnings as being too subject to accounting choices and changes. P/E is simply the current price of a share of stock divided by the "current" after-tax earnings per share. P/E can be confusing or misleading. Current earnings usually refer to the most recently reported quarter's or year's after-tax earnings, so they might be called *last quarter's*, *this year's*, *last year's*, or (preferably) *trailing* (past quarter, four quarters, or past 12 months) earnings. Even the "current" trailing annual earnings will be somewhat out of date, usually published weeks to months after the year-end close. From now on, I will use earnings to refer to trailing four-quarter (or *current*) earnings.

Earnings are generally reported quarterly, sometimes with a several-week delay. Even so, we would want to update earnings with each quarter's reported earnings, and refer to *the recent 12-months' earnings* or *the last four quarters' reported earnings* rather than waiting for (or using) the fiscal year's earnings only. Of course, we are long-term speculators, more interested in corporate growth and valuations over the years than with quarterly jumps and stumbles. We prefer to "smooth out" quarters of volatile earnings for the long-term trend. We do not want to buy a stock because of one quarter's "earnings explosion" only to have to sell it (or another) stock a few months later solely because of one quarter's "earnings disappointment."

Interpreting earnings can be devilishly tricky due to the potential for arbitrary and self-serving accounting decisions and practices. Writeoffs and writedowns; changes in reserves; changes in valuing inventory from last-in, first-out (LIFO) to first-in, first-out (FIFO); and other adjustments can play havoc with reported earnings, especially when comparing them to prior (or projected) years, as well as to another company, industry, or marketwide earnings/ratio averages.

Earnings are also subject to "dilution," such as when there are convertible bonds or convertible preferred stocks, warrants, or options outstanding. Earnings usually are reported in two ways; as primary after-tax earnings and as fully diluted after-tax earnings. Fully diluted earnings take into account the potential increase in common shares if all convertible instruments were changed into shares of common. Fully diluted earnings can mislead as warrants expire or convertible instruments are retired. Many corporations do not have fully diluted earnings, because they have no convertible instruments outstanding, but when they do, we use fully diluted earnings for our analyses. Otherwise, the figures we use are primary earnings.

There are also one-time, "extraordinary" earnings, such as from the sale of a major asset, which do not occur in the normal course of business. Because of their nonrecurring nature we tend to factor out extraordinary earnings, at least as far as earnings trends and projections are concerned. Likewise, there are extraordinary losses, which may distort the earnings picture for a period of time. Extraordinary gains and losses are more exceptional than normal; however, they can be recognized even in a simple analysis. In the case of fully diluted earnings, you would want to guard against comparing these numbers against undiluted numbers, as well as adjusting criterion P/E levels.

In spite of the various possible snares, I find that one can almost ignore the potential accounting variations, which may be masked by the simple P/E number, especially since this (or any) one criterion by itself does not a corporate analysis or selection make. Also, there is that wonderful statistical idea that if the quality of earnings for some corporations is overstated, the likelihood is that the quality of earnings for other corporations is understated. The average P/E for a large group of analyzed corporations probably reflects a relatively fair assessment of their earnings valuation in the stock markets on average, despite individual company accounting variations.

Sometimes higher average P/Es represent higher quality of earnings and more consistent growth patterns—"the market's" (participants') judgment as to the quality of the underlying company itself. Pharmaceutical companies traditionally sport relatively high average P/Es, while auto companies struggle with relatively low average P/Es. Some of these traditional levels are based on historical precedent, perceptions of the cyclical nature of a business, and the perceived potential for sustained high profit margins, given the economic outlook.

In general, a high relative P/E is at least a danger signal that the market is rewarding a company with its great confidence, but will tolerate no faltering in that company's progress and profits. In the jargon, the stock with a very high relative P/E may have limited upside but large downside price vulnerability.

A stock's P/E can be interpreted in several ways. P/E tells us what investors are willing to pay per $1 of earnings for a particular corporation at a particular time. For example, if a corporation has earned $1 per share in trailing (after-tax) earnings and its shares are trading for $10 each, then it is trading for 10 times earnings, or P/E 10. In this example, stock buyers are willing to pay 10 times earnings, and thus receive a 10 percent *earnings return* on their investment. Another term for an undervalued corporation (and its stock) is *out of favor*. The P/Es of out-of-favor corporations are relatively low for any number of different reasons, but often because investors do not believe these corporate earnings are as stable or valuable as those of other corporations, whose stocks reflect their popularity with higher P/Es.

Some investors emphasize buying high P/E stocks of large, well-known, or popular corporations for a variety of reasons, such as perceived economic strength and investment visibility. Many studies have shown that low P/E stocks tend to outperform high P/E stocks over longer periods of time. I am indebted to the April 7, 1989 edition of *Market Logic* for featuring a wonderful research report, "Earnings Yields, Market Values, and Stock Returns," by J. Jaffe, D. B. Keim, and R. Westerfield, published in *The Journal of Finance* (vol. 44, no. 1), which concludes "that both [P/E ratio and market-capitalization selection indicators] have independent forecasting value, and that investors can improve their odds of success in the market by using both."

I noted in my newsletter *TPS 253* (April 13, 1989) that this study is particularly strong in its use of 36 full years—from 1951 through 1986—of broadly based data using nearly all common stocks listed on the New York and American stock exchanges. Each year (from March 31 through the following March 31) stocks were sorted into five equally sized categories, for both P/Es and market values. Confirming previous studies, the study shows that low P/E stocks significantly outperformed high P/E stocks, while demonstrating that both categories experienced similar degrees of price volatility. "This means that investors did not have to assume greater risk to achieve the greater returns of the low P/E stocks." Table 2–1 shows the performance of the various groups.

There are a few caveats. The researchers found that the predictive value of P/Es worked better in the 1970s and '80s than in the 1950s and '60s, while the market cap effect was equally predictive throughout the 36-year period. However, the researchers found that nearly all the advantage achieved by small stocks was attributable to the single month of January (the "January Effect").

The clear admonition to buy low and sell high is easily understood by everyone. Difficulties arise when we try to quantify what is low and what is high, especially relative to P/Es. Not only are these relative terms, but they represent different levels for different corporations during different economic and market conditions.

Categorical guidelines or rules, such as, "Never buy a stock for more than 10 times earnings!" or "Only buy stocks in the lowest 20 percent of P/Es!", may have

Table 2–1. Annual Returns by P/E Ratio and Market-Capitalization Selection

P/E Groups	Annual Returns	Market-Cap Groups	Annual Returns
Lowest 20%	19.1%	Smallest 20%	19.4%
Next lowest 20%	17.3%	Next smallest 20%	15.5%
Middle 20%	13.9%	Middle 20%	14.8%
Next highest 20%	12.9%	Next highest 20%	14.5%
Highest 20%	13.9%	Highest 20%	13.1%

a substantial degree of merit, but may also be counterproductive when they keep us away from a stock that rarely if ever trades for less than 10 times earnings, yet has other severely undervalued corporate criteria. Many undervalued and great growth corporations tend to trade on average (or for brief periods) for one and one half to twice this P/E. If we are so mechanical as to exclude all stocks trading at greater than P/E 10 or not in the lowest 20 percent of market capitalization, we may well miss many wonderful opportunities based on assets, growth, or turnaround potential.

Three Guidelines for P/E Norms

The three guidelines I have in mind, which are appropriate for analysis of all fundamental criteria, are:

1.   Historic ranges of individual stock.
2.   Industry and market averages, past and present.
3.   Comparisons with other fundamental ratios

I am going to spend considerable space reviewing P/E considerations, because they are often similarly applicable and appropriate for considering other fundamental criteria. To avoid redundancy, these considerations won't be repeated for every criterion. There are at least three uncomplicated guidelines for determining what is high and low as far as P/Es—and many other fundamental criteria. We can first look to the stock under analysis and determine its historical range and average(s). This number can be found in several publications, such as *Value Line Investment Survey*, and *Standard and Poor's Stock Reports*, or easily calculated from annual reports which show the P/E range per year for several years. Even this specific approach may not provide much precision because of the tendency for stocks to trade in a wide P/E range annually and over the years.

The First P/E Guideline

For example, taking the Dow Jones Industrial Average (DJIA) as a proxy for the large-capitalization market—a much abused liberty, because the DJIA 30 stocks often do not reflect other large-capitalization stocks or industries—we can determine (or accept published calculations) that the DJIA has traded in a P/E range of 5 to 23+ (but on occasion well over 50) times earnings over many years, with a multiyear average of about P/E 15. During 1992–93, the DJIA actually registered at P/Es of over 50 for many months. These high P/Es were mainly caused by huge writeoffs and nonrecurring losses that were not excluded in their calculations, at least in *Barron's*. For example, in '92 General Motors took a $33.43 nonrecurring loss, while IBM had a net loss of $11.00 and another $14.23 loss in '94. By taking these writeoffs and losses, many corporations "cleaned" their books, lowering book value while making it more accurate. During this period the market traded in a relatively narrow range without a 10 percent decline in the DJIA despite the high P/Es and the lower book values.

We can see that when the DJIA is trading between P/E 5 to 12 it is in an historically low range, and when the DJIA is trading between P/E 18 to 23 or higher it is in a high range. We can extend this review to say that DJIA-like (large-capitalization blue-chip) stocks are generally undervalued below P/E 12 and overvalued above P/E 18, at least in terms of this one criterion and its historical levels. Of course there are many exceptions. Generally, the so-called cyclical stocks such as autos, papers, aluminums and steels trade in a lower P/E range, with other industry groups such as pharmaceuticals and technology stocks tending to trade in a higher P/E range than the DJIA averages.

This rather oversimplified analysis of DJIA-type stock P/Es actually fits in with the *30-percent principle*, at least for DJIA-type (large industrial) corporations. If such stocks trade 30 percent or more below their P/E norm (average), they are undervalued; if they trade more than 30 percent above their P/E norm, they are overvalued. *Fair valuation* may be defined as the average P/E, or a reasonable area, say 10 to 20 percent, above or below the average. For example, if the stock of a hypothetical corporation, International Widgets, Inc. (IWI), has a P/E norm of 12, then IWI's stock is into undervalued territory at 8.4 or less times earnings, and overvalued at 15.6 or more times earnings. *Caveat:* individual stocks may be quite undervalued or overvalued on any given criterion, yet not when examined as a whole.

Notice that the P/E spread from undervalued to overvalued in this example is 7.2 times earnings, but we would like to buy a stock in anticipation of its doubling in market value, which might seem to require going from P/E 8.4 to P/E 16.8, an increase in P/E of 8.4. However, that doubling of the P/E would only be necessary if the earnings remained absolutely constant, which they rarely do! What often happens is that between buying International Widgets, Inc. at 8.4 times earnings and seeing it subsequently trading for 15.6 times earnings, its nominal earnings have increased, sometimes dramatically. In such a case the actual market price will have more than doubled in the process, often without coming close to a double of the initial low P/E ratio.

One of the tables I often construct at investment seminars is the potential P/E growth table. For purposes of simplification, let's assume that we've found an out-of-favor corporation whose stock is trading for five times $2 per share earnings, or $10 per share. The P/E norm for the past 10 or so years has been determined to be 10. Our analysis shows that this corporation has the potential to grow at 15 percent per year (or more) for the next several years. What might happen to its stock in the

Table 2–2. P/E Potential Growth Table

(Price per Share Equals Earnings Times P/E)

Years	P/E 5	P/E 7.5	P/E 10	P/E 12.5	P/E 15	P/E 17.5	P/E 20
0 ($2)	$10	$15	$20	$ 25	$ 30	$ 35	$ 40
5 ($4)	20	30	40	50	60	70	80
10 ($8)	40	60	80	100	120	140	160

marketplace, given these assumptions? Remember, at 15 percent per year compounded quantities double in five years.

Table 2–2 illustrates what could happen. Suppose we bought a stock at $10 because its earnings were $2 per share (thus P/E 5) because we thought it should be trading at $20, at its "average" P/E 10. If, while we are waiting for our fair price, the corporation grows at 15 percent per year, then in five years it would probably earn $4 per share. If its stock advanced apace, that is, to trade at least 10 times earnings because the company showed a solid growth rate for five years and market valuations in general approached average P/Es, the shares would trade for $40, not merely doubling but quadrupling—a 300 percent gain in five years or 31.95 percent compounded annually.

If the corporation continued to grow at a strong but not phenomenal rate of 15 percent per year, in another five years it would probably earn $8 per share. Given this lucrative, solid growth rate over a decade, and a bullish market that rises to high but not necessarily record valuation levels, the stock would probably trade at 15 times its $8 earnings, or $120—a gain of 1,100 percent in 10 years—or 28.2 percent compounded annually. Of course, the market could go crazy after awhile and trade at 20 times earnings on average, carrying our stock along with it.

Ah, the deception of numbers. If you would have asked me what I would rather have, a 300 percent profit in five years or an 1,100 percent profit in 10 years, I would have immediately chosen the 1,100 percent. Alas, an 1,100 percent profit in 10 years is "only" a 28.2 percent compounded annual gain, while a 300 percent profit for five years is a 31.95 percent compounded annual gain for five years.

It would have been better, in theory and compounded annual returns, to have gone from $10 to $40 twice (in two successive five-year periods) than hold still 10 years for the $120. After reaching $40 in five years, that amount would have to become $160 (another four times the then capital of $40) in another five years, in order to maintain the 31.95 percent compounding for 10 years.

I say *in theory* because in practice we might have to pay taxes on the first position realized after five years. If our tax liability came to 33.3 percent of the $30 profit, we would then have only $20 left, after taxes, plus the original $10 capital, or $30 overall to reinvest (for the second five-year period of this example). Then, it would take a fourfold increase to bring us back to $120, after the second five years. In California or another high-tax state, we might also have to pay another 9 percent or more in capital gains tax, thus leaving us with less than $30 to reinvest for the second five years. Although this topic is reviewed a bit in Chapter 3 (on stock portfolio management), I reemphasize that a major benefit of long-term speculating is in minimizing tax "attrition" and excessive trading commissions.

By the way, I hope you don't think the kinds of observations in the above paragraphs are merely a superficial game with numbers. It is just such awareness of arithmetic details that can make the difference between a systematic, long-term accumulation of assets versus a random grab at convincing numbers that upon closer examination actually fall short of your expectations.

Another P/E Guideline: Industry and Market Averages

Instead of determining the fair or normative P/E from historical analysis of a corporation's (stock's) average P/E, we can make comparisons with current industry, sector, or marketwide averages. Again, these comparisons also may be revealing for other fundamental criteria. I tend to avoid industry averages because of the variability of individual corporations within an industry. The sample number of corporations in an industry may be too small for statistical significance, or the corporation being analyzed may not be comparable to the "average" corporation in that industry. You could check to see how other companies are trading, but then you would have to calculate several of their norms and note any significant differences among them—a potential tempest-in-a-teapot exercise in analysis.

More promising, especially for down-and-dirty (yet adequate) comparisons, are marketwide or major index P/E average or current ratios. Such a guideline applies to long-term averages or moderate levels associated with "normal" market periods. For example, the Standard & Poor's 500 Index (S&P 500) of 500 stocks, mainly but not all taken from the New York Stock Exchange, had a P/E of over 22 in late August 1987 (at the S&P 500's then all-time high), but was trading for less than 11 in mid-November 1988.

Market or major index P/Es relate to many other considerations such as the current, early, middle, or late position in a rising or falling market cycle, the interest-rate levels, the inflation readings, and the money supply levels. As you become aware of and work with individual stock P/Es and market or major index P/Es, you will likely develop a feel for what is relatively high or low at any given period.

Given that the S&P 500 Index average P/E for the past 69 years is 14–15, the S&P 500 was very historically overvalued above 22 P/E and undervalued below 11 P/E. If you blindly compared our hypothetical International Widgets Inc.'s (IWI's) P/E to the S&P 500 P/E at these extremes, without invoking the S&P 500's long-term P/E average, you might conclude that in 1991–1993, IWI's P/E could be 22 (or even 30 percent higher) before being overvalued, and that it would be undervalued at 15.4—which would be terribly distorted and misleading criterion levels.

On the other hand, if IWI's P/E was 7.7 in mid-1995, you could say it was trading at a 48 percent discount to the S&P 500's current P/E, or a 45 percent discount to the S&P 500's long-time average P/E. This might be an interesting and useful comparison, especially if IWI typically traded in concert with the S&P 500's varying P/E, or at a premium or discount to it. Likewise, comparisons could be made to the Dow Jones Industrial Average's current and average P/E, as well as broader and more representative indexes such as the New York Stock Exchange Composite Index. A transportation or utility issue could be compared to those indexes' P/Es, and likewise other industry issues to appropriate subsets in the over-the-counter market or the American Stock Exchange.

A Third P/E Guideline: Comparison with Associated Ratios

Estimating a fair or normal P/E for any given stock may involve the interrelationships of other fundamental and economic criteria. A rule of thumb suggests that a stock's P/E ratio can be the same number as its corporation's return on equity (ROE), sometimes called return on net worth. That is, if IWI's ROE is 15 percent, IWI could be fairly valued—at least in terms of its earnings' criterion—if its P/E was 15.

This rule of thumb might get you in trouble if you invoke it for extreme readings. If IWI's ROE jumped to 30 percent, I doubt that I would want to pay 30 times earnings (P/E 30) for its stock. On the other side, if IWI's ROE came in at 5 percent, I still might want to buy its stock at five times earnings (P/E), especially if I could buy IWI for 20 percent (one-fifth) of its equity. If I could buy IWI at 20 percent of equity, with only a 5 percent ROE, I would be getting a 25 percent *return on* (my) *investment* dollars in the stock. More about this relationship under the topic of book value, later in this chapter.

Some important criteria could be included in our estimating fair P/E levels, for those investors who wish to take a more academic or analytical approach than I believe is necessary. I mention a few of these criteria not to overwhelm the average reader, but rather to satisfy the more technical types. These criteria include inflation levels (actual and perceived) and Federal Reserve Board (the Fed, or FRB) policies, including money supply growth, free bank reserves, and interest rates. In *normal times*—which may be an oxymoron—a P/E norm (for either a stock, an industry, or the market overall) would exist in relation to "normal" interest rates as well as other historically average monetary conditions.

Ostensibly, as interest rates advance, the cost of doing business increases and the likelihood of increasing profits diminishes. Perhaps a P/E of 12–14 would be fair for IWI when the 30-year "long" Treasury bond trades to yield 8 percent or the 91-day T-bill yields 5 percent. With the long T-bond at 9 percent, and 3-month T-bills at 7 percent, perhaps an IWI P/E of 10–12 would be fair (assuming equivalent "levels" of monetary criteria). When the long bond yields 6 percent and the 91-day T-bill yields 4 percent, perhaps a P/E of 14–16 would be fair—*fair* meaning a fairly or fully valued, average criterion level under those conditions—and so forth for other configurations of the interest yield curve.

Again, I almost question the review of these relatively esoteric considerations, for they are perhaps more than our analysis requires. Such considerations as Fed policy and inflation are kinds of important information to be utilized analytically and intuitively rather than systematically in fundamental analysis. Fortunately, many other valuation criteria already factor in and reflect these economic and monetary considerations which affect the analysis of fair P/Es, so again, one can set them aside in a down-and-dirty, but sufficient, analysis of corporate valuations for stock speculation.

To the degree that we can generally ignore stock-market and macroeconomic considerations as we doggedly persevere in the systematic *purchase of undervalued stocks in a widely diversified portfolio to be held for long-term appreciation*, and subsequent sale of fully valued stocks, we can pay as much or as little attention as we like to information other than elementary corporate fundamental analysis.

P/E Levels Are Relative and Changing

It would be nice, as mentioned before, to say, "Only buy stocks that are trading for less than 10 times earnings or 30 percent below their 10-year average P/Es." I cannot do that. In fact, I believe such advice is too narrow and often counterproductive. Some stocks at some times, such as auto companies, are fully valued at P/E 9 or less, while others may be significantly undervalued at P/E 18 or more. Then there are the cases where a stock doesn't have a P/E because it has recorded deficit earnings (normally, negative P/Es are not used) or its P/E is ridiculously high because of a sharp drop in earnings or rise in market price.

I arrive at a stock's P/E norm based upon its average P/E for a number of years, often weighting the most recent years more heavily, considering its ROE, and integrating general market and major index P/Es. Obviously, no P/E norm is carved in stone, and all are subject to revision as corporate fundamentals fluctuate and long-term market conditions change. The P/E norm should reflect a P/E attributable to the stock in a "normal" market, adjusted for current and likely conditions. I will review some actual examples of determining a P/E norm in Chapter 9—detailing three specific stocks' analyses, based on my method of using fundamental criteria.

The Case for Book Value

Book value is generally defined as assets less liabilities. Again, the criterion seems simple enough, but soon one finds that neither all assets nor all liabilities are created equal. As *book value* (BV) is an accounting term, all sorts of accounting options and decisions go into the rendering of the final figure. There often arises the question of so-called intangibles, such as goodwill, patents, trademarks, and names. For our purposes, we can ignore the large amount of gross and subtle analysis that can go into determining the elements of book value, and the adjustments that could be made.

In general, I accept the book values stated in annual reports, *Barron's*, *Forbes*, various Standard & Poor's reports and publications, *Value Line Investment Survey*, and other financial publications. These sources frequently highlight cases where the book values may be severely overstated or understated.

I take it that most corporations' book values generally understate what their replacement cost values would be. Such replacement cost (or whole-business) values are usually made dramatically clear during corporate mergers and acquisitions, where some multiple of book value is almost always paid for the target company. Again, invoking my statistical attitude, within a large number of analyzed corporations, errors of overstated book values in some will tend to be more than balanced by understated book values in others, on average.

A small review of price/book value (P/BV) ratios shows that different companies within the same industry trade with a wide range of values. Also, different industries exhibit different average book value to share price ratios. There is no magic criterion or absolute guideline for an undervalued or overvalued P/BV. Truly, in fundamental analysis everything is relative, especially to each corporation but also to the current general market level, which itself is fluctuating and relative to general economic and monetary conditions.

We know that the Dow Jones Industrial Average of 30 large-capitalization "industrial" stocks, for example, has traded at a P/BV ranging from slightly below 1.00 at market lows to over 4.00 during 1929, but historically around 2.20 at many market highs. In early 1995, the DJIA was trading at 3.61 times book value; a year earlier it was at 3.37! When one factors in the huge writeoffs of the early '90s, these P/BV ratios are not as extreme as they look compared to historical ratios. Yet individual DJIA stocks show extremes which are masked by their averages, just as the wide range of P/BVs for individual secondary stocks is masked by their overall average. For instance, in March 1989, General Motors traded for a P/BV of 0.86, while Merck's P/BV was 8.84, and many more analysts were recommending Merck than General Motors.

I have been quoted more than once in national publications saying that I buy stocks when they are trading at 50 percent of their book value, with the implication that 50 percent of book value is my limit. Other conditions being amenable, I would love to buy the stocks of viable corporations trading at 50 percent or greater discounts from their book values. Still, I am frequently happy to pay more than several times book value if other fundamental criteria indicate extreme undervaluation and if that stock normally trades at several times book value (such as, stocks of service companies that do not need large plants and equipment).

Interestingly, the *30-percent principle* that can be applied as a trading criterion for P/Es—buy stocks 30 percent below their P/E norm and sell them 30 percent above—applies almost equally as well to P/BVs. If our hypothetical IWI normally (on average over a multiyear period) trades around 1.5 times its book value, then when it is trading for 105 percent of its BV it is "cheap" (undervalued) on this criterion, and when it trades at 195 percent of its BV it is "dear" (fully valued). Of course, it is not sufficient to base a stock's purchase on one criterion alone.

If you reviewed corporate fundamentals during the winter of 1973–74, you could have found a large number of solid corporations trading for 20 percent to 50 percent of their tangible book values. In long-term ("bear") market lows you might buy corporations for "20 cents on the dollar" and thereafter hold them until they are trading for "$2 on the dollar," that is, for two times their BVs. Although it can stagger the imagination, and be difficult to capitalize on at the time because conditions are so bleak, one can easily understand how, in a depressed stock market, great companies are auctioned at half or less than half of their net asset (book) value because people are afraid that the bad times will get worse and shareholders will be forced to liquidate in order to raise cash to meet their current obligations.

There is a curious economic pattern that occurs during both enthusiastic and fearful conditions—the vicious stock-market cycle version of the *self-fulfilling prophecy*. The self-fulfilling prophecy refers to events occurring mainly because we believe they are going to happen, and we curiously affect such outcomes. Suppose that interest rates are rising and money is getting scarce. The average person (or competent chief financial officer) who is considering borrowing funds in the near future will think, "I'd better make that loan today (or as soon as possible) because tomorrow (or next month) I will have to pay a higher interest rate or there might not be any funds available at all." Thus, numerous lemmings—many of whom may not even need a loan for quite a while—create a "run" on the system, depleting the available funds and forcing up interest rates, just as the phenomenon they feared (prophesied) would happen.

Suppose the stock market's rise is rational, based on improved corporate earnings and the early phase of a growing business cycle, such as happened in 1988–89. As this market advance progresses, the average market player—who has been out of the market, or underinvested, waiting for the bear market that was supposed to follow the Crash of '87 to occur—may well think, "I'd better get in on the good times before they get even farther away from me." As the ranks of these reborn bulls grow, the prices of stocks are bid up in an effort to obtain stocks before their prices go even higher.

The self-fulfilling "melt-up" trend might continue until a "blow off" top occurs, and a downward trend reversal sets in. Then, after a while, the negative self-fulfilling trend becomes dominant and drives prices down to ridiculous levels, as the market cycle is completed, only to begin another advancing cycle all over again.

For long spells, perhaps 40 percent of the time, the stock market stays in a trading range, neither rallying out of sight nor crashing to the ground. These relatively dull periods—such as the three years 1991–94, are generally good times to accumulate undervalued corporations because stocks trading for less than book value or low P/BVs, plus other undervaluedness, after a big, marketwide decline can take years to be revalued upward to their historic norms. Long, relatively dull periods of sidewise market action can be "base-building" plateaus from which to launch the next major advance. As the market averages increase, based on the increasing valuations of individual stocks, the criteria for what is undervalued or overvalued become modified to reflect current conditions.

In 1974, I was looking for industrial corporations trading for 50 percent or less than their book values. By 1982, I was looking for industrial and service corporations trading at or for less than their book values. Since 1989, I am satisfied to find undervalued corporations that are trading for less than 150 percent of book values (on average), especially when these book values are understated and several other fundamentals indicate significant average undervaluation.

I have been asked how I feel about the "future value" of companies trading at 150 percent or more of book value. After all, isn't our basic principle to buy stocks at 50 cents on the dollar or 50 percent of what we think they are worth? Actually, I am interested in acquiring companies—or small fractions of them as represented by some shares of their stock—for 50 percent or less of what I believe they will probably trade for in the next three to five years. In many cases we don't have to wait that long; in other cases no amount of time brings profits.

Even if a corporation is currently trading at 150 percent of its book value, that book value may be significantly understated, especially in terms of replacement costs or as a going business value. Then too, over the next few years the corporation may double in value, continue to trade at 150 percent of book value or more, and thus still double in its market price.

How to Read Revenues

A corporation may have much room for improvement and many problems, but if its sales or revenues are adequate or growing, it is more likely improvements can be made and problems solved than if revenues are inadequate and diminishing. I learned about the importance of the price/revenues ratio (P/R) from Ken Fisher in his book *Super Stocks*[1]. Ken calls it the price/sales ratio (P/SR), and spelled out many of its peculiarities, especially as it applies differently to different types and sizes of business. You will also find in his book many wise observations, keeping up with his family tradition—his father, Philip A. Fisher, wrote the classic, *Common Stocks & Uncommon Profits*.

Like all stock price valuation criteria which show what marketeers are willing to pay for a corporation's fundamentals, the P/SR (we call it the P/R) shows what it costs—in terms of the current price of a share of stock—to buy $1 of corporate sales or revenues. This is not unlike the P/E ratio, which shows what investors are willing to spend to buy $1 of earnings. Like the P/E, the P/R also indicates a stock's perceived worth or popularity, that is, how the investing public values a corporation. If our hypothetical International Widgits, Inc. (IWI) trades for a P/R of 1.0, that means the price of a share of IWI is the same as one share's worth of its revenues. If IWI's P/R was 0.5, that means "the market" is willing to pay 50 percent of IWI's revenues to own IWI shares—50 percent of the per share revenues equals the per share price.

Clearly, most of the caveats and considerations relevant to determining a fair ratio or norm and consequently undervalued/overvalued criteria for a corporation's P/E or P/BV apply similarly to its P/R. That is, each corporation has its historical average P/R, which can be compared to similar companies, its industry group, major

Table 2–3. The Popularity Monitor

	Stocks Are:		
	Very Unpopular, with PSRs Less Than	**Accepted, with PSRs over**	**Very Popular with PSRs over**
If Companies Are:			
Small, growth-oriented, of technology type	0.75	1.50	3.00
Multibillion-dollar-sales sized or without growth attributes	0.20	0.40	0.80
Inherently thin margin, such as supermarkets	0.03	0.06	0.12

Source: Adapted from *Super Stocks*, Kenneth L. Fisher (Homewood, IL: Dow Jones-Irwin, 1984), see pp.36–37.

[1] Kenneth L. Fisher, *Super Stocks,* (Homewood, IL: Dow Jones-Irwin, 1984).

market averages, or even the market as a whole. Certain averages, which are displayed in Table 2–3, have been worked out by Ken Fisher, but beware the fixed guideline, especially when it involves the gross categorizing of corporations. Two examples: The Singer Corp. no longer manufacturers sewing machines, and many people were unclear about Stop & Shop Companies, categorizing it only as a supermarket.

The historical precedents of superior market appreciation for low P/R stocks are most encouraging, as are such precedents for low P/E and low P/BV stocks.

I would take Ken Fisher's PSR/popularity numbers at face value as a general (or at least starting) guideline for undervaluation, fair, and overvaluation, subject to possible adjustment for unique conditions of individual corporations. When a giant industrial company is trading at cycle lows, at 20 percent of sales or less (price per share to revenues per share), it is both very unpopular and very undervalued according to this criterion. Then, when it trades at 40 percent of sales or so, it is "accepted" and in the range of fairly valued. Finally, when it trades at a very popular 80 percent of sales or greater, it is overvalued.

Ken Fisher writes in *Super Stocks*, "The absolute scale of PSR/popularity seems consistent—as stocks rise from obscurity to high regard. I have no explanation for this and report it merely as an interesting observation, worthy of further consideration." Often in fundamental or technical analysis, certain relationships are predictive and work, although their discoveries were accidental and empirical, with no satisfying rationale or theory to account for them. At such times the profound maxim applies: "If it works, use it; if it ain't broke, don't fix it!"

By itself, such a simplistic categorization might be misleading, and we would take some care by checking historical price/revenue ratios to see if a corporation under analysis approximated these categories. Often, several measures of popularity/valuation will be consonant, reinforcing a general picture. Obviously, not all undervalued stocks are unpopular, just as not all unpopular stocks are undervalued. As the logicians might say, there is no necessary bisymmetrical relationship between these two attributes. That is, we shouldn't confuse the appearance of popularity with the reality of overvalue, and likewise the appearance of unpopularity does not necessarily imply undervalue. Nonetheless, the popularity and valuation attributes frequently reflect each other in many other fundamental criteria as well as P/Rs.

As is true of so many guidelines for fundamental (or technical) criteria, we must guard against being too slavish to any given element. If International Widgits, Inc., were a retailing company with a market value of less than $200 million, we might not want to call its stock undervalued if its P/R was 0.5. If a review revealed that 20 percent of IWI's revenue came from royalties on its patents and 30 percent from the manufacture of exotic (high-technology) electronics equipment—which were sold in its and others' retail outlets—then we would be wrong to assign IWI strictly to the retailing industry. Likewise, we would not want to look for a retailing P/R level without accounting for IWI's royalty and manufacturing, niche, and growth potentials.

Often, if not usually, the guides for fundamental criteria are imprecise. Furthermore, the criteria can fluctuate significantly over the reported quarters and years and should not be applied too rigorously. We are looking for a recognizable picture of a corporation that is undervalued in general or on average. Any given criterion may indicate overvaluedness, either temporarily or systemically. Nonetheless, the weight of combined evaluative indicators will range along a spectrum from very undervalued to very overvalued, and depending perhaps upon economic and market conditions—and the requirements of our portfolio management strategies—we would choose sufficiently undervalued stocks to accumulate and approximately fully valued stocks to sell.

Does Cash Flow Outrank Earnings?

The name of the game in corporate speculating is earnings. Corporations are founded and operated ostensibly to earn profits for their shareholders. This notion can get lost in a complex society and a stock market where special-interest groups *other* than the corporation's shareholders believe the company exists for them and their interests. We have seen entrenched managements who run public corporations as if they were private partnerships, but this unfortunate condition seems to be changing for the better in the mid-1990s.

In this fourth quarter of the century, especially in the 1980s, with relatively *laissez-faire* regulation and willful indifference to antitrust laws on the books, many managements have worked against their shareholders to take "their" companies private or to sell out to "White Knights" in order to maintain their jobs and obtain golden parachutes and huge retirement benefits. To add injury to insult, rogue managements have used the leveraged buyout (LBO) to accomplish their desires, essentially basing the purchase of the corporation on its own assets—assets belonging to its shareholders. It seems managements have deliberately failed to maximize (or optimize) earnings, lowering the analyzed value of their corporations in order to grab them on the cheap, only to subsequently institute necessary reforms that bring on profitability. Thereafter, the company reemerges as a public corporation, with windfall profits for the pirates. Happily, such vulture capitalism seems to abating in the middle 1990s like a fashion that is no longer tolerated.

Because speculating in corporations involves many factors other than earnings, at least for substantial periods of time, the aware speculator considers value and growth potentials over recent earnings disappointments and periodic glitches in rising earnings trends. Fundamentals that may reflect a more accurate picture of the health of a corporation than do periods of fluctuating or low earnings are also to be taken seriously. *Cash flow* is one of the measures that may be more stable than earnings, and as such may be more important in determining undervalued corporations than P/E.

Cash flow is generally defined in accounting terms as the net income of a corporation before the deduction of book charges such as depreciations and amortizations. As depreciation and amortization charges—allocations of the cost of an asset over its theoretical useful life—are not actual cash outlays, they do not penalize the use of current income, or the cash available for conducting business operations, expansion, debt repayment, and investment in other enterprises.

Cash flow is another tricky accounting subject. If the principal item, depreciation, which is based upon original cost and "useful life," is insufficient to cover the asset's replacement costs, then earnings are probably overstated and the business may be facing (or developing) financial difficulties in maintaining and renewing its plant and equipment. On the other hand, if plant and equipment have appreciated in value over the years and are worth more than their depreciated value on the books, then earnings were probably understated and there are "hidden" asset values.

Yet again, as with other fundamental criteria, price/cash flow (P/CF) ratios are relative to their corporation's historic average, as well as comparisons with other corporations, market averages, and especially rule-of-thumb ratios. P/CF numbers are similar to P/Es but higher, because cash flow is net earnings plus tax-reducing depreciation and amortization charges. If International Widgets, Inc. (IWI) trades for 10 times cash flow on average—currently $10 per share, with a cash flow of $1 per share—that would be its fair cash flow value. Then, invoking the 30 percent over- or undervalue criterion, when IWI trades for P/CF 7 (seven times cash flow) it would be just undervalued; at P/CF of 13 it would be just overvalued.

Often, we can find corporations trading for almost half their average P/CF, which is a strong indication of undervaluation. If IWI traded at P/CF 5, that would mean at $10 per share it was generating $2 per share in cash flow, which yields a handsome 20 percent *return on cash*. As each integer of P/CF comes down, the return on cash expands greatly. At P/CF 4 the return on cash is 25 percent, and at P/CF 3 the return on cash is 33.3 percent. Of course, we are not to confuse these "returns on cash" with earnings returns.

Andrew Tobias in *Money Angles* agrees that cash flow is worth reckoning:

> In many respects more important than earnings, this is the simple-minded measure of how much cash is pouring in or draining out. Real-estate operations always report bad earnings (because of the depreciation they claim, for tax purposes, on their properties), but the cash just rolls in bigger and bigger each year (because the properties actually appreciate and the rents get raised).[2]

---

[2] A. Tobias, *Money Angles* (New York: Avon, 1985), p. 200.

An analyst would want to be aware of the cause(s) of any significant changes in cash flow, such as a massive rebuilding or a replacement program that would lead to greater depreciation deductions but would also eat up available cash, perhaps requiring massive borrowing and a burdensome interest and debt repayment.

Not all fundamental analysts think highly of cash flow as a measure of a corporation's worth. Benjamin Graham and Charles McGoldrick, authors of *The Interpretation of Financial Statements*, find fault with cash flow when it is presented on a per share basis, thus implying "that it represents the 'true earnings' of the business. Such an inference would be completely wrong." Of course, we shall not confuse cash flow with earnings, just as we do not confuse extraordinary earnings with operating earnings or with fully diluted earnings. We take to heart departed Ben Graham's careful, conservative ways, and consider his admonition:

> In our view the average investor would do well to ignore the cash-flow figure, as it is more likely to mislead than to enlighten him. Security analysts should study these figures mainly to determine whether the amortization charges need revision as being either too high or too low from the comparative standpoint.[3]

What some corporate pickers look for is free cash flow, or the money a corporation has available to work with. Technically, this is the cash flow surplus left after capital expenditures and other required costs necessary to support the business and anticipated revenues. Free cash flow is usually highest for corporations that have large depreciation expenses, which are tax deductible, but do not need to replace the equipment being depreciated. The aforementioned real estate companies, leasing corporations with equipment that outlives its depreciated "useful life," or pipeline companies, and even utilities whose major capital expenditures are behind them, are examples.

For our purpose, which is to find that handful of valuation criteria that will help us select undervalued corporations, without becoming accountants or wheeler-dealers, straightforward P/CF can be used to see if our other criteria check out. Of course, we needn't ignore information about free cash flow if we stumble over it in our research.

Each of the Big Three or Super Seven selection criteria offered here can be fraught with questions of quality and relevance. What is the quality of earnings, the quality of assets that make up book value, or the appropriateness (quality) of cash flow? All are important questions. Still, by finding several general criteria that reaffirm each other—and perhaps a few other safety checks like the amount of debt and repayment schedules a corporation carries—the likelihood of picking a winning stock is good.

---

[3] B. Graham and C. McGoldrick, *The Interpretation of Financial Statements*, 3d rev. ed. (New York: Harper & Row, 1987), p. 67.

Market Capitalization: Davids Do Better Than Goliaths

If you like irony, then the stock market is the place for you. After all the learned analysis, the hours spent hunched over financial reports, keeping track of corporations by interviewing officers, customers, vendors, and the competition, it turns out that very-small-capitalization stocks outperform very-large-capitalization stocks by significant and important percentages over long periods of time. From data reviewed on Table 2–1 comparing P/Es and market capitalizations, we see that for a 36-year period small-caps stocks—defined as the smallest 20 percent of market capitalization—gained 19.4 percent annual returns compared to only 13.1 percent for the largest 20 percent of market capitalization.

Confirming evidence, if more subdued, using somewhat different stock populations, comes from Ibbotson Associates, who conclude that small-company stocks have averaged 12.2 percent total return per year for the 69 years 1925–94. In the same period, large capitalization stocks, as represented by the S&P 500, have averaged 10.2 percent total return per year. More about Ibbotson's analyses, below and in Table 1–2.

Many authors and researchers have reported on this phenomenon in books, journals and, investment newsletters. For a detailed analysis, peruse Gerald Perritt's scholarly yet readable book, *Small Stocks, Big Profits*[4]. Perritt takes a serious, academic view that shows how "the small-firm effect" has produced superior results without a commensurate increase in risk. Efficient market theorists insist that investment returns are proportionate to risks taken, and use this dogma to "explain" how some investors outperform the market averages because they take greater risks.

I don't want to get involved with grand academic theories in this book, as I have considerable intuitive and practical problems with so-called standard measures of risk, especially when it is cast in terms of price or market volatility alone. The subject of risk in investing is more complex than the consideration given it by most investors I've met. Some kinds of risk are reviewed in Chapter 8, "Potpourri—A Stock Marketeer's Stew."

One of the best sources of documented results for long-term investment returns is the book *Stocks, Bonds, Bills, and Inflation 1995 Yearbook* (*SBBI*) annually published by Ibbotson Associates, Inc. (8 South Michigan Avenue, Suite 707, Chicago, IL 60603, 312-263-3434). From Chapter 2, "The Long Run Perspective," I have based several comparison results on *SBBI* figures. Especially interesting are the comparisons between the total returns of "Common Stocks, represented by the Standard and Poor's 500 Stock Composite Index (S&P 500)" and "Small Company Stocks, represented by the fifth capitalization quintile of stocks on the NYSE for 1926–1981 and the performance of the Dimensional Fund Advisors (DFA) Small Company Fund thereafter."

---

[4] Gerald Perritt, *Small Stocks, Big Profits*, (Homewood, IL: Dow Jones-Irwin, 1988).

Beginning with $1.00 at December 31, 1925, an index of S&P total returns closed 1994 at $810.54, which works out to a 10.2 percent compounded annual total return growth rate, while small company stocks closed 1994 at $2,842.77, a compound annual total return growth rate of 12.2 percent. In addition to showing that small-company stocks outperformed S&P 500 stocks by 2.0 percent per year on average for 69 years, that difference between 10.2 percent and 12.2 percent for 69 years results in a 350.72 percent greater dollar gain for small companies over big companies.

You might wonder if 69-year comparisons make much sense, as few of us will be investing or speculating for seven decades, besides which there is no guarantee that the next 69 years will echo the past 69. Fair enough, but I find it both comforting and encouraging to see that through all those years of wars, depressions, recessions, economic booms, technological and informational revolutions, governments, scandals, scoundrels and whatnot, large-capitalization stocks have advanced 7.1 percent above the 69-year average 3.1 percent annual inflation rate, while small-cap stocks managed a 9.1 percent after-inflation annual growth.

True, there were multiyear periods when stocks in general suffered losses, or when large-cap stocks did better than small-cap stocks or cash did better than both, but the long-term comparisons among the returns on equity and interest-bearing instruments such as "safe" Treasury bills (average 3.7 percent, for a real after-tax return of 0.6 percent) and long-term government bonds (average 4.8 percent, for a real after-tax return about 1.7 percent) can be astounding, especially considering the ravages of the post-World War II inflation, which reached a peak of 13.3 percent in 1979. "On a month-by-month basis, the peak inflation rate was a breathtaking 24.0 percent, stated in annualized terms, in August 1973." (*SBBI*, p. 32)

I can't remember when I first heard that "bonds are a form of legalized confiscation," but the long-term numbers strongly support that bitter assertion. After factoring in the costs of taxes and inflation-reducing purchasing power, the long-term bill, note, and bond holder—as well as the bank passbook and CD holder—except for brief transition periods, has been committed to a policy of systematic diminishment of future buying power.

The Bottom Line—Return on Equity

For some value investors, the bottom line is *return on equity* (ROE), also called *return on net worth* (or even return on *net asset value*), and for practical purposes could be *return on book value* when shareholder equity is represented by book value. Now we're talking about how much a corporation earns after taxes in terms of its owners' (shareholders') equity. This ROE percentage represents several important considerations, such as how well (profitably) management has run the business and how fast it is growing. Like every other financial figure it can be compared to prior years, other companies, and market averages. Alas, it can also be misleading if parts of the corporation, such as research and development, are being sacrificed to enhance (temporarily) our ROE figures.

If common stocks of large companies tend to generate a total return of about 10 percent per year, then it might seem that the average bottom line for corporations would be a 10 percent ROE. This crude analysis involves a major assumption—that stocks generally trade at their return on equity per share percentage over long time periods. In that case, shareholders would obtain the same return on a cost basis as the corporations earned on equity. As we have seen, shares rarely trade at equity per share or return on equity. The market is almost always overvaluing or undervaluing corporations according to these criteria.

The phenomenon of inefficient market pricing or not fairly valuing stocks most of the time creates great opportunities and permits the speculator's or investor's great gains and losses to occur. It is the backward-looking, trend-projecting, and herd (mob) instinct of a majority of market analysts and participants that fails to account for the individual case and tends to fight "the last war." This typical attitude toward the stock market is another misleading reverse form of the self-fulfilling prophecy.

When conditions have been favorable, analysts tend to raise their estimations of profits and returns, a tendency that sooner or later leads to error and excess. Conversely, when conditions have been negative, estimates are generally reduced, often swinging too much toward underestimation, until conditions appear better and stocks are in a firmly established uptrend, thereby leading to tardy commitments in advance of better times.

Corporations' returns on equity range from negative to high percentages. A young "emerging-growth" company might show a 50 percent or greater ROE, at least for a few years, although such growth rates are usually not sustainable as that company would soon dominate all commerce. Experience has shown me that a 15 percent ROE is a solid return for a moderate-size industrial company, which could be used as a baseline with the understanding that other fundamental factors may be more important in determining an undervalued stock than ROE. As there is variability of price/revenue ratios among corporations, so too there is a wide spread of ROE among corporations and often within a corporation over the years.

With ROE, we would generally like to see higher percentages, say 20 percent rather than 10 percent, unlike the lower ratios that spell undervaluedness in P/E, P/BV, and P/CF. However, there are interesting relationships of undervaluedness with relatively low ROEs. As previously pointed out in relation to the price/revenue ratio, if International Widgits, Inc. (IWI) is registering a 10 percent ROE—which I would consider mediocre as a return on equity—then I could still do well if IWI were trading at only 50 percent of its equity. In such a case, though IWI only managed 10 percent ROE, I would be getting a 20 percent return on my *invested capital* (equity), since I would be buying ROE for 50 cents on the dollar.

Sometimes relatively low measures of profitability can be a mask hiding a severely undervalued corporation. Sooner or later almost all corporations have bad years or special conditions that make them look bad in terms of earnings and ROE. In 1988, for the first time in its history, American Telephone and Telegraph reported a loss as it took a huge writedown for obsolete analog equipment that was being replaced by state-of-the-art digital equipment. Obviously, the ROE for American Telephone for 1988 would register its stock as hopelessly overvalued, if taken out of context. Clearly, the long history of a steady and substantial ROE—in this case restricted by regulatory commissions—augured well for a resumption after the special writedown. In fact, AT&T's stock quickly recovered in anticipation of even higher future profitability and ROEs. Given the relaxed regulatory processes underway, the utility and manufacturing company will have its service rates limited, but will probably be able to increase its overall returns.

Again, we want to keep our analysis as simple as is reasonable, perhaps limited to a few hours work per week, perusing readily available public sources of information. After we check out ROE, compare it with historical trend and rule-of-thumb levels, and check the *return on investment* of capital (what we have to pay for the equity and our return on equity), we have done all we need to do with this selection criterion.

Return on Assets (or, How the Corporation Manages Its Leverage)

A companion criterion to ROE is *return on assets* (ROA). This is an especially revealing number in corporations that have many assets compared to their equity, such as banks, savings and loans, insurance companies, and some highly leveraged industrial or service outfits.

Imagine a corporation—let's call it International Assets, Inc. (IAI)—that has $10 million in equity but manages $200 million in assets. Try as it might, IAI is only able to earn an (after-tax) ROA of 1 percent, or $2 million, apparently not a very good return. On the other hand, this profit gives IAI a 20 percent ROE, because it earned $2 million on its $10 million equity base. IAI, reporting such results, could be a savings and loan, a bank, or a financial management company.

In looking at ROE and ROA, we want to look not only at their absolute percentages but for any improvements (increasing percentages) over the past few years. Two corporations might have the same ROE and ROA at the same moment, but one may represent a rising trend and the other a declining trend. Though the trends might easily reverse in the future, between the two I would prefer the company with apparently improving returns, probably indicating improving management of equity and assets. On the other hand, I might look to see if the rising trend was at the expense of other criteria, such as a diminishment in maintenance and replacement spending, or big cuts in promotion and merchandizing spending, which might hamper the company in the future.

Or, we might simply be content to see that we have found a corporation that is undervalued on several criteria and meets our ROE or ROA minimums. "Let well enough alone" is often good advice for speculators. You may think me ambivalent or cavalier when, after mentioning some potential danger signal, I advise you not to worry because the minimum criteria will lead us to the promised stocks, which will pay for our passage to the good material life. My experience is that no matter how carefully I analyze corporations, about 25 percent of the time, my stock selections don't work out over the years. As many as 40 percent or more of them appear unprofitable in their first year after selection. Some selections that I think are golden turn out to be dross, while others that barely made the cut become big winners.

Not All Valuation Criteria Apply to All Corporations

Most of the selection criteria in this chapter apply to industrial, manufacturing, natural resource, and service industries. Financial institutions such as banks, savings and loans, insurance companies, brokerages, and financial services companies may be analyzed with several of the selection criteria already reviewed, but not all of them. For instance, cash flow analysis, or price/revenue analysis, for that matter, are not appropriate for financial companies. For financial corporations other criteria must supplant those—like current ratios or return on sales—that are not appropriate.

For savings and loan (S&L) analysis we might want to emphasize four other criteria. The ratio (percentage) of common shareholder equity (or net worth) to total assets measures the financial strength of an S&L's capital base, with 6 percent or more considered good. Average financial strength of net worth is 5–6 percent, with 3–4 percent below average, and below 3 percent considered bad. Another important S&L ratio is Net Interest Income to Total General and Administrative Expense, which indicates if interest income can meet expenses without requiring other nonrecurring income.

The ratio of nonperforming assets to total loans is one of the best tangible indications of effectiveness in sustaining loan quality, as delinquent loans and foreclosed properties impact negatively both earnings and management's time. Recently, nonperforming assets have been averaging well over 2 percent of total loans for both banks and S&Ls, so look for the ratio below 2 percent, with below 1 percent being outstanding. Finally, we can check out the "gap" as a percentage of total assets, which refers to the maturities (repricing) of assets and liabilities, which reflects balance sheet and interest-rate vulnerability.

I might well have skipped S&L analysis, as some stock pickers do by avoiding the industry altogether because of long-time negative publicity, but over the years many S&L and bank stocks have appreciated handsomely. It is in just such out-of-favor and depressed (undervalued) stocks that great returns can be gleaned, given good selection and patience. After the current travails have passed, the strong and well-managed S&Ls will emerge profitable and valuable, as they did after the high interest rates of the early '70s.

I want to alert readers that financial companies require different fundamental criteria than those for industrial corporations. For detailed reviews of S&L analysis, I suggest you study S&L annual reports, such as those of FirstFed Financial of California (FED) and Boston Bancorp (SBOS), but especially the 1994 annual report of Golden West Financial (GDW), which explains in understandable English and informative tables the nuances of the items mentioned above as well as other important fundamentals.

An Iconoclastic Clang

While first working on this chapter, I had the good fortune to read an interview with Walter J. Schloss and his son Edwin by Henry Emerson, editor of the *Outstanding Investor Digest*[5]. Walter J. Schloss Associates has racked up a gross annual return between 1956 through 1988 of 21.6 percent, compared to the S&P 500's Total Return of 9.8 percent per annum for the same period. Walter Schloss had worked with Ben Graham and Warren Buffett in 1954–55. Buffett has lauded Schloss as one of the "Super-Investors of Graham and Doddsville" (after the authors of the classic *Security Analysis*[6]). Of the many wonderful stories relating to Schloss' experiences and superior investing wisdom, I was particularly fascinated with his reminiscence about Ben Graham, often called the father of fundamental analysis.

After commenting on Graham's interest in ideas and new ways of doing things, and his renaissance nature, Walter Schloss said,

> Then, he discovered he could make good money by just buying stocks at two thirds of their working capital. My job was really finding those working capital stocks and then recommending which ones we should buy.
>
> After he found out he could make money this way, he kind of lost interest. It seemed like a good game. If he were alive today and

---

[5] Henry Emerson, *Outstanding Investor Digest*, March 6, 1989, (14 East 4th Street, Suite 501, New York, NY 10012).

[6] Benjamin Graham and David L. Dodd, *Security Analysis: Principles and Technique*, (New York: McGraw-Hill, 1940).

couldn't find working capital stocks, he'd very likely be looking around for something else.[7]

There are innumerable stock-selection schemes, some using only two criteria or even one as mentioned above. I sometimes wonder as I read of them if I haven't spent years in unnecessary computation and research. Then too, I read ostensibly sensible research reports that are based on anecdotal analyses of past events projected into the future, as if a good idea and a sharp entrepreneur is all an investor needs to know about. Somewhere between the oversimplified and the overcomplicated lies a middle path, but the ideal is probably closer to the simpler approaches.

Summary

I believe that what is important in stock speculation is to find significantly overlooked or out-of-favor corporations, buy their undervalued stocks, and continue holding them until many stock market participants recognize their fundamental values and growth potentials by bidding up their prices in accumulating them. My reformulation of the *cliché*, "Buy low, sell high," is a modified "Buy low, sell fully valued."

Obviously, the criteria for *low*, *high*, and *fully valued* are not fixed; they are relative to the present value and future prospects of the corporations as well as stock-market dynamics, the economic business cycle, and governmental policies. Still, we have many established fundamental valuation criteria that can be employed as meaningful, if imprecise, guidelines to select relatively undervalued stocks for purchase. These same criteria tell us when our stocks are fully valued and probably should be sold.

There is no limit to the amount of inquiry and effort analysts can expend evaluating a corporation, but it is not necessary to go into great or subtle detail. A selection of relatively gross measures is usually sufficient to make such evaluations and selections for successful stock speculation.

In this chapter we have looked at seven fundamental criteria: price/earnings; price/cash flow; price/revenues; price/book value; return on equity; return on assets; and market capitalization. We have considered that even with only three well-selected criteria a sufficient "down-and-dirty" analysis could be made.

It would be neat if we could give specific guidelines for these criteria, but such a set could be counterproductive as it might unnecessarily exclude undervalued stock selections due to one criterion or another. The important idea is that these criteria are relative to and reinforce each other, rather than any one being sufficient or necessary. At the risk of being counterproductive, I list below gross criteria to consider when comparing potential buy candidates. Remember, these guidelines are general and imprecise.

---

[7] *Outstanding Investor Digest*, March 6, 1989.

1. *Price/earnings.* Normally, industrial stocks trading below 10 times earnings or 30 percent below their P/E norm (average P/E). This item is reviewed further in the Chapter 9.
2. *Price/revenues.* Normally, stocks trading near their out-of-favor levels or below their accepted P/R levels (see Table 2–3).
3. *Price/book value.* Normally, stocks trading below their book value per share or 30 percent below their book value norm. Reviewed in Chapter 9.
4. *Price/cash flow.* Normally, stocks trading at less than six times cash flow or 30 percent below their cash flow norm. Reviewed in Chapter 9.
5. *Return on equity.* Normally, stocks trading at a 15 percent return on equity or better. (Likewise, a return of 15 percent or better on cost of shares.)
6. *Market capitalization.* Normally, stocks with a market capitalization of less than $200 million (computed as shares outstanding times price per share) are considered "small cap." While returns on small company stocks (below $100 million in market cap) are significant over long time periods, I tend to buy bargains in value and growth of any size market-capitalization stock, especially as a mix can aid in diversification (risk reduction) for those periods when large-cap stocks outperform small-cap stocks.
7. *Return on assets.* Normally, stocks trading for a ROA comparable to or higher than their historical ROA, although somewhat lower ROAs in stocks found to be otherwise undervalued may indicate room for improvement. Pay particular attention to the trend of this component, as well as in all the other criteria.

Consider the five-year growth rates of these seven criteria, and notice their consistencies or changes over time. For example, a 15 percent per annum growth in earnings would mean that earnings have doubled in the recent five years; however that average growth rate may show that five years ago earnings were growing at 5 percent while last year they grew at 25 percent, or vice versa.

One of the humbling realities of corporate analysis is that so much can go wrong with a corporation, even after extremely stringent criteria have been met or followed in its selection by a prudent speculator. One only has to look at mighty IBM or even giant General Motors. They are still great corporations, but not the monoliths they once were, and their share price declines over the years reflect their problems and downsizing. Also, so much can go wrong with stocks independent of their corporations as the marketplace becomes ebullient or depressed. I have found it a waste of time to spend too much effort on analysis, especially when experience shows that stock selection is perhaps 25 percent of the battle for effective speculation. Once you have "sufficient" information, accept it and go with it, because you will never find perfection in this process.

In order to avoid (or at least minimize) personal frustration from the fact that we can't always win, I take a statistical approach and accepting attitude, consistent with my actual experience. Some 25 percent of my selections have been losers—an acceptable number in terms of long-term holdings and superior long-term annual returns—over market cycles of five to eight years.

To cope with the reality of stocks that don't work out well, I employ widely diversified portfolios for the systematic risk reduction they provide (details follow in the next chapter). Still, if you have the time and feel the need to do more than this chapter calls for, you can consider the additional criteria reviewed in Chapter 9, wherein actual stock examples are noted.

3

Stock Portfolio Management

The word *portfolio* is used in many activities and has several definitions. Derived from the Latin and Italian words *to carry* and *leaf* or *sheet*, portfolios are portable cases for carrying loose papers, prints, government documents, and even stock certificates, which are becoming objects of the past. Nowadays, hardly anyone carries securities around. They are usually left with the stockbroker (most of whom use The Depository Trust Co.) or are put in a safe deposit vault. Still, it's rather romantic to speak of one's stock portfolio as if there were a briefcase, chock-a-block full of fabulous stock certificates, ready at a moment's notice to be carried off and exchanged for vast sums of cash.

Stock portfolio management (hereinafter "portfolio management") refers to much more than keeping track of one's stock positions or safekeeping one's stock certificates. It includes the coordinating and monitoring of our speculative strategies with guidelines for buy, hold, and sell decisions. Corporate analysis discovers undervalued stocks worth buying and also tells us when they are fully valued and thus become sell candidates in our strategy. Market timing tells us about dangerous periods, when we should not accumulate more stocks but rather become defensive, and lower-risk periods, when we should aggressively add to our portfolios if we can afford it. Portfolio management tells us how much to buy or sell, and which stocks to choose in order to balance and diversify our portfolios—our collection of stocks (businesses).

As with most "services" connected with Wall Street, purveyors of advice invent enticing marketing names for the most pedestrian of tasks. One doesn't decide to buy or sell, one develops an *asset allocation model* with complicated formulas and percentages—which translate into "Now's a good time to buy (or sell) some more." Asset allocation, however, is getting old hat for some, so now we hear of *tactical asset allocation* and perhaps cash *asset/liability management*. All this terminology is supposed to make you believe that a new height in scientific portfolio management has been achieved and therefore you should put your assets in the care of the sages who use it. While people have been allocating assets since the beginning of time, and it is vital to have a systematic discipline, buying a fancy approach doesn't assure you effective results.

Few of us have the money or available credit to buy all the bargains that fundamental analysis uncovers, especially at market lows. A persistent question faces the investor daily: How exposed to the stock market should I be and how do I manage that exposure among the many positions I have accumulated or want to obtain? Furthermore, there are techniques for enhancing or hedging the portfolio—taking various forms of "insurance" against sharp market drops—other than just buying and selling stocks. We will start with some of the basics and see how the simple decisions tend to get a bit more complicated with the passage of time, personal needs, the growth of portfolios, and stock market events.

PASADARM

Our overall speculative watchword or mantra is PASADARM, an acronym of the first letters of the words *Patience And Selection And Diversification And Risk Management*. Each element is as crucial as any other one, and they work together to form a total speculative approach, so the conjunctive And is logically meaningful. Our slogan used to be PASAD. I had considered risk management embedded in the fulfillment of the three basic principles. The trauma of the Crash of '87 convinced me that even more emphasis needed to be paid to the management of risk, especially market and leverage risk. Now, undervalued and fully valued stocks are also reviewed in the context of overbought and overvalued markets as well as oversold and undervalued markets. Portfolios are also considered in terms of personal cash flows, reserves, and prudent economic balance.

Speculative patience includes waiting for the right corporation at the right price before buying, then holding it years (if necessary) for its fair price before selling. Selection includes fundamental analysis in order to discover bargains— stocks trading at 50 percent or so of their estimated present or probable three- to five-year market price—so as not to overpay and to try to minimize the risk of deep downside price action. Diversification includes spreading risk over many corporations in different industries and sectors of the economy, as well as over time— which, oddly enough is a more important consideration than the actual number of different stocks held.

In the Crash of '87, I was shocked that the risk management principles built into patience, selection, and diversification did not provide enough protection. It became apparent that I would have to expand the original PASAD and systematically review risk management considerations, adding it as a basic and separate principle. Of course, all the elements of PASADARM are interrelated. If one element seems independent or exclusive, we should remember that it is interdependent with and inclusive of the others.

Patience Is Golden

How can we learn to be patient when most of our lives we are conditioned to be impatient? When the pervading ethos is that "time is money," the implication is that we had better not waste time unless we are willing to lose money—everything we do will either cost us or gain us, depending on how quickly we do it. Reflection might be okay for philosophers and meditation is acceptable for those outside the mainstream, but for the rest of us there are jobs to be done, trades to be won, and no time to waste.

"Whom do you trust?" could be a theme for our times, with the most common answer being, "No one!" If we can't trust anyone, nor by extension our institutions, how can we be patient with them? Too many stock-market investors believe, "We must get ours, and get out while the getting is good or suffer the consequences."

Consider the rise in sanctioned, legalized, and organized gambling—not to mention state-run lotteries—over the past few years. Perhaps our age of affluence, with its emphasis on winners and losers and the score kept in terms of dollars, has led to excess. Gambling is an enterprise of impatience. Place your bet and in a few seconds, hours, or days, you will know if you are a winner or a loser. Are the calculated risks of lotteries computed and published? Yes. Hardly ever do participants pay much attention to them. Chicago futures and options vie with Las Vegas and Atlantic City cards and dice as the gaming capitals of the world, especially since the advent of many so-called derivative instruments. These are often little more than bets on whether a stock, collection of stocks, or the stock market is going to advance or decline. I published this assertion six years before the recent scandals involving derivatives.

The psychology of impatience is a fascinating subject, involving anxiety, self-esteem, and conditioned behavior patterns, often involving self-punishment and leading to self-destruction. Students in elementary school often blurt out an answer they know to be wrong, because the teacher is impatient and they perceive it as more important to say something, anything, rather than to keep thinking a moment while under the scrutiny of an impatient teacher and class. How many of us in our ordinary conversations continue this practice of responding rapidly if haphazardly, often making statements about situations we know little about in an effort to facilitate social intercourse and allay another's impatience or anxiety? There are two problems here—speaking of what we know not and speaking without reflection—but I think they are both aspects of our life-long, conditioned impatience.

In order to control impatience, we have societal structures that require systematic participation in extended enterprises. Of course, some of these, like the 60-minute football game (which often requires over thrce hours to play) and the 48-minute basketball game (two hours), are compromises, as are the tie-breakers and three-set championships in tennis. How many spectators these days want to watch a tennis set go to 20 or 22 games or a match last five hours? Most people want near-instant gratification.

For a few "investors," very short-term day trading meets their tolerance for patience. They try to scalp a few eighths here and there, getting lucky or unlucky, but going home at night or on the weekend without the anxiety of what might happen to their investments or the market on the next trading day's opening. For other traders, *intermediate term* refers to a few days. *Long term* means a few weeks. For some investors, owning a stock for one year is the height of folly. These kinds of folk tend to watch the market whenever they can and eagerly await the first closing stock quotes to see how they've done, or would have done if . . .

For some people patience is the key, for others it's the lock that blocks them from consistently doing well in the stock market. True, patience can be costly when things are going wrong and prompt action is called for, but these occasions are rare and even then not necessarily as bad as they seem. Prudent investors and speculators should almost always be patient.

We want to be patient in the purchase of a position, waiting for it to trade at "our price." On the other hand, we do not want to put in limit orders when the stock's price is below our 50 percent buy limit, trying to save 1/4 or 1/2 point of the market price at the risk of bypassing the stock only to see a multipoint rise thereafter. We do not want to overpay for a stock out of frustration because we missed it at a lower price and fear that it may not again meet our 50 percent undervalued rule. It is disappointing to see a missed stock take off and finally meet our objectives, but bending our principles is likely to lead to a breakdown in our total strategy. Like buses and elevators, there will always be another stock, often even a better deal.

We want to be patient in holding a stock—not unduly influenced by market price fluctuations or the occasional poor quarterly earnings report—as we await fair prices for our equities. The great gains are made with the corporations that continue to be profitable and grow over the years, especially when our ownership of them is obtained at a discount to their fair value. The art of holding may well be more important than that of buying or selling. Holding invokes the phenomenon of time diversification, reviewed later in this chapter, a very interesting and fruitful companion to stock diversification.

Studies (see Tables 3–1A and B) have shown that time diversification can reduce both short-term market risk and short-term individual stock risk, and may be more important than stock diversification when all is said and done. We certainly want to be patient to allow time diversification to work its magic.

We even want to be patient (most of the time) in deciding to sell, either at our goal price or at a higher price, perhaps having used trailing stop-loss limits. Aside from the sometimes astute but often misleading motto, "Cut short your losses and let your profits run," the major rationale for value investing is to see those values realized in the market. How can they be realized if we sell a stock before its time? Stocks, like wine, or crops, have their seasons and their harvests. While the occasional stock may turn sour or the harvest be damaged in a selling storm, over the long run our vintage strategy will produce award-winning results.

The best way to teach speculative patience is by successful examples. The only way to learn investment patience is to practice it systematically. Alas, the stock market is full of examples, in a sense nothing but examples, and almost any reasonable sounding thesis can be made to seem plausible by using one set of examples or another. Still, there are the long-term records of famous value and growth speculators—who call themselves investors—as well as the highly convincing long-term statistics that are scattered throughout this book and in much of the literature about the subject.

Time Diversification

A subject that seems as appropriate under the rubric *patience* as it does in the section on diversification or the discussion of risk is time diversification. It is surprising that *time diversification* is a rarely reviewed concept as it may be more important than stock diversification. *Market Logic*, September 21, 1984, reports on a study published in the *Journal of Portfolio Management* (vol. 6, no. 3) quantifying risk reduction through time diversification compared to stock diversification. Apparently, "time diversification is at least as important as stock diversification when it comes to reducing risk."

Testing portfolios varying in size from 1 to 100 stocks, with holding periods from six months to six years, "[The researchers] concluded that a 1-stock 'portfolio' held for one year was less risky than a 100-stock portfolio held for a single six-month period." The authors also found that *holding a 10-stock portfolio for four years was one-third as risky as holding a 100-stock portfolio for one year.*

There is a common sense rationale for the statistical probabilities of time diversification. For any relatively brief period, the market can have a selloff that carries most stocks down without regard to each of their corporation's fundamentals. This is called *market* or *systematic risk*. But over longer time periods, the

Table 3–1A. Results of Time Diversification in TPS Actual Margin Account

Period	Date:	Qtrly %	6 mos.	12 mos.	24 mos.	36 mos.	48 mos.	60 mos.	72 mos.	84 mos.	96 mos.	108 mos.
1	2nd–77	53.97										
2	3rd	−11.94	35.59									
3	4th	25.59	10.59									
4	1st–78	7.11	34.52	82.39								
5	2nd	22.46	31.17	45.06								
6	3rd	32.28	61.99	117.91								
7	4th	−27.95	−4.69	25.01								
8	1st–79	42.26	2.50	66.04	202.83							
9	2nd	4.97	49.33	42.32	106.46							
10	3rd	13.60	19.25	22.23	166.34							
11	4th	−3.64	9.46	63.46	104.35							
12	1st–80	−37.58	−39.85	−28.28	19.09	117.20						
13	2nd	45.43	−9.22	−0.63	41.43	105.16						
14	3rd	45.83	112.08	27.56	55.91	239.75						
15	4th	−12.60	27.46	15.70	89.13	136.43						
16	1st–81	35.12	18.09	150.46	79.64	198.26	444.00					
17	2nd	30.75	76.67	125.17	123.75	218.46	361.96					
18	3rd	−56.15	−42.67	−37.29	−13.63	5.57	130.04					
19	4th	28.12	−43.82	−0.75	14.84	87.72	134.67					
20	1st–82	−13.35	11.02	−36.35	59.41	14.34	89.84	246.26				
21	2nd	−25.94	−35.83	−63.95	−18.82	−19.33	14.81	66.55				
22	3rd	42.99	5.90	17.56	−20.40	1.54	24.11	170.44				
23	4th	72.76	147.03	58.53	57.34	82.05	197.58	272.02				
24	1st–83	46.41	152.94	167.86	70.49	327.00	206.26	408.51	827.47			
25	2nd	44.81	112.02	423.74	88.82	325.18	322.50	501.32	772.30			
26	3rd	3.70	50.17	279.83	346.55	202.35	285.68	371.40	927.22			
27	4th	−0.97	2.69	117.73	245.16	242.58	296.37	547.92	709.98			
28	1st–84	−16.64	−17.45	23.97	232.05	111.35	429.34	279.66	530.38	1049.75		
29	2nd	−30.55	−42.11	−40.55	211.38	12.26	152.79	151.19	257.50	418.61		
30	3rd	26.19	−12.36	−27.65	174.80	223.06	118.74	179.03	241.05	643.17		
31	4th	19.49	50.78	−12.71	90.06	201.30	199.05	246.01	465.60	607.07		
32	1st–85	4.92	25.37	9.87	36.20	264.83	132.21	481.60	317.14	592.61	1163.25	
33	2nd	10.25	15.67	74.42	3.70	443.11	95.81	340.91	338.13	523.55	804.55	
34	3rd	−15.02	−6.31	17.46	−15.02	222.77	279.47	156.93	227.75	300.59	772.91	
35	4th	53.33	30.30	50.72	31.57	186.47	354.13	350.75	421.52	752.49	965.72	
36	1st–86	67.97	157.55	141.30	165.12	228.66	780.33	460.33	1303.38	906.56	1571.26	2948.21
37	2nd	5.73	77.59	131.41	303.61	139.96	1156.78	353.11	920.28	913.85	1342.94	1993.18
38	3rd	−14.75	−9.87	132.14	172.67	97.27	649.29	780.90	496.44	660.83	829.93	1926.39
39	4th	−3.27	−17.54	46.45	120.73	92.69	319.53	565.07	560.11	663.75	1148.46	1460.73
40	1st–87	44.85	40.11	26.29	204.74	234.82	315.06	1011.78	607.64	1672.34	1171.19	2010.65
41	2nd	−7.60	33.84	10.37	155.40	345.46	164.84	1287.10	400.09	1026.07	1018.97	1492.55
42	3rd	4.66	−3.29	35.50	214.55	269.46	167.29	915.27	1093.59	708.16	930.91	1160.03
43	4th	−68.34	−66.86	−55.65	−35.05	−2.11	−14.55	86.06	194.95	192.75	238.72	453.68
44	1st–88	34.71	−57.35	−58.76	−47.91	25.69	38.09	71.19	358.55	191.86	630.99	424.29
45	2nd	10.48	48.83	−50.69	−45.57	25.95	119.68	30.61	584.04	146.62	455.32	451.81
46	3rd	−2.12	8.14	−53.88	−37.51	45.07	70.40	23.28	368.24	450.48	272.72	375.45
47	4th	3.08	0.89	50.16	−33.41	−2.47	46.99	28.32	179.38	342.90	339.59	408.61
48	1st–89	18.00	21.63	31.53	−45.75	−31.49	65.32	81.64	125.17	503.14	283.90	861.49
49	2nd	15.96	36.83	38.06	−31.92	−24.86	73.88	203.28	80.31	844.37	240.47	666.65
50	3rd	12.30	30.22	58.40	−26.95	−1.02	129.78	169.90	95.26	641.68	771.95	490.38

Table 3–1A. Results of Time Diversification in TPS Actual Margin Account (cont.)

Per-iod	Date:	Qtrly %	6 mos.	12 mos.	24 mos.	36 mos.	48 mos.	60 mos.	72 mos.	84 mos.	96 mos.	108 mos.
51	4th	−21.46	−11.80	20.69	81.22	−19.63	17.70	77.40	54.86	237.18	434.52	430.53
52	1st–90	−15.29	−33.47	−13.36	13.96	−53.00	−40.64	43.23	57.37	95.09	422.55	232.60
53	2nd	−4.08	−18.75	−28.33	−1.06	−51.21	−46.15	24.61	117.35	29.22	576.79	144.00
54	3rd	−54.83	−56.67	−71.17	−54.34	−78.94	−71.47	−33.76	−22.20	−43.71	113.80	151.35
55	4th	4.42	−52.83	−61.68	−53.75	−30.55	−69.20	−54.89	−32.01	−40.65	29.22	104.85
56	1st–91	76.99	84.81	−19.93	−30.62	−8.75	−62.36	−52.47	14.69	26.01	56.21	318.43
57	2nd	−3.91	70.07	−19.78	−42.51	−20.63	−60.86	−56.80	−0.04	74.35	3.66	442.89
58	3rd	−1.85	−5.69	74.30	−49.76	−20.42	−63.30	−50.27	15.45	35.61	−1.89	272.65
59	4th	6.30	4.33	77.44	−32.00	−17.93	23.24	−45.35	−19.96	20.64	5.31	129.29
60	1st–92	23.29	31.06	23.60	−1.03	−14.25	12.79	−53.48	−41.25	41.76	55.76	93.08
61	2nd	6.90	31.80	37.51	10.30	−20.95	9.13	−46.18	−40.60	37.45	139.75	42.54
62	3rd	−10.25	−4.06	25.74	119.17	−36.82	0.07	−53.85	−37.46	45.17	70.51	23.36
63	4th	37.45	23.36	62.59	188.49	10.56	33.44	100.37	−11.14	30.13	96.14	71.22
64	1st–93	15.12	58.23	51.81	87.65	50.26	30.18	71.23	−29.38	−10.81	115.21	136.46
65	2nd	−4.17	10.32	36.09	87.14	50.11	7.58	48.52	−26.76	−19.16	87.06	226.27
66	3rd	13.10	8.38	71.50	115.64	275.87	8.35	71.62	−20.85	7.25	148.96	192.43
67	4th	13.01	27.81	41.00	129.25	306.79	55.90	88.15	182.53	25.30	83.50	176.57
68	1st–94	−2.50	10.18	19.42	81.30	124.09	79.44	55.46	104.49	−15.66	6.51	157.01
69	2nd	−5.21	−7.58	18.13	60.76	121.06	77.32	27.08	75.45	−13.48	−4.51	120.97
70	3rd	6.53	0.98	11.26	90.82	139.93	318.21	20.55	90.95	−11.93	19.33	177.01
71	4th	−11.54	−5.76	−12.91	22.81	99.67	254.29	35.78	63.87	146.06	9.13	59.81
72	1st–95	15.81	2.45	3.45	23.54	87.55	131.82	85.63	60.83	111.54	−12.75	10.19
73	2nd	31.32	52.08	43.10	69.04	130.04	216.33	153.75	81.85	151.06	23.81	36.65
Down Qtrs:		28	25	20	20	18	8	9	11	7	3	0
Periods:		73	72	70	66	62	58	54	50	46	42	38
Percent/Time:		38.36	34.72	28.57	30.30	29.03	13.79	16.67	22.00	15.22	7.14	0.00

aphorism "Value will out" tends to prove true. We can see how time diversification has worked in reality by glancing at the 18.25 years of quarterly results of The Prudent Speculator Portfolio (see Table 3–1A).

First let's look at my actual margined account (a.k.a. TPS Portfolio) where we note that 28 of the past 73 quarters (38.36 percent) have been down. This is in keeping with the generalization that the market declines about one-third of the time. Of the 72 six-month periods, 25 (34.72 percent) were down, but for the 70 12-month periods only 20 (28.57 percent) were down—a distinct trend showing the effects of time (long-term) diversification. In the 66 24-month periods, 20 (30.30 percent) were down, while for the 62 36-month periods, 18 (29.03 percent) were down. When we observe 48-month periods, there are eight losing three-month periods or 13.79 percent of the time. It takes nine years (108 months) until there are no down quarters, although at 96 months there are only three periods of a small −1.89, −4.51, and −12.75 percent losses.

Table 3-1B. Results of Time Diversification in TPS Hypothetical Cash Account

Period	Date:	Qtrly %	6 mos.	12 mos.	24 mos.	36 mos.	48 mos.	60 mos.
1	2nd–77	25.68						
2	3rd	–5.33	18.98					
3	4th	13.03	7.01					
4	1st–78	4.49	18.11	40.52				
5	2nd	11.55	16.56	24.72				
6	3rd	15.45	28.78	52.10				
7	4th	–11.45	2.23	19.16				
8	1st–79	18.19	4.66	34.78	89.40			
9	2nd	4.04	22.96	25.71	56.79			
10	3rd	8.08	12.45	17.68	79.00			
11	4th	0.68	8.81	33.80	59.44			
12	1st–80	–13.58	–12.99	–2.16	31.87	85.30		
13	2nd	17.19	1.28	10.20	38.53	72.79		
14	3rd	19.09	39.56	21.43	42.90	117.36		
15	4th	–3.00	15.52	16.99	56.54	86.53		
16	1st–81	17.25	13.73	58.73	55.29	109.31	194.13	
17	2nd	16.36	36.43	57.60	73.68	118.33	172.31	
18	3rd	–22.91	–10.30	2.02	23.88	45.79	121.75	
19	4th	11.52	–14.03	17.29	37.22	83.61	118.78	
20	1st–82	–2.10	9.18	–2.07	55.45	52.09	104.99	188.05
21	2nd	–6.45	–8.41	–21.26	24.09	36.75	71.91	114.41
22	3rd	15.13	7.70	17.59	19.96	45.67	71.43	160.75
23	4th	21.83	40.26	28.46	50.67	76.27	135.86	181.05
24	1st–83	16.68	42.15	53.10	49.94	138.00	132.85	213.84
25	2nd	19.51	39.44	95.59	54.00	142.71	167.47	236.23
26	3rd	3.29	23.44	75.47	106.34	110.51	155.62	200.82
27	4th	0.98	4.30	45.44	86.84	119.14	156.38	243.05
28	1st–84	–6.38	–5.46	16.70	78.67	74.98	177.74	171.73
29	2nd	–8.96	–14.77	–11.10	73.88	36.90	115.76	137.78
30	3rd	10.42	0.53	–4.96	66.76	96.09	100.06	142.93
31	4th	8.53	19.84	2.14	48.56	90.84	123.84	161.87
32	1st–85	3.34	12.15	12.75	31.57	101.44	97.28	213.14
33	2nd	5.10	8.61	30.16	15.71	126.31	78.19	180.83
34	3rd	–3.76	1.15	13.44	7.81	89.18	122.45	126.95
35	4th	18.06	13.62	23.40	26.05	83.33	135.50	176.22
36	1st–86	26.98	49.91	51.63	70.96	99.51	205.45	99.14
37	2nd	4.03	32.10	50.09	95.35	73.67	239.67	167.45
38	3rd	–7.60	–3.88	44.10	63.47	55.36	172.61	220.56
39	4th	–0.76	–8.30	21.13	49.48	52.68	122.06	185.26
40	1st–87	19.29	18.38	13.79	72.55	94.54	127.03	247.59
41	2nd	–2.56	16.24	6.59	59.98	108.22	85.10	262.04
42	3rd	3.23	0.59	19.08	71.59	94.66	85.00	224.62
43	4th	–36.48	–34.43	–23.78	–7.68	13.93	16.37	69.25
44	1st–88	15.62	–26.56	–26.13	–15.94	27.47	43.72	67.71
45	2nd	6.20	22.79	–19.49	–14.18	28.80	67.65	49.04
46	3rd	0.20	6.41	–21.85	–6.94	34.10	52.13	44.58
47	4th	2.69	2.90	26.34	–3.70	16.64	43.94	47.03
48	1st–89	9.83	12.78	20.02	–11.34	0.89	52.98	72.48
49	2nd	8.98	19.69	23.16	–0.84	5.69	58.63	106.47

Table 3-1B. Results of Time Diversification in TPS Hypothetical Cash Account (cont.)

Per iod	Date:	Qtrly %	6 mos.	12 mos.	24 mos.	36 mos.	48 mos.	60 mos.
50	3rd	7.31	16.95	31.90	3.08	22.75	76.88	100.66
51	4th	−9.10	−2.46	16.75	47.51	12.43	36.19	68.06
52	1st–90	−5.73	−14.31	0.21	20.27	−11.15	1.11	53.31
53	2nd	−0.10	−5.82	−8.14	13.14	−8.91	−2.91	45.72
54	3rd	−19.35	−19.43	−30.96	−8.94	−28.83	−15.26	22.12
55	4th	2.23	−17.55	−22.35	−9.34	14.54	−12.70	5.74
56	1st–91	32.56	35.52	9.18	9.42	31.32	−2.99	10.39
57	2nd	1.20	34.15	10.61	1.61	25.14	0.75	7.39
58	3rd	−1.98	−0.80	34.43	−7.19	22.41	−4.33	13.92
59	4th	1.06	−0.94	32.89	3.18	20.47	52.21	16.01
60	1st–92	8.51	9.66	8.78	18.77	19.02	42.85	5.53
61	2nd	5.54	14.52	13.44	25.47	15.27	41.96	14.30
62	3rd	−3.60	1.74	11.57	49.98	3.55	36.58	6.74
63	4th	14.87	10.73	26.81	68.52	30.85	52.77	93.02
64	1st–93	7.31	23.27	25.41	36.42	48.95	49.27	79.15
65	2nd	−1.24	5.98	17.36	33.13	47.25	35.27	66.60
66	3rd	6.46	5.14	29.60	44.60	94.38	34.20	77.01
67	4th	6.51	13.39	20.17	52.39	102.51	57.25	83.59
68	1st–94	−0.52	5.96	11.40	39.71	51.98	65.94	66.29
69	2nd	−1.68	−2.19	10.91	30.15	47.65	63.31	50.02
70	3rd	3.92	2.17	8.26	40.31	56.54	110.43	45.28
71	4th	−4.30	−0.55	−2.73	16.89	48.24	96.99	52.96
72	1st–95	7.74	3.11	5.35	17.36	47.19	60.11	74.81
73	2nd	15.03	23.92	22.73	36.11	59.74	81.21	100.43
Down Qtrs:		24	19	13	10	3	5	0
Periods:		73	72	70	66	62	58	54
Percent/Time:		32.88	26.39	18.57	15.15	4.84	8.62	0.00

Frankly, this is a harsher record than the market in general because of the high leverage used in TPS Portfolio and the huge drops of both 1987 and 1990. These events are detailed later in this book. To get a more reasonable perspective we can turn to time diversification in the Hypothetical Cash Account, which is the margined account as if traded only with cash (no borrowed leverage).

Without going into as much detail, Table 3–1B shows that of 73 quarterly periods 24 were down—32.88 percent. Down periods are fewer throughout the periods and by 60 months there are no down periods. Even this table may overstate down periods because in the Hypothetical Cash Account stocks were considered sold as they were in the margined account, but would not have had to be sold in a cash account in order to meet maintenance (margin) calls. Thus, a somewhat greater stability would likely have resulted in a true cash account using the same stocks as were traded in the margin account.

By the way, Figures 3–1A and 3–1B also provide a long-term picture of TPS Portfolio's total return performance, which is reviewed in greater detail in the Introduction (see Table I–2).

While this-real time analysis using TPS Portfolio results is not the same as a rigorous statistical analysis of a random sample of all stocks, or of the DJIA 30 stocks, it is solid enough evidence, as far as I am concerned, of the apparent reduction of individual stock and short-term market risk brought about by time diversification, especially as, in this case, stocks tend to be held in TPS Portfolio for over eight years on average.

Misleading Performance Numbers

As you may know, when a cash dividend is paid on a stock on the New York Stock Exchange, on the ex-dividend date (three market days before the record date), the price of that stock is reduced by an amount equal to the dividend (to the next nearest eighth of a point). Thus, three trading days before Chrysler pays its current 50 cent quarterly dividend, its stock goes "ex-dividend" and is reduced in market price at the opening by the specialist responsible by 1/2 (50 cents) per share. Thus, at its 1995 dividend rate, by the end of one year Chrysler has had its shares reduced $2 yet the dividend returns are not reflected in the stock's price! If Chrysler (or any dividend-paying stock) happened to close "unchanged" from one year to the next, an investor merely inspecting its market price would think there was no return (gain) from holding the stock even though shareholders might have received a several percent "total return" from dividends.

When we start using nominal averages and index numbers for performance comparison examples we must be careful to stipulate just how we are calculating results for adjustments, as in the example with Chrysler. Taking just the raw numbers, for example, the S&P 500 Index closed at 459.27 on December 30, 1994, for an apparent loss of 7.18 points (–1.54 percent) for 1994. Using this nominal index return exclusively ignores the dividends paid out and their reinvested potential. At year-end, the S&P 500 dividend yield was 2.90 percent. Rather than having a very slightly down year the S&P 500 Index actually had a slightly up year in terms of total return of 1.31 percent. Admittedly not a handsome amount, but accurately calculated and compounded over the years, a significant amount.

Reading the Dow Jones Industrial Average

We usually do not account for the actual total-return performance of the 30 stocks in the DJIA, or with regard to their market-capitalization weighting, which involves a large series of adjustments to account for stock dividends, split shares, and the replacement over the years of stocks in the average. These adjustments have resulted in the DJIA divisor which, in April 1989, was 0.682. That means, in theory, it only took a 68.2 cent move in an average weighted DJIA stock for the DJIA to advance one point, but a weighted market-capitalization formula rarely if ever finds a day's divisor the same.

Updating to February 3, 1995, the DJIA divisor was 0.37153418, a little more than half its April 1989 value. There have been many stock splits and stock dividends since April 1989. I chose February 3, 1995 for this mini-analysis because that was the day after the Federal Reserve raised interest rates for the seventh time in 12 months, yet the market rallied in a major way, probably believing it would be the final increase of the cycle or at least for a while. The DJIA closed up 57.87 points, to 3928.64, for an imputed index gain of 1.50 percent. However, adding the value of each of the 30 stocks amounted to $1,458.375, up $19.875 for the day (only 1.38 percent). Calculation shows that the "divisor" according to the dollar amounts involved was 0.343, while the divisor according to nominal DJIA points was 0.371.

So what? First, the DJIA was not up 57.87 dollars, as commentators sometimes say, but rather $19.875. It was not up 1.50 percent in dollar terms, but only 1.38 percent. These numbers may seem trivial on a one-day basis, but they can be quite misleading when compounded over the years.

Considering the exclusion of dividends from the DJIA, the most commonly reported DJIA performance understates its actual total-return performance. As common stocks in the S&P 500 have averaged a 10.2 percent total return gain over the past 69 years, with almost 50 percent of that gain made up of reinvested dividends, you can imagine how skewed the figures are without those dividends. *Stock Market Logic*[1], by Norman Fosback, has a fascinating table that shows the accumulated differences of accounting for the Dow Jones Industrials (1) by price return alone, (2) by dividend return only, and (3) by a total return, between January 2, 1897 and mid-September, 1975 (see Table 3–2).

Fosback points out that the dividend return, while less risky than the price return, amounts to about half of the total return over long periods. Just accounting for 1988, Lipper Analytical Securities Corporation's "Total Reinvested Percent Change"—assuming quarterly reinvested dividends—arrives at a DJIA figure of 16.21 percent, versus the 11.85 percent nominal change in the index. If we simply added the average of each quarter's dividend yield (as reported in *Barron's*) of 3.59 percent, we would arrive at a "market price plus dividend return" of 15.44 percent for the year. Even the small annual difference of 0.77 percent between Lipper's 16.21 percent total return and 15.44 percent including dividends (but not

---

[1] Norman Fosback, *Stock Market Logic*, (Fort Lauderdale, FL: The Institute for Econometric Research, 1984).

Table 3-2. The Dow Jones Industrial Average "Returns"

	Price Return	Dividend Return	Total Return
DJIA on January 2, 1897	29.85*	29.85*	29.85*
By mid-September 1975 they had grown to . . .	816.10	1196.59	32684.99
a growth of over . . .	27-fold	40-fold	1095-fold
which is a compounded annual rate of return of	4.29%	4.80%	9.30%*

*Adjusted for 12/12/14 change in DJIA components.

Source: Adapted from Norman G. Fosback, *Stock Market Logic* (Fort Lauderdale, FL: The Institute for Econometric Research, 1984), p. 276.

reinvested) can make a significant difference over a long period—for example 16.58 percent if compounded over 20 years, or a gain of $1,000,000, without dividends reinvested; reinvested dividends would add $165,800.

Stock Selection

Stock-selection criteria and considerations are dealt with in detail in Chapters 2, 3, and 9, which emphasize corporation selection (stock picking) through fundamental analysis. The basic idea is quite simple. We are looking for bargains—undervalued stocks of viable corporations—with good future prospects.

One of the wonders of the modern world is how a functioning corporation's common shares—which are units of ownership that represent its assets and earnings potentials—can trade in the stock market for less than 50 percent of its fundamentally assessed current value one year, and yet a few years later trade for perhaps 200 percent of its increased intrinsic value. Scores or hundreds of such undervalued corporations can be discovered each and every year, in good times and bad, waiting for the astute speculator to buy at a discount and, in the course of events, usually sell at a premium.

One could buy the shares of the strongest and best-run corporation, sooner or later benefiting from its growth, dividends, and increased share prices. If such a corporation's stock was overvalued at the time of initial purchase, the shareholder might have to wait many years to obtain a superior total return. In theory at least, the corporation would have to increase in value to and beyond its initially overvalued shares' cost. In actuality, overvalued stocks often become even more overvalued, supporting the "greater fool theory," which states we can probably sell these expensive shares at an even greater price to a greater fool than ourselves.

The greater fool theory is for some an effective way of playing the market as trend or momentum followers. *High-relative-strength stocks* are stocks that have advanced faster and farther than the market on average and therefore seem likely to continue to do so, for awhile at least. These are stocks momentum players deal with; popular stocks that are bid higher with slight regard, if any, for their fundamental values. With these stocks some investors are able to capture the overvalued price rises, at least until their trends reverse, often falling faster than the market because of their overvaluations. The famed "Nifty Fifty" group of very high P/E stocks of the 1960s are an example, a bubble that continued for several years before crashing into the great bear market of '69–'74. Still, if you can get on the bandwagon while it's surging ahead and jump off before it topples, you can garner some relatively quick and massive gains. However, this is no strategy for a prudent speculator.

Because there are so few basic ideas needed to succeed in the stock market (if they are but followed consistently and applied systematically), you will encounter them repeatedly in this book and in many other such books. Hopefully their redundancy will not bore you or cause you to gloss over them. *To be a successful prudent speculator is to do something when appropriate, to do nothing when that is called for, and to make ideas the touchstones for motivating strategies.* Although this is a book on the stock market and investing in it, its basic focus is on corporations and becoming partners in them, through the utter convenience of being able to trade their stocks at our pleasure, when we determine it to be to our advantage, in our own good time.

The investor who has not had the privilege of owning a semisuccessful business is probably at a slight disadvantage to the speculator who has experienced first-hand how lucrative businesses can be. Businesses are often far more rewarding than they might appear on profit-and-loss statements or income-tax filings. Scandalous stories abound of major corporations paying few or no taxes while making huge reported profits and rewarding their top managers with obscene bonuses and perquisites.

Such high profits and low taxes are made possible through a variety of accounting devices such as tax loss carryforwards, depreciation (including accelerated writedowns and investment tax credits), and bad loan reserves. Consider also that management benefits and bonuses are a pre-tax cost of doing business, so such deductible "expenses" reduce corporate taxable profitability.

In my modest experience of owning two small print shops and an investment advisory business, I have seen my taxable profits reduced by the effective use of depreciation, travel and entertainment expenses, and pension and profit-sharing plans, even as each business increased in value as a going concern. My small businesses are examples to me of what is writ large in huge corporations. It is not surprising that companies can be sold for much more than two times their depreciated and amortized book values, even as their earnings do not appear outstanding, when it would cost much more to replace their physical plants and build their trademarks, patents, and customer bases.

Of course, it is not at all necessary to have been a small business owner to understand the hidden, depreciated assets, undervalued land on the books at cost, and "goodwill" value of corporations. Becoming slightly familiar with the financial reports of an analyzed corporation, even just the grossest items, can point the way to recognizing undervaluations and potential capital gains in such corporations' stocks in the course of time.

Asset Investing

However small the percentage of ownership, becoming "partners" of undervalued corporations offers at least two main approaches to picking bargain stocks. Let's call the first approach asset plays or current valuations. The second approach is *growth* or projected valuations.

I have left the following review almost verbatim from its 1989 writing to show how dramatic and yet how recurring undervaluations can be. As I reread this section to update and revise this book, I was shocked at the numbers involved.

If it's true that Ford Motor Company (F), for example, has a book value around $13.60 per share (split-adjusted figures, as are all that follow) and is trading at $4 per share—it traded between $3.50 and $4.75 in 1981—then investors were able to select Ford shares for 29 cents on the dollar more or less. In fact, Ford traded for less than 40 percent of its book value from middle-1980 through the beginning of 1982, and as low as 26 percent of book value in late '80 and again in late '81.

Considering that Ford's book value had been growing at the rate of 8.5 percent for the previous 10 years (1970–80) and 10 percent for the previous five years (1975–80), there was a good chance that its underlying fundamental value, as represented by its book value, would become even greater over the next several years. A purchase in the early '80s could lead to a greater than 100 percent gain, as the stock trading a few years down the road tended to reflect its assessed valuation.

In fact, Ford's book value did grow substantially over the years, so that the $13.60 of 1981 became $43.87 by the end of 1988. Ford's book value increase for this period is 226 percent. More important for stock speculators, Ford's (split-adjusted) share price climbed from a low of $3.50 in '81 to a high of $55 in '88, for a gain of 1,471 percent, not counting some substantial dividends along the way.

Many investors found it difficult to buy Ford shares in the early '80s. The domestic auto industry was out of favor, to say the least, and Ford had lost $2.85 per share for '80, $1.96 per share for '81, and $1.21 per share for '82. Ironically, while Ford was losing money in '82, and did not pay a dividend for that year, its shares advanced from their low of $3.625 at the beginning of the year to over $9 near year-end, for a market price appreciation of 148 percent. In the early '80s, Ford Motor Company was an asset play, at least. Of course, Ford was a whole lot more, as time revealed.

Ford split its stock two-for-one in mid-1994, so split-adjusted prices, earnings, and ratios were half what they were after the early 1988 two-for-one stock split. Ford, as well as General Motors and Chrysler, is highly sensitive to the economic and auto cycle of boom and bust. As with the losses incurred during 1980 through 1982, Ford also had losses for 1991 (–$2.40) and 1990 (–$0.73). From the $55 high in '88 (adjusted $27.625), and slightly higher in '89, Ford's stock tumbled to $11.875 at the end of '91. While still losing money in '92, Ford advanced to $24.50 that year, $33.125 in '93, and an all-time high of $35 ($70 pre-split) in '94.

In mid-1995, Ford is trading around $30 per share, with a book value of under $20.00; it is no longer an asset play. However, it has been making money hand over fist ($2.28 in '93; $5.20 in '94; estimated $5.50 for '95) and has good prospects for increased earnings for another year or two. It has a 30 percent return on equity while trading for only 5.5 times earnings, and so it is and has been for some time a growth play, even if it does not adhere to traditional cyclical investing standards. But there should come a time in the next year or so when Ford's earnings will peak, when Ford and the market will be overbought and overvalued. Then the wonderful company's stock should be prudently sold in anticipation of the next auto cycle. Ironically, when Ford is no longer making a profit (or at least not very much of one) and its stock has declined significantly, perhaps 50 to 80 percent from its cyclical high, it will be time to buy it again, going against the crowd that won't touch it.

A similar analysis could be presented concerning Chrysler, perhaps even more dramatic as Chrysler's stock has climbed from $9.75 in '91 to a high of $63.50 in '94, before backing off to $43.125 in the selldown of auto stocks in mid-1994.

We should be constantly aware of the reality that, just as stocks trade much of the time at a big discount to their fundamental values, they also trade on many occasions at a significant premium to these valuations. Although not presently the case with Ford or Chrysler, a corporation—even if it doesn't seem to be reaching its potential—nevertheless can provide a handsome capital gain as others recognize its takeover, merger, breakup, or growth value.

Growth Investing

The second major approach to picking bargain corporations is often called growth investing. A company may be doing well or poorly, having "hit a glitch" as the Fishers (Philip and Ken) might say, but with continuing prospects for a rewarding future. Since it is generally accepted that increased earnings are the ultimate goal of for-profit corporations, a large number of fundamental investors concentrate on finding emerging growth, junior growth, growth, and accelerating growth stocks, the prices of which do not yet reflect their reality or potential.

Here too, I leave the 1989 analysis, with some 1995 followup afterwards. Happily, we can again turn to Ford Motor Company—from the early '80s to 1989—for an example of growth investing. Since Ford already has $80 billion or so in sales and $25 billion or so in market capitalization and is a giant corporation, its stock would not be considered junior, emerging, or even a high-growth candidate. Still, in 10 years (1979–1988) Ford's earnings have grown at 14 percent, while its dividend has grown at 33 percent per annum for the past five years. In mid-1989, Ford was trading at 4.5 times current earnings, compared to *Value Line's* average annual P/E ratio of 7.0, and my belief was that Ford should trade at 8 to 10 times earnings when it becomes fully appreciated. Therefore, Ford was a currently recommended stock in 1989 for its growth potential rather than as an asset play.

We do not live in an Aristotelian world of either/or, and though we often distinguish between growth and asset plays, many undervalued stocks have both characteristics. Ford is not the asset play it was in the early '80s. It had a [mid-1989] book value around $46.56 per share, compared to a price of $50 per share. Thus, Ford traded at 107 percent of book value. Considering Ford had traded at 154 percent of its book value before the Crash of '87, it could easily have traded at $71.70 (based on summer 1989 figures without any increase in its book value) in reaching that level again. Furthermore, since Ford's book value has grown at 16 percent in the past five years, its book value could have doubled in the next five years at just under 15 percent per year.

We could have also projected a conservative example, saying Ford only managed its 10-year book value growth rate of 7.5 percent. In that case, in five years (by 1994), Ford's book value could become $66.84; and if it traded for the aforementioned 154 percent of book value, Ford shares would be priced at $102.94, more than twice their 1989 market price. Hey, it looks like Ford was a bit of an asset play after all, at least for the patient speculator.

Now, in 1995, to repeat, we find that Ford has a book value around $20 and is trading around $30 per share. What happened? Ford took a big writedown in '92. It also split its shares two-for-one in 1994 (just as it had in 1988). It looks like our 1989 optimism of Ford's book value growth was not well founded. Yet, with a "leaner, meaner Ford" having written a lot of water out of its book value—as so many corporations have over the past five years—we can be comfortable with a higher price/book value ratio than its historical average ratio.

We again can see that *even a couple basic criteria such as price/earnings and price/book value, invoked above, are adequate for finding currently undervalued corporations*, and for believing in their financials and future, holding them through ugly stock-market periods, and finally selling them at enormous capital gains, often receiving substantial dividend income along the way. It's simple in theory, and it works in practice much of the time if one's emotions and personality don't interfere.

Stock Diversification—A Principal Strategy

We may have put the cart before the horse in reviewing time diversification in the preceding paragraphs. Generally, diversification refers to stock or industry diversification, including sector diversification. There are two distinct schools of portfolio construction and management which can be summarized by the terms *concentration* and *diversification*.

Those who favor concentration believe in owning relatively few stocks at any one time. Instead of putting many eggs in many baskets, the concentrationists put a few eggs in one basket. They are very careful in the initial selection process, because if they are wrong in even one stock the impact on their equity would be significantly detrimental. Some of them also believe that few can adequately analyze and understand more than a handful of corporations, let alone keep sufficient tabs on them after buying them.

Gerald Loeb in his informative, if somewhat dated, book *Your Battle for Stock Market Profits*[2], believes in the concentrated approach:

> As to individual stocks, I believe in owning very few. I do not want to buy stock unless I buy enough to show me a worthwhile profit if I am right and potentially hurt me if I am wrong. In practice, if things go my way I would tend to buy more. If things go against me, I would aim to sell out and minimize the damage. I only want to select an individual stock to buy with a unique extra reason that suggests it is the best buy. This is the opposite of building a "portfolio" of "core stocks," that is, a long list of popular leaders in popular groups. (p. 90)

Several personal attitudes are apparent in Mr. Loeb's quotation above, and we may contrast them with our own diversification beliefs as well as with other concentrationists who deviate strongly from one point or another of his.

Warren Buffett, a believer in holding core stocks, has said that every investor should be given a book of 20 tickets at birth and have one torn out for every stock bought so that when all tickets are used up no more stocks can be acquired. That might certainly concentrate one's attention on careful and judicious stock selection, although not necessarily.

---

[2] Gerald M. Loeb, *Your Battle for Stock Market Profits,* (NY: Simon and Shuster, 1974).

In contrast to these estimable and successful gentlemen, *I am a firm believer in diversification—almost the wider the better—in order to minimize individual corporate risk* sometimes called unsystematic risk (as contrasted with market or systematic risk). Even before I learned about risk reduction from diversification, I had an intuitive or common sense notion that if you only had a small percentage of your estate at risk in any one position, and if that position went against you badly, then you wouldn't be hurt much overall. My initial sense of stock diversification was that I'd want at least 30 stocks, because 30 was the number that elementary statistics texts claim is a minimum meaningful population or number of events. Later I was to learn of such studies and tables as Table 3–3, reprinted here through the courtesy of *Stock Market Logic*

I find it interesting that my original, naive choice of having at least 30 stocks would turn out statistically to eliminate about 96 percent of individual stock risk. But there is an important caveat about the basic number of stocks: they must be scattered among different, specific industry groups. If we have five airlines, five paper companies, five gold mines, five banks, five savings and loans, and five oil companies, we would have 30 different stocks, but we would not have the equivalent unsystematic risk reduction implied by that number of positions. Each of those industry groups generally tends to act in concert, so the above example could have the effect of having only six or so diversified positions rather than 30.

Having sufficient corporation and industry diversification in a new portfolio creates certain practical problems, especially given the amount of cash and the selection of undervalued stocks available at any given moment. From time to time we find ourselves "overweighted" in certain industries because that's where the bargains are. Over the years, as portfolios evolve and grow, other undervalued

Table 3–3. Diversification and Reduction of Risk

Number of Stocks in Portfolio	Percentage of Risk Eliminated
2	46%
4	72
8	81
16	93
32	96
64	98
500	99
All Stocks	100

Source: Adapted from Norman G. Fosback, *Stock Market Logic* (Fort Lauderdale, FL: The Institute for Econometric Research, 1984), p. 254.

stocks are added to the portfolio, sometimes replacing some of the overweighted positions, resulting in a more balanced stock diversification.

In the Meltdown of '87, TPS Portfolio was much too overweighted in savings and loan, bank, and other interest-sensitive stocks. Even though the bargains may be concentrated in a few industries, eternal vigilance is needed to maintain a better industry group balance than just the "best bargains" criterion.

We certainly can have more than one corporation in the same industry, especially when, for example, two tire companies reflect a different niche in the market with their major products, one specializing in the original equipment manufacturing (OEM) market and the other mainly serving the replacement and repair markets. The less our portfolios are represented by a wide spectrum of manufacturing, financial, retail, personal service, natural resource, and other principal industry groups, the less diversification is at work despite our large number of different stocks.

And yet, referring again to Table 3–3, even if we hold only 15 or 16 diversified industry positions—which might involve 20 to 30 individual stocks—isn't a 93 percent risk-elimination level enough for us? Of course it is. If our selections are halfway decent, and our multiyear market timing (time diversification) protects us against serious but temporary marketwide declines, we will do very nicely, thank you. Still, I want to own as many undervalued stocks as I can because of my intuition and experience that casting a wider net increases the possibility of catching more winners. Even if my wide net also catches more losers, I am not terribly concerned because winners generally win more than losers lose, and by a substantial measure.

It is simple to observe—but not simpleminded to consider—that a $10 stock can only lose $10, or 100 percent, or it could gain many times $10 over the years. Most of us do not realize the extent to which many stocks have appreciated, because the gains may be hidden by stock splits (and the occasional special large stock or cash dividend that is paid).

As previously mentioned, we must monitor our researched stocks and question how their current prices came to be when they appear cheap to us. The apparently low prices may be the result of a stock split, in which case there is no change in the fundamental value. One original share at $70 is equal to two split shares at $35, although there may be some psychological advantages, such as making lower-price shares available to more shareholders. Or the previously priced $70 shares' current $35 price may be due to a significant marketwide decline, in which case the stock may have been driven into undervalued, buy-candidate territory.

Other reasons for wide diversification for the small investor or beginning student of speculation—as I was when I began dabbling more than 26 years ago— include each of our individual limitations in time, capital, information, knowledge, and sophistication. Most of us have neither the time to study each corporation in depth nor the talent to recognize most subtle and esoteric situations. Most of us do not have *entrée* to interview captains of industry or, if we do hear them at annual meetings, cannot discern reality from company cheerleading. Remember, corporate officers are partisans, boosters of their companies, who see and publicize few if any problems that cannot be solved or be regarded as opportunities in disguise. Also, they eschew practicing candor or being forthcoming, following the Brass Rule: "Thou shalt not knock thy company."

Some individual investors/speculators do have the time and inclination to track companies constantly, recognizing subtle but meaningful—let alone gross— changes in their fortunes and prospects. Perhaps some talented stock pickers can be concentrationists and keep a careful watch over 5 or 10 positions without regard to diversification. Even the most astute, devoted, and hard-working stock pickers make errors in judgment as otherwise competent managers and well-run corporations suffer glitches in their operations. Perhaps a promising new product, which has been heavily promoted and inventoried, fails badly in public acceptance and causes a corporation unexpectedly large losses and setbacks. There are many currently good-looking companies that are potential disasters waiting to occur.

Barry Ziskin, one of the better stock pickers and portfolio managers, uses a rigid, seven-criteria test for stock selection. Though he had managed 30 percent returns on equity for years, he saw two stocks that met his strict requirements, Amfesco Corp. and Commodore International, take a tumble in 1986.

By the way, the annual reports of Ziskin's Z-Seven Fund[3] are like mini-textbooks on conservative investing, explicating his methods for managing his closed-end mutual fund and clients' portfolios. While I appreciate the logic and efficacy of Ziskin's seven criteria, I don't use them systematically myself, finding them too restrictive for my taste and too sophisticated for my accounting.

The Initial 5 Percent Rule

I strongly advise at the outset to have no more than 5 percent of a portfolio in any one equity. If the portfolio has no more than 5 percent in any one position—not counting cash or equivalents such as Treasury bills at times—then it will have at least 20 or more stocks when it is fully formed.

Unfortunately for the small speculator who has only $5,000 or $10,000 available—and does not choose to use margin leverage in order to buy more equities—it is impractical to buy 20 stocks. First, there is the penalty of relatively high commission percentages on small amounts of stock. If you were to buy 20 positions with $5,000—that is, about $250 each for 20 different stocks—you would have to pay between $400 to $600 in "minimum" commissions at a discount brokerage house.

---

[3] Z-Seven Fund, Inc., 2651 West Guadalupe, Suite B-233, Mesa, AZ 85202.

This works out to between 8 and 12 percent of your purchase costs, and you would be faced with paying comparable commissions when you decided to trade those stocks. Perhaps your $5,000 worth of stocks did well in market price (on average) before you sold. You would again pay $400 to $600 on the $10,000 of sales. This means that your stocks would have to appreciate between 16 and 24 percent just for you to break even—quite a load with which to be burdened, although not insurmountable.

There used to be another penalty involved for the very small investor, the odd-lot differential, which refers to the tradition of charging you an "eighth" (12.5 cents)— coming and going, buying and selling—for stock lots of fewer than 100 shares. One hundred shares are called *round lots* for most positions. In some cases for very high-priced stocks, less than 100-share lots, such as 10 shares, may be designated "round." Over time, these relatively high commission percentages and differentials combined to lower the net total return performance of a small investor's portfolio.

If you do not have the cash (or cash plus margin) to buy over $20,000 worth of stocks, you would probably do well to begin with mutual funds, at least as far as diversification and commission expenses are concerned (see Chapter 10). Even then I would like to see $10,000 spread among at least three or four funds, and $20,000 diversified into at least six funds. Although each fund will probably have sufficient stock and industry diversification, ranging from dozens to hundreds of different corporate positions, each fund will have its bias and approach that empha-sizes one kind of company or stock category over another. More on the dangers of open-end mutual funds in Chapter 10.

Selecting stocks is a serious activity. So too is selecting mutual funds. The selection of mutual funds is beyond the purview of this chapter, although many of the criteria for stock selection can be applied to mutual fund selection.

The initial 5 percent limit guideline mentioned above seems straightforward, but soon requires some interpretation and decisions. Suppose you bought 25 stocks in your $50,000 diversified portfolio, which meant you spent "on average" (an often-used expression implying less than high precision) some $2,000 per position. Sometime later, say after a year, if your portfolio had appreciated 20 percent and thus was priced at $60,000, most likely you would have some stocks that had advanced significantly and others that had declined significantly. Perhaps your best-performing stock position doubled in market price and was valued at $5,000, but that would be 8.3 percent of the portfolio ($5,000/$60,000). Would the 5 per-cent rule call for your selling $2,000 worth of this most-appreciated stock in order to bring its market value down to 5 percent of the portfolio? No, it would not.

Applying only to *initial* purchases, the 5 percent rule is waived in the case of appreciated stocks that are still significantly undervalued according to their fundamen-tal corporate analysis. I suggest you consider a 10 to 20 percent limit of any appreciat-ed position in your portfolio. The idea is to avoid the chance of being badly damaged if one or a few positions go sour, and if your "best stock" begins to represent more than 15 percent, a sharp (50 percent) drop in it would really set back the portfolio's overall performance. Then too, as a great stock appreciates and your portfolio appreciates, 15 percent of the larger portfolio is more than triple an original 5 percent position. Besides, you don't have to sell all or even most of the highly appreciated stock— just bring it down to 10 percent or less of the portfolio and reinvest the proceeds in other undervalued stocks, thus increasing stock diversification.

Suppose that after this pleasant hypothetical example of a 20 percent appreciation year you find you have additional funds available for stocks, there are undervalued buy candidates, and the market is not especially threatening. What would be the limit for additional purchases to your $60,000 portfolio? At first glance you might say $3,000, because that is 5 percent of the current market value of the portfolio. But say you intended to add $20,000; you are actually considering an $80,000 portfolio, so you are then "permitted" to buy up to $4,000 positions.

Of course, you are not required to spend 5 percent per position; that is a rough maximum guideline for portfolios of less than $50,000. In the preceding example of adding $20,000 to a $60,000 portfolio, you might well consider buying six or seven $3,000 positions, rather than just five $4,000 positions with your $20,000 additional capital. You also have the option to buy new shares or to add to current positions that may have declined in market price even while their fundamental values have been increasing.

As the portfolio increases in value, I would definitely tend to initiate smaller than 5 percent positions. Table 3–4 represents my personal guideline for initial percentages and stock diversification. Obviously, small portfolios may need to exceed the 5 percent rule in order to avoid excessive commission expenses. Remember, stock diversification might better be called industry diversification. *With 30 stocks try to be in at least 12 to 15 industry groups.*

Averaging Up and Averaging Down

Averaging, in the present context, refers to adding to positions already owned, usually at a different price per share than the original cost basis. Not unlike the unexamined prohibition against the use of leverage (borrowed funds in margined accounts) is the motto "Never average down!" Anytime you get an "always" or "never" in stock-market advice, you're probably getting an overstatement at best and almost *always* a bum steer. I disagree that buying more shares of a stock that has declined significantly is necessarily "throwing good money after bad." In averaging down, the second purchase may be a far wiser move than the first purchase has so far turned out to be.

Table 3-4. Initial Position Diversification and Percentage per Portfolio Size

Portfolio Size	Number of Stocks	Dollar Percent
$25,000	12–15	6.0–8.5%
50,000	15–20	5.0–7.0
100,000	20–30	3.5–5.0
200,000	25–40	2.5–4.0
500,000	30–50	2.0–3.5
1,000,000	50–100	1.0–2.0

If you own the stock of a prospering corporation, that prosperity may extend to the price of its stock, so that now it trades for appreciably more than you paid, and yet it is still undervalued according to fundamental analysis. With other appropriate conditions, such as the priority of first considering other stocks with greater undervaluations, and the percentage limit guideline of this position in the portfolio, it makes perfectly good sense to increase your position in such a stock. As you buy the stock at a higher price, you are *averaging up*. If the first 100 shares cost $10 per share, and now you buy another 100 shares at $20 per, your average cost will be $15 per share for the 200 shares.

There may be a small psychological letdown after averaging up because your augmented position no longer reflects a doubling of its total cost basis, although you still have a gain in the total position in the example above. Such psychological twinges should be of little consequence in a speculator's long-term portfolio.

As long as a stock's price continues to represent less than 50 percent of its corporation's fundamental value (or anticipated three- to five-year market price)—no matter how much it has advanced beyond your cost basis or its original goal price—it is a buy candidate competing for a place to improve the balance of your portfolio. However, if there were an equally or almost equally undervalued stock not in the portfolio, I would tend to want to add that currently unowned stock before increasing current positions, thus slightly widening the net.

If our prospering corporation's stock continued to do well enough but then began to slow in its appreciation or falter, then perhaps the other added stock would take up the slack. Of course, there is almost always the case where the already owned, advancing stock continues to advance nicely, even into overvalued territory, while the newly purchased undervalued stock declines significantly. In such an event we are likely to express the famous "Why did I . . . when I shoulda" laments: "Why did I buy Improving Prospects Unlimited at all—it lost 50 percent of its market price over the past 24 months—when I shoulda bought more shares of Slow and Unsteady Limited, which appreciated 500 percent in the past two years?"

It is certainly okay to hold so-called losers and average down for the right reasons. As Sir John Templeton said:

You will always find in our list some stocks selling below cost, but we're not holding them just because they're below cost. We're holding them because we think they are the best bargains, the lowest prices in relation to the long-term earning power of that corporation.

We really try to avoid the question of is it above or below what we paid for it. That has nothing to do with whether it's a good value or not. [4]

Warren Buffett, aside from being arguably the most astute investor of current times, is noted for his wit and down-to-earth observations. A card player, Buffett enjoys the idioms associated with that activity, and has said if you're in a poker game for a half-hour and you don't know who's the patsy, you're the patsy. *Webster's New World Dictionary* defines patsy as "a person easily imposed upon or victimized." In the present context, Buffett has said:

If your stock goes down 10 percent and that upsets you—it obviously means you think the market knows more about the company than you do. In that case you're the patsy.

If it goes down 10 percent and you want to buy more because you know the business is worth just as much as when you bought it before, perhaps a little bit more with the passage of time, so you buy more, they're the patsy.[5]

Most investors tend to get emotionally biased when it comes to buying a stock currently or previously owned that has not done well. I've suffered from this syndrome myself, as related in my early trading of Whittaker Corp. (see Chapter 7). The Whittaker example showed I was not a prudent investor or speculator when I first started buying the overvalued stock and when I last sold the undervalued stock. Since I had been so hurt and embarrassed in my trading in Whittaker, I was unable to recognize or act upon one of the great buys of late 1974.

Ideas and terms like *averaging up*, *averaging down*, *doubling one's position*, *taking profits*, and *taking losses*, should have little emotional influence on portfolio management. To repeat our song, *we buy undervalued stocks to be held for the long term in widely diversified portfolios until they are fully valued* or until very severe and threatening overvalued and overbought markets suggest taking defensive measures.

---

[4] *Outstanding Investor Digest*, October 30, 1988, p. 11.

[5] *Outstanding Investor Digest*, June 30, 1988, p. 12.

The Basics Are More Important Than Being Clever

Our basic investment approach of finding and buying stocks of undervalued corporations can be done quite easily, although not perfectly. To the degree we try to bring in intellectual or academic cleverness, such as outguessing megatrends, the economy, the stock market, inflation, or the next fad, we endanger our strongest suit. All we have to do is our bottom-up (individual company) approach, and sooner or later, most of the time, our undervalued corporations will become fairly valued, as reflected in the rising prices of their stocks over a multiyear period.

Clearly, in 1995 inflation is a major concern of the investment world, especially the Federal Reserve. Inflation refers to several components, such as wages, wholesale and retail prices, commodities, interest rates, and service costs. One simple description of inflation is too many dollars chasing too few goods. The relationship of productivity increases versus wage increases is very important, as the balance of goods to dollars is maintained or lost. You would have to be a very bright and learned economist to keep track of and understand many of the elements that contribute to inflation or deflation, and then you might be able to guess right 50 percent of the time. I am told that economists are rarely right 50 percent of the time. Meanwhile, you run the strong chance of zigging when you should have zagged, being out of the market when it fools the majority and takes off as it has during the first seven months of 1995.

For example, a headline in the *Investor's Daily* (March 16, 1989) stated: "Oil Prices Head Higher, Defying Predictions." Instead of crude oil prices continuing to drop in November 1988 from the $13 per barrel low to below $10 as then predicted, they climbed to over $21 per barrel in April 1989. Those who sold—or declined to hold or buy—oil stocks before year-end because of the low crude prices missed handsome gains in most of the major oil companies over that following five-month period, and beyond.

As if trying to outguess crude oil demand, supply, and prices weren't bad enough, some investors presumed that rising oil prices would be negative for airline stocks, which is often the case because fuel is a major expense for airlines. However, the airlines had a banner first quarter, on average, in both profitability and in their stocks' appreciation, powering the Dow Jones Transportation Index to all-time highs, surpassing pre-Crash of '87 levels. Such clever analysis often doesn't work out in practice, as so many other elements enter into the picture to distort the seemingly simple and apparent if-then relationships.

In the prior edition of this book, I wrote "It will be interesting to see if we are in the much-predicted recession by the time this book is published in the fall of '89—a recession that many economists and market prognosticators were sure would follow the Crash of '87, each subsequent quarter of '88, and '89." [A recession finally occurred during the second half of 1990.] Would a recession make much difference to the long-term value investor? Not according to Warren Buffett, who was asked whether a recession was imminent at the Berkshire Hathaway annual meeting in May of '88. His answer:

> "I don't know . . . But it just doesn't make any difference. If I had spent my time trying to figure out when the next recession would occur, Berkshire's stock would probably be around $15 a share instead of its current $3,675 . . . I wouldn't believe anybody's fore-cast—especially my own."[6]

By the way, Berkshire shares traded for over $6,300 each in May 1989. By February 1995, Berkshire Hathaway traded as high as $25,200 per share—perhaps overvalued, as they decline some 10 percent into mid-1995, then advanced again.

Although rising interest rates are generally not supportive of rising stock prices, there are many periods during which both advanced in tandem, such as the first eight months of 1987, for most of 1988, and during the first quarter of 1989. It seems that the level of interest rates, the strength of their advance, and the percep-tion of future stability or change in direction all contribute to that incalculable bal-ance that tips market fluctuations. Ironically, after seven hostile Federal Reserve raises of short-term interest rates, between February 4, 1994 and February 2, 1995, which led to increases in long-term interest rates several major averages and indexes hit all-time highs through mid-1995, although many individual stocks were trading below their 1994 highs. A large part of this advance was caused by long-term rates dropping—a very strong bond-market rally—after the Fed's seventh increase.

A phenomenon that often confuses stock marketeers is the discounting or anticipating mechanism that the market represents. Markets top out and begin declining during periods of prosperity and enthusiasm, just when it looks like the good times will go on and on. Markets bottom out and begin advancing during recessions, depressions, and otherwise generally gloomy periods when it looks like the economic viability of America is in grave straits.

There are many cycles, periods, and movements that are neither intuitive nor apparent from daily and weekly stock-market activity. There are long stretches (years and decades) when stocks are "overowned," maintaining and keeping up demand and prices until monetary conditions cannot support such excesses. Then too, when stocks are "underowned," financial institutions and individuals, newly discovering the market or overcoming previous bad experience, seem compelled to invest excess reserves in stocks under all but the most adverse conditions.

In 1989, as the 1980s came to a close, there was a seeming shortage of stocks caused by the massive amounts of shares retired due to mergers, acquisitions, buy-

---

[6] *Outstanding Investor Digest*, June 30, 1988, p. 13.

outs, and buybacks, unmatched by relatively few new issues. Over $400 billion in stocks had been "retired" from the stock market since January 1984. This five-year reduction in the "supply" of stocks can have only bullish implications for the longer term, especially as stocks are already underowned by historic averages and investable funds continue to grow.

Curiously, in the 1994–95 period there is another major buyback of stocks— this time by their own corporations, rather than through mergers, acquisitions, and buyouts—thus putting some supply-demand pressure on stock prices and tending to elevate earnings-per-share ratios. Of course, at any time such a process can be reversed as more new issues or secondary distributions are made by corporations in an effort to capture overvalued bids for equities.

To Sell or Not to Sell?—That Is the Question

Most people I've read or listened to agree that *knowing when to sell and selling are the most difficult and troublesome aspects of investing.* The glib may say that selling is merely the other side of the investment coin—heads I buy, tails I sell—but that really doesn't capture the asymmetrical relationships among buying, holding, and selling. Selling is often analytically and psychologically tough, and probably as important a discipline as buying. I say selling is probably as important as buying because I believe in the idea that a well-bought corporation may almost never need to be sold or will provide many good selling opportunities at a handsome profit in the fullness of time. Still, there are many guidelines for doing selling well.

Because so many people have trouble selling, we'll review some of the psychology involved. After deciding to buy stocks but before committing to any trade, we have the luxury of taking our time to review the enormous number of choices available. In Warren Buffett's imagery, we can stand at the plate all day waiting for just the right pitch at which to swing. As individual and independent speculators, no one is forcing us to buy stocks or hold them only if they show superior quarterly performance, as often happens to institutional investors. As long as we are selecting buy candidates, checking them out, and watching their market meanderings, we are safe in the world of the potential position.

Once we buy a stock, we must then decide to hold. Holding one or a group of stocks is an existential exercise for some, a decision each day on whether to continue holding or to sell. It is one thing to peruse a buy list and take one's time in picking and choosing; it is quite another to peruse one's holdings, watching them rise and fall, especially when they decline in price, often for no apparent reason, while the market advances on average. This process can be so nerve-wracking for some investors that they take a mechanical way out and place stop-loss sell orders. That way, if the stock's price drops a certain amount or percentage, adios and farewell, it's history.

I find it fascinating to hear investors admit, dripping with sincerity and candor, that they made a mistake when a stock they picked dropped 10 percent (or whatever amount) in its market price. They believe they are showing how disciplined they are by automatically selling such "mistakes" without additional review or hesitation. Perhaps they have convinced themselves that when the market speaks, they listen. The tape does not lie. For them, the market's language is price, and the market is always right. I disagree vehemently. The market doesn't speak; people speak. The market is merely a mechanism for bringing together heterogenous numbers of people, many of whom see the stock market as a game, trying their luck in that big casino in the Big Apple, the Windy City, or other places.

The market is not always right, except in terms of the most sophomoric and tortured logic. In reality, the stock market is usually wrong. Many people assume that a stock's price is the result of an efficient process of informed, rational trading. If that were the case, why would we trade stocks at all? If that were the case, why do some corporations trade today at 5 to 50 percent or more—or less, for that matter—than their price of yesterday? You might say that so-and-so decided to make a bid for the company. Is so-and-so a philanthropist, "giving" away much more than the recent stock price for the benefit of owning the corporation in question? Or was the market "wrong" in pricing that stock yesterday because it is "correct" today?

Short-term stock price fluctuations often have little or nothing to do with long-term corporate or general economic conditions. Daily price movements are in effect seemingly random, although daily commentators strive for apparent reasons to explain price fluctuations. Understanding participants, in this complex adaptive system called the stock market, take a more sanguine view than professional commentators who are paid to sound knowledgeable and must come up with plausible-sounding reasons. We might content ourselves with the Vedantist saying that "things happen," when asked to explain events. Or we may be best off saying with a twinkle in the eye, "The price dropped because there were more sellers than buyers," or vice versa.

While much of portfolio management is mathematical and mechanistic, the keys to maintaining long-term perspectives and perseverance are based on developing a realistic attitude and exploring one's own mindsets. *Probably the most general mistake, and therefore the weakest link in portfolio management, is selling too soon.* Either because a stock has declined in market price and we are afraid it's going lower, or because a stock has advanced in market price and we are afraid our good fortune cannot continue and the unrealized gains will soon vanish, many investors lock-in small losses and limit themselves to relatively modest gains. This practice is a recipe for not doing well in the stock market. Each loss must be made up—plus four commissions—before one breaks even, so if the gains generally aren't significantly greater than the losses, one will end with little to show for all the effort, commitment of funds, and risk.

Many conscious and unconscious attitudes we carry into stock speculation may sabotage our best efforts. One significant inhibiter of clear thinking is the concept of getting even.

The Getting Even Fallacy

I have often encountered the *getting even fallacy* from market participants. This attitude takes two distinct forms, each containing fatal errors in reasoning and practice. The first class of investors, after sustaining a price decline, say and think that they are waiting to get even in order to get out of a position or the market in general. The other class are those shareholders who are willing to sell out their "losers" now because, even if their stocks have a strong potential to double in market price, they would only become "even" with their original costs.

Let's start with the terms *realized and unrealized capital gains and losses.* A realized gain or loss occurs when a position is sold and the net costs are subtracted from the net proceeds. If the proceeds realized from the sale, after brokerage commissions and transfer taxes or fees, are greater than the purchase costs (which also include brokerage commissions) then one has a realized capital gain. Obviously, in the opposite case, where the proceeds are less than the costs, one has a realized capital loss. Realized gains and losses have tax consequences (outside a sheltered portfolio such as an IRA) and become part of your income tax return. Realized capital gains and losses are the clear and tangible outcomes of the closed transactions defined by simple arithmetic.

Unrealized capital gains and losses refer to the differences between the market values of your positions compared to the costs of those positions. Until those positions are sold and the gains or losses realized, there are no tax consequences, except in the rare event of a return of equity which exceeds the cost basis of the stock. What is quite arithmetically clear often becomes emotionally confused, especially when slogans like, "It's not a loss until you sell!" are believed. (The potentially troublesome effects of such a misleading attitude are also touched on in Chapter 5, on margin.)

People who believe they do not have capital losses until they are "realized" are often inconsistent because they believe they do have capital gains before those are realized. In the words of a popular song of some years past, they are accentuating the positive and eliminating the negative, but at the expense of reality. If you can treat these two impostors, as Kipling would say—unrealized gains and losses (triumphs and despairs)—with equanimity, your investment decisions will be more rational.

Gains and losses are just that, whether realized or not, and those who do not wish to accept the reality of their unrealized positions are often led into making poor speculative decisions. Most important, current gains and losses have no necessary relationship to the fundamental values of corporations. Thus, making investment decisions because of unrealized gains or losses in market price is missing the whole point of long-term value and growth investing.

What is important to the prudent stock speculator, at any given moment, is the fundamental value of the corporation—and therefore the value of its stock—in which a position is held. For example, I held Ford Motor Company (F) in my portfolio with a cost basis of $13.01, which closed March 31, 1989 at $48.875. The fact that there was an unrealized gain of over 275 percent had nothing to do with why I continued to hold Ford shares or when I might decide to sell them. The operative factor for holding was that my analysis of Ford at that time showed its potential to trade between $97 and $100 in the next three to five years. Therefore, it was a currently recommended stock and *I might even have bought more shares at near four times my original cost basis*, except that Ford already amounted to one of the largest positions in my portfolio. To buy more Ford would have violated the diversification principle of not buying more than 2 to 3 percent in any one position in a portfolio the size of mine.

On the other hand, I held General Development (GDV) in my portfolio at a cost basis of $18.88 per share; GDV closed on July 29, 1988, at $12. Again, I held GDV (and might have bought more shares, thus averaging down) because its estimated three- to five-year market price was then $34 per share. Logically, I did not care what GDV cost me in the past. As long as it was currently trading for half or less than its projected goal price I could buy more shares, and thereafter hold it until its market price met its analyzed goal price or market conditions dictated selling. By April 31, 1989, GDV closed at $14.625, but its goal price had declined to $24 per share, so it was then a strong hold but no longer a buy. In time, GDV's goal price might well advance and make it a buy again, or decline and make it a sell. Alas, in time, GDV shares became worthless. Win some, lose some.

I might be remiss not to mention such disappointments as Financial Corp. of America (FIN) and Maxus Energy (MXS), among many positions that have not worked out well. I held FIN at a cost basis of $8.82; it closed on July 29, 1988, at $1. I had believed that FIN could be turned around and become a valuable property, but finally concluded my long-held expectation was unlikely to occur and "realized" my loss. Even though there was little to be received at $1 per share, I would not hold the stock hoping to get even or even to make a double from the clearly depressed price. Several months later, FIN was reorganized by the FSLIC and the common shares became worthless. Likewise, I had concluded that with all Maxus Energy's potential, its fundamental analysis led me to want to redeploy the $7.75 per share or so of proceeds—original cost basis $11.63 per share—into a more promising position.

Most overvalued stocks that we sell continue to advance in market price, at least for a while. We should not be chagrined or disappointed by such patterns. Only by accident can we catch tops and bottoms in stock prices and market movements. It may feel bad to miss that extra appreciation, but consider what potential appreciation may be gained from new, undervalued stocks bought with the proceeds, especially over time. We should go with the probabilities that say trim the overvalued stocks—even when they produce a realized loss—in favor of repositioning in undervalued stocks with much greater potential.

So, we do not *hold* stocks to get even, to show a profit, or to put off realizing a loss. *We hold stocks because they are undervalued.* We do not sell stocks because their current goal prices are below our cost basis. *We sell stocks because they are fully valued or overvalued, no matter what our cost basis*, so that we can redeploy the proceeds—with realized gains or losses—into undervalued positions.

It truly grieves me when investors reason that it is correct to liquidate stocks and even portfolios because even if our current projections come true, that would only lead to a stock or a portfolio becoming even in two or three years.

Let's say that because of an unusual run of poorly performing selections and the market crash of October 1987 your portfolio declined 50 percent from its cost basis. Let's say that if things went well—of course no guarantees, and future performance may not equal past performance or even be profitable—you might double your post-crash equity in four years (about 18 percent compounded annually), or perhaps in three years (about 24 percent compounded annually). The investor who says, "You mean, even if things go well I will have to wait three or four years, and then only get even?" has not understood value and growth speculating and the reality of the situation. And besides, what is he or she going to do with the funds remaining? Put them in a bank account to earn a 4 to 6 percent return before taxes and inflation?

Our unrealized losses are real, as the proceeds from selling out will attest. In this example, our capital is 50 percent gone—it's spilt milk. What matters is what we can do about it from now on. If we can return to making handsome compounded annual gains for the next several years, we will not only "get even" but recover and prevail.

I bought Ambase Corporation (ABC, formerly Home Group) at $18.625 per share, and it was trading around $13.75 on June 28, 1989, but had a goal price of $28. I wouldn't consider selling it merely because it would have to appreciate about 50 percent for me to just become even. I considered buying more, or at least holding my current shares, because of the probability that I could gain over 100 percent or more from current levels with my ABC shares over the next few years. Conditions may change and I might have to sell Ambase for less than the current price, but as long as it was undervalued and I didn't project a crash, I held it. Alas, I sold my 400 shares of Ambase at $6.25 on August 6, 1990, for a total loss of $3,719.51, in order to meet a maintenance call. I see that Ambase closed at 3/16 on March 31, 1995, so I was lucky to have to sell it because it never got to our sell goal price.

Many stocks trade for 30 to 50 percent of their originally recommended or purchased prices only to become huge winners over the years. Consider the early disappointing price history of Puerto Rican Cement (PRN). I bought 500 shares of PRN in November 1983 for $6.75 per share. PRN hit a high of $12.25 in 1984, but fell to a low of $6.00 in 1985. PRN hit a high of $38.50 before the Crash of '87 and thereafter traded at a low of $16.50, thus twice declining more than 50 percent in less than four years. On March 31, 1989, PRN closed at $46.50, for an unrealized gain of 589 percent in less than five years. What would my long-term record be if I had sold out when I got even in '86? What would my performance for 1988 have been if I sold out after the crash because I could hope for little more than getting even with the pre-Crash unrealized gain? I still hold 600 shares of Puerto Rican Cement, with a split-adjusted cost basis of $2.25 per share and a current price on June 8, 1995 of $30.50 per share with our goal price at $34.50 per share, which I hope to see realized in '95 or early '96.

Successful speculators sometimes make convincing, sagacious statements. George Soros, fabled for his speculative successes, has asserted that he never tries to get even. What's past is over and done. What's important is to get on with the process.

Warren Buffett, often mentioned in these pages because of his great and continued success, commented at the 1988 Berkshire Hathaway annual meeting about the probability of a 50 percent decline in one's common stocks. "You ignore that possibility at your own peril. In the history of almost every major company in this country, it has happened. *You shouldn't own common stocks if a decrease in their value by 50 percent would cause you to feel stress.*"[7]

Every market day we are faced with considering our stock positions, unless we are truly long-term "partners" in our corporations. If we focus on our corporations rather than the stock market, we may only consider our stock positions weekly, monthly, quarterly, or even annually. Should we sell, hold, or buy more? Most of the time the answer to these questions is the same as yesterday's—I will hold until I believe the position is fully valued or market conditions become too threatening. From time to time, cash becomes available to invest, and market conditions seem propitious or at least neutral, so I will have to decide whether to buy more undervalued shares of already owned positions or instead buy other undervalued stocks. These decisions involve reviews of diversification, limits of concentration, comparative undervaluedness, and perhaps current economic conditions.

Some misguided marketeers say if you wouldn't buy the stocks you own today, then you should sell them—you shouldn't keep holding them. I find this either/or thinking illogical and inefficient. If I find a corporation, which fundamental analysis suggests will likely trade at $25 within three to five years, then my discipline permits me to buy that equity up to $12.50 per share. Suppose I am able to purchase some of this potential $25-corporations' shares at $10, and a few weeks later they

---

[7] *Outstanding Investor Digest*, June 30, 1988, p. 9.

are trading at $13, just above my current buy limit. Though I might not buy any more shares unless and until that stock's goal price increases to twice or more than its current market price (or its market price decreases to 50 percent or less than its current goal price), I would certainly want to hold those shares—with their rapidly unrealized 30 percent gain—for their perceived greater worth.

My experience has shown that in a majority of cases the fundamentally analyzed goal prices will tend to increase during the years, in keeping with a corporation's growing value. Long-term capital gains often turn out to be much more than the original goal price—a doubling or better of the initial purchase price—due to continued corporate growth over the years and the expansion of market valuations (such as increasing P/Es) in strong upward-trending stock markets.

No superior stock speculation system that I know of is effortless or completely automatic, although many are simpler than others. Decisions may become more difficult as formerly undervalued positions approach their analyzed values (goal prices). Should we hold a stock that has only 5 or 10 percent more potential appreciation according to our current analysis, or should we sell it and redeploy the proceeds in stocks that have 100 percent or more potential appreciation? Oddly enough, it may be (and often is) prudent to stick with the 10 percent undervalued stock, considering commissions, tax consequences, relative strength or momentum of the stock, and general market conditions.

Sir John Templeton, talking about when to sell a stock, touches on this topic.

> When we change from one stock to another, about one third of the time it would have been better to stay in the old stock. It has always been that way. And I really can't hold out much hope for you that it's going to improve. I don't know any investment counsel organization who is right more than two thirds of the time.[8]

As previously mentioned, undervalued stocks are also known as out-of-favor stocks and often take months or even years to become fully appreciated in the market. A formerly undervalued corporation's stock that has overcome market indifference and is advancing nicely towards its fair value may provide a greater proximal gain than would a newly discovered out-of-favor equity, even though the new-found bargain apparently has greater total percentage performance prospects over the next several years. Because of this momentum and maturation factor, the question arises of whether to hold the well-performing stock for its potential overvaluation.

Holding well-performing stocks for overvaluation may seem to negate our basic strategy of going with the probabilities—that is, selling fairly valued stocks and buying undervalued stocks—unless you can claim that the near-term probabili-

---

[8] *Outstanding Investor Digest*, August 30, 1988, p. 11.

ties are greater for an appreciation in a strong, upward-trending stock than in the long-term potentially out-of-favor, undervalued one. Just as the market usually goes too far in discounting stock values, making them unbelievably cheap, so it often errs on the swings into overvaluation, making many stocks unbelievably expensive.

I realize that talking about holding fairly valued stocks because they are in a strong uptrend is just a razor's edge away from talking about buying or holding high-relative-strength stocks in strongly uptrending markets. The crucial differences between that technique and holding stocks beyond their fair value is that we know the corporation's fundamentals and its potential; we have owned our shares since they were deeply undervalued; and that our goal price is actually based on fair (or average) valuations, not premium valuations.

If significant questions remain about a fairly valued stock continuing to advance in a strong uptrend, just take the capital gains (or losses) and move on to the next candidate. If you do want to try to "let your profits run," consider entering trailing stop-loss orders. A stop-loss order becomes a market order when its price limit is traded, usually getting you a price near your indicated limit. If the stock opens down, perhaps many points, your loss order would be executed at its turn at the then-prevailing price. These "stops" were often poor protection during the volatility of the Crash of '87, when very many stocks dropped 10 to 40 percent in price, only to recover much or most of their intraday price dips the same day or a few days later.

Generally, I do not like limit orders, either to buy or to sell. Some investment advisors recommend an initial arbitrary sell order at 10 percent or so below your purchase price—protection against making a big mistake in a stock's selection—but that technique will lock-in that loss if the stock temporarily drops to your limit before recovering. Worse yet, in order to save an 1/8 or 1/4 point when buying a position, you might "lose" several points as the stock advances smartly away from your buy limit.

After being whipsawed out of a position, we are often averse to buying that position again, and if we do, it must earn its loss plus two commissions for us to break even. For example, you buy 100 shares of the common stock of a hypothetical Volatile Times Unlimited (VTU) at $20 and immediately put an $18 stop-loss sell order on it. The stock trades to $18 or below and your position is sold. Assuming your sell was executed at $18, you lost $200 plus two commissions, perhaps $250 or more total (at a discount brokerage). Lo and behold, a week or two later this undervalued stock is trading at $20 again and your analysis continues to indicate it is worth at least $40. What do you do? You "should" take a new position in VTU, but now it would have to advance to $23 or more (the previous loss plus four commissions) before you begin to profit.

So you take a second position in VTU at $20 (or perhaps a little higher before your mind is made up and your order is filled), set a sell order at $18, and you are sold out again. I'm fairly certain that most investors would not buy that stock a third time when it again traded at $20. Thereafter, you could feel bad as you watched the stock double in price over the next year or two, just as your original analysis had indicated was likely. The maxim, "Cut short your losses!", is like a two-edged sword, capable of cutting short recoveries and long-term capital gains and locking in losses. Yes, there will be times when a stop-loss could save a lot of money in a stock that just goes south and never comes back. But on balance, *I find stop-losses counterproductive except in the instance of upward trailing stops in a fairly valued to somewhat overvalued stock* in which you are "letting your profits run," with an automatic out.

In 1986 and 1987 we saw many examples of scary advances into overvaluation. Some people felt the market was overvalued in late August 1986 as the DJIA closed above 1900, and thus were frightened out of the market by the sharp selloff in early September 1986, after a seven-day down period between September 5 and September 12, including the then-shocking 86.61-point DJIA drop on September 11, with 237.6 million shares traded. By 1995, September 11, 1986 would be considered a low-volume day and a drop of 86 Dow points would be hard to come by, given the market collars that go into effect after a 50-point DJIA move in either direction, inhibiting program trading.

Many others began liquidating shares and leaving the stock market when the Dow Jones Industrial Average surpassed the 2000 "barrier" on January 8, 1987 (2002.25), noting how even more historically overvalued this blue-chip group was than the previous September. But the DJIA advanced another 35 percent before topping out on August 25, 1987. The most astute marketeers were able to capture much of that "overshoot rally" and some, not many, were able to avoid giving it all back in the October '87 Crash. By the way, in terms of the total returns of the DJIA and S&P 500 Index, 1987 was an up year by a few percentage points.

I hope you will never again look at a stock you own that is trading at 50 percent or less than what you paid for it—but has the well-analyzed potential to double or better in a few years—and think to yourself, "Why own this loser? Even if it does well, I will just get even." Rather, look at such an undervalued situation and think, "This is the first day of the rest of my speculative life and this stock can potentially earn 100 percent or more of its current price during the next few years." That is an uncommonly handsome return on investment. Past gains or losses in stocks are history. What counts now are the stock's current indications.

Total Risk Management

In order to intelligently review risk management, we need a good understanding of what risk is, at least as applied to investing and speculating in the stock market. It is too simplistic to say that risk is bad or that we want to avoid risk, because we cannot. The classic jokes about keeping your money in your mattress or burying it in the backyard carry with them equally classic cases about fires burning up mattresses (and their contents), or kids digging in the backyard discovering unexpected treasures. Clearly, the cookie jar is also risky.

Cash being burnt, stolen, or lost is an obvious risk. Losing buying power to inflation year after year is a more subtle type. The person who squirreled away $2,000 in cash (in a safe "risk-free" deposit vault) 25 years ago, when $2,000 could have bought a new automobile, now realizes that cash would barely make the down payment on a good used car. Pity the poor pensioner who looked forward to retirement 20 years ago because of a generous $1,000-a-month pension, who today can hardly make ends meet.

While there are historical periods of deflation—such as 1932, when the Consumer Price Index registered –10.3 percent, in effect raising the purchasing power of cash by that amount or more, given hard times—those periods are few and far between, and not on the horizon. All of us today are faced with the risk of inflation-inflicted poverty if we live long enough on modest, fixed incomes. Of course, if deflation and depression arrive, simple cash can grow in purchasing power.

One continuous risk to wealth we cannot avoid is *opportunity risk*. Choosing one way of investing an asset over another, we forego the opportunity potentials of the alternative. If you buy a $10,000 one-year certificate of deposit, for most intents and purposes your capital is tied up in the CD, although you are able to cash it early, at some penalty. If you keep $10,000 in a passbook or checking account because it's good to have an emergency reserve, you have bypassed the opportunity to buy $10,000 worth of stock, on which, by the way, you could borrow $5,000 (or 50 percent of its market value) on a few hours' notice for an emergency.

For a few years after the Crash of '87, many investors and advisors had been singing the praises of 9 to 10 percent interest, depending upon the fluctuating yields of 30-year Treasury bonds, 91-day Treasury bills, CDs, money market funds, or what have you. "How silly," the stock market bears say, "to speculate in dangerous stocks when you can obtain 9 percent or more in absolutely safe, government-insured returns." Never mind that S&P 500 stocks showed a total return of 16.8 percent in '88, while small-company stocks recorded a total return of 22.9 percent. Nine or so percent then represented the long-time average returns from blue-chip stocks, but could be had without risk, the prophets of riskless investing crooned. Without which risk? Without market risk, or individual stock risk, but not without opportunity risk.

In 1988, for example, official inflation as represented by the Consumer Price Index (CPI) was 4.4 percent for the year. Most of my friends are convinced the CPI understated inflation, based upon their experiences at the supermarket, the airline counter, the movie or theater box office, and numerous other places of exchange, not to mention their checkbooks and budgets. On the other hand, Alan Greenspan, Chairman of the Federal Reserve Board, said in early 1995 that he believes the CPI overstates inflation by 0.5 to 1.0 percent or more.

Even so, if from a 9 percent gross gain you deduct Federal income tax of 28 percent (or more, not to mention state taxes), or 2.52 percent of the pre-tax return, and then 4.4 percent loss of buying power from the 106.48 percent after-tax, pre-inflation value of each dollar, you end up with 1.8 percent after-tax, after-inflation return. Not so bad; at least you're in the black, if inflation for you was no more than 4.4 percent and you were not in the special 33 percent or higher tax bracket, or had no state and local taxes to pay on CDs or money market funds. By mid-1995, inflation was running between 2.5 and 3.5 percent depending upon the index followed.

As 1-, 2-, 5-, and 10-year CDs came to maturity in 1995, people who had enjoyed relatively high interest rates (of 8 to 10 percent, or more) were faced with redeploying their funds in much-lower paying instruments. Many a lifestyle was reduced significantly and peremptorily.

Clearly, if in mid-1995 you left substantial amounts in a 3 to 5 percent passbook or checking account—free from risk of loss because of government guarantees up to $100,000 or more—you may have actually lost after-tax, after-inflation, "real" purchasing power. So much for avoiding risk management with these kinds of investments.

We have already reviewed unsystematic or individual stock risk that is mitigated by stock diversification, and systematic or market risk that is minimized by time diversification. Most academics and members of the investment community identify individual stock risk with volatility, so that the greater the fluctuations in market price, the greater the risk associated with a stock. I just don't buy this statistical definition. Large fluctuations in price can be attributed to positive events as well as negative ones. Consider the effect of buyout offers or unexpectedly high earnings reports, interspersed with rejected buyout offers and unexpectedly low earnings reports. These temporary events and fluctuations, often positive for the corporation, do not add more risk in terms of fundamental values and ultimate gains than before they occurred.

A friend of mine, Kenneth G. Buffin, Fellow of the Institute of Actuaries, and Fellow of the Royal Statistical Society, gave me an unpublished paper he wrote in April 1987, "Investment Risk Concepts," which states, "A coherent universal theory of investment risk has yet to be developed." Buffin points out that among the different risks in the investment process is "the 'ruin probability' risk that the value of the invested asset will be lost, due to such causes as financial default or bankruptcy." We can imagine investing most of our resources in a home mortgage, becoming unemployed, using up all our reserves and being forced to lose all the equity in the house due to foreclosure. Another ruin probability occurred for some writers of naked stock-index put options during the Meltdown of '87 as their losses became dozens of times greater than the premiums they obtained in selling those contracts. Of course, such put options are just one kind of derivative instrument, much in the news these past few years and responsible for the ruin of many firms and individuals.

So too, in a heavily margined stock account, especially where there is little or no diversification, one could be wiped out in an exceptional event such as the Crash of '87, even though the margin was not as great nor the losses generally as devastating as in 1929. Still, homes, businesses, commodity accounts, and even heavily leveraged stock accounts are subject to ruin probability risk considerations. (In the case of margined stock accounts, this subject is reviewed in detail in Chapter 5.)

Interest-rate sensitivity is another risk, but it is most directly and immediately associated with bonds and other interest-bearing instruments. Bond prices are inversely proportionate to interest rates, so that if interest rates go up, the market price of bonds will come down. For example, if a $1,000 bond yields 8 percent ($80 per year, usually paid at $40 every six months) and interest rates were to rise to 12 percent, that bond would fall in market price to $667 in order to yield 12 percent, an equity depreciation of 33.3 percent. Curiously enough, stocks often do not decline during periods of rising interest rates, at least for a lengthy period, although rising interest rates are hostile to stock prices.

The seven interest-rate increases promulgated by the Federal Reserve starting February 4, 1994, through February 1, 1995, inhibited the major market averages from surpassing their January 31, 1994, highs until FRB Chairman Alan Greenspan testifying in February 1995 before Congressional committees suggested that the tightening process was at or near an end. Meanwhile, 1994 was the worst year in 34 years for U.S. Treasury bond prices, which dropped over 20 percent in price for a total return loss of 14 percent or so after counting interest income. Many people and organizations—including Orange County, California—were badly hurt, betting with highly leveraged bonds and derivatives that interest rates would not go up or remain as high as they did.

Portfolio risk management should include our total financial picture. We must not jeopardize our homes, reserves, and living standards in order to "go for broke" in the stock market. We can take our calculated chances, especially when they are taken based on probable and favorable reward-to-risk ratios of systematic fundamental speculation in undervalued stocks in widely diversified portfolios to be held for long-term capital gains. (Now where have I heard that before?) We will sometimes get burnt, but most of the time we will likely do well, overcoming the occasional setback with consistent vigilance, patience, and time.

I always advise potential clients not to invest in the stock market if they know they will need the funds within one year, even though conditions look promising and the reward-to-risk ratios seem very large. Perhaps my criterion should be two or three years. Anything can go wrong over the short to intermediate term, and the overextended investor might be forced to sell or take great losses during a low point in the cycle. I urge new speculators to make a three- to five-year commitment to their stock portfolio "business." Time and again, if one is able to withstand cyclic lows, and even add to positions during such trying times, a year or two or three later the portfolio makes up the initial declines and is on the way to handsome long-term returns. Not only are the risks managed, but the rewards as well.

Your Stock Portfolio Is Your Business

I find it helpful to think of my speculating with stocks as being in business. I am in the investment business by virtue of my stock portfolio. I am not betting on stocks as one might bet a sports teams—to see how high they might finish in the standings. I am deciding what businesses I would like to own (to the small degree that I can afford some of their common shares) and how to apportion my available capital among the available stock candidates.

When I started speculating in a systematic way—beginning with the publication of *The Prudent Speculator* advisory letter in March 1977—I had just $8,006 in equity capital and $16,200 worth of stocks in "inventory." Along the way I had managed through gains, additional capital, and margin to control a little over $2 million in holdings, based on a little under $1 million in equity. Much of this was lost during the severe selloffs of 1987 and 1990. Some was used for personal expenses, homes, cars, and vacations. At this writing, I have about $1.36 million in stocks, with $922,000 in equity, including my IRA. My stock business has always used debt extensively, which has led to great gains and great losses. Every so often, sometimes daily, sometimes weekly or less frequently, I check to see whether I should be shifting my capital or changing my debt level, and whether or not to add to or reduce my stock inventory.

I try to make businesslike decisions and avoid emotional or irrational responses to the pressures of the moment. Almost every day there is a terrible or wonderful story about one or more of the positions I hold. One day the story is that Lockheed Corp. is a takeover candidate and its stock rises by a point or more. Another day an eminent market observer points out that the defense industry is likely to have a little depression of its own as federal budget deficits cause substantial cuts in defense appropriations, and the stock of Lockheed drops a point or more. Oddly enough, this example, first written five years ago, is still appropriate. However, with downsizing and merging, the defense industry giants have done okay on balance and on March 16, 1995, Lockheed merged with Martin Marietta, forming Lockheed Martin, a powerhouse organization. Owners of Lockheed shares received 1.63 new shares in LMT.

While it can be important to be aware of merger and acquisition activities as well as industry and macroeconomic trends, there is usually not a one-to-one relationship between even a correct analysis of these items and the long-term price of a corporation's stock. For some years now (both in 1989 and 1995), a principal concern has been rising inflation, which has often led to rising prices of gold and silver. Alas, the prices of gold and silver through 1989 had been in a general downtrend and through 1995 trading in a narrow band in spite of the threatening inflation rates and unrest in various parts of the world. In 1989 I wondered if perhaps they were about to change trends? Well, in mid-1995 we can also ask that question, but I do not find the precious metals all that precious or important to my investing/speculative approach.

We are constantly being threatened by events worldwide that could be bad for our stock market or certain stocks in our portfolio but rarely are, and then for only a relatively manageable period of time. I am reminded how our auto industry has been threatened by invasions of first German then Japanese cars, as well as oil crises. At least three times in the past 15 years prophets of gloom and doom have counted out our auto companies. Yet, in 1995 they are among the strongest and most profitable manufacturing corporations. Yes, there were some harsh selloffs, in some cases tied to the auto cycle or business cycle, augmented by recessions and the pressure of foreign imports, but in time these have proved to be great opportunities.

For many years preceding 1989 the valuations of the Japanese stock market had been called a financial bubble ready to burst, an accident waiting to happen that would swamp the rest of the world's financial institutions, especially our own stock market. Perhaps this analysis will someday be correct. Perhaps the dire predictions will come to pass. However, the Japanese stock market did lose over half its value of the past several years, but that hasn't seemed to greatly affect the world's financial institutions or our stock markets.

In 1995 we face the horrendous economic problems of Mexico and several other Western Hemisphere countries, including Canada. At this writing, the dollar is out of favor and recently traded at its lowest value compared to the Japanese yen, the German mark, and the Swiss franc. The economics of this situation are complicated and mean different things to different people. If you want to travel abroad, your dollars will hardly buy half as much as they would have 10 or 20 years ago. If you are exporting, your products in dollar terms will be inexpensive for foreigners to import and sell. If you are importing or buying imports, they will cost more and add to inflationary pressures and the trade deficit. While all of these conditions are important, successful corporations cope with them and continue to be profitable on balance.

There is a silver lining to many of our present economic problems. For example, with a historically low and undervalued dollar—perhaps by 30 percent in general—we can see the potential for a turnaround, an increase in its exchange-rate value, and thus an increase in the value of American equities and dollar denominated assets. After so many years of being under this cloud, we should have many years of improving dollar effects. Then too, after-tax returns that exceed our inflation rates help to cope with the dollar's low international values, especially if one spends most of one's money in America on American-made items and services.

The business of stocks, which is to say the business of businesses, can be conducted almost independently of the stock market. We understand that dubious economic forecasts, even if correct, often have different effects from those expected. The Crash of '87 convinced many that we were headed for a prompt recession due to its severity; but the recession did not come as a result of that financial trauma and not for over two years. We buy and hold corporations at a discount until their stocks trade at fair value or a premium to it. We are prepared, as in business, to have bad seasons, poor years, and even failures. By our diversifying among many carefully selected enterprises, failures are minimized and the poor years are overcome through long-term holding periods that include many more good years.

Sometimes our selection process catches an unusually large number of corporations that fail to work out as projected. More often, our selection process catches an unusually large number of corporations that exceed our expectations. Through the use of stock and time diversification, we have been able to outperform the long-term total return percentages. By using debt to increase our inventory of businesses (stocks), we are generally able to enhance the unmargined total return, although enduring greater volatility in the process.

Like any business, we are concerned about tax consequences. Happily, tax laws are generally written to favor invested capital, although you might not believe this when you think of the double taxation of dividends and the current lack of capital gains exclusions. Even there, the capital gains rate is lower than the top income tax rates. Although most stocks appreciate in price year after year, there is no tax until they are sold, even though you may be able to use up to 50 percent of your gains by borrowing (margining) against your shares. The margin interest is deductible in the year incurred (paid) against investment income and capital gains for that year. Unfortunately, many shareholders find themselves with huge gains in their stocks and are thus inhibited from selling them because of the taxes.

Better to pay taxes on fully valued or overvalued shares than pay no tax at all because those once fully valued shares later lose much or all of their gains in their (or the market's) next down cycle. Timing can help mitigate taxes, although one should not let tax considerations distort good investment practices. For instance, if stocks are sold during the year—before tax-loss selling season in November and December—that loss can be a deduction in a few months on the following April's income tax filing (or for adjusting quarterly payments). And, absent estimated tax payment requirements that otherwise may be specifically applicable to your situation, if stocks are sold for a gain early in the year, those profits are part of that taxable year and apply to the payment due April 15 of the following year.

The January Effect

There is an ironic twist to tax timing—as well as to investing in general—in what is known as the *January Effect*. The January Effect refers to the frequent tendency for the market to strongly advance in that month, an anomaly that has defied a complete explanation. Some surmise that investors and institutions begin reinvesting for the new year, starting off with a new slate in the hopes of doing better than (or as well as) the previous year. Some attribute the January Effect to the ending of December's tax-loss selling and the reinvested proceeds generated from December's selling, as well as year-end bonuses.

It is amusing to think that one could do heavy buying in late December and hold those shares through January or early February before selling them, thus capturing the January Effect and not paying taxes on those gains until the following year. This "technique" might be particularly effective as applied to small company stocks. As the *SBBI 1989 Yearbook* puts it:

> Unlike returns on large stocks, the returns on small stocks appear to be seasonal. Small stocks outperform larger stocks during January more often, and by larger amounts, than in any other month.[9]

> . . . Virtually all of the small stock effect occurs in January. The other months, are, on net, negative for small stocks. Excess returns in January relate to size in precisely rank-ordered fashion. This January phenomenon seems to pervade all size groups.[10]

Of course, I am not advocating a business style such as trying to capture five or six weeks' gain per year. In fact, January 1995 had a "January Defect"—as the Russell 2000 Index of small-capitalization stocks was negative by −1.40 percent while the Russell 1000 Index of large-capitalization stocks was positive by 2.40 percent. Who knows what next January will bring? Long-term positions would have no chance to capture time diversification with such a scheme. Still, it might be fun to throw "gambling money" into tax-sold-out secondary stocks in mid-December to see if one might

---

[9] This "January Effect" was first documented in Donald B. Deim, "Sized-Related Anomalies and Stock Return Seasonality: Further Empirical Evidence," *Journal of Financial Economics* (March 1983), pp. 13–32.

[10] Roger G. Ibbotson, and Rex A. Sinquefield, "Stocks, Bonds, Bills and Inflation (SBBI), 1982," updated in *Stocks, Bonds, Bills and Inflation 1989 Yearbook™*, Ibbotson Associates, Inc., Chicago. p. 114. All rights reserved.

not capture a 15 to 20 percent gain in the next six to eight weeks, especially if you have that kind of adventurous capital and it wouldn't disturb your long-term portfolio.

Summary

Our slogan for the business of speculating in the stocks of other businesses is PASADARM, which represents *Patience And Selection And Diversification And Risk Management*. Stock portfolio management consists of integrating these inter-related elements.

Patience is probably the most difficult quality for the average investor, as most seem to focus on and emphasize stock prices and shorter-term trends. Patience includes waiting for a corporation's stock to become sufficiently undervalued in market price to buy, then living with the stock position, as in a partnership, allowing enough time (often years) for the corporation to grow as its stock's value comes to be fairly valued in market price. While practicing patience, you must also be able to withstand the traumas that occur when 25 percent or more of the stocks in your portfolio fail to produce a profit.

Selection, a subject of much published comment, is probably the easiest element to master in a successful stock speculation system. Mostly, stock selection requires a substantial (but not overwhelming) amount of bookkeeping homework. There are no great secrets, but experience and expertise come through systematic application of analyzing corporate financial fundamentals as well as recognizing valuations, tangible and intangible. Chapter 2 deals with the major criteria and Chapter 9 goes into greater detail including lesser but potentially important criteria, with specific examples.

Diversification refers to stocks, industries, and time. Stock diversification is the spreading of individual stock and corporate risk by obtaining as many different stocks in different industries as is reasonable and feasible with one's resources. Time diversification is the holding of positions for as long as their fundamental analyses indicate their undervaluation and potential appreciation, because studies have shown market risk is thereby reduced. Few investors seem aware that time diversification is more important than stock diversification. Generally, the longer you own a stock (of a viable business), the less risk you engender (see Tables 3–1A and B).

Risk management actually incorporates the previous three elements and adds an emphasis on general economic and market conditions. Stock markets—to greater or lesser degrees—can be *overbought* and thus vulnerable to a selloff, or *oversold* and thus likely to advance. The stock market, major segments of it, or individual stocks can be *overvalued* and thus likely to decline, or *undervalued* and thus likely to advance, again to varying degrees. Combinations of overbought and overvalued markets can point to cyclical tops and dangerous market levels, just as oversold and undervalued conditions indicate market bottoms and great buying opportunities.

There are techniques for guarding against selloffs. In addition to reducing exposure appropriately, insurance hedging through the use of stock-index put options and other instruments can be invoked. This subject is part of risk management, risk insurance, and is reviewed at some length in Chapter 4.

There are many logical and psychological guidelines to follow and errors to avoid. Certain common sense and reasonable attitudes, such as approaching investing as a process of buying companies (or small pieces of them called shares) rather than trying to guess stock price movements, enhance one's chances for handsome, long-term capital gains in widely diversified portfolios of undervalued stocks.

I must add one item not obvious in PASADARM and that is *belief*. Investing and speculating in the stock market is not a religious experience, either positive or negative, but it does require belief in the markets and in one's system. Through practice, error, experience, and results, I have come to believe in what I am doing and have been consistently and tremendously rewarded for my efforts. I have seen others dabble, plunge, or even try to be systematic, but they did not truly believe and, at crucial moments, their impulsive actions led to losses rather than rewards. If you feel that you don't understand what is going on—although no one can understand everything—and that your activities are based upon blind luck or supernatural intuition, you are unlikely to prosper in the stock market.

4

Technical Market Analysis

Under penalty of perjury, let me affirm that I am not now nor have I ever been a stock-market technician. Whether I become one in the future depends upon two things: How long I live and whether I can discover a consistent technical formula or combination of indicators that work as well as my evolving fundamental approach has worked for 18 years.

Although I should be satisfied with my eclectic fundamentalist approach, I cannot ignore the impressive and cogent technical work of such people as Elaine Garzarelli, Norman Fosback, Ned Davis, and Dan Sullivan, among several others.

I remain firmly in the Ben Graham/Warren Buffett/Ken Fisher/Peter Lynch/David Dreman stock-market camp—don't try to outguess the stock market's fluctuations. Therefore, I see technical analysis of the stock market as a secondary enterprise rather than a primary one. Lynch (with John Rothchild) wrote in *One Up on Wall Street*, "The market ought to be irrelevant. If I could convince you of this one thing, I'd feel this book had done its job."[1] For confirmation, Lynch quotes Buffett as having written, "As far as I'm concerned, the stock market doesn't exist. It is there only as a reference to see if anybody is offering to do anything foolish."[2] Buffett means by this that from time to time people are willing (or forced) to sell shares at a fraction of their fundamental values, while at other times there are those making inflated offers to buy shares no prudent man could resist selling.

I have made my technical disclaimers and voiced my disdain for the short-term fluctuations of the stock market. My increasing concern—since the Crash of

---

[1] Peter Lynch, *One Up on Wall Street* (New York: Simon & Schuster, 1989), p. 78.

[2] Lynch, *One Up on Wall Street*, p. 78.

99

'87 and the Selloff of '90—of not having mastered additional techniques for improving my stock speculation success has led me to systematically perform daily and weekly technical analysis, as well as interest- and inflation-rate analysis. These technical efforts are pursued to improve my fundamental market timing and overall performance. Table 4–1, "Daily Data Printout," is a copy of a daily printout summarizing the closely watched NYSE, Amex, and OTC data and some computations of them, commonly known as technical indicators.

Like fundamental criteria, which taken individually rarely support a conclusion at the same time or to the same degree, technical indicators are often at odds with each other. Also, as is true of the effect of fundamental indicators, different technical criteria are more or less predictive at different phases of the market-economic-regulatory cycles, so it would be arbitrary and perhaps misleading to order them in terms of importance.

Rest assured that you needn't be a mathematician to do my kind of technical analysis. If you can add, subtract, multiply, and divide—or better still, let a calculator or personal computer do the computations—then you can handle the ratios and formulas that follow. It does help to have a basic facility with fractions, ratios, and percentages (all of which can express the same relationship), but most spreadsheet software (and business calculators) have a simple key sequence for making those calculations. For example, in the computer spreadsheet SuperCalc5, you merely type std(A1:A10) to compute the standard deviation of the values in cells A1 through A10. (By the way, Computer Associates Inc., one of the companies reviewed in Chapter 9, publishes SuperCalc5.) Other software, such as Lotus 1-2-3 and Excel, have similar simple functions for obtaining standard deviations and the like.

Advances and Declines

We can start with some simple ideas and some obvious numbers and build upon these. We focus on the New York Stock Exchange because it provides the greatest liquidity, volumes, historical statistics, and readily available data. Most of the relationships described for the NYSE would be used in analyses of the over-the-counter markets or the American Stock Exchange. Every market day about 3,000 issues are traded on the NYSE. In 1989, that number was 1,900 to 2,000, so in just six years NYSE listings have grown 50 percent. When an equity issue—a common stock, preferred stock, or master limited partnership—trades, only one of three things can happen with its market price. At that day's close each issue can have advanced, declined, or remained unchanged in price compared to its previous close (not necessarily the previous day). Thus, we obtain and record advance/decline/unchanged numbers from readily available public sources such as *The Wall Street Journal*, the *New York Times*, other metropolitan dailies, the weekly *Barron's*, or on-line data services.

While some interesting analysis can be done with the number of unchanged issues to show the flatness or ambiguity of a market day or period, most students of the market focus mainly on advances and declines, and by natural extension the advance/decline (A/D) line. The A/D line is made on a graph by recording the points of daily or weekly net advances. Our approach doesn't normally use the unchanged issues numbers. Fosback points out how to derive useful information from the unchanged issues with the "Going Nowhere" indicator:

> The Unchanged Issues Index is calculated by dividing the number of issues which are unchanged in price by the total number of stocks traded. The ratio is usually expressed in percentage form. A typical reading might be 15 percent, although the index has ranged from as little as 5 percent to upwards of 25 percent. Low readings are considered bullish and high readings bearish.[3]

Advancing-in-price issues represent buying—or at least more buying than selling at the moment—on the basic notion that an excess of buyers over sellers (or greater demand than supply) tends to bid up prices. Conversely, selling is represented by stocks declining in price. On any given day the fluctuations represented by buyers and sellers often appear to be random, as orders pour in from all over the world, some to trade "at the market" (the current asking price) or at a price limit with the trader hoping to get a better deal than the current bid or ask price for a sale or a purchase.

When shares being offered and bid for—a process that creates selling and buying, or supply and demand, pressures—are in temporary balance, a stock may trade unchanged, at the same price as the previous trade(s). Or, when a large limit order ("I'll buy 30,000 shares at 10!") overhangs the market, a stock may trade unchanged at $10 for awhile (until sellers supply 30,000 shares at $10 or less).

The absolute number of advances and declines can be important and sometimes indicative in and of itself. Somewhat noteworthy are the days when over 1,500 advances or declines are generated. Even more noteworthy are the days when there are 1,000 net advances less declines, or vice versa. Such results indicate tremendous buying or selling pressure. Such absolute numbers will have to be adjusted to account for the continuing larger number of issues trading.

Still more noteworthy of late are instances of three or more consecutive days of 1,500 advances or declines, especially if some of these days contain the net 1,000 figures. A classic example occurred between October 6 and 12, 1987, with five days in a row of over 1,000 declines (when fewer than 1,900 issues were traded), which was one piece of scenery setting the stage for the bloodbath that

---

[3] Norman G. Fosback, *Stock Market Logic* (Ft. Lauderdale: The Institute for Econometric Research, 1984), p. 125.

Table 4-1. Daily Data Printout

1988	Adv	Dec	UpVol	DownV	NYCI	DJIA	NewH	NewL	Arms	10A	100A	25A	25OA	A/D	10A/D	25A/D	10 NYCI	% Away	25 NYCI	% Away	10 DJIA	% Away	25 DJIA	% Away
11/1	717	743	68397	52465	156.98	2150.96	32	13	0.74	0.91	0.92	0.83	0.80	-26	-789	511	157.76	-0.49	156.00	-2.54	2160.12	-0.42	2139.97	-2.54
11/2	568	777	71309	64512	157.00	2156.83	48	25	0.78	0.88	0.97	0.84	0.80	-109	-547	294	157.84	-0.53	156.20	-1.55	2162.07	-0.24	2142.82	-1.10
11/3	781	652	75321	54979	157.08	2170.34	54	27	0.87	0.93	0.93	0.86	0.82	129	-1060	-230	157.65	-0.36	156.33	-1.77	2160.99	0.43	2144.86	-1.49
11/4	472	993	25637	96939	155.70	2145.80	25	29	1.80	1.03	1.05	0.87	0.81	-521	-1643	-991	157.28	-1.00	156.41	-2.04	2157.22	-0.53	2146.18	-1.91
11/7	314	1200	22652	92727	154.28	2124.64	10	35	1.07	1.07	1.09	0.89	0.82	-886	-2259	-1459	156.82	-1.62	156.46	-2.25	2152.65	-1.30	2146.96	-2.09
11/8	852	578	86789	32503	154.84	2127.49	16	29	0.55	1.01	1.03	0.88	0.82	274	-1968	-1065	156.42	-1.01	156.53	-1.86	2148.06	-0.96	2147.97	-1.93
11/9	493	949	34357	99035	153.92	2118.24	12	35	1.50	1.07	1.09	0.91	0.84	-456	-2234	-1809	155.97	-1.31	156.55	-1.67	2143.37	-1.17	2148.44	-1.89
11/10	715	666	56674	40791	154.09	2114.69	22	32	0.77	0.96	1.11	0.91	0.83	49	-1330	-1930	155.76	-1.07	156.55	0.17	2140.75	-1.22	2148.72	0.07
11/11	292	1235	9572	113635	151.24	2067.03	9	31	2.81	1.17	1.01	1.01	0.89	-943	-2536	-3614	155.21	-2.56	156.33	0.40	2132.47	-3.07	2145.39	0.63
11/14	561	912	51217	65245	151.04	2065.08	7	38	0.78	1.17	1.03	1.01	0.89	-351	-2840	-3947	154.62	-2.31	156.09	0.43	2124.11	-2.78	2141.64	0.69
11/15	715	709	54418	40166	151.33	2077.17	15	34	0.74	1.17	1.04	1.00	0.88	6	-2808	-3711	154.05	-1.77	155.87	-0.71	2116.73	-1.87	2138.46	-0.57
11/16	316	1237	13877	133117	148.96	2038.58	3	51	2.45	1.34	1.17	1.05	0.89	-921	-3620	-3915	153.25	-2.80	155.64	-0.19	2104.91	-3.15	2134.96	-0.07
11/17	635	844	56567	61203	149.24	2052.45	10	43	0.81	1.33	1.16	1.06	0.91	-209	-3958	-4206	152.46	-2.11	155.40	0.04	2093.12	-1.94	2131.72	0.07
11/18	841	552	79900	21375	150.18	2062.41	8	32	0.41	1.19	1.10	1.03	0.88	289	-3148	-4010	151.91	-1.14	155.19	0.44	2084.78	-1.07	2128.89	0.54
11/20	565	930	41795	58496	150.10	2065.97	24	63	0.85	1.17	1.09	1.04	0.89	-365	-2627	-4455	151.49	-0.92	154.96	1.53	2078.91	-0.62	2125.91	1.60
11/21	729	714	58253	47003	150.55	2077.70	24	48	0.82	1.20	1.05	1.05	0.90	15	-2886	-4788	151.07	-.34	154.69	0.97	2073.93	0.18	2122.62	0.69
11/22	893	514	79367	18660	151.41	2092.28	30	27	0.41	1.09	1.05	1.02	0.88	379	-2051	-4058	150.81	0.40	154.49	2.92	2071.34	1.01	2120.82	2.85
11/25	520	783	25087	35896	150.63	2074.68	23	20	0.95	1.10	0.97	1.04	0.92	-263	-2363	-4963	150.47	0.11	154.16	3.41	2067.34	0.36	2116.56	3.16
11/28	710	726	66320	33325	151.25	2081.44	27	33	0.49	0.87	0.98	1.03	0.92	-16	-1436	-5041	150.47	0.52	153.83	3.26	2068.78	0.61	2112.48	2.74
11/29	938	551	87696	24387	152.43	2101.53	30	32	0.47	0.84	0.87	1.02	0.91	387	-698	-4384	150.61	1.21	153.58	3.45	2072.42	1.40	2109.73	3.02
11/30	995	470	113623	23254	153.90	2114.51	31	28	0.43	0.81	0.78	0.99	0.88	525	-179	-3842	150.87	2.01	153.38	3.26	2076.16	1.85	2107.37	2.74

Table 4-1. Daily Data Printout (cont.)

1989	Adv	Dec	UpVol	DownV	NYCI	DJIA	NewH	NewL	Aims	10A	10OA	25A	25OA	A/D	10A/D	25A/D	10 NYCI	% Away	25 NYCI	% Away	10 DJIA	% Away	25 DJIA	% Away
1/23	553	912	33091	88586	160.13	2218.39	57	12	1.65	0.82	0.85	0.87	0.81	-359	672	3691	160.26	-0.08	158.00	-1.80	2221.89	-0.16	2191.57	-1.86
1/24	1009	477	136311	33318	161.99	2256.43	64	7	0.51	0.79	0.81	0.87	0.80	541	1424	3710	160.62	0.86	158.28	-1.20	2228.21	1.27	2195.80	-1.05
1/25	820	648	105423	54911	162.33	2265.89	65	7	0.88	0.80	0.73	0.88	0.81	200	1435	3667	160.93	0.87	158.52	-1.75	2234.16	1.42	2199.53	-1.52
1/26	960	512	143949	46383	163.60	2291.07	110	6	0.69	0.79	0.73	0.85	0.78	448	1555	4308	161.32	1.41	158.83	-1.95	2241.04	2.23	2204.53	-1.81
1/27	929	611	175908	58467	164.78	2322.86	164	10	0.54	0.77	0.72	0.84	0.75	318	1642	4765	161.79	1.85	159.19	-2.32	2250.71	3.21	2210.86	-2.28
1/30	876	570	100997	41824	165.36	2324.11	104	7	0.64	0.76	0.72	0.83	0.74	306	1906	5113	162.30	1.89	159.59	-2.21	2260.66	2.81	2217.41	-2.19
1/31	960	541	130932	39583	166.63	2342.32	107	13	0.54	0.73	0.73	0.83	0.73	419	2515	5169	162.96	2.25	160.01	-2.77	2273.43	3.03	2224.34	-2.77
2/1	753	718	95744	89129	166.47	2338.21	120	14	0.98	0.78	0.74	0.83	0.75	35	1990	5450	163.46	1.84	160.44	-2.89	2283.38	2.40	2231.36	-2.91
2/2	771	662	91146	65334	166.35	2333.75	92	5	0.83	0.77	0.78	0.83	0.75	109	1927	5376	163.93	1.48	160.87	-2.47	2292.84	1.78	2238.06	-2.47
2/3	792	642	91142	55464	166.50	2331.25	93	4	0.75	0.77	0.78	0.85	0.76	150	2167	5016	164.41	1.27	161.25	-3.09	2302.43	1.25	2244.00	-3.36
2/6	636	786	62951	66328	166.19	2321.07	83	10	0.85	0.69	0.78	0.81	0.74	-150	2376	4515	165.02	0.71	161.65	-3.79	2312.70	0.36	2250.10	-4.69
2/7	1095	425	162712	30847	168.02	2347.14	144	9	0.49	0.69	0.70	0.75	0.71	670	2505	5488	165.62	1.45	162.15	-2.80	2321.77	1.09	2258.20	-3.57
2/8	762	722	78546	83313	167.69	2343.21	137	8	1.15	0.73	0.77	0.78	0.73	40	2345	4666	166.16	0.92	162.55	-2.77	2329.50	0.59	2264.82	-3.28
2/9	504	1003	64469	124237	166.13	2323.04	72	7	0.97	0.77	0.80	0.79	0.75	-499	1398	3937	166.41	-0.17	162.87	-2.67	2332.70	-0.41	2270.12	-3.34
2/10	301	1233	32644	127874	164.01	2286.07	23	11	0.94	0.81	0.88	0.80	0.75	-932	148	2548	166.34	-1.40	163.09	-2.69	2329.02	-1.84	2273.79	-3.27
2/13	602	861	60742	59342	164.15	2282.50	16	17	0.64	0.82	0.85	0.77	0.73	-259	-417	2068	166.21	-1.24	163.31	-3.01	2324.86	-1.82	2277.11	-3.68
2/14	763	668	72860	55925	163.94	2281.25	32	14	0.85	0.85	0.85	0.77	0.74	95	-741	2374	165.95	-1.21	163.53	-2.67	2318.75	-1.62	2280.64	-3.25
2/15	907	556	102000	34580	165.21	2303.93	52	18	0.55	0.81	0.91	0.78	0.74	351	-425	2536	165.82	-0.37	163.77	-2.45	2315.32	-0.49	2284.54	-2.72
2/16	816	591	101062	50249	165.51	2311.43	57	12	0.66	0.79	0.85	0.77	0.74	225	-309	2433	165.74	-0.14	164.00	-2.40	2313.09	-0.07	2288.10	-2.71
2/17	946	513	95399	39343	165.45	2324.82	55	15	0.70	0.79	0.87	0.77	0.74	433	-26	2635	165.63	-0.11	164.22	-2.40	2312.45	0.54	2292.05	-2.94
2/21	611	872	53646	65396	166.06	2326.43	50	13	0.82	0.79	0.88	0.78	0.74	-261	-137	2332	165.62	0.27	164.45	-1.74	2312.98	0.58	2296.12	-3.55
2/22	332	1197	15283	129925	163.55	2283.93	19	10	2.30	0.98	0.94	0.84	0.76	-865	-1672	1657	165.17	-0.98	164.60	-1.89	2306.66	-0.99	2298.89	-2.62
2/23	741	694	89405	40828	164.09	2289.46	25	20	0.45	0.92	0.94	0.84	0.76	47	-1665	1144	164.81	-0.44	164.70	-1.82	2301.29	-0.51	2300.92	-2.69
2/24	327	1191	27125	123175	161.72	2245.54	22	24	1.25	0.95	0.99	0.85	0.76	-864	-2030	108	164.37	-1.61	164.70	-1.86	2293.54	-2.09	2301.18	-2.86
2/27	616	800	67013	55137	161.95	2250.36	19	20	0.63	0.91	0.96	0.85	0.75	-184	-1282	14	164.16	-1.35	164.71	-2.78	2289.97	-1.73	2301.78	-3.62
2/28	911	531	79337	43691	162.49	2258.39	25	17	0.94	0.94	0.91	0.82	0.75	380	-643	753	164.00	-0.92	164.81	-1.71	2287.55	-1.27	2303.38	-2.04
3/1	633	816	59410	93422	161.74	2243.04	33	13	1.25	0.97	0.93	0.85	0.78	-183	-921	29	163.78	-1.24	164.80	-1.50	2283.73	-1.78	2302.84	-1.60

followed. After a one-day respite, there were another five 1,000+ declines in a row, this time with more than 1,000+ net declines on October 14 and October 15, leading up to the pre-Crash collapse of Friday, October 16, wherein 1,638 more declines than advances occurred.

The configuration of October 1987 declines is unique, and a similar recurrence is not likely. Yet, there have been many other less dramatic periods where the A/D line has provided important indications of market turns and trend reversals. Especially telling are extreme numbers, such as six-to-one or nine-to-one advance/decline days, which indicate tremendous momentum strength on the upside or weakness on the downside. Such extreme days may signal a cycle top or a washout bottom, arguing for an imminent market trend reversal.

To make stock speculation as simple and straightforward as feasible, we need to recognize the implications of extreme readings and interrelationships with other technical indicators. In practice it only takes 15 or fewer minutes a day to keep track of them, at least with the aid of a personal computer.

From advances and declines we obtain A/D figures, usually expressed as advances less declines. If there were 1,200 advances and 1,000 declines—with perhaps 700 unchanged—the daily A/D would be 200. As is the case for a large number of technical events, daily results often appear random and usually are not particularly predictive. Longer period trends and averages, such as 4-, 10-, 25-, 40-, 150- or 200-day, are interpreted as defining and projecting trends or indicating new (reversed) trends. Some technicians favor certain multiday periods and A/D parameters over others.

A crude rule of thumb (pretty much unchanged over the past six years) is that when there are 2,000 or more advances than declines in a 10-day period "the market" (namely, the New York Stock Exchange) has become slightly overbought. Likewise, 2,000 more declines than advances for 10 days indicates a slightly oversold market condition. When considering 25 days, excesses amounting to 3,000 in one direction or the other indicate overbought or oversold conditions. Obviously, the greater the net of advances or declines within each period, the greater the overbought or oversold condition.

The longer the period observed, the more long-term its implications. Ten-day excesses relate to short-term fluctuations, short-term being considered a few days to a few weeks. Twenty-five-day excesses refer to intermediate-term potentials, or several weeks to several months duration. Obviously, there can be all manner of crosscurrents in such indicators, which are sometimes mediated by other less-conflicted indicators, to be considered in due course.

For practical examples of the technical indicators reviewed in this chapter we reference the periods November 1988 and January 23 through March 1, 1989 (see Table 4–1), a more settled—one hesitates to say normal—period than that of the

Crash of '87 or the selloff of '90. This period yielded a relatively clear buy signal before a 14 percent rally, and then a topping cycle sell signal. On November 7, 1988, with the DJIA at 2124.64, there were 2,259 more declines than advances for 10 days (–2,259) and 1,459 net declines for 25 days (–1,459). Strictly on A/D analysis—we'll review and associate the A/D line with other indicators—we could say "the market" (the NYSE) was oversold according to the 10-day A/D and moving toward oversold for the 25-day A/D.

By November 16, with the DJIA at 2038.58 (4.05 percent lower than November 7), the 10-day A/D was net –3,620 and the 25-day A/D was net –3,915, both indicating a significantly oversold condition. Between November 7 and November 16 there were three days with over 1,200 declines, suggesting a selling-out (if not sold-out) market. Of course, the selling could continue—shades of October 1987—but the idea is that such accumulated selling means (1) much damage has been done, and (2) we are approaching a lower-risk area or a sold-out market. Without wanting to prejudge this two-element analysis, I will mention that other indicators gave confirming buy signals on November 16, as described below.

Both empirical observations and common sense notions attest to the theory that the stock market is a homeostatic mechanism. That is, it always tends toward equilibrium and tends to regress toward the norm after having been pushed or pulled to extremes. We compare the fluctuations of technical indicators (and the market) to a pendulum with A/Ds and other criteria oscillating from one side to the other, usually going too far in its swings before starting back toward the midpoint or average.

In a homeostatic stock market theory, overbought markets—which usually have also advanced in price due to buying pressures—will sooner or later sell off as the "exhausted buyers" give way to profit taking and the normal level of selling. Thereafter, oversold markets will sooner or later rally as "bargain hunters" and the normal level of buying overwhelm the "sold-out" sellers.

When we study the extreme paradigm Crash of '87 period (see Chapter 6), we see how overbought and then oversold the New York Stock Exchange can become. We note that there were 9,141 net declines for 10 days on October 19 and 11,578 net declines for 25 days on October 28, numbers that seem to make a mockery of calling 2,000 net declines in 10 days a short-term oversold indicator, or 3,000 net declines in 25 days an oversold market, intermediate term. Still, as the market returned to more average oscillations, the traditional parameters were again meaningful, representing more "normal" overbought and oversold conditions.

Just as one or a few undervalued fundamental criteria may not be sufficient to recommend a stock, so too with technical criteria—one or two may not give a clear trend signal, especially if they are out of sync with several other indicators. It is important to remember that it is the gestalt—the overall pattern, often coordinated with many nonmarket indicators—that suggests we take aggressive, passive, or defensive action in the stock market, based upon unknown but probable future direction.

Much is made about the advance/decline line (the basic breadth measure) as a confirming or disconfirming indicator to a market's major average's continued direction, especially when it registers new highs. You may read that new highs in the Dow Jones Industrial Averages were not confirmed by the daily A/D line, which topped out several months (or years) earlier. Such relationships, known as *disparity indexes*, *divergences*, or *disconfirmations*, may be important or not, depending upon recognized or unperceived other relationships and anomalies. You should be careful not to accept single technical pronouncements at their purported face value, even from otherwise astute stock-market commentators.

There is more than one way to construct an A/D line, but what concerns me here is the apparent conflict between the daily and the weekly A/D numbers. One day I received *The Addison Report,* dated March 22, 1989, and learned that editor Andrew Addison was bullish long-term, augmented by his interpretation of the A/D line.

> One of the primary reasons for this optimism is the action of the NYSE weekly advance/decline line. Unlike its daily counterpart, it has been a consistent leading indicator for the market. While most analysts focus on the daily A/D, the weekly A/D has continued to surge to new all-time highs since January. At the market's post-crash recovery high in mid-February, the weekly A/D was 1,255 advances above its prior all-time high in August 1987, when the Dow closed at 2722.[4]

On the same day I received Stan Weinstein's completely technically oriented newsletter, *The Professional Tape Reader*, dated March 24, 1989, and read that all is not well in A/D land.

> Another important long-term negative is the ongoing negative divergence that exists between the D.J. Industrial Average and all three of our advance-decline lines . . . It has now been one full year since the A/D lines peaked after hitting their post-crash recovery highs. Since then the DJIA has registered a series of new recovery highs but all have been unconfirmed by the daily A/D lines.
>
> . . . We've followed both A/D lines (daily and weekly) for many years, and, surprisingly, what we've noted over the years is that strength in the weekly line usually correlates with intermediate-term up-moves, while persistent strength (or weakness) in the daily fig-

---

[4] Andrew Addison, *The Addison Report*, March 22, 1989, p. 2. (P.O. Box 402, Franklin, MO 02038.)

ures have longer term meaning. Note that at the August 1987 peak there was no negative divergence in the weekly A/D figures but there was one in the daily numbers.[5]

How can the daily A/D line be in a long-term downtrend when the weekly A/D line is in a long-term uptrend for the same period? Easy. Suppose whenever the "average stock" declines it loses 12.5 cents (1/8 of a point), but whenever it advances it gains 25 cents (1/4 of a point), on balance. During the course of the "average week," the average stock loses on three days and gains on two; its daily A/D line is down while its weekly A/D reading is up, as the stock is net up for the week. Or, a stock could suffer three 12.5-cent down days but gain one 50-cent up day, again down on its daily readings but up for the week. Actually, there is a long-term downward bias to the daily A/D line.

For a solid but not pedantic review of the A/D line and its use as a *disparity index*—comparing its trend to another stock market average—I refer you to Norman G. Fosback's excellent, thorough yet readable book, *Stock Market Logic*. Fosback points out that, "To facilitate historical compatibility . . . (1) each week divide the difference of advances minus declines by the total number of issues changing in price; and (2) accumulate the weekly ratio readings . . . Without this adjustment the A/D line is biased by the long-term increase in the number of issues traded."[6]

Fosback states that the negative Disparity Index is flawed and thus indicates about twice as many bear markets as actually occur.

> Technicians should note, too, the Disparity Index is better at forecasting market tops than market bottoms. The 1946–1949 experience is actually the index's only leading buy signal in the last 50 years. In large part this is accounted for by a long-term downward bias in the advance/decline line making uptrends difficult to achieve. (For example, the A/D line is much lower today than it was 20 years ago.) The downward bias produces frequent periods of negative divergence, with the A/D line moving lower and the DJIA trending higher.[7]

So much here for A/D line analysis, although I revisit it again in relation to the Crash of '87 in Chapter 6. Meanwhile, I still like to see what the simple 10- and 25-day A/D lines—as updated daily (see Table 4–1)—show in terms of overbought/oversold numbers in order to compare them with other indicators.

---

[5] Stan Weinstein, *The Professional Tape Reader*, March 24, 1989, p. 1. (Radcap, Inc., P.O. Box 2407, Hollywood, FL 33022.)

[6] Fosback, *Stock Market Logic*, p. 117.

[7] Fosback, *Stock Market Logic*, p. 117.

It is not necessary to be aware of all these relationships in order to obtain predictive or confirming signals from daily and weekly A/D lines. Each week *Barron's* provides technical data, "more than you want to know," in its "Market Laboratory/Stocks" section near the back pages, one table of which list the weekly A/D numbers (and weekly new highs/new lows, a subject reviewed below) for the NYSE, AMEX, and NASDAQ. Recording and reviewing these totals should give you a clearer picture of the market's recent, current, and trending breadth, according to those indicators.

Up and Down Volumes

A principal guru of volumes is Joseph Granville, who has had a colorful career, to say the least, and continues to write books, modify his volume analysis, and publish his advisory letter, the *Granville Market Letter* (P.O. Drawer 413006, Kansas City, MO 64141). Alas, Mr. Granville's analyses have led him to be on the wrong side of the market several times and for long periods in the past 25 years. Of course, many technicians emphasize the basic importance of volume, including Richard Arms, Jr., and his Arms Index, reviewed below.

"Price follows volume" is the slogan of on-balance-volume analysts, and intuitively that elliptic and ambiguous slogan can make sense. That is, if large volumes of stocks are being traded, buyers are buying and sellers are selling. As there is usually more money available than there are stocks at their current prices, especially when stocks are considered the place to be, large volumes tend to go with advancing prices—until they don't, such as in selloffs and crashes. The problem here is that stocks can be undergoing accumulation or distribution but it's not always clear which is happening.

Accumulation refers to smart or "strong hands" buyers picking up the stocks that are being sold by not-as-smart or "weak hands" sellers, such as begins to happen at market lows. *Distribution*, of course, is just the opposite: "Smarties" are taking profits near a market top while the "dummies" are rushing to join the party shortly before it ends. Received opinion has it that it's bullish to see higher prices on higher volumes and bearish to see lower prices on lower volumes. That may not always be the case. In fact, it may be better to note stock-price trends during periods of decreasing trading volumes, on the theory that informed (smart) trading usually occurs during quiet market days on declining volume.

Accumulation seems clear enough when large majorities of stocks are advancing on high volumes. At or near market tops, that may be the misleading picture of the relatively narrow (30-stock) Dow Jones Industrial Average, while beneath the surface sellers are becoming more plentiful, with the number of advancing stocks—price increases in size and breadth—diminishing, as fewer stocks make new highs and the advance/decline lines fail to confirm the recurring highs in the DJIA. At other times, when the market appears to be in equilibrium or a so-called trading range where the averages advance a bit, then decline a bit, without making significant trending movement in either direction, the resolution is not clear.

Between the end of 1990 and the beginning of 1995, we have seen an unusually long trading-range market where the major averages did not decline more than 10 percent during the period. This market included several periods of severe drops in many industries and groups, such as 20 percent declines in the Dow Jones Utilities Average, auto stocks, and the bond markets in 1994. While some sectors advanced and then declined during the four years, other sectors, especially technology and computers (with some noticeable setbacks), advanced to compensate and create the narrow moves in the major averages.

Fosback points out in reviewing the Negative Volume Index (NVI) that "the direction the market assumes on days of negative volume changes supposedly reflects accumulation (buying) or distribution (selling) of stock by those who are in the know."[8] Fosback averages the NVI index over the past year and compares the current figure. "When the weekly NVI is graded bullish by this technique, the odds are better than 95 in 100 in favor of a major bull market."[9] The NVI is not a good bear market indicator. I do not follow the NVI except in passing (noting its update in *Market Logic*). Believing we must question popular slogans on technical market phenomena, I include NVI commentary as one alternative to the high-volume-high-price slogan.

I do follow the daily and weekly observations of the up and down volumes, and the total volume of trading. Mostly, I see the technical effects of volume in the Arms Index, described below. I am happy to see those volume confirmation days of nine-to-one on the upside that augur for strongly advancing markets to follow; and I am concerned about seeing six-to-one (or greater) down-to-up volume that indicates extreme selling pressures. Oddly enough, sometimes a great down-to-up-volume day can also indicate a "selling climax" or sold-out market, thus suggesting a cycle low and the likelihood of an uptrend to begin.

The Arms or Trading Index

The Arms Index, whose creation is credited to Richard W. Arms, Jr., of Albuquerque, New Mexico, has many aliases including the Short-Term Trading Index (STTI) and the Trading Index (TRIN, MKDS). (The symbols in parenthesis are access codes for various data retrieval and quotation systems.) The Arms Index

---

[8] Fosback, *Stock Market Logic,* p. 120.

[9] Fosback, *Stock Market Logic*, p. 122.

is basically the relationship among advancing and declining issues to their up and down volumes, expressed as a ratio. In Table 4–2, if the ratio of advances to declines is the same as the ratio of up volume to down volume, the result will equal 1.00. In theory this would represent a neutral market day. When the Arms is above 1.00 there has been more bearish action, more selling pressure than buying. Numbers below 1.00 indicate a bullish configuration; that is, more buying pressure than selling. You will notice that the relationships are the number of advancing issues with up volume versus the number of declining issues with down volume. On many an otherwise down market day the Arms Index may be reading more buying than selling ratios. As one observes the Arms from moment to moment, one can see buying or selling pressures and make that conclusion for the New York Stock Exchange intraday or daily price-volume relationship. Naturally, most long-term investors would like to see the Arms below 1.00, and way below 1.00 if fully invested.

Alas, what is good or encouraging news—a low Arms Index and advancing prices—for one or a few days can turn out to be bad or threatening news as strong buying days follow one another. That is, if the market continues to be strongly bought day after day it soon becomes *overbought*. Now "overbought" is a general and easily understood concept, but not necessarily a precise term, as we have already noted in referring to the advance/decline line. Many differing time periods and ways of massaging Arms data are generated by different technicians, with the 10-day moving average (10-MA, see Table 4–1) probably most commonly used.

From Mr. Arms' appearance on *Wall $treet Week*, October 10, 1986, we learned that a 10-MA Arms of 1.25 or greater in a *normal market* means that we can buy with *relative safety* (emphases mine). Four times in the 20 years preceding 1986, the 10-MA Arms was as high as 1.50 in bear markets. The Arms Index is more useful for buying than for selling, according to its author. By the way, Mr. Arms placed much importance on trading volume and held a theory that the market makes cyclical lows every 9 billion shares (about every four months at 1986 levels). Mr. Arms published a book on his findings, *The Arms Index (TRIN)* , which I have enjoyed studying.

Table 4–2. Calculating an Arms Index

$$\frac{\dfrac{\text{Advances}}{\text{Declines}}}{\dfrac{\text{Up Volume}}{\text{Down Volume}}} \quad \frac{\dfrac{1300}{1000}}{\dfrac{130 \text{ million}}{100 \text{ million}}} = \frac{1.30}{1.30} = 1.00$$

[10] Richard Arms, Jr., *The Arms Index (TRIN)* (Homewood, IL: Dow Jones-Irwin, 1989), p. 1.

I calculate the Arms Index in two ways, paying attention to several multiple-day moving averages (see Table 4–1). The common way to compute a *moving average* is to sum a number of daily Arms Indexes and then divide by that number of days. Then, each new day is added and each oldest day is removed, so that the succession of 10-day averages becomes a moving average. Let us refer to the daily averaging and its successive multiday averages as the *Regular Arms moving averages* (e.g., 4–A, 10–A, 25–A, etc.).

Another way of developing a moving average—especially useful for the Arms Index figures—is to sum 4, 10, or 25 days each of advances, declines, up volumes, and down volumes, and then calculate these multiday totals according to the formula in Table 4–2. When calculating totaled multiday elements, we arrive at the Open Arms moving averages (4–O, 10–O, 25–O, etc.). The *Open Arms moving averages* often represent what is going on, since daily fluctuations, especially in volumes traded, can produce large fluctuations and undue weighting on the Regular Arms moving averages.

In the hypothetical and exaggerated example shown in Table 4–3, we suppose that one day there are 1,300 advancing issues (advances) and 1,000 declining issues (declines), with 200 million shares of up volume and 60 million shares of down volume, resulting in a daily Arms of 0.39. Suppose the next day there are 1,000 advances and 1,200 declines, with 70 million up volume and 230 million down volume, for an Arms of 2.74.

If we calculated a Regular Arms 2-day moving average, we would get 1.57, but if we calculated an Open Arms 2-day moving average, we would get 1.12, as displayed in Table 4–4.

Table 4–3. Regular Arms 2-Day Moving Average Example

	Day 1	**Day 2**	**2-Day Moving Average**	
Advances	1,300	1,000	Day 1 Arms	0.39
Declines	1,000 = 0.39	1,200 = 2.74	Day 2 Arms	+2.74
Up Volume	200	70	Total 2 Days	3.13
Down Volume	60	230	Average 2 Days	1.57

Table 4–4. Open Arms 2-Day Moving Average Example

	Day 1	**+**	**Day 2**	**=**	**Cumulative**	**=**	**2-Day Open Arms**
Advances	1,300	+	1,000	=	2,300		
Declines	1,000	+	1,200	=	2,200	=	1.12
Up Volume	200	+	70	=	270 million		
Down Volume	60	+	230	=	290 million		

We can see from this brief hypothetical example a great enough difference to give a buy signal (above 1.25) from the 2-day Regular Arms but not from the 2-day Open Arms. Similar (if not so dramatic) variations can occur for 10- and 25-day Regular Arms moving averages (10–A and 25–A, etc.) compared to 10- and 25-day Open Arms moving averages (10–O and 25–O, etc.). As it happens, with experience reflecting market action in the '90s, we have developed slightly different "oversold" buy-signal levels for the Open Arms, specifically 1.15 for a 10–O compared to 1.20 for the Regular Arms. Actually, I prefer to use 1.20 on the 4-day and 10-day Regular Arms as indicating an oversold market and suggesting a short-term rally to soon follow, though these numbers can get almost unbelievably high as witnessed during the Crash of '87. From here on, let's refer to the Regular Arms as the *Arms* as distinguished from the *Open Arms*. Although both the Arms and the Open Arms Indexes can stay in oversold territory for a long time before a market or cycle bottoms out, we can see that the likelihood of a rally increases with each passing day of larger Arms ratios. And in "normal" markets, which ebb and flow in sideways to slightly trending ranges, the Arm's moving averages are nicely indicative, especially when coordinated with overbought-oversold criteria such as the A/D line and others reviewed below.

For overbought markets (and therefore sell signals), we look for a 10–A moving average below 0.80 and a 10–O (Open Arms) moving average below 0.75, again without implying that these levels are precisely indicative. For the 25–A, a concern is raised at 0.84, while the 25–O is considered overbought below 0.80. The Arms Indexes have often stayed in overbought territory for months, sometimes stimulating some technicians to get out of the market well ahead of a selloff. We can see this early warning at various periods, for instance early in 1987.

In the November 1988 through March 1989 example in Table 4–1, we see that by November 7 the 10–A was 1.07, slightly oversold, with the 10–O at 0.99 in the neutral range. At 0.89 and 0.82, the 25–A and the 25–O registered somewhat overbought levels. Thus, according to the Arms' moving averages, the NYSE was not yet signalling buy or sell. By November 16, we see the 10–A hit 1.34, a definite short-term oversold buy signal, while the 10–O and 25–A were somewhat oversold, and the 25–O was overbought-neutral.

By January 27, 1989, after the bulk of this rally had run its course, the Arms' moving averages ranged from the 25–A's somewhat overbought reading to very overbought for the rest, certainly issuing a sell signal at these levels. In case one felt that other indications called for an "overshoot rally"—a continuation of the rally despite strong overbought readings—the numbers registered seven days later should have overcome any ambiguities or doubts. Of course, the market, like the proverbial 600-pound gorilla, can do anything it wants to do and conceivably could have rallied even higher for a few days (or weeks) given some extraordinary positive turn of events.

When the DJIA approached a post-Crash resistance high on February 7 at 2347.14, the Arms' moving averages were uniform in deeply overbought readings, giving strong sell signals. Indeed, the 10-O at 0.66 registered most overbought for a long time. Also, the Arms' sell signals were confirmed by other indicators such as the A/D line and others reviewed further on.

We should consider ourselves properly warned when the Arms and Open Arms are deeply overbought, especially when these warnings are augmented by other technical indicators. We can even make some short-term predictions on reversals in trends based on the Arms and other indexes at extreme readings and "spiking" occasions. Mr. Arms admits that the index seems to give better buy signals than sell signals. His is a balanced view of technical analysis that fits in well with volume theories and integrating the A/D line, as he explains:

> It is assumed that price tells what is happening, while volume tells how it is happening. To look at either factor alone, not taking the other into consideration, gives an incomplete, and often erroneous, picture of the market. It is the partnership of volume and price which makes the index so effective. Just looking at the advance/decline figures can sometimes be quite misleading. One sees that more stocks are up than down and assumes that the market is, therefore, strong. Actually there are many times when this is far from true, and the truth is only revealed when one looks at the volume figures. Then one may see that the up stocks are trading on low volume while the down stocks are trading on heavy volume. Under the guise of a strong market, the sellers actually have the upper hand.[11]

New Highs and Lows

Every market day some issues close at a higher or lower price than they have for the preceding 52 weeks and are called yearly, 12-month, or 52-week new highs or new lows. Do not confuse new highs/new lows for the current year (reported by some services) with 52-week new highs/new lows. In an upward-trending market there will be many more new highs than new lows, reaching better than nine-to-one ratios on 10- and 25-day moving averages during strong bull market advances. When there are more new lows than new highs, the market is either declining or threatening to decline. Interior weakness often shows up in the new highs/new lows ratios before the major averages top out and before their closing moving averages turn down and plunge below their 150- and 200-day moving average lines.

---

[11] Richard Arms, Jr., *The Arms Index (TRIN)* (Homewood, IL: Dow Jones-Irwin, 1989), p. 1.

When all-time new high or recovery new high averages coincide with fewer new 52-week highs, it is especially disappointing and worthy of attention. This relationship is one of the strongest, simplest, and most obvious disconfirmation indicators (of apparent market strength) at our disposal. A good example of this kind of disconfirmation occurred on July 17, 1995, when DJIA closed at a new high of 4736.29 with only 167 new 52-week highs compared to the DJIA's high close of 4702.39 with 339 new 52-week highs on July 10, 1995. We can study these July numbers on the "Technical Summary Criteria for Short-Term Market/OEX Timing," Table 4–5. On lines 10 and 31. During the two days following July 17, the DJIA sold off 107.32 points or 2.27 percent. Intraday on July 19, the Dow was down 134.19 points or 2.86 percent with massive selling of over 400 million shares down to only 53 million shares up, and 2,142 declines to only 344 advances. Quite a summer squall.

I should point out that a one-day 2.86 percent selloff can be a sickening event and yet trivial for the long-term investor, who has a three- to five-year or longer outlook for positions in the portfolio. One of my arguments about technical market timing is that to attempt to sidestep 4 to 7 percent corrections is very tricky and not likely to succeed over the long term. One might hold off buying stocks during a sell signal and emphasize buying stocks during a buy signal, but even then there is no guarantee that the stocks bought will advance with the market or the stocks not bought will decline with the market. Obviously, if a stock is worth owning, it's worth owning through many 4 to 7 percent fluctuations in either direction. One might be able to use a signal such as that given on July 17, 1995, for speculating in OEX stock index put options or other put instruments (derivatives) which tend to rise in value as the market declines. Such activities are beyond the scope of our techniques for prudent speculating.

As with other daily numbers and ratios, cumulative ratios and moving averages can be constructed for the yearly new highs and new lows. On our daily technical summary (Table 4–5), lines 10 and 11 show the 52-week new highs and new lows for that day. Lines 13 through 16 display a moving average of the ratio of yearly new highs divided by yearly new highs plus yearly new lows (NH/NH + NL), for 5-, 9-, 17-, and 23-day moving averages. While I have studied this series to see how sensitive and predictive it is for indicating short-term trend reversals, as part of our continuing effort to time the market as a defense against sharp and possibly extended selloffs, I have not yet found it all that valuable.

When all four NH/NH + NL moving averages are increasing, the trend is up; when all four are decreasing, the trend is down; and as each period's moving average turns one way or the other, we have evidence of a change in momentum and a potential change in direction.

Lines 17 and 18 are merely the sum of yearly new highs less new lows for 10 and 25 days. Elsewhere, these sums are calculated as a ratio, but it is mainly the trend direction that is useful in suggesting strengthening or weakening markets. Let me remind you again, when I write of the market or markets in relation to these

Table 4-5. Technical Summary Criteria for Short-Term Market/OEX Timing

1	Date:	071095	071195	071295	071395	071495	071795	071895	071995	072095	072195	072495	072595	072695	072795
2	OEX	530.96+	528.76–	534.71+	534.56–	533.50–	536.58+	532.88–	526.22–	527.94+	529.52+	531.11+	534.74+	534.13–	537.71+
3	UPPER	532.52	532.40	534.08*	535.40	530.19	537.68	538.52	538.57	538.64	538.88	539.31	539.99	540.14	540.97
4	20D Avg	519.49+	520.69+	521.93+	523.09+	524.15+	525.22+	525.86+	526.14+	526.55+	526.72+	527.04+	527.81+	528.64+	529.52+
5	LOWER	506.45	508.98	509.77	510.77	512.13	512.76	513.19	513.71	514.45	514.56	514.77	515.63	517.15	518.07
6	OEX 5-D	526.19+	527.76+	530.52+	531.81+	532.53+	533.62+	534.45+	532.75–	531.42–	530.63–	529.53–	529.91+	531.49+	533.44+
7	OEX 9-D	522.85+	524.11+	525.72+	527.44+	525.15+	530.91+	532.24+	532.03–	531.79–	531.63–	531.89+	531.89+	531.85–	532.31+
8	OEX 17D	521.40+	522.37+	523.52+	524.36+	525.12+	526.11+	525.52+	526.60+	527.11+	527.82+	528.46+	529.38+	530.33+	531.32+
9	OEX 23D	517.54+	518.51+	519.77+	521.21+	522.45+	523.62+	524.55+	525.17+	525.72+	526.12+	526.58+	527.23+	527.58+	528.15+
10	NEW HI	339+	196–	270+	226–	137–	167+	97–	40–	71+	92+	112+	160+	188+	220+
11	NEW LOW	8–	17+	9–	3–	10+	6–	12+	24+	8–	11+	14+	6–	5–	8+
12	NH/NH+N	0.98+	0.92–	0.97+	0.99+	0.92–	0.97–	0.89–	0.63–	0.90+	0.89–	0.89–	0.96+	0.97+	0.96–
13	H/H+L.5	0.97–	0.96–	0.96–	0.96+	0.96–	0.95–	0.95–	0.88–	0.86–	0.85–	0.84–	0.85–	0.92–	0.94–
14	H/H+L.9	0.93+	0.93–	0.95+	0.97+	0.96–	0.96–	0.95–	0.91–	0.91–	0.90–	0.89–	0.89–	0.89–	0.90–
15	H/H+L17	0.92+	0.92+	0.92+	0.93+	0.93–	0.93+	0.93–	0.91–	0.91+	0.92+	0.92+	0.93+	0.93–	0.93+
16	H/H+L.23	0.92+	0.92+	0.92–	0.92+	0.93–	0.93+	0.92–	0.91–	0.91–	0.91+	0.91–	0.91+	0.91+	0.92+
17	NH-NL10	1428+	1513+	1706+	1884+	1943+	2046+	2048+	1901–	1771–	1527–	1294–	1269–	1191–	1180–
18	NH-NL25	3450+	3392–	3494+	3614+	3642–	3740+	3757+	3643–	3603–	3549–	3529–	3528–	3569+	3622+
19	NYCI	298.03+	297.19–	299.93+	299.79–	298.90–	300.01+	298.38–	294.91–	296.36–	296.67+	297.99–	299.92+	300.27+	302.13+
20	UPPER	298.22	298.43	299.46*	300.24	300.68	301.33	301.70	301.68	301.70	301.81	302.05	302.39	302.58	303.09
21	20D Avg	292.04+	292.62+	293.21+	293.78+	294.29+	294.79+	295.10+	295.26+	295.50+	295.58+	295.78+	296.20+	296.67+	297.20+
22	LOWER	285.86	286.81	286.96	287.32	287.90	288.26	288.51	288.84	289.29	289.36	289.50	290.00	290.77	291.30
23	NYCI 10	293.54+	294.11+	295.03+	295.84+	296.60+	297.42+	297.96+	298.13+	298.12–	298.02–	298.01–	298.29+	298.32+	298.55+
24	% AWAY	1.53–	1.05–	1.66+	1.34–	0.77–	0.87+	0.14–	–1.08–	–0.59–	–0.45–	–0.01+	0.55–	0.65–	1.20–
25	NYCI 25	290.98+	291.35+	291.82+	292.33+	292.83+	293.47+	293.98+	294.25+	294.57+	294.89+	295.21+	295.52+	295.86+	296.28+
26	% AWAY	2.42–	2.00–	2.78+	2.55–	2.07–	2.23+	1.50–	0.22–	0.61+	0.61–	0.94+	1.49+	1.49–	1.98+
27	NYCI150	269.37+	269.70+	270.05+	270.40+	270.77+	271.14+	271.49+	271.82+	272.14+	272.46+	272.78+	273.11+	273.44+	273.79+
28	% AWAY	10.64–	10.19–	11.07+	10.87–	10.35–	10.65+	9.90–	8.49–	8.90+	8.89–	9.24+	9.82+	9.81–	10.35+
29	NYCI200	265.46+	265.67+	265.90+	266.13+	266.34+	266.56+	266.78+	266.98+	267.20+	267.43+	267.67+	267.92+	268.15+	268.38+
30	% AWAY	12.27+	11.86–	12.80+	12.65–	12.23–	12.55+	11.85–	10.46–	10.91+	10.93–	11.33+	11.94+	11.98–	12.57+
31	DJIA	4702.39–	4680.60–	4727.29+	4727.48+	4708.32–	4735.29+	4686.28–	4628.87–	4641.55+	4641.55	4668.67+	4714.45+	4707.06–	4732.77+
32	UPPER	4696.02*	4705.41	4726.25*	4743.23	4753.09	4765.71	4772.42	4771.85	4771.01	4771.17	4774.17	4778.53	4778.39	4781.17
33	20D Avg	4564.14+	4575.84+	4587.98+	4599.80+	4610.43+	4621.71+	4628.34+	4632.25+	4636.97+	4639.57+	4643.71+	4651.87+	4660.09+	4668.89+
34	LOWER	4432.26	4446.28	4449.72	4456.37	4467.77	4476.70	4484.25	4492.65	4502.93	4507.30	4513.25	4525.21	4541.79	4556.61
35	DJIA 10	4602.68+	4615.62+	4634.08+	4651.15+	4666.38+	4685.30+	4695.11+	4696.48+	4694.23–	4688.11–	4684.74–	4688.13+	4686.10–	4686.63+
36	% AWAY	2.17–	1.41–	2.01+	1.64–	0.30–	1.09+	–0.19–	–1.44–	–1.12–	–0.99–	–0.34–	0.56–	0.45–	0.98+

Table 4-5. Technical Summary Criteria for Short-Term Market/OEX Timing (cont.)

	Date:	071095	071195	071295	071395	071495	071795	071895	071995	072095	072195	072495	072595	072695	072795
37	DJIA 25	4543.56+	4551.73+	4561.41+	4572.03+	4582.04+	4594.53+	4604.12+	4609.90+	4615.91+	4621.73+	4628.04+	4634.47+	4640.73+	4648.16+
38	% AWAY	3.50–	2.83–	3.64+	3.40–	2.77–	3.09+	1.78–	0.41–	0.56–	0.43–	0.88+	1.73+	1.43–	1.82+
39	DJIA 150	4140.80+	4147.05+	4153.60+	4160.21+	4167.03+	4174.00+	4180.45+	4186.54+	4192.51+	4198.35+	4204.09+	4210.25+	4216.52+	4222.72+
40	% AWAY	13.56–	12.87–	13.81+	13.64+	13.00–	13.47+	12.10–	10.57–	10.71+	10.56–	11.05+	11.98–	11.63–	12.08+
41	DJIA 200	4062.78+	4067.02+	4071.42+	4075.74+	4079.89+	4084.30+	4088.51+	4092.42+	4096.63+	4100.90+	4105.36+	4109.95+	4114.38+	4118.66+
42	% AWAY	15.74	15.09	16.11+	15.99	15.42–	15.96+	14.62–	13.11–	13.30+	13.18–	13.72+	14.71+	14.41–	14.91+
43	Advance	1384	1045–	1493+	1044	921–	1210+	759–	344	1484+	1191–	1454+	1351–	1252+	1490+
44	Decline	985+	1332+	827–	1230+	1321+	1086–	1558+	2142+	868–	1040+	826–	948–	1031+	840–
45	Unchng	658+	660+	694+	734+	751+	725–	711–	530–	661+	746–	716–	727+	729–	680–
46	Unchng%	0.22–	0.22–	0.23+	0.24+	0.25+	0.24–	0.23–	0.18–	0.22+	0.25+	0.24–	0.24+	0.24+	0.23–
47	Up Vol	220779–	136113–	279014+	193441–	116227–	167138+	97084–	53376–	237571+	200800–	182083–	234630+	199775–	226869+
48	DownVol	153116+	203359+	88658–	158850+	155214–	116014–	229299+	400695+	107619–	173621+	92178–	100534+	152056+	90838–
49	OnBalV.	67663–	–67246–	190356+	37591–	–38987–	511244–	–132215–	–347319–	129952+	27179–	89905+	134096+	47719–	136031+
50	VOLUME	508230–	464561–	508107+	478959–	386175–	402056+	455877+	589818+	463115–	500096–	398068–	465951+	478635+	434068+
51	ADV–DEC	399–	–287–	666+	–186–	–400–	124–	–799–	–1798–	616+	151+	628–	403–	221–	650+
52	10D A–D	2869+	3510+	4251+	3814–	3562–	2863–	1746–	–394–	–783–	–1514–	–1285+	595–	–1040–	–204–
53	25D A–D	4199–	3080–	3711+	3974+	3694–	4780+	3661–	1005–	1693+	1647–	2271+	2281+	2669+	3208+
54	ARMS	0.97+	1.17+	0.57–	0.68+	0.93+	0.77–	1.15+	1.21+	0.77–	0.99–	0.89–	0.61–	0.92+	0.71–
55	ARMS 4	0.84+	0.92+	0.91+	0.85–	0.84–	0.74–	0.88+	1.02+	0.98–	1.03+	0.97–	0.82–	0.85+	0.78–
56	Open 4	0.83+	0.89+	0.87–	0.82–	0.80–	0.71–	0.87+	1.10+	1.03–	1.04+	1.05+	0.82–	0.87+	0.79–
57	ARMS 10	0.99+	0.94+	0.87–	0.83–	0.84+	0.80–	0.87+	0.90+	0.92+	0.92+	0.91–	0.86–	0.89+	0.90+
58	Open 10	0.93+	0.93+	0.85–	0.82–	0.83+	0.79–	0.83+	0.88+	0.90+	0.92+	0.93+	0.87–	0.91+	0.93+
59	ARMS 13	0.96+	0.97+	0.97+	0.95–	0.89–	0.85–	0.86+	0.89+	0.86–	0.89–	0.90–	0.90–	0.90–	0.88–
60	ARMS 25	0.90–	0.91+	0.90–	0.88–	0.88+	0.87–	0.89+	0.92+	0.91–	0.92–	0.92+	0.92+	0.93+	0.91–
61	Open 25	0.86–	0.88+	0.86–	0.84–	0.84–	0.84–	0.85+	0.89+	0.89–	0.89+	0.90+	0.90–	0.90+	0.89–
62	NAI55	0.92–	0.93–	0.93+	0.92–	0.92+	0.91–	0.92+	0.92+	0.92–	0.93+	0.92–	0.92–	0.92+	0.92–
63	OEXputV	139728	113137	146504	157719	142889	142527	178342	418614	262643	188729	98248	114124	106896	67057
64	OEXcalV	110239	76754	129373	150612	97768	128353	164197	242249	198296	156367	82774	80487	82792	67885
65	OEXp/c	1.27	1.47	1.13	1.05	1.46	1.11	1.09	1.73	1.32	1.39	1.19	1.42	1.29	0.99
66	10dapv	125837	120432	122218	124332	124173	130115	145746	174867	185593	191873	184935	175849	168686	157558
67	pv/10pv	1.11	0.94	1.20	1.27	1.15	1.10	1.22	2.39	1.42	0.85	0.53	0.65	0.63	0.43
68	10dacv	85234	83982	89139	95118	96127	103052	117238	133590	142785	127520	142674	11375	125322	115690
69	cv/10cv	1.29	0.91	1.45	1.58	1.02	1.25	1.40	1.81	1.39	0.92	0.58	0.61	0.66	0.59
70	OEXpoi	632552	653491	657452	682333	686176	711326	729081	734801	743330	770157	328097	357098	383369	401774
71	OEXcoi	401870	400880	406840	412434	417251	419388	421841	423930	439273	448528	222185	244181	253458	262812
72	poi/coi	1.57	1.63	1.62	1.65	1.64	1.70	1.73	1.73	1.69	1.28	1.48	1.46	1.51	1.53

figures I am really referring to the New York Stock Exchange, from which all these numbers are taken.

For a practical example involving the yearly new highs and lows (NH/NL), we return to the figures generated during the period of November 1, 1988 to March 1, 1989 (Table 4–1). On November 16, 1988, the DJIA closed at 2038.58, with only 3 new highs and 51 new lows. That was the fewest number of new highs since August 11, 1988, when there were only 2, with the DJIA at 2039.30. As reviewed above, on November 16, 1988, the 10-day Arms (10–A) registered a buy signal of 1.34, and there were 3,620 and 3,915 more declines than advances for 10 days and 25 days, respectively, which also represent buy-signal levels on these indicators. So with November 16's closing we can see several confirmed buy signals, confirmed also by the 10- and 25-day relationships of the DJIA and NYSE Composite Index to their closing numbers (reviewed below).

We observe that on January 27, 1989, the DJIA had advanced nicely to 2322.86, a 13.9 percent gain, with 164 new 52-week highs and 10 new lows. Noticing other indicators we see our 10–A, 10 O, 25–A, and 25–O Arms Indexes at 0.76, 0.68, 0.84, 0.76, respectively, screamingly overbought, especially on the 10–O. We also see 4,712 more advances than declines for 25 days, and the NYSE Composite Index (NYCI) and DJIA at somewhat overbought levels.

Even though the DJIA advanced seven days later to 2347.14 on February 7, 1989, another 24 points (1.05 percent), only 144 new highs were generated, 12 percent fewer than at the previous peak. With both the Arms and A/D indicators further overbought, a signaled decline was imminent. The DJIA sold off 100+ points by February 24, closing at 2245.54 with 22 new highs and 24 new lows. Then the DJIA rallied to 2340.71 on March 16, but with only 120 new highs—24 fewer new highs than on February 7—to 15 new lows, indicating another unconfirmed advance. Thereafter the DJIA sold off again 97.67 points.

A very small number of yearly new highs suggests a market or cycle bottom, especially if the new lows are huge (over several hundred). A classic example of this relationship occurred on Black Monday, October 19, 1987, when there were 10 new highs to 1,068 new lows, and the next day, when there was one new high to 1,174 new lows, a bottom-washout ratio of historic proportions.

Two signs that Black Monday was a cyclical bottom occurred thereafter. On the following Monday (October 26) when the DJIA "retested" its previous low, reaching 1793.93, there were no new highs but "only" 467 new lows. And on December 4, 1987, the DJIA declined again to 1766.74 (a failed retest of its Meltdown Monday October 19, 1987, low—with no new highs and only 281 new lows. By the way, that day was the '87 bear market low for the NYCI at 125.91 (which closed at 128.62 on October 19) and for other indexes such as the OTC Industrials Index at 290.47 (which closed at 369.73 on October 19).

If you absorbed all those figures in the paragraphs above, you can see how the pattern of decreasing 52-week new highs, in spite of increasing recovery high readings for the DJIA (and other major indexes), suggested disconfirming breadth weakness and the likelihood of a correction according to the new highs/new lows indicator alone. When these patterns are reinforced with other indicators, the probabilities—although I cannot quantify them with any precision, especially in terms of time—become so great that a trend reversal is in the offing. Now we turn to another interesting set of numbers and relationships, the DJIA and NYCI moving averages.

The DJIA and NYCI Moving Averages

If I were trying to be a full-fledged technician, I would be using the Standard & Poor's (S&P) 500 Index, and perhaps the S&P 400 Index, instead of the NYCI. When I got started tracking such things I was focused on the New York Stock Exchange and its Composite Index and its Average Price per Share of Common Stock (APSC)—that number they tell you about on TV when they say the average price of a share of stock changed so many cents today.

In the beginning, I mainly studied NYSE listed corporations because of their stocks' liquidity being generally greater than those on other exchanges and over-the-counter markets. Other reasons for focusing on the NYSE included its more stringent admission and reporting requirements and more readily available public information. All were considered initial safety advantages. Now that I think about it, I understand how some people limit themselves to only New York listed stocks or to only the 30 DJIA corporations. One could make a successful speculating career in dealing with just those 30 companies, buying them when they are out of favor and undervalued and selling them when they are very popular and fully or overvalued.

As a matter of record, there is an interesting, published technique on how to beat the performance of the DJIA by buying its: (1) 10 highest yielding stocks; (2) 5 high-yield/lowest-priced stocks; or (3) the Penultimate Profit Prospect (the second lowest-priced high yielder). This system explained in *Beating the Dow*[12], is a tempting alternative to the labor-intensive techniques of being a prudent speculator. Apparently, anyone could use this simple mechanistic technique.

By the way, stock market tradition uses prices based on the bit—you know, 12.5 cents ("Shave and a haircut, two bits"), a hangover from currencies divided into pieces of eight—and reports in archaic 1/8s (16ths, 32nds, 64ths, etc.) instead of using the dollars and whole cents of today's decimal system. From time to time

---

[12] Michael O'Higgins with John Downes, *Beating the Dow* (New York: Harper Perennial, 1992).

someone raises this issue, but Wall Street seems to remain entrenched rather than incur the expense of changing just for the sake of logic and clarity.

Even as a neophyte, I knew I had to have some index or average more representative than just the DJIA with its 30 large-capitalization stocks—out of 1,700 or more (at the time) other common stocks on the NYSE. (Now, in 1995, there are over 3,100 issues listed on the NYSE, so the DJIA is even less representative of the overall market.) So I chose the NYCI. I also keep daily track of the S&P 500 Index, S&P 100 Index (aka OEX), Amex Index, OTC Composite, Value Line "G," and Russell 2000 Index of smaller capitalization stocks.

It is relatively common knowledge among technicians that major indexes tend to oscillate about 3 to 4 percent or more above and below 10- and 25-day moving averages before reversing in "normal" market environments. When we review the Crash of '87 in Chapter 6, we'll see how extreme such oscillations can become, and even how we must adjust to their extreme readings for long periods thereafter.

For over 3,600 consecutive trading days, I've kept moving averages of the DJIA and NYCI for 5, 7, 10, 25, 50, 100, 150, and 200 days. These records have been helpful from time to time in recognizing the general condition of the market. Since the Crash of '87, I have redoubled my efforts at becoming defensive in overbought (and overvalued) markets, partially through a more rigorous analysis of these and other technical indicators, as well as interest and inflation rates and Federal Reserve policies and actions.

There are any number of ways of developing moving averages other than simply dividing the sum of elements by the number of elements summed. Many technicians "weight" MAs by attributing higher values to more recent days (or years, etc.), or calculate with "smoothing constants" to obtain exponential MAs. I use simple arithmetic for my MAs, but I mention these alternatives to alert you to avoid comparing plain vanilla MAs with weighted or exponential MAs. To see how the DJIA and NYCI moving averages work in terms of overbought/oversold indications, we return to the example of November 1, 1988 to March 1, 1989 (see Table 4–1).

These overbought/oversold (OB/OS) figures represent the percentage of the daily close's distance away from its moving averages. When the daily close is above its MAs, that is positive, unless by too great a percentage, which indicates it is into overbought territory. A close 3 percent or more above a 10-day MA or 4 percent or more above a 25-day MA is significantly overbought and signalling a likely downward fluctuation—a short-term sell signal. Conversely, a daily close of 3 percent or more below a 10-day MA or 4 percent of more below a 25-day MA signals a short-term oversold buy condition.

As can be seen in Table 4–1, on November 7, 1988, the 10–MAs and 25–MAs of the NYCI and DJIA recorded –1.6 percent, –1.4 percent, –1.3 percent, and –1.0 percent, respectively. While these closes were all below their MAs—indicating declining daily closes and slightly oversold conditions—they did not yet suggest a buy signal (rally) with such modest numbers.

By November 16, the 10- and 25-day NYCI and DJIA OB/OS numbers had deteriorated to –2.8 percent, –4.3 percent, –3.2 percent, and –4.5 percent, respectively, registering significantly oversold, especially on the 25–MAs. With three out of four OB/OS indicators in oversold/buy signal territory, plus several other indicators signalling oversold/buy, we had a strong probability of an upcoming rally. Thereafter, as previously noted, the NYSE rallied through January 27, 1989, and a bit beyond.

By January 27, 1989, the 10-week rally of the NYSE, left the NYCI and DJIA 10–MAs and 25–MAs at +2.0 percent, +3.7 percent, +3.2 percent, and +5.1 percent, respectively—significantly overbought readings, on balance. While the DJIA was able to advance another 25 points after January 27 through February 7, the 25–MAs remained significantly overbought at +3.8 percent and +3.9 percent, suggesting the previously signaled correction was still likely, especially when considering the other technical indicators in concert (reviewed above). Sure enough, the DJIA began an immediate decline of just over 100 points by March 1, at which point it began to register slightly oversold percentages again.

Experience shows that at various times the OB/OS levels—also know as *trading bands*—are more effective if interpreted with 3.0, 3.5, 4.0 or higher percentages. That is, sometimes the market reverses after a 3.0 percent reading is developed and sometimes not until an OB/OS band registers over 4.0 percent. In an effort to fine-tune a criterion OB/OS level, John Bollinger, the former resident technician at the old Financial News Network (FNN, now taken over by CNBC), came up with an intriguing idea. Instead of fixing on a single percentage or several fixed bands away from the MA, why not generate some relative percentages "that vary in distance from the average as a function of the market's volatility"?

After considerable empirical testing and review, Bollinger determined that using 20-day MAs with bands two standard deviations (STD) away gave various clues to future market movements when these bands were approached or penetrated in either direction. Bollinger actually analyzes his bands in combination with convergence/divergence analyses of several other indicators, which are beyond my scope and interest; nevertheless, I find the basic technique intriguing. In an unpublished handout from a Technical Analysts of Southern California (TASC) presentation, Bollinger points out:

> (1) Sharp moves tend to occur after the bands tighten to the average (volatility lessens). (2) A move outside the bands calls for a continuation of the trend, not an end to it. (3) Bottoms (tops) made outside the bands followed by bottoms (tops) made inside the bands call for reversals in trend. (4) A move originating at one band tends to go all

the way to the other band (this observation is useful for projecting targets for moves early on).

One can also use a 30-day (or any duration) moving average to develop Bollinger Bands. The 30-day moving averages are a little less sensitive than the 20-day bands, but make an interesting exercise and reinforcement when both give overbought/oversold signals.

On our daily technical summary (Table 4–5), we keep three sets of 20-day moving average Bollinger Bands, one each for the OEX Index (S&P 100), the NYCI, and the DJIA. Mostly, I observe these printouts in coordination with the other indicators to see where the daily close is in relation to their MAs and band-widths. Measuring direction as well as amplitude can add to one's interpretation of the market's condition and trend.

As I am intrigued by the possibility of fluctuating bands based on volatility providing or augmenting signals that may be superior to arbitrary percentage lim-its, I want to include this indicator at this point. Clearly, one would not need to refer to Bollinger Bands (or any bands, necessarily) to have sufficient technical indicators signalling OB/OS conditions.

We also pay attention to the daily closes of the NYCI and DJIA in relation to their various MAs, especially the 150– and 200–MAs. One widely used definition of a bull market is when the daily major averages are closing nicely above their 200 MAs. Sometimes this leads to confusion, as when the DJIA is closing above its 200–MA while the S&P 500 is closing below its 200–MA, or vice versa. It's also comforting to note that the 200–MAs are in a rising trend. When the 200–MAs are declining and the major averages are closing beneath them, we are in a bearish configuration.

A classical trend-following signal is that when the daily close penetrates the 150–MA or 200–MA (take your preference), the major market trend is reversing in that direction. While there is some merit to this configuration, the case is stronger if these long-term MAs are moving in the same direction as the percentage dis-tance of the daily penetrations. As you can see from Figure 4–1 and Figure 4–2, in 1988 there were two whipsaw penetrations that failed to inhibit the primary trend. On the other hand, the 150–MAs and 200–MAs were penetrated two days before the October '87 Crash, giving good (if rather late) bailout signals, especially as the secondary stocks continued to decline on average until early December.

In Chapter 6 on the Crash of '87, we will see how these indicators first sig-nalled a potential selloff, but then prematurely signalled a turnaround, thus trap-ping some (many?) market technicians by encouraging them to hold or buy into the crashing market before its bottoming out. Other fundamental, sentiment, interest and monetary conditions will be mentioned that should be considered as augment-ing or ameliorating the strength of strictly technical signals.

Figure 4–1. The DJIA 150/200-Day Moving Averages

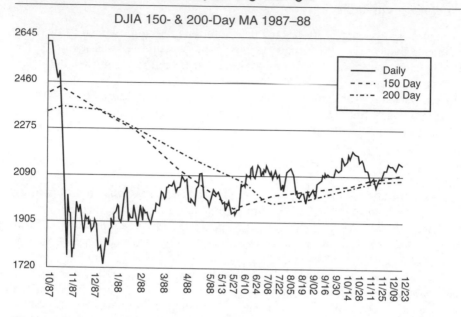

Figure 4–2. The NYCI 150/200-Day Moving Averages

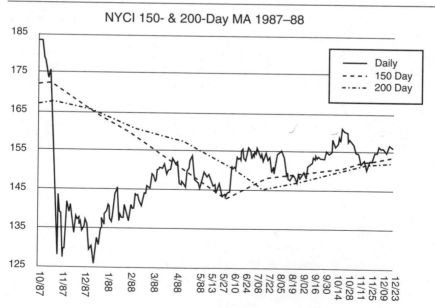

OEX Analysis

As mentioned in the chapter on portfolio management, I want to use OEX Index put options to hedge portfolios when I'm concerned about the market selling off sharply—7 percent or more in a relatively short time. The Standard & Poor's 100 Index (S&P 100) forms the basis for the OEX option contracts. The S&P 100/OEX has certain characteristics that both reflect and diverge from other major market averages and portfolios that are constructed mainly with stocks other than those 100 issues in the index. It would be nice to be able to use the OEX both in concert with general market movements and as an insurance hedge for my (or your) particular portfolio.

For our technical analysis review, let us look at the daily technical summary (Table 4–5). Since the OEX analysis may be the second most sensitive and short-term trading indicator I follow (after the Arms Indexes), I begin the top of the page with it. Line 2 is the OEX (S&P 100) close for the day. Line 3 is the upper band, two standard deviations above the OEX's 20–MA, which is Line 4. Line 5 is the lower band, two standard deviations below the OEX's 20–MA.

As one observes these oscillations exceed the upper and lower bands—bands that expand and contract with the changes in two times their standard deviations—one can sometimes note confirming trends or reversing indications, as mentioned by Bollinger above. The penetration of the Bollinger Bands, especially the Bollinger Bands of the NYCI and the DJIA, requires artful interpretation in the context of other indicators. It can be instructive to compare the relative band penetrations with the absolute percentage difference between the closes of the NYCI and DJIA and their 10– and 25–MAs, as well as with the size of the standard deviation figure. So far, larger standard deviations suggest upcoming selloffs, while small standard deviations can be associated with likely rallies, although not always.

The Endless Quest

I have learned much and quoted frequently from the work of Norm Fosback and others in an effort to develop techniques for effective market timing, especially in terms of risk management. I have not quoted from the work of Ned Davis, whom I admire greatly and have followed closely through several of his Ned Davis Research publications[13].

Ned Davis Research produces several thousand charts each month, representing an almost unbelievable number of technical and fundamental relationships and indicators of probable stock, bond, economic, and international trends. His is a

---

[13] Ned Davis Research publications (Davis, Mendel & Regenstein, Inc., 800–241–0621 or 404–252–4008).

model-building approach that yields suggested market-exposure levels, including buy and sell signals. For example, "Big Mo [a composite longer-term momentum guide] was built from 73 Standard & Poor's industry group models, with its latest reading derived by dividing the number of bullish groups by the group total and scaling the results."[14] Such models' trading signals are compared with the movements of major averages over many years and cycles, with their track-record percentages reported.

Technical stock and market analysis is a well-established profession, with many superior practitioners. However, too many (in my opinion) are worse than useless because of their inconsistencies. Some of the better technicians, such as Robert Nurock, editor of *Bob Nurock's Advisory*[15], developer and keeper of the Elves' Technical Market Indicator, and the oft-mentioned Norm Fosback, of *Market Logic* and several other publications, combine their basic technical approach with complementary fundamental and macroanalysis.

Perhaps I should just fess up and admit that I am a "closet technician," even if many of the great fundamentalist investors I try to emulate have pronounced technical analysis unworkable or worse. Like so many labels, technical analysis means different things to different people and practitioners. My interest in technical analysis is mainly to try to avoid such devastating trend reversals as the Crash of '87 and the selloff of '90, not to mention great bear markets such as those of 1929, 1937, and 1973–74.

Technicians generally believe that all influences affecting stock prices are represented and reflected in the graphs and charts, even though they may not be identified specifically in terms of time or amplitude. Obviously we have not used many graphs in this review of technical analysis, nor many of the wonderful slogans used in practice. The maxim, "The trend is your friend!" seems incomplete to me, requiring an additional phrase, "until it's not!", which is to say until it reverses with a vengeance. Some technical tautologies such as, "There is nothing more bullish than an advancing market," are pleasant. The definition of an uptrend as a pattern of "higher highs and higher lows" on the chart is irrefutable, although it seems like hindsight, which may or may not continue to be true. It is easy to be skeptical about technical analysis, especially about chart reading.

Summary

Trading action in the stock markets—specifically in the New York Stock Exchange—produces daily results and periodic patterns that may be indicative of future trading activities. Technicians attempt to find recurring relationships and

---

[14] N. Davis, *Stock Market Explanation Book* (Atlanta: Ned Davis Research, Inc., 1989), p. 30.

[15] *Bob Nurock's Advisory* (P.O. Box 460, Santa Fe, NM 87504-0460).

patterns that may be useful in timing the price directions of stocks and markets. Many variables impinge upon stock prices and market movements that are neither mathematically precise nor clear in their temporal influences. Mass psychology, government policy, economic cycles, and international events affect stock-market outcomes, especially in the shorter term.

A technician's faith in the numbers for predicting likely stock or market direction is not unlike the fundamentalists' faith in their analysis of corporate valuations. Neither really needs to know what a corporation "does" in order to make a buy, hold, or sell judgment of that corporation's stock.

This book is not a complete treatise on fundamental analysis, and it is even less a manual of technical analysis. However, in spite of my being a firm fundamentalist on stock selection, I am deeply interested in learning whether technical analysis can consistently help me to avoid investing shortly before significantly sharp or extended market declines and to speculate aggressively shortly before and during extended market advances. To that end I keep and study the several sets of technical indicators mentioned in this chapter.

The advance/decline line constructed from the net of daily advancing minus declining stocks yields market breadth readings of strength and weakness. The on-balance volumes of daily up-volumes less down-volumes also show strength and breadth configurations. Combining the daily advance/decline ratio divided by the daily up/down volumes' ratio yields the daily *Arms Index* (*TRIN*), which shows both subtle and gross relationships of buying and selling pressures. These Arms Index moving averages show overbought and oversold market conditions (as do the moving averages of the A/D line and on-balance volume), which yield marketwide buy and sell signals, especially in confirmation with other technical indicators.

Another important technical ratio is the 52-week new highs to new lows, which is often an early warning confirming or disconfirming indicator of the strength of a market trend or its potential reversal. At extreme levels the new highs/new lows ratio can signal cycle or major market-trend reversals in either direction. An interesting short-term trend model is the ratio of new highs divided by new highs plus new lows for 5, 9, 17, and 23 trading days. When these results are coupled with short-term OEX moving averages for the same periods, one can obtain early indications of momentum changes and potential trend reversals.

Experience shows that trends rarely carry much more than 3 to 4 percent away from the 10- and 25-day moving averages of the Dow Jones Industrial Average (DJIA) and the New York Stock Exchange Composite Index (NYCI). Comparing the various technical elements and ratios with the relationships of the DJIA and NYCI moving averages can provide a meaningful and often predictive picture of the general overbought or oversold condition of the market. In severely overbought markets, which usually coincide with advanced price levels and market or cycle tops, beware of an impending consolidation or a trend-reversing correction (decline). In severely oversold markets, which usually coincide with depressed price levels and market cycle bottoms, beware of an impending trend-reversing rally.

In an effort to develop an insurance hedging program using OEX stock index put options, I continue to study the action of the Standard & Poor's 100 Index, the basis for the OEX options' contracts. Invoking moving averages and Bollinger Bands of OEX, DJIA, and NYCI relationships, I attempt to augment and confirm buy and sell indications based on the other technical indicators reviewed.

None of these technical indicators provides guaranteed signals. Some of them seem more predictive of advancing than declining markets. All of them may be early or late—that is, overbought markets can stay overbought and become even more overbought for long periods; oversold markets can stay oversold and become even more so for long periods. There is no end to the number of models, graphs, ratios, and indicators that have been and could be developed for prognosticating future market movements.

The more one studies technical indicators, the greater the tendency to find important ones contradicting each other, as is described somewhat in Chapter 6 which reviews aspects of the Crash of '87. Some individuals and organizations have a superior record of calling major market turns, such as Elaine Garzarelli's calls to be out of the market before the Crash of '87 and the Selloff of '90. Many calls were early, late, or missing completely on occasion. Still, I will take any help I can get and continue to search for magic bullets that might improve my fundamental stock-selection returns by alerting me to become defensive before major market declines and aggressive before major market advances. I will continue to analyze technical information that will help keep me invested during choppy, fluctuating, upward-trending markets.

5

The Myths and Magic of Margin

My personal ("TPS") common stock portfolio has been fully margined since I began acting as a professional investment adviser in March 1977. A margined account—where money is borrowed against the market value of a portfolio in order to buy more stocks or to use for other reasons—is one of the tools I choose to use in my approach to speculating. However, using margin leverage isn't necessary in order to obtain better-than-market-average performance (see the long-term results in Table 1–2). The use of margin has many advantages and some disadvantages beyond merely doubling your gains or losses. I hope you can read this chapter with an open mind, setting aside preconceptions and foregone conclusions.

Margin leverage may not be your cup of tea, or it may be the technique that provides you many extra cups of tea. As is the case with speculation, many people turn a glazed eye and a deaf ear on the subject of margin. Memories or stories of 1929-type wipeouts, or confusion with the thin margins (good faith money) and big losses associated with commodities and futures contracts, lead the unsophisticated investor to identify these tragedies and very high risks with margined stock accounts. Today, margined stock accounts can only borrow up to 50 percent of the market value of marginable stocks (on the portfolio as a whole) and can be managed without excessive risk.

True, you don't need to know about or use margin, but then you don't need to know about business, investing, or speculating in stocks either to have a perfectly good life. If you want to increase the prospects of systematically enhancing your investment capital, however, you might do well to consider the careful and effective use of margin leverage. Actually, *margin* refers to one's equity or cash and *leverage* refers to the funds borrowed from your broker, but convention refers to this process as using margin in a margined account, so I will submit to convention and refer to this process as *margin* instead of *margin leverage*.

Is Margin Dangerous?

One of the most amazing attitudes toward stock investing and speculating that I have encountered is the generally hostile mindset toward the use of margin. Otherwise bright, astute, and successful investors (who are of course speculating when they buy common stocks) have a my-mind-is-made-up, don't-bother-me-with-the-facts attitude when margin is mentioned. Even Peter Lynch, formerly the extremely successful manager of the Fidelity Magellan Fund, in his enlightening and wonderful book, *One Up on Wall Street*, has no entry for "margin," but there is one for *leverage, real estate*:

> It's no accident that people who are geniuses in their houses are idiots in their stocks. A house is entirely rigged in the homeowner's favor. The banks let you acquire it for 20 percent down and in some cases less, giving you the remarkable power of leverage. (True, you can buy stocks with 50 percent cash down, which is known in the trade as "buying on margin," but every time a stock bought on margin drops in price, you have to put up more cash. . . . The real estate agent never calls at midnight to announce: "You'll have to come up with twenty thousand dollars by eleven a.m. tomorrow or else sell off two bedrooms," which frequently happens to stockholders forced to sell their shares bought on margin. This is another great advantage to owning a house.)[1]

That is *One Up's* total discussion of margin, which is understandable since apparently Mr. Lynch doesn't use or recommend margin leverage. Unfortunately, the author's statement contains a false and misleading assertion—"every time a stock bought on margin drops in price, you have to put up more cash." In fact, stocks bought on margin are generally calculated on the total portfolio market value, and it would have to drop 30 percent in price from its original purchase price before additional cash (or sale of stock) is required. Of course, if you only bought one stock, then that stock would have to drop 30 percent in market price before additional cash (or sale of stock) is required.

To the novice investor, it sounds like Mr. Lynch is saying if you buy $20,000 worth of stocks using margin, and their market value decreases at all, you will be

---

[1] Peter Lynch with John Rothchild, *One Up on Wall Street*, (New York: Simon & Schuster, 1989), p .66.

called "at midnight" and told that you have to come up with more dollars by 11 A.M. *Maintenance calls*, the correct term, are usually made during business hours or by telegram. Even if you did get one, generally, you are allowed one or more business days to meet a maintenance/margin call, and with some brokers the margin call is "cured" (or met) if the market value of your portfolio increases in price sufficiently by the next day.[2]

But notice the negative connotations and scariness in Lynch's brief mention of margin. According to Lynch, not only will you be called at midnight, but this "frequently happens" to the "idiots in their stocks" who are "forced to sell their shares bought on margin." Actually, you would only be forced to sell as many shares of any stock in your portfolio as necessary (if you didn't have the cash to add) to meet the call.

Peter Lynch is one of my stock-market heros and role models. I try to emulate his techniques and successes, along with those of Warren Buffett, John Templeton, Kenneth Fisher, David Dreman and a few other long-term, equity-oriented, stock-picking portfolio managers. However, it grieves me to see such an astute stock marketeer give such short and negative shrift to the topic of margin. Still, the majority view is down on margin, especially for the protection of the small, inexperienced investor.

Using Margin Effectively Requires Study and Commitment

To use margin effectively you must understand it thoroughly and believe in it strongly. You must be aware that using margin generally incurs greater risk and portfolio volatility than would occur in a comparable unmargined portfolio. Why take additional risk and suffer through potentially gut-wrenching volatility when adequate to handsome returns can be obtained without margin? Because substantially greater rewards are likely through the prudent application of margin, given the consistent use of effective speculating techniques reviewed in this book. Over long periods of time the market goes up, and margin is effective in leveraging returns.

Over those long periods of time when the market advances, the reality of having one and one-half or two times as many shares—including wider diversification of issues—provides not just increased total returns but much greater flexibility in portfolio management as well. During those shorter periods when the market

---

[2] NYSE and NASD rules require the collection of maintenance calls "promptly but in any event within a reasonable period of time." House (brokerage) rules may require payment within three business days. This can be shortened if any of the following conditions apply: (1) an undue concentration in one or more stocks, (2) a single stock position (sole collateral), (3) equity below 25 percent (NYSE), (4) any short position in account, (5) market volatility (e.g.: October 20, 1987, all margin calls were due "next day" [Oct 21]; calls in short or mixed accounts were due "same day" [by noon Oct. 20]), (6) a significant decline in client's creditworthiness, (7) an extremely large debit balance ($500,000+).

declines, although your losses are leveraged (magnified), they are usually still manageable and temporary if you do not sell out. Leveraged recovery is likely in the next up cycle. Beyond that, if you can be defensive at blatantly overvalued and overbought periods, you can diminish the downside risks.

Even during the Crash of '87, modest and conservatively managed margin accounts were not sold out or did not suffer irreversible losses that couldn't be made up in the following year or two. Because a portfolio must decline 30 percent overall from its initial (maximum) 50 percent margined level, even the 22 percent drop of Black Monday itself was not necessarily sufficient to create a margin call, but more about this in detail a little later on.

Occasionally, the use of margin may actually decrease portfolio risk by permitting sufficient diversification among more stocks than one's cash alone would buy. When I started out with about $8,000 in cash in 1977, I could effectively own about six stocks because trading commissions and odd-lot differentials then would eat up too much of the potential gains in smaller positions. Diversification with only six stocks would permit a 77 percent or so risk reduction (see Table 3–3). By using margin, I was able to buy and hold 12 stocks, thus reducing unsystematic risk—individual stock risk compared to overall market risk—by 87 percent or so. Thereafter, I was able to diversify more, further reducing my individual stock risk.

The audited statement of TPS Portfolio (see Table I–2) shows that for 18.25 years, my actual margined (TPS) portfolio gained 22.92 percent compounded annually (including margin interest and trading commission expense as well as dividend income), while a hypothetical portfolio of the same trades done using only 100 percent cash would have a market appreciation of 16.95 percent compounded annually. Clearly, a 16.95 percent compounded annual return for 18.25 years, which is the equivalent of almost a 14-fold increase, is nothing to sneeze at. But a 22.92 percent compounded annual return for 18.25 years is very strong, and amounts to a greater than 32-fold increase. A few extra percent each year over many years really adds up.

Being leveraged to the hilt going into the Crash of '87, my (TPS) Portfolio showed a loss of 55.65 percent for that year, and during the crash period the interim percentage was even greater. I did have to sell many stocks, even after putting up $90,000 in cash to meet margin calls. I would not have been completely "sold out," but the stocks in my portfolio would have been reduced to about $200,000 to $270,000 less if I hadn't added that cash. Happily, the tremendous declines were partially diminished by the strong comeback beginning in December of '87, and were further mitigated by a 50.16 percent total return for 1988 and a 20.69 percent total return for 1989.

I do not expect to see that type of waterfall crash again as witnessed in October 1987. For one thing, there are now "collars" on the NYSE that inhibit programmed trading after a 50-point change in the DJIA, and various other breaks on larger moves both in New York and Chicago (where future derivatives are traded) to give the market makers and specialists time to let things cool down and make adjustments.

I have formulated principles and taken steps to avoid being so vulnerable again. These principles and practices, reviewed in previous chapters and below, include maintaining reserves to meet potential margin calls, not permitting equity to fall below 40 percent, and watching out that low-priced stocks—which lose their loan values as they decline below $10 (in some cases) and $5 (almost always) per share—do not threaten my portfolio's marginability due to a sudden market drop. With our revised selling discipline, I expect to be in better shape the next time similar vulnerable market conditions prevail.

Alas, a similar overleveraged condition occurred in July 1990. How can I tell you that margin can be prudently handled when I have been so imprudent twice in its handling? By example, so that both you and I do not make this error again! I missed a sell signal in early July 1990 that might have cushioned the blow of the horrendous sharp selloff, especially in secondary stocks, from mid-July through mid-October 1990.

I do not plead extenuating circumstances as an excuse for the 60.52 percent loss in 1990. In hindsight, I might have handled the problem quite differently both in my portfolio management (sales, and hedges with OEX put options) and in my management of cash flows (selling from my IRA account or borrowing funds from other sources). In the end, I am convinced that the speculative system I employ with the use of margin is good and effective, and any major stumbles along the way were largely because I let down my guard and even abused the system. Fortunately, no money management clients were as heavily margined as I.

Conceptual Points of View

When I tell people that I have been fully margined for the past 18 years, most of them are amazed and many are disbelieving (some of them are even polite). For many investors, margin represents undue risk and visions of people being wiped out *à la* 1929. Few people with whom I've talked seem to understand the effective use of margin with common stocks and even fewer—including stockbrokers, who should know the ins and outs—understand its sometimes tricky mechanics. When I refer to "stockbrokers," I include registered reps (representatives or brokerage sales personnel), financial consultants, account executives, vice presidents, or whatever titles your brokerage house uses.

It should be common knowledge that our great American economy was built, is based, and continues to grow on borrowed funds—in the case of the federal government, vast borrowed funds, unfortunately. Every day, governments (federal, state, and local) borrow funds and service huge amounts of debt in order to take care of present needs and build for the future. We know of such borrowing as Treasury bills, notes, and bonds, municipal bonds, and other governmental and quasi-governmental "paper." Every day, banks, savings and loans, and other financial institutions borrow and lend, often only overnight, in order to meet reserve requirements or short- and long-term needs.

The modern corporation would not exist if it weren't for the debt markets, which are far larger than the equity markets. It is customary for businesspersons to borrow to start businesses, meet short-term needs and long-term expansions, add staff, open new branches, spend for research and development, or just smooth out seasonal cash flows. Almost every large corporation's equity is based on the sale of stock to the public, but future growth and operations usually depend upon raising additional capital by issuing bonds, selling commercial paper, or borrowing from banks. If you are in business, you likely seek loans or credit under the rubric of taking a *businessperson's risk*.

Perhaps a more meaningful example of the use of margin—aside from business use—is the purchase of a car or house. If everyone waited until they could purchase a car for cash there would be far fewer cars sold, and therefore produced, at least for the four or five years while we saved for them. But most of us do not hesitate to put a 10 or 20 percent down (margin) payment and borrow the difference, agreeing to pay off the debt plus interest with monthly payments. Often, we make major purchases without putting any money down, as reflected in all-time high levels of credit-card debt.

Likewise, most people would have to save for 20 or 30 or more years in order to buy a house for cash. And while they were saving there would be fewer houses built, and these houses would probably cost more as the inefficiencies of a cash or barter market and the ravages of inflation took their tolls. Peter Lynch lauds real-estate leverage, but that leverage can be as beneficial or damaging to the individual as stock-market leverage. If the real-estate buyer cannot meet the mortgage payments, the property could be repossessed (or liquidated at a loss) costing the buyer both the down payment and accumulated equity.

So, most of us buy our cars and houses (and many large purchases) with the extensive use of personal credit. Not only do we have the benefit and use of such items now, but we help to keep the economy going. The people who build the cars, houses, and provide the other services we want or need are able to earn their livelihoods—because of our credit purchases—and in turn buy our products or services, also most often with credit. We have a credit economy and, until or unless it gets too far out of whack, it helps us achieve the high standards of living we now enjoy.

Meanwhile, investing in common stocks is part of this generally felicitous economy driven by government, industry, small business, and personal credit. Entrepreneurs with good ideas and products or services that meet society's needs and wants are able to implement their dreams and create realities by sharing expenses, risks, and profits (or losses) with shareholders. Even though shares of stock are not considered debt—they are equity or ownership, as contrasted with bonds and loans—company founders nevertheless are literally indebted to shareholders for supplying the wherewithal to pursue the company's projects. In a sense, the entrepreneurs have borrowed against their ideas and talents, and in the process have given up a percentage of their company's anticipated profits in exchange for the money shareholders provide.

As a stock speculator, you are in business—the business of investing in other businesses through the mechanism of stocks. Shares become your inventory. When conditions are appropriate you want to add to inventory, buying more at bargain prices in order to have more to sell when prices are higher, thus increasing your total net worth. It is one more small, logical, businesslike step that, after you have purchased a widely diversified portfolio of businesses that you believe are under-valued, you borrow against your inventory of businesses—your stock portfolio—in order to optimize your profit potential.

It is sound business practice to prudently increase the variety and quantity of your inventory, especially if you can obtain bargains that will provide merchandise for profitable future sales. In terms of stock, you spread your risk among even more enterprises; the stock of each corporation may advance or decline at different times, but on average, over long periods of time, the various stocks will tend to hedge against overall losses and balance each other's positive outcomes. As the saying goes, "Buy your summer hats in winter, when they are cheap." True, you may have a slow summer or an occasional "fire sale," but on average you will obtain handsome profits from your merchandizing of stocks.

The above paragraphs describe what the use of margin—the borrowing of funds to buy additional stocks—means to me. In the beginning, when I only had a few thousand dollars and thus could only buy a few stocks, I was concerned that I wasn't sufficiently diversified. Rather than own only 5 or 6 different stocks, I would prefer to own 10 or 12 (and more). Later, even though I didn't have any more available cash, I was able to add more (different) stocks to my portfolio because of its increased market value and resulting increased buying power (50 percent of the unrealized gains) of my margin account.

Since margin worked so well for me in the beginning, when I was simply trying to increase portfolio diversification, I have come to see it as a workable practice for widely diversified portfolios of any size. My litany of margin includes the simple hypothetical example that in any given year, for any four carefully selected, undervalued stocks, one will decline, one will break even, one will do okay, and one will be a big winner. Of course, for any specific four stocks among those owned, this pattern may not occur, as all four could turn out to be losers or winners. Still, the paradigm (average for a large number of positions) is that the winner gains 100 percent (or more), the okay stock gains 25 percent, the breakeven stock gains zero, and the failed stock loses 50 percent. When the dust settles on such a scenario, we see that for every $1 invested in each stock, or $4 total, we end up with $4.75 ($2 + $1.25 + $1 + $0.50), which amounts to an 18.75 percent gain.

Thus, a cash account gain of 18.75 percent could turn into a margin account gain of 27 percent or more depending upon the level of interest rates, dividends, and leveraged employed. The more sets of "four" undervalued stocks in inventory, and more importantly, the longer these stocks are held, the more likely such superb performance will result.

The Mechanics of Margin

Here's how margin works in terms of its basics. At this time (and since 1974), you must have $2,000 in cash as a minimum amount to open a margin account with a brokerage firm. There is no charge for opening a margin account (just as there is no charge for having multiple cash accounts), but a margin agreement, spelling out the details of the account, must be signed. You should read the margin agreement carefully (it is usually in small print) in order to understand what is going on. Although I never have, you may be able to negotiate the standard margin agreement if your account is large enough (one of my clients did), altering some clauses that do not meet with your approval. Brokerage houses have somewhat differing limits affecting margin, such as the definition of a *marginable stock* and actions affecting margin (maintenance) calls.

After your margin account is approved (opened) by your broker, you may buy marginable stocks, paying only 50 percent of their cost, including brokerage commissions, in cash or equivalents such as other stock put into your account. This is called Regulation-T, promulgated by the Federal Reserve Board (FRB). Its percentage has varied over the years (see Table 5–1), but it has been at 50 percent since January 1974. If the FRB felt that speculation was too rampant it could raise the initial margin deposit required. Occasionally, an individual stock will have a 100 percent margin requirement (100 percent cash) due to its volatility, short interest (shares lent to short sellers), or pending announcement or investigation.

A marginable stock is generally any common stock listed on any major stock exchange plus a large number of over-the-counter stocks that have been designated

Table 5-1. Initial Margin Deposit Required (Market Value %, Effective Date)

	3/11/68	6/8/68	5/6/70	12/6/71	11/24/72	1/3/74
Margin stocks/short sales	70	80	65	55	65	50
Convertible bonds	50	60	50	50	50	50

as marginable by the Federal Reserve Board. There are varying limits as to which stocks a brokerage house will margin. Some brokerages require stocks to trade at $5 per share or more, while others will margin down to $3 per share. Still other brokerages will require a minimum $3 per share equity on stocks trading at $10 per share or less.

Thus, if you have $10,000 in cash, you could buy up to $20,000 of marginable stocks (including commissions) because the broker will lend you up to $10,000, or 50 percent of the market value of the purchased shares, which are held by the broker as collateral. Your shares must be held in your account in "street name," while you retain voting rights and receive dividends. Most margin agreements permit the broker to lend stock held in street name to others for short sales, but all this is opaque to you and does not affect your account. Another name for your loan on the broker's books is *debit balance*. The broker debits your account for any funds withdrawn or borrowed, and credits your account with any cash, dividends, or proceeds received.

Advantages of Using Margin

If, for example, your $20,000 stock portfolio should increase in market value 20 percent, thus appreciating $4,000, that would represent a 40 percent gain on your original $10,000 equity. This is an unrealized gain in terms of tax consequences and is untaxed until and unless the positions are sold. Your market value would then be $24,000, your debit (loan) would remain unchanged at $10,000 (plus applied margin interest), and your equity would increase to $14,000 (plus dividends, less margin interest). Your account would then have $2,000 excess equity (the amount of equity in excess of Reg-T 50 percent). Your broker, at your request, could send to you up to $2,000 in cash (usually that day if ordered early enough, before the closing of the broker's cashier window). Or you could choose to use your $2,000 excess equity to purchase $4,000 worth of stock (including commissions).

Not only does your margin account permit you to leverage stock positions, it also permits you—without delay—to borrow for any purpose whatsoever up to your line of credit (loan value) which is based on 50 percent of the market value of your marginable shares. Furthermore, the margin interest charged for this collateralized loan is probably the lowest percentage you could obtain anywhere.

Increased (and increasing) buying power generated by an appreciating stock portfolio can be a very important aspect of portfolio management that is not always understood by the majority of investors. If yours is a *cash account* (where all transactions are settled for cash by the third business day) and it increased 20 percent in market value, you'd also have a 20 percent unrealized gain. But you are not able to use this gain in order to buy other stocks unless you sell some shares to realize the gain, to raise cash for the new purchases. When you sell profitable shares, you cre-ate a tax liability and thus have fewer dollars available for reinvesting, at least at tax time. If you want to replace the sold shares with other shares costing the same amount, you can enter a same day trade, but you still create a tax liability.

Otherwise, if you need cash to meet an emergency, the proceeds from any sales in a cash account are usually not available for withdrawal for three trading days (potentially five calendar days with an intervening weekend, plus any inter-vening market holiday). The unrealized gain becomes a realized gain creating its tax liability, and the sold stock is no longer available to appreciate further (or to decline in price, for that matter).

If you like all the stocks in your cash account portfolio and have no invest-ment reason to sell any of them, you will nevertheless have to choose which to eliminate if you need some cash or want to buy other stocks and do not have addi-tional cash to pay for them. However, with a margined account you often can leave your undervalued stocks undisturbed and still add other promising shares, using the buying power created by portfolio appreciation or accumulated dividends.

Disadvantages of Using Margin

There is no free lunch on Wall Street. Well, hardly any. Margined or leveraged stock results cut two ways. Just as a 25 percent increase in the market price of a portfolio yields a 50 percent increase in its equity—at the 50 percent margined level—so a 25 percent decline in market price would result in a 50 percent decline in equity at the same margined level. This leverage can lead to even greater destruc-tion on rare occasions such as the Crash of October '87 or the Selloff of '90.

Some market observers have commented that a leveraged position carries trad-ing commissions that one would avoid by buying stocks with cash alone. This seems a niggling criticism to me, because one would want to have enough cash to buy those additional stock positions and to pay those commissions. Saying that buying on margin increases one's commission expense is almost like saying mak-ing profits increases one's income tax. I await the happy day when I must pay $1,000,000 in taxes on margined gains. The additional commissions for additional stocks are a minor percentage of the cost basis for the stocks and of the net pro-ceeds received from their sale.

Another criticism of using margin is the interest expense that accrues relent-lessly, month after month, increasing one's debit balance and liability. Well, there's no free dessert on Wall Street, either. I, and many businesspersons, would willingly incur a 6 to 9 percent interest cost in order to buy something expected to appreciate 18 percent, for a net 9 to 13 percent gain per year, after interest expenses. The downside is, even if my portfolio breaks even in terms of its market value, I might be down 3 to 4.4 percent or more. Much of one's margin interest expense is covered by one's dividends, especially since there are twice as many dividends in the 50 percent margined portfolio, with only half the portfolio subject to margin interest.

The Dreaded Margin Call

Leveraged declines bring us to the famous subject of *margin calls*. A "Reg-T call" is actually the initial Regulation-T requirement (or original margin call for 50 percent cash payment) previously mentioned. When most people refer to margin calls due to declining market values, they mean *maintenance calls*. As part of the agreement to lend up to 50 percent of the market value of the marginable stocks in your portfolio, the broker requires you to maintain a certain equity level (ownership amount) in relation to the market price of your margined stocks.

The New York Stock Exchange mandates that brokers do not permit equity levels to fall below 25 percent of market value, but many brokerages have a "traditional" 30 percent minimum level and some have higher requirements and special conditions, especially instituted after the spectacular maintenance calls generated by the Crash of '87. You should be aware of minimum maintenance levels (from here on simply called *maintenance* or *margin*) and the potential calls for additional equity based on them, because they really can undermine a margined account at a crucial time.

Say you bought $100,000 worth of stock, putting up $50,000 in cash, and the market went against you, so that later your market value had declined to $70,000. Alas, you would have suffered $30,000 in unrealized losses, as the accountants say. Remember, unrealized does not mean unreal, although the euphemistic term *paper losses* is widely used. The slogan, "You haven't lost anything until you sell" (while true as far as the Internal Revenue is concerned) reflects the potentially dangerous idea that somehow so-called paper losses are not real, especially when they create maintenance calls.

In this hypothetical example, your equity has shrunk (how's that for a euphemism?) to $20,000. But you are required to maintain your equity at 30 percent of your current market value. Thirty percent of your $70,000 portfolio is $21,000—$1,000 more than your actual remaining equity. At this time, your broker would telephone (rarely if ever at midnight), write, or telegraph you "requesting" at least $1,000 to bring your account into compliance with its maintenance requirement. If you do not come up with the $1,000 in cash or deposit fully paid certificates of marginable securities into the account, your broker may liquidate enough of your account to meet its maintenance requirement.

Stock portfolio maintenance calls often strike terror in the hearts of the uninitiated. A margin call can give rise to visions of being "sold out" and losing everything. To the sophisticated margin user, a maintenance call need not be a big deal. After all, you borrowed some money and the broker wants you to pay back a portion of it. That is the rational and healthy way to react to a maintenance call. Nor will you be sold out completely if you fail to come up with the cash in time (assuming your portfolio is not "underwater," that is, with no remaining equity). You may select the shares to be sold, or let your broker make that decision if you are unavailable or too traumatized to make the selection. I would suggest that you make the selection, taking profits or losses in the least currently undervalued stocks.

Meeting a maintenance call by selling stock can be shocking when you realize that you will have to sell about three and one-third times as much stock as the amount of the maintenance call because you now "own" less than 30 cents on the dollar of the stock in your portfolio. Thus, it might be better if you could meet the call with cash, especially if you do not want to part with many of the shares in your portfolio likely to be deeply depressed and undervalued. Unnecessarily selling stocks generates brokerage commissions and tax consequences. Conversely, it may be a good thing to prune the portfolio a bit and let go of your least undervalued stocks. When the market turns up you can buy them again, or other stocks, with the increased buying power generated by increasing market prices and the credits developed in the Special Miscellaneous Account (SMA) (reviewed later).

Although a 30 percent or greater drop in the market value of one's fully margined portfolio is a terrible setback, it is *not* the end of the world, nor the end of one's potentially successful speculating career. In a widely diversified portfolio of well-selected, undervalued stocks, which is managed with an eye for major declining markets, the likelihood of the total portfolio dropping 30 percent is not all that great. Obviously it can happen, as evidenced by the Crash of '87 when the Dow Jones Industrial Average declined 36.13 percent in eight weeks, from 2722.42 on August 25 to 1738.74 on October 19.

Consider the possibility of a 30 percent drop in the DJIA from, for example, the 4700 level, which would mean 1410 points, to DJIA 3290. While such a decline might again occur, it might take several months, and could be recognized before it had gone very far. The margined speculator should be able to take defensive moves, such as insuring short-term protection with stock index put options (see comments in Chapter 8), getting off margin, or reducing total stock exposure. As the market declined and one's equity level declined below 50 percent (or 40 percent for a more aggressive speculator), cash (if available) could be added or stocks sold to bring the equity levels up to 40 to 50 percent or higher, thus avoiding the trauma of having forced liquidations under the pressure of maintenance calls in a turbulent market selloff.

Margin Requirements and Negotiability

Most people refer to margin as the amount of cash one borrows from the brokerage company against the market price of a stock portfolio, but that can be confusing. Technically, margin refers to the percentage of cash or equity that must be deposited when stocks are purchased. Otherwise marginable stocks that are currently *restricted* require "100 percent margin"—100 percent cash. Current Reg-T is for 50 percent margin, thus requiring 50 percent cash. If the market gets too speculative in the view of the Federal Reserve, they may change the initial margin requirement from 50 to 60 percent (or more), which would mean that 60 percent (or more) cash would be required; thus, 40 percent (or less) would be the maximum initial brokerage loan.

Because of the conventional use of the word "margin" and its technical denotation, confusion often arises when discussing the degree of margin in a margined account. If I say I am 100 percent margined, I probably mean that I am fully margined and have used up all my buying (borrowing) power, rather than that I have paid 100 percent cash for all my positions. This imprecise meaning conflicts with the definition of margin as the percentage of cash required.

If I say I am 60 percent margined, I might commonly be understood to mean that I have used up 60 percent of my loan value, or that my equity equals 60 percent of my market value. For example, if my market value is $100,000, my initial loan value is $50,000, 60 percent of which is $30,000. With a $30,000 debit (loan), my equity is $70,000—70 percent of my market value. It gets confusing. With a 70 percent equity-to-market value level, one has used 60 percent of the loan value. To avoid such confusion it is probably best to always refer to one's equity percentage level (for this example, "I am at 70 percent equity").

Since margin applies to the entire marginable portfolio—which is held in a margin account, as distinct from other stocks that are held in a cash account—one need not worry about any particular stock declining 30 percent or more and requiring a maintenance call for that one position. One might have to watch an equity level that will fall below the required minimum $2,000, but by then we probably should not be "on margin" at all.

The margin leverage user incurs interest expense on borrowed funds, just as you do borrowing from a bank. The margin interest rate is probably the lowest rate an individual could find for borrowing funds. Margin interest is usually based on the *broker loan* or *call money* rates (interchangeable terms), plus an additional percentage. The call money rate is usually slightly below the prime rate, but depending upon the size of the loan or the amount of commissions generated annually in your portfolio, the brokerage house will add from 0 percent to 3 percent on top of the current call money interest rate.

The call money rate changes from time to time depending upon the relatively frequent fluctuations of short-term interest rates. If you do not pay your margin interest each month with cash, the accrued interest will increase your debit balance (what you owe your broker). The accumulating margin interest will have its own compounding effect over the months and years unless offset by stock dividend income retained in your account. By not withdrawing my dividend income, I keep my margin interest (and debit balance) under more control.

Although I do not pay my margin interest or debit balance monthly, or even yearly, I have suggested making a payment of one's margin interest for the year by check just before the end of the year to establish to the Internal Revenue Service that the interest expense was incurred and paid during the taxable year. Few people do this, and I know personally of no cases where the IRS has disallowed a margin interest deduction as reflected on one's monthly brokerage statements, but I've been told more than once that for safety's sake it is a good practice. I have also been told by CPAs that such an exercise is unnecessary, that they know of no cases of disallowal of margin interest even though it hadn't been specifically paid during the taxable year. You can always "borrow" this payment back by having the broker send you the equivalent amount early in the next year, assuming your account remains above its maintenance level. Thus, you would not be out of pocket for more than a few days while establishing a paper trail of expense and payment, ready to present your cancelled check if audited.

Margin interest rates may be negotiable. Many people today pay higher margin interest rates than they would if they bargained with their brokers. Full-service and discount brokers may show you a schedule based upon amount of debt or volume of trading, but you can cut through this "boilerplate" sometimes by negotiation. For instance, on a $50,000 debit balance, upon which you are being charged 2 percent over call money, you can ask to have your margin interest at 1 percent or 1/2 percent above call, which happens to be a currently competitive percentage at some discount brokerages.

If your broker says he or she can't give you lower rates, suggest that you might move your account. In the face of losing both your margin interest business, which is a big profit center for most brokerages, plus the commissions your account generates, your broker or the branch manager may reconsider. Or, you may choose to shop for a better deal in the very competitive climate of stock brokers who need clients more than the other way around. After all, there is no need for you to pay hundreds or thousands of dollars extra each year in margin interest just because of a published schedule or an unchallenged, quoted standard figure.

Usually margin interest charges are not (and need not be) paid until you are ready to get off margin or to close the account. In theory, the margin debt is callable, and you should carefully read the margin agreement papers you will have to sign in order to use margin, so that you are aware of the possibilities. However, in the past 18 years, working with a great number of brokers, I have never had or heard of a margin debit called, except to meet the minimum maintenance requirement. Still, the invoking of the call provision is a remote possibility, especially if we have a devastating market crash and the brokerage house itself (or its lender) must raise cash.

Special Memorandum Account (SMA)

SMA is an abbreviation for *special memorandum account* (or special miscellaneous account), a sometimes complicated accounting for certain credit and debit amounts. For several years I thought SMA meant "surplus" in the margin account. I got this idea because brokers told me that the cash available for withdrawing from my accounts was based on my SMA. SMA and *cash available* are often—but not always—the same, especially as there can be "false SMA" credits in your margin accounting. This paradox will be explained in due course.

Before reviewing the intricacies of margined accounts and SMA, let us cover some of the basic ideas and terminology. I've already mentioned market value (MV), which is the value of the account according to the previous day's closing market prices of each item. Accounts are *marked-to-market* (valued at current market prices) daily. In a cash account, the market value of your holdings plus any cash credits amount to your *equity* (EQ), or *net asset value* (NAV).

The following review (and Tables 5–2 through 5–8) refer only to *long margin accounts*. Buying long is the basic transaction of buying a stock to own it, in expectation of selling it later at a higher price in order to realize a capital gain. Do not confuse short selling accounting with long margin accounting. *Selling short*—which requires a margin account and has specific limitations of its own—is the process of having your broker borrow shares of a stock you do not own so that you can sell them in the expectation of replacing them with a later, "covering" purchase at a lower price so as to profit from the difference.

Once you start working with long margin purchases and begin borrowing, you create *debit balances* (DR), or what you owe the broker, as opposed to *credit balances* (CR), which represent what you are owed by the broker. The basic formula for portfolio valuation and ownership is MV plus CR less DR equals EQ, as illustrated in Table 5–2. Dividends increase equity by decreasing debit balances. Market price fluctuations increase or decrease market value and equity. Margin interest and cash withdrawals increase debit balances and decrease equity. When there is a debit balance, credit balances are usually journalled over to decrease the debit balance, which is why CR is not shown in Table 5–2.

Table 5–2. Portfolio Valuation and Ownership

Stocks at market value (marginable)	100,000
Debits (loans, margin interest)	(60,000)
Equity (net worth)	40,000

If your stocks are priced at $100,000 and you owe $60,000, you own the difference; therefore, your equity is $40,000.

If you were to sell the whole portfolio the next day, it is not clear that you would come away with today's $40,000 equity. First of all, portfolios are marked to closing prices rather than the bid price, which is the price you would get if you offered stock for sale, often lower than the closing price. Secondly, the market might open lower and decline sharply that day so you could find yourself selling into lower prices. Thirdly, you will have to pay trading commissions so, all in all, you might end up with 2 percent or less than you expected, based on your indicated equity of the previous day. Beside the 1 to 3 percent commissions (depending upon the number of shares traded and brokerage house commissions) deducted from the proceeds of the total portfolio's sale, a 4 percent slippage due to market declines and bid prices (quite rare) could reduce your portfolio by perhaps $4,000 and your equity by perhaps 10 percent. On the other hand, the market might rally strongly and you could cash out a bit more than today's equity.

What happens next in accounting for SMA can seem tricky. Whenever a margined portfolio receives a dividend payment, that amount is credited to both your SMA and your actual margin account. You are entitled to the dividend, and could have the brokerage house mail it to you. (Some houses only do this monthly, unless a special request is made.) But you may choose not to withdraw your dividends, preferring to let them apply against and thus diminish the debit balance (your margin loan). Letting dividends accrue helps to offset the margin interest that is applied to your account. Margin interest is computed at least monthly, but sometimes more frequently in a volatile interest-rate environment, as it is based on changes in the broker call money rates.

Clearly, if you do not have your dividends routinely forwarded to you, they are usually still available to you later upon request. But while they remain with the broker, they are credited against your debit balance. If you currently do not have a debit balance, they accrue as a credit balance, often earning money-market interest. Different brokerages have different procedures for paying interest on credit balances; some require a minimum amount or have a "sweep" policy of periodically buying money market shares with cash (credit) balances. Still, at any moment, you may withdraw those dividends that have been accounted for in your SMA, provided their withdrawal would not drive your equity below the 30 percent maintenance level (or below the $2,000 minimum).

To guard against attempting a cash withdrawal or stock purchase based on apparent SMA, which would reduce your equity to less than 30 percent—or whatever your brokerage's minimum maintenance level percentage is—a cash available amount (a.k.a. maintenance excess, firm maintenance excess, or house excess) is computed with each update of your margin account. When your maintenance excess (ME) is less than your SMA, then the ME represents all the cash you can withdraw or use for additional purchases. In other words, you will only be permitted to withdraw the lesser of SMA or maintenance excess. Hypothetical SMA-Margin Accounting Tables 5–3 through 5–8 present examples of the accounting for a set of possible margin account transactions. I will use consistent, comparative examples based on the beginning condition in Table 5–3.

Table 5–3 shows the details of the initial transaction. After the first 12 months, assuming (for simplicity's sake) no change in market value, the effects of margin interest expense (not paid) and dividend income (not withdrawn) would be as shown in Table 5–4.

Thus, this hypothetical account after the first 12 months, assuming no trades, change in market value, cash additions or withdrawals, but accounting for margin interest expense (not paid) and dividend income (not withdrawn) would be as represented in Table 5–5.

Note that SMA is not reduced by margin interest expense. Posting margin interest increases one's debit balance and decreases one's equity—and one's maintenance

Table 5–3. SMA-Margin Accounting—Initial Transaction

Beginning buys/market value	$100,000
Beginning debit/broker loan	(50,000)
Beginning cash/equity	50,000
Equity/Maintenance	
50% SMA (cash available)	0

Table 5–4. Effects of Dividend Income and Interest Expense—12 Months Later

Margin interest expense @8%	(4,000)	(to debit balance)
Dividend interest income @3%	3,000	(from all stocks)
Net increase in debit balance	(1,000)	

Table 5–5. Portfolio Valuation and Ownership—12 Months Later

Portfolio market value	100,000	
Debit balance	(51,000)	Net increase $1,000
Account equity	49,000	Equity/Maintenance 49.0%
SMA (cash available)	3,000	Dividend accrual to account/SMA

excess and borrowing power. However, once a credit has been posted to SMA, such as a dividend or proceeds from the sale of stock or cash added to the portfolio, that credit can only be decreased by a cash withdrawal or by using SMA credits for the purchase of stock. The dividends received remain available as long as maintenance excess is sufficient. If one had withdrawn the $3,000 worth of dividends, the debit balance would have increased to $54,000 and equity decreased to $46,000.

Although one needn't wait any given period of time, let's see what might happen to our hypothetical margin account by the end of the first year. Assuming the portfolio had appreciated 20 percent in market value, and no dividends had been withdrawn, the overall margin account would be represented by Table 5–6.

In theory, you should be able to borrow at least 50 percent of the portfolio's gains, as each time the portfolio is marked-to-market (priced at market value) any "excess equity" is journalled to its SMA, as are all dividends and cash payments received. SMA is computed based on the greater of market value times 50 percent plus or minus your (credit or debit) balance, or previous SMA. In practice, a brokerage may say it will only lend you 50 percent of the current market value of your margin account. In Table 5–6, your maximum allowed loan value is $60,000, but since you already owe $51,000 (see Table 5–5), you would be permitted to withdraw only $9,000, based on loan value plus your $3,000 dividend credit in SMA.

Or, looking at the account from the point of view of equity, you are required to have $60,000 in equity ($120,000 times 50 percent, the Reg-T percentage). As you actually have $69,000 in equity, your account has $9,000 "excess equity" available for you to use, plus dividends accrued.

Some brokerages have rules that do not permit SMA payouts if your equity is below a certain minimum maintenance level, such as 35 to 40 percent. No brokerage house will pay SMA if to do so would drive the account below its minimum maintenance levels of 30 percent (or 35 percent, for example, at Charles Schwab). Note that you can draw out the full $12,000 in the SMA without having to sell any stocks or otherwise disturb the portfolio. Table 5–7 shows how your account would look if you did drain it of its SMA.

One might take all the SMA available to meet an emergency, to pay for a vacation, or to purchase additional stocks. If the brokerage calculates the SMA at $12,000, then you could buy another $24,000 worth of stock, based on the initial 50 percent Regulation-T limit for the new purchase. Assuming we were very

Table 5–6. Effect of a 20% Market Appreciation

Portfolio market value	120,000	20% market gain
Debit balance	(51,000)	Net increase $1,000
Account equity	69,000	Equity/Maintenance 57.5%
SMA (cash available)	12,000	(see review in text)

aggressive (believing our selected stocks and the market undervalued and in a long-term uptrend), we might use most or all of the buying power (true SMA times two) for augmenting the portfolio. Note that buying power is usually twice the SMA, unless using the apparent SMA would drive the account below its broker-age's maintenance level. Thus, at the end of the first year, if we spent our $12,000 SMA to buy $24,000 worth of stock, Table 5–6 would look like Table 5–8.

For the seasoned margin user, spending appreciated (but unrealized) gains to buy more stock that brings one back toward a 50 percent margined level need be no more dangerous than the original decision to become fully margined, assuming similar propitious market and valuation conditions continue to exist. Some people, who probably are averse to borrowing in any event, would claim that you are risking more than your original equity, because now (Table 5–8) you owe $75,000 instead of $51,000—the original $50,000 plus $1,000 more margin expense than dividend income plus $24,000 in additional stock purchased. In absolute terms you have more capital at risk, but in relative terms you remain near the original percentage risk. As I often point out, speculating in the stock market is a process of percentages. Furthermore, you should have greater diversification, thus spreading the risk.

SMA accounting can be confusing because of its double nature. When you draw funds out of your margined account, those amounts reduce equity, increase the debit balance, and reduce SMA. The tricky part of SMA accounting is that it *exists independently* of the actual debit balances affecting the equity in your margin account.

To review, if you begin a margin account with $50,000 cash, both your margin account and your SMA register $50,000. If you buy $100,000 worth of stocks with that $50,000 cash credit—using that $50,000 worth of SMA—your SMA is debited $50,000, thus leaving you with zero SMA. Of course, your equity is $50,000 and the market value of your portfolio is $100,000, but you have no more buying power

Table 5–7. Portfolio Valuation and Ownership after SMA Payout

Portfolio value	120,000	
Debit balance	(63,000)	Borrowed additional $12,000
Account Equity	57,000	Equity/Maintenance 47.5%
SMA (cash available)	0	Exhausted

Table 5–8. Effect of Using SMA to Purchase Additional Stocks on Margin

Portfolio value	144,000	Bought $24,000 more stock
Debit balance	(75,000)	Borrowed $24,000 more
Account equity	69,000	Equity/Maintenance 47.9%
SMA (cash available)	0	Exhausted

(excess equity) at that time. If during the course of a year $3,000 in dividends were paid in (credited) to your account, and $4,000 in margin interest charges were debited, and there was no change in the market value of your portfolio, you would then have $49,000 in equity, but also $3,000 in SMA. If you drew out your $3,000 (dividends) in SMA, you would then have $54,000 in margin debit, $46,000 in equity, and no SMA.

If by year's end your portfolio advanced 20 percent in market value, it would be worth $120,000. You would have a $20,000 unrealized gain, on which you might borrow another $10,000 or so depending upon the brokerage house. In Table 5–6, to be conservative, you can borrow $9,000, given that your debit balance had increased by $1,000 due to its $4,000 margin interest charge less $3,000 received in dividends. Thus, your SMA would now show $9,000 from appreciation plus $3,000 from dividends, which means you could draw out $12,000 for any purpose.

In doing so, you would increase your debit balance by $12,000 (Table 5–7). If you decided to use that $12,000 to buy $24,000 worth of stock, you would be borrowing an additional $24,000 from the broker—the $12,000 cash loan from SMA and another $12,000 loan based on 50 percent of the value of the newly bought stock—so your account would look like Table 5–8, with a debit balance of $75,000. This $75,000 represents the $12,000 cash drawn out plus the additional $12,000 borrowed, or $24,000 added to your year-end $51,000 debit balance. Of course, you would now have $144,000 worth of stock working for (or against) you. You might call this use of leverage *pyramiding* your unrealized gains.

A Visit to the Downside

However, if during the course of this hypothetical year the market value of your portfolio decreased by 28 percent, to $72,000 (instead of increasing by 20 percent to $120,000 as in Table 5–6), then you would have only $21,000 in equity—below the minimum maintenance level of 30 percent equity to market value, that is, facing a maintenance call. Even though your SMA still showed $3,000 (from the dividends), you would not be able to withdraw it because you have no firm excess. Under these conditions, the $3,000 SMA in your margin account would be "False SMA," unavailable for withdrawal or as buying power. Using the year-end figures from Tables 5–4 and 5–5, accounting for dividends and margin interest, the account would look like Table 5–9.

Given the configuration in Table 5–9, your maintenance call should be $600, because 30 percent of $72,000 is $21,600, and you have only $21,000 in equity. Note that, as your debit balance builds up due to unpaid margin interest, it takes less than a 30 percent portfolio decline to exceed your minimum maintenance requirement. (More about meeting maintenance calls a little later.)

Table 5-9. Effect of a 28% Portfolio Depreciation

Portfolio market value	72,000	28% capital loss	
Debit balance	(51,000)	Net increase $1,000	
Account equity	21,000	Equity/Maintenance 29.2%	
False SMA (not available)	3,000	Dividend accrual	

Even false SMA has potential future value. If your portfolio thereafter appreciated in market value from $72,000, say to $80,000, then your equity would also increase $8,000, from $21,600 (including the $600 maintenance call payment) to $29,600 and you could withdraw the $3,000 (of formerly false SMA) still in SMA plus the $600 payment, freed by sufficient market appreciation. In this example, a market value of $80,000 requires at least $24,000 in equity for minimum maintenance. Your renewed $29,600 equity—maintenance level 37 percent—would become $26,000 after withdrawing the $3,600 in SMA, leaving your equity at 32.5 percent of market value (see Table 5–10).

Many brokerage houses will not pay out SMA on accounts below 35 percent equity, but some do. Actually, Charles Schwab requires a minimum firm maintenance of 35 percent, so many of these examples would have to be recalculated for a Charles Schwab margin account or other brokerages which have higher than 30 percent firm maintenance levels. Of course, at 32.5 percent of equity you are very close to a maintenance call if your portfolio should take even a small dip.

Methodically, you could use this $3,600 to buy $7,200 more in stocks. Updating Table 5–10, the changes would make the portfolio look like what is shown in Table 5–11.

Of course, your portfolio at 33.9 percent maintenance level would be somewhat vulnerable to a maintenance call. Its market value would only have to drop

Table 5-10. A Small Market Appreciation Returns SMA

Portfolio value	80,000	Appreciation of $8,000
Debit Balance	(50,400)	Maintenance payment $600
Account equity	29,600	Equity/Maintenance 37.0%
SMA (cash available)	3,600	Dividends plus maintenance payment

Table 5-11. Effect of a Subsequent Small Margined Purchase

Portfolio value	87,200	Bought $7,200 more stock
Debit balance	(57,600)	Increased $7,200
Account equity	29,600	Equity/Maintenance 33.9%
SMA (cash available)	0	Used $3,600 to buy stocks

$4,900 to put your equity at its 30 percent minimum maintenance. At such times, you must be very careful that your broker does not require that you bring your equity up to a 35 percent (or higher) maintenance level when your equity falls below 30 percent of your market value—a policy of some brokerages.

Such a policy can spell trouble when working on the edge with margin. Suddenly, for example, if the portfolio in Table 5–11 declined $5,000, instead of having to come up with $60 (30 percent of $82,200 = $24,660, less equity of $24,600, leaves the portfolio $60 below minimum maintenance) to meet a maintenance call at the 30 percent level, you would need to come up with $4,170 (35 percent of $82,200 = $28,770 less $24,600 equity leaves this portfolio $4,170 below minimum maintenance). And, if you didn't have the cash or fully owned marginable stock to add, you would have to sell 3 1/3 times as much stock (about $13,761 worth) because your equity (ownership) is only 30 percent of the market value of the stock in your margin account.

Such a maintenance call condition could occur at or near a market bottom, when you "should" be buying deeply undervalued stocks rather than having to sell them. The forced sale of stock also creates additional commissions and tax consequences, while the diminished portfolio reduces your chance for a rapid comeback when the market turns up. For these reasons, I have made it a policy not to have my account with a brokerage that has a jump to a higher equity (minimum maintenance level) after a minimum maintenance call is issued, as I did in 1987. Make it your policy, too!

Even if the brokerage does raise the required equity level to 35 percent after a maintenance call, you may be able to negotiate this policy, especially if you have a large, widely diversified portfolio. If you do negotiate such arrangements, be sure to get them in ironclad writing, as brokers have a way of changing conditions *post hoc*, without prior notice. With a widely diversified, margin account portfolio, the overall decline is not as likely to be as sharp as that of a "portfolio" of two or three stocks that could each quickly decline over 30 percent in market price during a strong setback.

There is another generally unperceived vulnerability in margined portfolios in a declining market. For a stock to be margined, most brokerages require that it must trade at $5 a share or more. At some brokerages, stocks that fall below $10 per share must have a $3 minimum maintenance (equity) per share, not 30 percent. Table 5–12 shows how Merrill Lynch carried low-priced stocks in margin accounts.

At other brokerages, otherwise "marginable" stocks that fall below $5 per share are immediately journalled from the margin to the cash account and required to have 100 percent margin—that is, their minimum maintenance is 100 percent cash. Thus, they have no loan value, so they no longer count as equity toward the maintenance level of your margined portfolio. These potentially substantial withdrawals of

Table 5–12. Merrill Lynch Equity Requirements on Low-Priced Stocks in Margin Accounts

Stock	Value	Minimum	Required Equity
100 shares @ $12 per share	$1,200	$360	30%
100 shares @ $8 per share	800	300	$3 per share
100 shares @ $2 per share	200	200	100%

"loan value" can really add to the rapid decline in your margin account's equity maintenance level in a market selloff.

Suppose your margined portfolio has $100,000 market value and $50,000 equity, with 20 positions (stocks) of about $5,000 each, but five of those stocks have a market price just over $5 per share (say they are trading at an average $6 per share). If the market and in turn your portfolio should suffer a 20 percent decline, you might not expect a maintenance call because you might presume the accounting would be as shown in Table 5–13.

But if those five positions averaging $6 per share declined to under $5 per share, some $20,000 or so worth of stocks less than $5 per share could be journalled out of the margin account into the cash account, requiring 100 percent margin (no loan value). Such a margin account would then look like Table 5–14.

Ouch! You would have to come up with $8,000 in cash or sell over $26,000 worth of margined stock to bring the maintenance level to its 30 percent level. Of course, now that those stocks under $5 are in the cash account, you would get dollar-for-dollar when selling them because they are not margined and represent their full market price. Still, you could be forced to liquidate much more stock than you expected or wanted to, given this scenario.

We can foresee several problems and possible solutions to this potential for a margined account to be quickly driven below maintenance level, especially if

Table 5–13. Presumed Normal Effect of a 20% Decline in Market Value

Portfolio value	80,000	Declined $20,000
Debit balance	(50,000)	Unchanged
Account Equity	30,000	Equity/Maintenance 37.5%

Table 5–14. Potential Effect of a 20% Decline in Some Low-Priced Stocks

Total portfolio value	80,000	
Margin account value	60,000	$20,000 to cash account
Debit balance	(50,000)	Unchanged
Margin account equity	10,000	Equity/Maintenance 16.7%

many of the margined stocks are likely to be driven below marginable price minimums into the nonmargined (cash) account. One way to minimize problems would be to have only stocks trading for more than $10 per share in your margin account. You could request that all stocks under $10 per share be held in your cash account, even though they are marginable. This arrangement could be awkward and counterproductive in a rising market, as perfectly solid stocks trading just below your cutoff—but well above their marginable cutoff price—would be unavailable for their market-value buying power in the margin account.

Another strategy, undoubtedly better, is to make sure that you have either a cash reserve or line of credit sufficient to meet maintenance calls (even perhaps to pay off the total debit, thus converting your margin account into a cash account). Better yet, carefully monitor your equity level and do not allow it to fall below 40 percent, especially if the market looks vulnerable to a serious tumble.

The Best Defense May Be a Good Offense

One technique to protect your margin account against maintenance calls is to buy more stock, either paying all cash or the 50 percent initial required margin. If you buy more stock in a margined portfolio for cash, you raise your equity level by the amount of the new stock. Suppose you had cash available and were willing to commit another $15,000 to your portfolio. If you paid down your debit balance by $15,000 (see Table 5–11) to $42,600, your equity would become $44,600 and thus be 51.1 percent of the $87,200 market value. However, if you bought $15,000 worth of new shares for cash, you would raise your equity to 43.6 percent of market value (see Table 5–15). This kind of result would apply proportionately to any margin account's maintenance level.

But if you determined that the market was turning up and not only did you want to avoid a maintenance call due to a temporary dip, but also wanted to take advantage of the impending or current rally, you might buy $30,000 worth of stock with the available $15,000 additional cash commitment. In this example, even though you borrowed another $15,000 in order to buy $30,000 in stock, by adding the $15,000 in cash you still were able to raise your equity level to 38.1 percent, even as you owed and owned more. Revising Table 5–11, Table 5–16 shows how the account would look.

Table 5–15. Effect of Buying Additional Shares for Cash (refer to Table 5–11)

Portfolio value	102,200	Bought $15,000 shares for cash
Debit balance	(57,600)	Unchanged
Account equity	44,600	Equity/Maintenance 43.6%
SMA (cash available)	15,000	$15,000 added to portfolio

While your margin account might still be vulnerable at 38.1 percent equity, that is a big improvement over the previous 33.9 percent level, and you have more stock working for (or against) you. Actually. you also have a little less leverage working against you in a down market with 38.1 percent equity than with 33.9 percent. Still, your margined portfolio could then decline about $13,500 (11.5 percent) before violating its 30 percent maintenance level.

In all the above examples, one would have to consider the effects of the periodic posting of margin interest, which increases the debit balance and decreases equity and, on the other hand, the effect of posting dividends (or cash infusions), which decrease the debit balance and increase equity. Unless there is an intra-month change in the broker loan rate (call money plus broker's premium), monthly margin interest charges are usually posted to the account once a month, although their daily accrual is kept track of by a month-to-date interest figure. If a margin interest charge of $544.50 (in Table 5–17, 0.75 percent of $72,600 when that was its debit balance) were posted to the account near its 30 percent maintenance level, that reduction in equity and increase in debit balance would trigger a maintenance call. As these debits are posted, they could build up, so that even if the vulnerable portfolio wasn't driven into a maintenance call due to lower market prices, a maintenance call might still occur due to the account's increasing debit balance.

A Hidden Benefit—Carry Forward SMA Credits

Meanwhile, having seen how SMA works, and even how you can have false SMA, you should be aware that if you had to sell stocks to meet a maintenance call, 50 percent of the proceeds from those sales would be credited to your SMA as they go to pay down the debit balance. Even if such SMA credits can't be withdrawn or used because your account is still at or below the 30 to 35 percent maintenance

Table 5–16. Effect of Purchasing Additional Stocks on Margin (refer to Table 5–11)

Portfolio value	117,200	Bought another $30,000
Debit balance	(72,600)	Borrowed additional $15,000
Account equity	44,600	Equity/Maintenance 38.1%
SMA (cash available)	9,440	Equity less 30% maintenance

Table 5–17. Effect of a Subsequent 11.5% Decline in Portfolio Value

Portfolio value	103,700	Declined 11.5%
Debit balance	(72,600)	Unchanged from Table 5–16
Account equity	31,100	Equity/Maintenance 30.0%

level, these SMA credits are not lost and may be of strategic value later, as the market value of your portfolio increases. We've already seen how this works with dividends "locked up" in false (unavailable) SMA.

Assuming one did reach the sad state of being at or near 30 percent equity, there is a potential silver lining. When the market turns up—which it always has, sooner or later—and your portfolio begins to advance, every dollar increase in market value carries the leverage to result in a 3 1/3 increase in equity, because each dollar of stock you control represents only 30 cents of your equity at the outset. Now, instead of the 50 percent or 2-to-1 leverage of the initial margined position, you are at 30 percent or 3 1/3-to-1 leverage in your current margined position. If your portfolio advanced 20 percent in market price from its 30 percent equity level (Table 5–17), you would get the effect shown in Table 5–18.

SMA would have accumulated from accrued dividends not withdrawn and from the previous sale of stocks. If your broker permitted you to use all your SMA as long as your equity remained above 30 percent maintenance, you could then use your maintenance excess to buy more stocks, although at the 41.6 percent level that might be imprudent, as any more purchases would drive your equity closer to the minimum maintenance level and another potential maintenance call. Still, you could begin to buy some stocks with SMA, especially if your portfolio's value continued to appreciate.

Either with or without additional margined stock purchases, the long-suffering margin account that has withstood the ravages of a strong market decline and survives at just above the 30 percent maintenance level can be well positioned to participate fully in the next market rally. For the aggressive speculator using margin, additional positions can be bought as increases in market value first release false SMA and later provide additional new SMA (when equity moves above 50 percent of market value), which translates into excess maintenance equity and new buying power.

The Great Potential of Pyramiding

Buying additional shares through the use of increased buying power is a form of pyramiding. Some use the term *pyramiding* to refer to "averaging up," that is, buying more shares of a stock—either with cash or margin buying power—as the stock's price increases. That is not the sense in which we use it here. You can pyramid your

Table 5–18. Effect of a Subsequent 20% Appreciation in Portfolio Value

Portfolio value	124,440	103,700 × 20% increase
Debit balance	(72,600)	Unchanged from Figure 5–17
Account equity	51,840	Equity/Maintenance 41.7%
Gain on 31,100 equity	20,740	66.7% increase in equity

pre-tax paper profits (unrealized gains) to seek even greater future profits by buying more stocks. To many "investors" who find margin unduly risky, pyramiding would be even more unacceptable a practice. Notice, however, that even with the increased purchases based upon unrealized gains you could still be at a 50 percent (or higher) margined level, and at no more relative risk than at your original leveraged level.

If the original premise of wanting to own as many undervalued stocks as you can afford is valid, then pyramiding is merely a consistent application of our fundamental principle of diversification. Nevertheless, pyramiding should be used only to purchase severely undervalued stocks in a long-term bullish or neutral-trending stock market environment. Even if a portfolio represented all the sufficiently undervalued stocks our analysis can currently find, it would probably be unevenly weighted in some positions versus others. Over time, some stocks advance smartly in price and, as a percentage of the portfolio are much larger than other stocks. We could make use of margined/pyramiding buying power to add to underowned and underweighted (yet still undervalued) positions in a continuing effort to adjust and balance our widely diversified portfolios.

We have already learned about the efficacy or magic of simple compounding (Chapter 1, in the section entitled "The Miracle of Compounding"). Now we can marvel at the wizardry of pyramiding—at least when it works! We can also become alert to its dangers. In Table 1–2, we saw how various compounded, annual, reinvested returns would accumulate over the years, gaining magnitude and momentum with time. Now we can augment those figures even more by pyramiding such (unrealized) gains for even more astounding potential total returns (see Tables 5–19 and 5–20).

Of course, the pyramided returns table is theoretical (ideal) and does not include the considerable potential attrition caused by taxes. To the degree that the average holding period is very long—5 to 10 years is not unreasonable—tax consequences will be minimized somewhat, especially compared to many short-term trades on which taxes must be paid the next year. If one's reinvestment capital's profit is set back 30 to 40 percent a year in taxes, so too will compounding and pyramiding be affected. Assuming one could consistently gain a pre-tax return of 20 percent per year, then if 40 percent of this return was "lost" each year in taxes there would still be a 12 percent after-tax gain available for reinvestment, instead of the whole 20 percent at work for several years before realized gains are taxed.

If one only turned over (sold) a position every five years, the compounding and pyramiding effects would endure for five years before the effect of a setback in post-tax capital was generated. A five-year, total pre-tax compounded gain of 148.8 percent (at 20 percent per annum) would end up at 89.28 percent after being taxed at 40 percent. That works out to about 13.6 percent per year compounded after tax, compared to 12 percent after paying taxes annually. To compute and dis-

Table 5-19. Pyramiding: Beginning with $2,000 and Buying Additional Stock on Margin Only with Appreciated Gains (Note: $2,000 cash buys $4,000 stock with $2,000 borrowed.)

After Year	Mark Val	@10%	Debit	Equity	Mark Val	@12.5%	Debit	Equity	Mark Val	@15%	Debit	Equity	Mark Val	@17.5%	Debit	Equity
0	4,000		2,000	2,000	4,000		2,000	2,000	4,000		2,000	2,000	4,000		2,000	2,000
1	4,800	400	2,400	2,400	5,000	500	2,500	2,500	5,200	600	2,600	2,600	5,400	700	2,700	2,700
2	5,760	480	2,880	2,880	6,250	625	3,125	3,125	6,760	780	3,380	3,380	7,290	945	3,645	3,645
3	6,912	576	3,456	3,456	7,813	781	3,906	3,906	8,788	1,014	4,394	4,394	9,842	1,276	4,921	4,921
4	8,294	691	4,147	4,147	9,766	977	4,883	4,883	11,424	1,318	5,712	5,712	13,286	1,722	6,643	6,643
5	9,953	829	4,977	4,977	12,207	1,221	6,104	6,104	14,852	1,714	7,426	7,426	17,936	2,325	8,968	8,968
6	11,944	995	5,972	5,972	15,259	1,526	7,629	7,629	19,307	2,228	9,654	9,654	24,214	3,139	12,107	12,107
7	14,333	1,194	7,166	7,166	19,073	1,907	9,537	9,537	25,099	2,896	12,550	12,550	32,689	4,237	16,344	16,344
8	17,199	1,433	8,600	8,600	23,842	2,384	11,921	11,921	32,629	3,765	16,315	16,315	44,130	5,721	22,065	22,065
9	20,639	1,720	10,320	10,320	29,802	2,980	14,901	14,901	42,418	4,894	21,209	21,209	59,575	7,723	29,787	29,787
10	24,767	2,064	12,383	12,383	37,253	3,725	18,626	18,626	55,143	6,363	27,572	27,572	80,426	10,426	40,213	40,213
11	29,720	2,477	14,860	14,860	46,566	4,657	23,283	23,283	71,686	8,272	35,843	35,843	108,575	14,075	54,288	54,288
12	35,664	2,972	17,832	17,832	58,208	5,821	29,104	29,104	93,192	10,753	46,596	46,596	146,577	19,001	73,288	73,288
13	42,797	3,566	21,399	21,399	72,760	7,276	36,380	36,380	121,150	13,979	60,575	60,575	197,879	25,651	98,939	98,939
14	51,357	4,280	25,678	25,678	90,949	9,095	45,475	45,475	157,495	18,173	78,748	78,748	267,136	34,629	133,568	133,568
15	61,628	5,136	30,814	30,814	113,687	11,369	56,843	56,843	204,744	23,624	102,372	102,372	360,634	46,749	180,317	180,317
16	73,954	6,163	36,977	36,977	142,109	14,211	71,054	71,054	266,167	30,712	133,083	133,083	486,856	63,111	243,428	243,428
17	88,744	7,395	44,372	44,372	177,636	17,764	88,818	88,818	346,017	39,925	173,008	173,008	657,255	85,200	328,628	328,628
18	106,493	8,874	53,247	53,247	222,045	22,204	111,022	111,022	449,822	51,902	224,911	224,911	887,295	115,020	443,647	443,647
19	127,792	10,649	63,896	63,896	277,556	27,756	138,778	138,778	584,768	67,473	292,384	292,384	1,197,848	155,277	598,924	598,924
20	153,350	12,779	76,675	76,675	346,945	34,694	173,472	173,472	760,199	87,715	380,099	380,099	1,617,094	209,623	808,547	808,547
		74,675		0.2000		171,472		0.2500		378,099		0.3000		806,547		0.3500

Table 5-20. Pyramiding: Beginning with $2,000, Adding $2,000 Each Year Plus Full Margin Leverage
(Note: $2,000 cash buys $4,000 stock with $2,000 borrowed)

After Year	Mark Val	@10%	Debit	Equity	Mark Val	@12.5%	Debit	Equity	Mark Val	@15%	Debit	Equity	Mark Val	@17.5%	Debit	Equity
0	4,000		2,000	2,000	4,000		2,000	2,000	4,000		2,000	2,000	4,000		2,000	2,000
1	6,800	400	3,400	3,400	7,000	500	3,500	3,500	7,200	600	3,600	3,600	7,400	700	2,700	4,700
2	10,160	680	5,080	5,080	10,750	875	5,375	5,375	11,360	1,080	5,680	5,680	11,990	1,295	3,995	7,995
3	14,192	1,016	7,096	7,096	15,438	1,344	7,719	7,719	16,768	1,704	8,384	8,384	18,187	2,098	6,093	12,093
4	19,030	1,419	9,515	9,515	21,297	1,930	10,648	10,648	23,798	2,515	11,899	11,899	26,552	3,183	9,276	17,276
5	24,836	1,903	12,418	12,418	28,621	2,662	14,311	14,311	32,938	3,570	16,469	16,469	37,845	4,647	13,922	23,922
6	31,804	2,484	15,902	15,902	37,776	3,578	18,888	18,888	44,819	4,941	22,410	22,410	53,091	6,623	20,545	32,545
7	40,165	3,180	20,082	20,082	49,220	4,722	24,610	24,610	60,265	6,723	30,133	30,133	73,672	9,291	29,836	43,836
8	50,197	4,016	25,099	25,099	63,526	6,153	31,763	31,763	80,345	9,040	40,172	40,172	101,458	12,893	42,729	58,729
9	62,237	5,020	31,118	31,118	81,407	7,941	40,703	40,703	106,448	12,052	53,224	53,224	138,968	17,755	60,484	78,484
10	76,684	6,224	38,342	38,342	103,759	10,176	51,879	51,879	140,382	15,967	70,191	70,191	189,607	24,319	84,803	104,803
11	94,021	7,668	47,011	47,011	131,698	12,970	65,849	65,849	184,497	21,057	92,249	92,249	257,969	33,181	117,984	139,984
12	114,825	9,402	57,413	57,413	166,623	16,462	83,311	83,311	241,846	27,675	120,923	120,923	350,258	45,145	163,129	187,129
13	139,790	11,483	69,895	69,895	210,279	20,828	105,139	105,139	316,400	36,277	158,200	158,200	474,848	61,295	224,424	250,424
14	169,749	13,979	84,874	84,874	264,848	26,285	132,424	132,424	413,320	47,460	206,660	206,660	643,045	83,098	307,523	335,523
15	205,698	16,975	102,849	102,849	333,061	33,106	166,530	166,530	539,316	61,998	269,658	269,658	870,111	112,533	420,055	450,055
16	248,838	20,570	124,419	124,419	418,326	41,633	209,163	209,163	703,111	80,897	351,556	351,556	1,176,650	152,269	572,325	604,325
17	300,606	24,884	150,303	150,303	524,907	52,291	262,454	262,454	916,044	105,467	458,022	458,022	1,590,477	205,914	778,239	812,239
18	362,727	30,061	181,363	181,363	658,134	65,613	329,067	329,067	1,192,858	137,407	596,429	596,429	2,149,144	278,333	1,056,572	1,092,572
19	437,272	36,273	218,636	218,636	824,667	82,267	412,334	412,334	1,552,715	178,929	776,357	776,357	2,903,344	376,100	1,432,672	1,470,672
20	526,726	43,727	263,363	263,363	1,032,834	103,083	516,417	516,417	2,020,529	232,907	1,010,265	1,010,265	3,921,515	508,085	1,940,757	1,980,757
		241,363		20%		494,417		25%		988,265		30%		1,938,757		35%

play the many potential permutations would be excessive because there are so many possible tax levels and holding periods. This is why most performance charts most of the time only show pre-tax gains and compounding.

Table 5–20 shows the potential accelerated growth engendered by adding $2,000 cash per year to the original $2,000 equity, including pyramiding of subsequent unrealized (untaxed) gains. One would have "contributed" $40,000 over 20 years, but notice the theoretical difference between this and the unaugmented pyramiding shown in Table 5–19. In the case of "simply" pyramiding at 10 percent (compounded annually), one would have a total return of $61,896—perhaps enough for a four-year college tuition—assuming no subsequent diminishment due to taxes.

When taxes on the profits on the 20 percent of the portfolio being turned over annually, began to be levied after several years, these taxes perhaps could be paid with additional funds as part of a continuing investment plan. With $2,000 added yearly, the theoretical gain would be $333,376, more than five times greater than the unaugmented (unpyramided) gain. Again, tax consequences would diminish these idealized gains significantly, depending upon holding periods and long-term capital gain rates over the years. Still, the after-tax gains would be exceptional.

Tax Laws Still Favor Investment Debt

Even though the tax laws have been tightened over the years to eliminate some egregious tax-sheltered programs and "wholesome" capital gains preferences, they still favor debtors, at least in the home mortgage and investment "mortgage" (leveraged) fields.

I am not a tax attorney or accountant, and I am not giving tax advice or counsel in my asset-management business or in this book. From my understanding, margin interest is deductible against investment income, including dividends and capital gains. Generally, the dividend yields gained from a total portfolio will tend to offset much if not all of the margin interest, which is based on only 50 percent (or less) of the total portfolio.

Dividends generated by the whole portfolio—subject to ordinary income taxes—are matched against margin interest expense deductions and become a diminished tax consequence. The effect of this trade-off is having twice as much stock held for long-term appreciation which is not taxed until sold and then at the lower capital gains rate. Through the use of margin, 50 percent of appreciated "unrealized" gains can be drawn out and employed without being taxed until these gains are "realized" by their stocks being sold. In former years this was a bigger advantage than it is now (summer 1995) because of the former capital gains exclusions.

If a lower capital gains tax is ever reinstated, this relationship will again heavily favor setting off dividend income against margin interest in order to concentrate upon long-term capital gains being generated in a larger portfolio than could be afforded without margin leverage.

Realized capital losses currently can be offset against $3,000 of ordinary income per year. Uncle Sam is still subsidizing a portion of net capital losses claimed up to $3,000 per year. For tax consequences, the accounting can get complicated, due to the various possibilities of alternative minimum tax, passive income, and so on, but I think of this offset as a potential savings of 28 to 40+ percent of $3,000 (or $840 to $1,200) tax-saving loss and carryforward over the years.

In the long-term outlook, working with the multiyear nature of a large, volatile portfolio, one should consider the effects of unrealized losses and investment expenses, especially to the degree that they can be carried forward to offset realized gains and tax liabilities in subsequent years. I have pointed out several times that one of the advantages of long-term speculating is the lack of tax consequences until a sale is made, while the ongoing margin interest expense is still deductible (against investment income) as incurred each year. Let us not forget the advantage of capital "losses" in one year, which have a value in reducing taxes in subsequent years and thus are not the absolute losses they may seem to be at the time they are realized.

Summary

The use of margin leverage—often shunned and criticized by the uninitiated—is a potentially effective technique for enhancing speculative gains but carries with it the added risk of heavy losses. I like to think of my margined portfolio as having twice as many corporations working for me as I could otherwise have if I had been able to buy shares only for cash. Of course, when there is a general market decline, I may have twice as many stocks working against me. There are also periods when the corporations I have selected do not do as well as the general market, but, over time, my selections have tended to significantly outperform the market averages.

When the margin technique is working well, the leveraged, pyramided portfolio can produce exceptional (almost unbelievable) returns. But there are many pitfalls, especially for the unwary, which demand attention to minimize the risk of being deeply hurt, if not wiped out. I do not see that widely diversified portfolios of undervalued stocks would likely be wiped out. In a terrible market meltdown, such as September–November 1987, widely diversified margined portfolios could sustain 50 to 75 percent losses in equity and survive, albeit greatly reduced in equity and stocks.

I have attempted to show the potentials and the dangers of using margin. There is a strong tendency for the print and TV media to criticize the use of margin, as if it were equivalent to throwing dice in Las Vegas. I believe that few of these commentators know what they are talking about when they repeat scary slogans about margin without even hinting at its potential benefits. Many of the horror stories of the excesses of leverage do not belong to the stock market, although some do. The futures and commodities markets require only one-tenth to one-fifth of the initial margin (cash) required by Regulation-T, (50 percent) so that a 10 to 20 percent or greater move against a commodities or futures position, which usually requires only 10 percent or less "good faith" margin, could not only wipe out all one's equity but create an even greater liability. A 10 to 20 percent decline in a normally margined stock account would not even require a maintenance call.

I firmly believe that the dedicated individual stock speculator can make good use of margin if its pitfalls, limitations, and potentials are well understood, anticipated, and managed effectively. Using margin to varying degrees can enhance significantly one's total returns over the long term as part of a consistent strategy of dealing in undervalued stocks in widely diversified portfolios while being defensive in seriously overbought and overvalued stock markets.

6

The Crash of '87 and the Selloff of '90

It is said that we learn more from our mistakes than our successes. Well, here are a couple of whoppers.

The stock market suffered a very large and rapid decline in the Fall of 1987. At the time it was called a crash, but 18 months later we heard the New York Stock Exchange and others refer to it as a *market break*. To understand what went on, one has to be as much a semanticist as a statistician. Between August 25, when the Dow Jones Industrial Average recorded its then all-time high close at 2722.42, and Meltdown Monday, October 19, when it closed at 1738.74, this most-widely watched indicator declined 983.68 points (36.13 percent). Among other things, that means that over one third of the market value among America's 30 great blue-chip corporations was erased in less than two months. The event staggered the financial community, and predictions of economic chaos were magnified by a crisis-hungry media.

The crash was actually worse than these closing numbers attest in that the DJIA was higher intraday on August 25 and declined even further on the morning of Tuesday, October 20, after Meltdown Monday's 508.00-point (29.22 percent), one-day collapse. The NYSE finally stabilized on Tuesday, and the DJIA was able to gain back 102.27 points (5.88 percent) for the day by the close. Never before in the history of the stock market had this intensity of trading (selling) been seen, with over 600 million shares changing hands on October 19 and over 608 million shares traded on October 20.

Many of the heretofore most astute market analysts and portfolio managers were caught fully invested going into the unexpected crash. Many technicians had predicted a correction of the August '87 high of 2722.42, expecting it to drop

159

between 5 and 10 percent but likely no lower than 2400.00. Of course, several analysts had been warning of a market top, and a few called for a big market correction. But many of them had been issuing warnings for several months and even over the previous two years as the market reached high valuations and overboughtness on one criterion or another. I believe the overwhelming majority were surprised at the timing of the decline and shocked by its intensity, and no one I know of contemplated a 500-point, one-day decline on 600 million shares of volume.

Can the Crash of '87 teach us to protect ourselves against a similar recurrence in the future? There are at least five principal areas to review. Fundamental analysis of stock valuations and, by extension, the market's valuation level yield an important series of observations. Monetary indicators that are based on interest rates and Federal Reserve policies often point to long-range trends as well as short-term reversals. Sentiment indicators correlate with historical market movements supporting current trends and suggesting reversals of those trends. Technical analysis of market activity also offers indications of the strength of current trends and projects potential changes and future trends.

We can also consider the general economic environment, including government policy, as a fifth indicator of the stock market's probable course. In addition, we can consider—albeit after the fact—the uncontrollable market mechanisms that had been put in place a few years prior to the Crash such as programmed trading and so-called insurance hedging, which helped turn what probably would have been an ordinary and orderly correction into a meltdown.

Fundamental Analysis and Stock Market Valuation Levels

There is a not-so-subtle, after-the-fact argument, often repeated by those who had withdrawn from the market several months (or years) before October '87, that the market was extremely overvalued and therefore a crash was to be expected. Even these "I-told-you-so" gurus did not expect a 22 percent drop in one day with over 600 million shares traded. The bulk of these arguments rests on the price/earnings (P/E), price/book value (P/BV), and dividend yield of the DJIA and S&P 500 Index. While many of these and other fundamentals were no doubt high, based on trailing earnings, some were not particularly high at all based upon the next year's estimated earnings and other criteria.

With the DJIA at 2722.42 on August 25, 1987, its P/E ratio was being reported at different levels, often overstated. According to *Barron's*, the 12-months earnings for the DJIA at June '87 was $126.23. Using the August DJIA all-time high, we get a P/E of 21.6. Some market commentators referred back to the 1986 calendar year's earnings of $115.59. Using these 1986 year-end figures, the August '87 DJIA high had a P/E of 23.6.

A fundamentalist consensus is that whenever the DJIA trades for over 20 times earnings (P/E 20), it represents nearness to a market (cycle) top, but this is not always the case, at least for a significant pre-top period. For example, during the whole year of 1961 the DJIA was never below 22.9 times earnings, yet it rose from 615.89 (December 31, 1960) to 731.13 (December 29, 1961, the last trading day of the year)—18.7 percent, not including dividends.

During the 1992–94 period, the DJIA traded many months from P/E 50+, partially because of a large number of nonrecurring charges (writeoffs and write-downs), down to P/E 17, without a significant (10 percent) market selloff, which led technicians to continually predict a big market selloff not unlike 1973–74. If we do see a big market selloff as this book goes to press (mid-1995), remember to minimize the P/E argument, which has failed for well over three years.

Barry Ziskin, the successful stock portfolio manager and president of the Z-Seven Fund, has a perceptive analysis of the market's valuation level in '87, published in his *Third Quarter 1987 Addendum Report to Shareholders*.

> Many analysts are at a loss to explain the October market crash, and therefore claim that it occurred because stocks were overvalued at the end of the third quarter. . . . I wish to challenge this "overvaluation" notion right now. The P/E ratio for the S&P appears to have been quite high when based on old earnings information; however, a more farsighted approach taking into account current earnings by S&P 500 companies instead of past corporate profits, which have been depressed since the 1982/1983 mini-depression, indicates a moderate (neither undervalued nor overvalued) P/E of 16.93 on this year's earnings just before the stock market's October crash. Late in the year of 1987, it may be even more appropriate to base the market's P/E multiple on conservatively estimated 1988 earnings. On this basis, average historical annual growth of 7 percent would lift the earnings of the S&P 500 to $20.34 in 1988, indicating a pre-crash P/E multiple of only 15.82 times. . . . It is interesting to note that only once in history was the S&P's ratio as low as it was just three years ago at the start of the most recent bull market—that was back in 1949 at the beginning of the longest major stock market advance in history, one which lasted 13 consecutive years before its first 20 percent decline. Looking at the 10 year trend of the P/E ratio of the S&P 500 within a historical context, the case is clearly established that the 1984–1987 stock market upcycle began at severely undervalued levels and has not yet reached overvalued extremes.[1]

[1] Z-Seven Fund, *Third Quarter 1987 Addendum Report to Shareholders*, p. 3.

Ziskin's comments dovetail with my next observation that the stock market is a discounting mechanism, a process of anticipating the future of business profits and the economy, and as such is one of the strongest "leading indicators" in that government series of leading indicators. Toward the end of 1986, consensus projected earnings for the DJIA for 1987 was running about $135. My projection for 1987 was for DJIA 2700, or 20 times the consensus earnings projections. The following spring of 1987 there were higher consensus earnings projections for 1988 of $190–$200, which led to my anticipating 3600 in 1988. DJIA earnings for 1988 turned out to be $215.46.

As the Reagan revolution of *laissez-faire* business practices gathered steam, with leveraged buyouts, mergers and acquisitions, restructurings, and the favorable tax treatment of debt interest versus dividend payments, it became obvious that book values were generally understated, especially in terms of replacement costs and going business values. A rule of thumb has been that when the DJIA sold at over two times book value, the market was also near or at a top. In 1929, the DJIA traded at over three times its book value. Given corporate growth and projected valuations, the DJIA trading at over two times book value in August of '87 (and for several months before then) did not appear dangerously excessive to me.

Another rule of thumb is that when the DJIA dividend yield is below 3.0 percent, the DJIA—and by extension the market—is overvalued according to this criterion. The market was clearly overvalued on the dividend yield indicator in October '87—and for several months before then as the DJIA continued to make all-time new highs—as both the DJIA and S&P 500 were at 2.8 percent. I rationalized this low figure with the idea that corporations were not raising dividends, but rather conserving cash to grow faster or buy back their undervalued shares in the market.

Monetary, Sentiment Indicators, and Technical Trends

I am relying on the October 16, 1987, edition of Norm Fosback's newsletter, *Market Logic,* for many of the following numbers and assessments. Explaining each of the items in detail is beyond the scope of this review. I mention these many indicators and comments only to give an overview of technical conditions shortly before the crash.

The Corporate Bonds—Commercial Paper Index was "bullish at +1.8 percent, although weakening in the face of rising short-term rates."

The Discount Rate/Federal Funds Index was bearish at −1.4 percent. The Discount Rate-T-Bill Index was bearish at −0.3 percent.

Free/Total Reserves (10-week) ratio "is positive and favorable at +0.7 percent but remains in a moderately unfavorable downtrend. Neutral overall."

Interest Rates Trends were "undeniably up, a bearish underlying factor for stock prices."

Real M2 was in a bullish uptrend. The Prime Rate-Federal Funds Index was bullish at +1.8 percent and would remain so unless the fed funds rate moved above the prime rate.

The Tumbles & Stumbles—an indicator of changes in Federal Reserve discount rates, margin requirements, or reserve requirements—was on a buy signal since December 21, 1984.

And the Yield Curve, with three-month T-bills at 6.6 percent; five-year T-notes at 9.3 percent; and long-term T-bonds at 9.9 percent, was maintaining a "Bullish upward slope intact."

Market Logic (October 16, 1987) reported, "The sentiment indicators are bullish, including favorable reports on credit balances, margin debt, and insider trading." There were some clouds, as advisory (newsletter) optimism rose to 62 percent bullish, a poor omen, "although there has not yet been time for this week's free fall in prices to be reflected in an inevitable defection from the bullish camp." While credit balances were down $270 million from September, "the new total is just above the 12-month moving average, which defines a continuing bullish uptrend." Margin debt was "extremely bullish" at a record $44.17 billion, far above its 12-month moving average. Mutual fund cash reserves were high, signifying "impressive buying power in the hands of institutional investors." The Insiders Index was very bullish with well over 50 percent purchases, "far above their 35 percent normal buying rate."

Market Timers Index was turning negative, while Public/Specialists Short was nicely favorable, and the Put/Call Ratio was "moderately bullish long-term." The Put/Call Premium Ratio was moderately unfavorable, but the various Short Interest Ratios ranged from a neutral monthly DJIA at 1.54 to a very bullish annualized NYSE at 2.96. The *technical trends* that *Market Logic* followed were turning bearish or close to sell signals in the aggregate, with a couple holding on to threatened bullish uptrends, and the weekly A/D line "holding above its 50-week average, a condition that has strongly bullish cyclical implications."

After all was said and done, *Market Logic* recommended an 80 percent invested level and projected its NYSE Total Return Index to go 25 percent higher in six months in its October 16, 1987, edition, exactly the same as in its October 2, 1987, edition. Its recommendation (since April) of a 20 percent interest-earning cash reserve "remains advisable while we await the next, and perhaps final, up leg of the great bull market." Very thoughtful, considered, and reasonable advice, given the total picture at that time.

The Advance/Decline Balance

We have already surveyed in some detail (in Chapter 4) the technical indicators that we had been keeping and watching closely for several years before the Crash and that we continue to monitor in order to anticipate the next major selloff or bear market. These indicators had led us through bad-looking times before, such as the sharp, two-day setback in September 1986, and the shocking one-day selloff in January 1987. Although, as long-term speculators, we were not into market timing in order to avoid 4 to 7 percent fluctuations, we were interested in not buying into topping markets or selling at market lows.

We planned on being able to reduce exposure or hedge (buy some insurance) with OEX stock index put options when conditions warranted. We had bought puts—prematurely as it worked out—in January and February 1987, but went through the April–May decline unhedged. By October, it looked like the September correction from the August highs had built a base sufficient for the next leg up in the bull market.

One of the many failed, misleading, or "fooler" indicators leading up to the Crash of '87 was the balance of advancing issues to declining issues, known as the advance/decline line (A/D). To review, the A/D is merely the daily total of declining issues subtracted from the daily total of advancing issues. On a given day this difference can indicate a broadly strong, weak, or neutral market, and is one of the so-called breadth indicators. In 1987, with fewer than 2,000 issues traded on the NYSE, 1,000 or more advancing issues indicated strong bullish participation, while a similar number of declining stocks indicated strong bearish activity. The greater preponderance of over 1,000 issues in either direction indicated greater strength or weakness.

As with most daily indicators, which have some descriptive and little predictive value, the multiple-day results reflect trends and degrees of overbought or oversold tension. Overbought (as previously reviewed) indicates that, after a period of significantly more buying than selling that has driven up stock prices, buyers become sated or exhausted (perhaps "bought out" as reserve funds are spent), so that selling (profit taking) and a market downturn is likely to follow. Contrarily, after a period of on-balance selling has carried the market down, fewer sellers are left to compete with bargain-hunting buyers; thus, the market is oversold and likely to advance. After extended selling of stocks, cash funds have been built up with which to fuel the next rally.

If 10 days of daily A/Ds result in over 2,000 more advances than declines, the market is said to be overbought short term. Different technicians have different quantitative signals and look at various time periods. Although there are many definitions resulting in disagreement and ambiguity, in general *short term* refers to a few hours, a few days, or a few weeks; *intermediate term* refers to several weeks to several months; and *long term* refers to nine months to several years.

In a way, it's a shame that these time periods have not been standardized. We must be careful to understand what they represent in any given context. The former

Financial News Network (FNN), for example, defined short-term periods for stocks as 10 days to 10 weeks, intermediate term as 10 weeks to 10 months, and long term as over 10 months. Short-term traders, for many of whom 10 days is an age, and some self-described long-term traders, for many of whom six to nine months is about their tolerance limit, would demur from FNN's stipulations.

Two marketeers could have seemingly opposite predictions—or a single prognosticator could offer apparently contradictory outlooks—that actually would turn out to be compatible once the time spans have been specified. For example, in the summer of 1989 I was mildly bearish short term (for the next week or two), but bullish intermediate (for the next several months after the next week or two) and long-term (over the next three to five years). I expected that after a current mild correction and a substantial advance there would be an important decline (still in the intermediate-term reference) before a major, long-term advance unfolded.

Now, in the summer of 1995, I am short-term concerned (neutral/bearish), intermediate-term bullish, and long-term bullish (for the next 12 to18 months). Obviously, a strong intermediate- or long-term outlook is more important than a short-term outlook. Still, expected small corrections sometimes turn into larger unexpected corrections. That is why balancing market momentum against valuations levels is important. In the Crash of '87, the series of down days that developed overbought (buy) signals could have been read as a momentum change in trend sell signal.

Returning to A/Ds, as shown in Table 6–1, if 25 days of daily A/Ds result in 3,000+ more advances than declines, the market is overbought intermediate-term. Likewise, if the market shows 3,000 more declines than advances, it is oversold intermediate-term. It would be oversold short-term if there were 2,000+ more declines than advances for 10 days, and vice versa for advances over declines. We must remember that these are guidelines and not all that precise. Quick reviews of 10- and 25-day trading periods will show that markets advance and decline (reverse trends) without reaching overbought or oversold A/D levels. Perhaps worse, markets get very extended in either direction and can stay that way for weeks and months.

If we look at market data for the period between August 21, 1987 and December 11, 1987 (Table 6–2), we see amazingly large numbers develop as the

Table 6–1. Advance/Decline Overbought-Oversold Criteria

	10-Day Net	25-Day Net
Overbought (sell signal)	+2,000	+3,000
Oversold (buy signal)	–2,000	–3,000

Table 6-2. Daily Data Printout During Crash Period (8/21/87-12/11/87)

1987	Adv	Dec	UpVol	DownV	NYCI	DJIA	NewH	NewL	Arms	10A	100A	25A	250A	A-D	10A-D	25A-D	10 NYCI	% Away	25 NYCI	% Away	10 DJIA	% Away	25 DJIA	% Away
8/21	803	776	97068	76348	187.51	2709.50	132	10	0.81	0.85	0.78	0.85	0.80	27	1019	1255	184.54	1.61	180.26	4.02	2679.99	1.10	2589.30	4.64
8/24	578	1019	49794	83427	186.27	2697.07	90	8	0.95	0.92	0.81	0.84	0.79	-441	-92	1381	185.21	0.57	180.71	3.08	2686.11	0.41	2597.67	3.83
8/25	1023	594	152208	45833	187.99	2722.42	135	16	0.52	0.93	0.85	0.82	0.77	429	-140	2406	185.88	1.14	181.28	3.70	2690.31	1.19	2607.85	4.39
8/26	683	897	76003	109879	186.94	2701.85	106	19	1.10	0.95	0.86	0.83	0.78	-214	-127	2382	186.16	0.42	181.82	2.81	2693.56	0.31	2617.12	3.24
8/27	548	1032	43709	102796	185.26	2675.06	39	17	1.25	1.02	0.93	0.84	0.79	-484	-877	2217	186.34	-0.58	182.31	1.62	2691.92	-.63	2625.24	1.90
8/28	395	1231	22406	124225	182.99	2639.35	29	24	1.78	1.08	0.93	0.89	0.80	-836	-1607	1240	186.47	-1.86	182.68	0.17	2687.31	-1.78	2631.40	0.30
8/31	1007	601	109648	40484	184.45	2662.95	37	23	0.62	1.05	0.91	0.87	0.79	406	-1152	1447	186.30	-0.99	183.08	0.75	2683.55	-0.77	2638.16	0.94
9/01	428	1197	35047	131497	181.21	2610.97	52	22	1.34	0.99	0.88	0.90	0.81	-769	-1022	451	185.93	-2.54	183.32	-1.15	2679.18	-2.55	2641.81	-1.17
9/02	443	1216	51266	128281	180.12	2602.04	24	31	0.91	0.98	0.88	0.91	0.82	-773	-1813	-856	185.70	-3.00	183.45	-1.81	2672.80	-2.65	2644.31	-1.60
9/03	625	984	48754	97401	179.34	2599.35	24	37	1.27	1.06	0.94	0.94	0.84	-359	-3014	-1556	185.40	-3.27	183.49	-2.26	2662.06	-2.36	2645.59	-1.75
9/04	513	1060	33433	83948	177.58	2561.38	19	43	1.22	1.10	0.97	0.95	0.85	-547	-3588	-2245	184.98	-4.00	183.45	-3.20	2647.24	-3.24	2645.16	-3.17
9/08	252	1532	31766	199007	175.59	2545.12	10	74	1.03	1.10	1.01	0.95	0.85	-1280	-4427	-3139	184.21	-4.68	183.35	-4.23	2632.05	-3.30	2644.68	-3.76
9/09	848	763	75490	69427	175.79	2549.27	9	68	1.02	1.15	1.13	0.95	0.85	85	-4771	-2763	183.22	-4.05	183.28	-4.09	2614.73	-2.50	2644.78	-3.61
9/10	1103	494	129079	34950	177.46	2576.05	22	43	0.60	1.10	1.06	0.95	0.86	609	-3948	-2524	182.15	-2.57	183.24	-3.15	2602.15	-1.00	2645.16	-2.61
9/11	1153	449	137554	25133	180.02	2608.74	44	37	0.47	1.03	0.98	0.95	0.86	704	-2760	-2298	180.93	-0.50	183.23	-1.75	2595.52	0.51	2645.74	-1.40
9/14	833	752	85870	49078	180.54	2613.04	43	49	0.63	0.91	0.93	0.93	0.85	81	-1843	-2370	179.98	0.31	183.21	-1.46	2592.89	0.78	2646.58	-1.27
9/15	430	1159	22959	101326	177.98	2566.58	31	56	1.64	1.01	0.97	0.98	0.87	-729	-2978	-3769	179.46	-0.82	182.99	-2.74	2583.25	-0.65	2643.81	-2.92
9/16	528	1034	34982	138858	176.51	2530.19	29	60	2.03	1.08	1.01	1.05	0.94	-506	-2715	-4752	179.21	-1.51	182.61	-3.34	2575.18	-1.75	2637.80	-4.08
9/17	691	838	62096	66796	176.48	2527.90	34	62	0.89	1.08	1.01	1.05	0.95	-147	-2089	-4672	178.56	-1.17	182.24	-3.16	2567.76	-1.55	2632.14	-3.96
9/18	702	876	80887	88256	176.30	2524.64	40	49	0.87	1.04	0.97	1.06	0.97	-174	-1904	-5112	178.09	-1.01	181.81	-3.03	2560.29	-1.39	2625.47	-3.84
9/21	489	1069	30289	126957	174.25	2492.82	25	58	1.92	1.11	1.02	1.09	0.98	-580	-1937	-5586	177.73	-1.96	181.32	-3.90	2553.44	-2.37	2617.77	-4.77
9/22	1058	555	167525	24777	178.48	2568.05	31	79	0.28	1.04	0.86	1.06	0.94	503	-154	-5034	177.43	0.59	180.98	-1.38	2555.73	0.48	2612.46	-1.70
9/23	1010	605	129685	68503	179.53	2585.67	53	56	0.88	1.02	0.84	1.02	0.91	405	166	-3730	177.09	1.38	180.80	-0.70	2559.37	1.03	2609.70	-0.92
9/24	734	828	65755	78193	178.86	2566.42	54	56	1.05	1.07	0.88	1.03	0.91	-94	-537	-3842	177.38	0.83	180.58	-0.95	2558.41	0.31	2605.73	-1.51
9/25	689	789	67820	54095	179.14	2570.17	43	67	0.70	1.09	0.90	1.03	0.92	-100	-1341	-4784	177.76	0.78	180.26	-0.62	2554.55	0.61	2600.26	-1.16

Table 6-2. Daily Data Printout During Crash Period (8/21/87–12/11/87, cont.)

1987	Adv	Dec	UpVol	DownV	NYCI	DJIA	NewH	NewL	Arms	10A	100A	25A	250A	A-D	10A-D	25A-D	10 NYCI	% Away	25 NYCI	% Away	10 DJIA	% Away	25 DJIA	% Away
9/28	1010	593	127045	46771	180.74	2601.50	78	53	0.63	1.09	0.89	1.02	0.91	417	-1005	-4394	177.90	1.60	179.99	0.42	2553.39	1.88	2595.94	0.21
9/29	636	940	68232	86266	180.06	2590.57	51	77	0.86	1.01	0.87	1.02	0.91	-304	-580	-4257	177.81	1.27	179.74	0.18	2555.79	1.36	2591.68	-0.04
9/30	921	674	92730	71689	180.24	2596.28	43	66	1.06	0.91	0.82	1.04	0.94	247	173	-4439	177.83	1.36	179.43	0.45	2562.40	1.32	2586.64	0.37
10/01	1029	526	146820	30778	182.97	2639.20	87	35	0.41	0.87	0.77	1.01	0.90	503	823	-3722	178.04	2.77	179.28	2.06	2573.53	2.55	2584.13	2.13
10/02	838	731	94871	58082	183.43	2640.99	92	41	0.70	0.85	0.75	0.99	0.89	107	1104	-3131	178.41	2.81	179.20	2.36	2585.17	2.16	2582.77	2.25
10/05	688	855	82129	59968	183.44	2640.18	83	39	0.59	0.72	0.67	0.94	0.86	-167	1517	-2462	179.06	2.45	179.22	2.35	2599.90	1.55	2582.80	2.22
10/06	338	1332	22570	144432	178.98	2548.63	44	57	1.62	0.85	0.78	0.98	0.88	-994	20	-3862	179.77	-0.44	179.00	-0.01	2597.96	-1.90	2578.23	-1.15
10/07	546	1020	57221	105254	178.55	2551.08	13	54	0.98	0.86	0.80	0.97	0.87	-474	-859	-3567	180.69	-1.18	178.90	-0.19	2594.50	-1.67	2575.83	-0.96
10/08	404	1193	25764	152152	176.32	2516.54	21	78	2.00	0.95	0.85	1.01	0.90	-789	-1554	-3583	180.74	-2.44	178.74	-1.36	2589.52	-2.81	2572.42	-2.17
10/09	498	1058	45060	98768	174.64	2482.21	16	89	1.03	0.99	0.87	1.00	0.89	-560	-2014	-3784	180.64	-3.32	178.56	-2.19	2580.73	-3.82	2567.73	-3.33
10/12	377	1210	29581	95968	173.52	2471.44	8	112	1.01	1.03	0.89	1.00	0.88	-833	-3264	-4070	180.39	-3.81	178.39	-2.73	2567.72	-3.75	2564.14	-3.62
10/13	959	629	128399	33037	176.02	2508.16	14	88	0.39	0.98	0.84	0.97	0.84	330	-2630	-2460	179.94	-2.18	178.41	-1.34	2559.48	-2.01	2562.66	-2.13
10/14	287	1406	19695	180980	171.26	2412.70	5	123	1.88	1.26	0.88	1.00	0.86	-1119	-3996	-3664	179.22	-4.44	178.23	-3.91	2541.12	-5.05	2557.19	-5.65
10/15	298	1441	29766	218132	167.45	2355.09	6	189	1.52	1.17	1.03	1.04	0.90	-1143	-5642	-5416	178.81	-6.35	177.83	-5.84	2512.71	-6.27	2548.36	-7.58
10/16	111	1749	3616	329776	159.13	2246.74	5	327	5.79	1.58	1.21	1.25	0.93	-1638	-7387	-7758	177.91	-10.56	176.99	-10.09	2473.29	-9.16	2533.88	-11.33
10/19	52	1973	1129	602781	128.62	1738.74	10	1068	14.07	3.33	1.61	1.79	1.14	-1921	-9141	-9760	176.36	-27.07	174.92	-26.47	2383.14	-27.04	2498.90	-30.42
10/20	509	1445	329398	250583	133.04	1841.01	1	1174	0.27	2.59	0.95	1.74	1.00	-936	-9083	-9967	173.93	-23.51	173.12	-23.15	2312.38	-20.38	2469.88	-25.46
10/21	1756	210	422·577	19574	145.02	2027.85	2	108	0.39	2.83	0.81	1.67	0.90	1546	-7063	-7915	168.45	-13.91	171.86	-15.62	2260.06	-10.27	2449.79	-17.22
10/22	361	1540	35249	346618	139.45	1950.43	1	172	2.31	2.86	0.86	1.73	0.94	-1179	-7453	-8947	163.86	-14.89	170.38	-18.15	2203.44	-11.48	2426.69	-19.63
10/23	670	1048	89414	134393	139.22	1950.76	1	144	0.96	2.86	0.86	1.73	0.95	-378	-7271	-9151	160.50	-13.26	168.89	-17.57	2150.29	-9.28	2403.73	-18.84
10/26	134	1791	1862	301434	127.88	1793.93	0	467	12.11	3.97	0.88	2.14	0.96	-1657	-8095	-10228	156.82	-18.45	167.04	-23.44	2082.54	-13.86	2375.78	-24.49
10/27	941	821	173950	64985	130.51	1846.59	0	341	0.43	3.97	0.84	2.14	0.95	120	-8305	-10611	153.27	-14.85	165.12	-20.96	2016.42	-8.40	2346.94	-21.30
10/28	591	1153	115873	146651	130.31	1846.82	0	477	0.65	3.85	0.83	2.14	0.93	-562	-7748	-11578	148.71	-12.37	163.15	-20.13	1959.84	-5.77	2317.38	-20.31
10/09'	1405	366	234773	16212	136.28	1938.33	2	169	0.27	3.72	0.85	2.10	0.90	1039	-5566	-10445	144.16	-5.46	161.45	-15.59	1918.16	1.05	2292.26	-15.44
10/30	1611	224	249283	30158	140.80	1993.53	1	39	0.87	3.23	0.88	2.11	0.90	1387	-2541	-8958	140.06	0.53	159.92	-11.95	1892.84	5.32	2269.19	-12.15

Table 6-2. Daily Data Printout During Crash Period (8/21/87–12/11/87, concluded)

1987	Adv	Dec	UpVol	DownV	NYCI	DJIA	NewH	NewL	Arms	10A	100A	25A	250A	A–D	10A–D	25A–D	10 NYCI	% Away	25 NYCI	% Away	10 DJIA	% Away	25 DJIA	% Away
11/02	1093	629	115683	47386	142.74	2014.09	1	34	0.71	1.90	0.75	2.11	0.91	464	−156	−8911	136.95	4.23	158.40	−9.88	1920.37	4.88	2245.70	−10.31
11/03	493	1211	34524	179220	140.11	1963.53	1	37	2.11	2.08	0.88	2.16	0.93	−718	62	−9325	135.11	3.70	156.80	−10.64	1932.63	1.60	2220.61	−11.58
11/04	713	933	81788	102305	139.11	1945.29	2	39	0.96	2.14	1.00	2.16	0.92	−220	−1704	−9792	136.53	1.89	155.15	−10.34	1924.37	1.09	2194.57	−11.36
11/05	1281	450	172743	38710	141.81	1985.41	2	45	0.64	1.97	0.87	2.17	0.93	831	306	−9464	137.23	3.34	153.51	−7.62	1927.87	2.98	2168.42	−8.44
11/06	807	814	56363	97076	140.04	1959.05	0	21	1.71	2.05	0.89	2.21	0.95	−7	677	−9578	136.64	2.49	151.77	−7.73	1928.70	1.57	2141.15	−8.50
11/09	412	1285	16210	135030	136.35	1900.20	2	46	2.67	1.10	0.81	2.29	0.96	−873	1461	−10284	136.88	−0.39	149.89	−9.03	1939.32	−2.02	2111.55	−10.01
11/10	416	1277	34386	136732	134.06	1878.15	3	75	1.30	1.19	0.88	2.28	0.96	−861	480	−10151	136.96	−2.12	148.09	−9.47	1942.44	−3.31	2084.73	−9.91
11/11	995	587	96818	33268	135.46	1899.20	2	39	0.58	1.18	0.89	2.26	0.97	408	1450	−9269	137.81	−1.70	146.37	−7.45	1947.68	−2.49	2058.65	−7.75
11/12	1296	386	176395	18196	138.88	1960.21	3	20	0.35	1.19	0.93	2.20	0.96	910	1321	−7570	138.16	0.52	144.87	−4.13	1949.87	0.53	2036.39	−3.74
11/13	692	912	40970	121569	137.60	1935.01	3	25	2.25	1.33	1.06	2.25	0.98	−220	−286	−7230	138.68	−0.78	143.39	−4.04	1944.01	−0.46	2014.51	−3.95
11/16	866	701	78556	51591	138.16	1949.10	0	29	0.81	1.34	1.08	2.24	1.00	165	−585	−6232	138.94	−0.56	141.97	−2.69	1937.52	0.60	1993.61	−2.23
11/17	399	1204	23101	112255	136.21	1922.25	1	56	1.61	1.29	1.00	2.29	1.00	−805	−672	−7367	138.62	−1.74	140.38	−2.97	1933.39	−0.58	1970.18	−2.43
11/18	1031	537	97853	40370	137.58	1939.16	2	56	0.79	1.27	0.99	2.24	1.01	494	42	−5754	138.16	−0.42	139.03	−1.04	1932.77	0.33	1951.23	−0.62
11/19	366	1287	12612	131884	134.72	1895.39	3	60	2.97	1.50	1.12	2.30	1.00	−921	−1710	−5532	137.77	−2.21	137.72	−2.18	1923.77	−1.48	1932.85	−1.94
11/20	714	826	92248	71665	135.56	1913.63	3	88	0.67	1.40	1.02	2.10	0.96	−112	−1815	−4006	137.62	−1.49	136.78	−0.89	1919.23	−0.29	1919.52	−0.31
11/23	903	694	86811	41153	136.13	1923.08	4	68	0.62	1.20	0.94	1.56	0.85	209	−733	−1876	136.91	−0.57	137.08	−0.69	1921.52	0.08	1926.90	−0.20
11/24	1139	502	127240	37630	137.93	1963.53	5	48	0.67	1.13	0.87	1.58	0.91	637	765	−303	136.46	1.08	137.28	0.48	1930.06	1.73	1931.80	1.64
11/25	745	813	54882	67019	139.90	1946.95	2	49	1.12	1.19	0.91	1.61	0.99	−68	289	−1917	136.44	2.54	137.07	20.06	1934.83	0.63	1928.56	0.95
11/27	514	957	18812	51753	135.16	1910.48	6	28	1.48	1.30	1.00	1.57	0.91	−443	−1064	−1181	136.82	−1.22	136.90	−1.27	1929.86	−1.00	1926.96	−0.86
11/30	201	1576	7012	255085	129.69	1833.55	2	211	4.64	1.54	1.09	1.72	0.95	−1375	−2219	−2178	137.27	−5.52	136.52	−5.00	1919.71	−4.49	1922.27	−4.62
12/01	819	771	81236	45675	130.50	1842.34	1	86	0.60	1.52	1.06	1.26	0.89	48	−2336	−473	136.90	−4.67	136.62	−4.48	1909.04	−3.49	1924.21	−4.25
12/02	753	755	72921	46266	131.21	1848.97	1	95	0.63	1.42	1.00	1.27	0.92	−2	−1533	−595	136.01	−3.60	136.65	−3.98	1901.71	−2.77	1924.29	−3.91
12/03	268	1390	14526	181191	127.01	1776.53	2	169	2.40	1.58	1.10	1.34	0.95	−1122	−3149	−1155	135.34	−6.15	136.52	−6.97	1885.45	−5.78	1921.48	−7.54
12/04	362	1306	45653	120852	125.91	1766.74	0	281	0.73	1.36	1.02	1.36	1.00	−944	−3172	−3138	134.84	−6.62	136.11	−7.49	1872.58	−5.65	1914.61	−7.72
12/07	925	698	96164	33594	128.23	1812.17	2	194	.46	1.34	1.02	1.34	1.02	227	−2833	−4298	133.78	−4.15	135.60	−5.44	1862.43	−2.70	1907.36	−4.99
12/08	1151	473	131759	63609	131.42	1868.37	1	128	1.17	1.39	1.03	1.36	1.03	678	−2364	−4084	132.90	−1.11	135.15	−2.76	1856.96	0.61	1901.53	−1.74
12/09	1119	501	129189	40242	133.56	1902.52	1	74	0.70	1.39	1.03	1.30	0.98	618	−2383	−2748	132.17	1.05	134.89	−0.98	1850.86	2.79	1899.09	0.18
12/10	512	1085	37765	136063	131.07	1855.44	3	92	1.70	1.45	1.07	1.33	1.00	−573	−2888	−3101	131.70	−0.48	134.57	−2.60	1841.71	0.75	1895.50	−2.11
12/11	829	674	91397	40755	131.79	1867.04	2	70	0.55	1.36	1.02	1.33	1.02	155	−2290	−3777	131.26	0.40	134.17	−1.77	1837.37	1.61	1890.76	−1.25

crash builds, numbers that were never generated before. On August 21, the 10-day A/D (10A/D) is 1,019, while the 25-day A/D (25A/D) is 1,255, both just slightly overbought readings. Oddly enough, when the DJIA makes its all-time closing high on August 25 (2722.42), the 10A/D is a –140, while the 25A/D is somewhat overbought at 2,406, neither issuing an A/D "sell signal." As the DJIA sells off and reaches 2545.12 on September 8, the 10A/D registers an extremely oversold reading of –4,427, while the 25A/D is definitely oversold at –3,139. In theory, these are strong buy signals and one would expect the market to advance very soon.

In fact, the DJIA does rally for the four trading days after September 8, but then sells off again, so that by September 21, at DJIA 2492.82, the 10A/D is at –1,937 "almost oversold"—but the 25A/D registers –5,586, an extremely oversold intermediate-term strong buy signal! Sure enough, for the next nine trading days the DJIA rallies strongly—as it is "supposed" to do—to 2640.99 on October 2, up 148.17 points (almost 6 percent). In the process, the 10A/D turns positive (1,104) as the oversoldness of the 25A/D is mitigated to a less oversold –3,131, suggesting a continuation of its buy signal. According to these criteria, one might well expect the market's advance to continue until the 25A/D attained a neutral reading or turned positive.

No such luck. Instead of a continuing technical rally, the market tumbled for the next week, with the DJIA closing at 2482.21 on October 9. This renewed decline drove the 10A/D to a barely oversold –2,014 and expanded the 25A/D to a strongly oversold –3,784. It was time for another technical rally from clearly oversold territory. After all, the market had "corrected" 240 DJIA points, over 8.8 percent, from its August 25 all-time high.

The following week, ending October 16, made a shambles of the market and the shorter-term A/D indicator, which had "worked" so often over the years. After a fake-out advance on October 13, the market suffered three successive days of declines greater than net 1,000. Especially ambiguous—from an A/D point of view—was Friday the 16th, when there were 1,638 more declines than advances. This was seen by some technicians as a selling "climax," and several of them issued buy signals for Monday, October 19, 1987. And why shouldn't they, at least as far as A/D experience and indications were concerned? There were other technical indicators suggesting a washed-out selling climax—as the 10A/D registered a hardly believable –7,387 to confirm the 25A/D's extreme –7,758.

Monday the 19th taught us that "hardly believable" and "extreme" readings had still to make their appearances. On Meltdown Monday there were 1,921 net declines, driving both 10A/D and 25A/D to over –9,000 as the DJIA "bottomed" at 1738.74 on a closing basis. By October 28, the 25A/D registered its greatest negative reading –11,578. All of these historically oversold A/D readings since Meltdown Monday indicated that the market "should" advance, but who could believe them after being so misled in the days—especially the Friday—before the market's crash?

The market made successful retests of (did not exceed) its DJIA lows one week later on October 26 and again on December 4, which was the actual low for more representative market indexes such as the New York Stock Exchange Composite Index of all common stocks. Ironically, both the 10A/D, at –3,172, and the 25A/D, at –3,138 were issuing oversold buy signals on December 4, the day that may be counted as the end of the bear market of '87, or preferably, the end of the sharp August 25 to December 4 "correction" in the long-term bull market that began in October/December 1974 at DJIA 577.60, some 2,145 DJIA points beneath its closing high of August 25, 1987. If one considers that the '87 selloff traversed some 983.68 DJIA points, then one can still accept that potential wipeout as "merely" a 45 percent "correction" in a long-term, secular bull market. Ironically, 1987 was an up year for the S&P 500 Index (the index most used by professionals), with a total return of 5.23 percent. Those who were invested in the S&P 500 and ignored the whole drama still came out ahead for the year, according to the total return S&P 500 Index.

The Arms Index

The Arms or Trading Index, including its buy and sell signal parameters, was analyzed in Chapter 4. To review, the Arms Index is computed by dividing advancing issues by declining issues, then dividing that quotient by the quotient of up volume divided by down volume (see Table 4–2). In theory, 1.00 is neutral, representing as many stocks advancing on up volume, proportionately, as stocks declining on down volume. A guideline is that on any given day, an Arms below 1.00 indicates buying pressures, while an Arms above 1.00 indicates selling pressures; the farther from 1.00 in either direction, the stronger the indication.

There are several ways to compute the Arms Index as a moving average. The 10-Day Arms (10–A) and 25-Day Arms (25–A) are simple arithmetic averages of 10 and 25 days of daily Arms. To obtain the 10-Day Open Arms (10–O) and 25–Day Open Arms (25–O), first sum 10 (or 25) days' worth of each of the four elements and then derive their ratios. The Open Arms averages smooth out large variations among the daily figures, where, for example, one day's volume may be almost twice as much as another day's in the average.

For the 10–A and 25–A, below 0.80 indicates overbought (pressure building for a selloff) and above 1.20 indicates oversold (pressure building for a rally), in general. The Open Arms tends to generate smaller numbers: For the 10–O, below 0.75 and for the 25–O, below 0.78, are dangerously overbought limits; above 1.15 for the 10–O and 1.10 for the 25–O are oversold buy signals.

This technical tool also is mangled by the Crash of '87, and fails to give a clear or timely indication of the impending selloff. Let us consider Arms Indexes for August 11, 1987 (not on Table 6–2.). The daily Arms registers 0.45, indicating strong buying pressure, and driving the 10-Arms to 0.71, the 10–O to 0.70, the 25–A to 0.79, and the 25–O to 0.76—all very overbought, all issuing short- and intermediate-term sell signals. But the DJIA continues to trend higher to its fateful rendezvous with 2722.42 on August 25. Now, at its DJIA top, the Arms Indexes are registering 0.93, 0.85, 0.82, and 0.77, respectively, only the 25–O remaining overbought.

As the market begins its descent from its all-time highs, the Arms Indexes "improve," and by September 9 the short-term indexes are somewhat oversold and threatening to issue short-term buy signals as the 10-A registers 1.15 and the 10–O notches up to 1.13, with the DJIA at 2549.27. In fact, this strength in the 10–O leads Peter Eliades, editor of *Stock Market Cycles*, to write an article for *Barron's* on the likelihood of a long-term buy signal having been issued, based on the 10-day Open Arms reaching 1.12 (see Table 6–2).[2] The DJIA does jump up 63.77 points during the following three trading days, but then declines to a Blue Monday close of 2492.82 on September 21, down 56.45 from September 9.

Between September 21 and October 2, the DJIA rises to 2640.99, up 148.17 points (5.9 percent). The 10–A is 0.85, the 10–O 0.75, the 25–A 0.99, and the 25–O 0.89; thus, only the 10–O is in clear sell-signal territory. This is a less overbought configuration than the August 11 series of 0.71, 0.70, 0.79, 0.76, after which the DJIA advanced from 2680.48 to its all-time high. Alas, the 2640-level proves to be "overhead resistance" and, in the next nine trading days, the DJIA falls to 2246.74 on "Black Friday," October 16. In the process, the four Arms Indexes we've been reviewing register 1.68, 1.21, 1.25, and 0.98—screaming short-term and long-term buy signals in all but the 25–O. This was another reason for some technicians to believe the market had bottomed on October 16 and would rally the following week. Neither they nor I know what mischief was afoot in the futures pits in Chicago.

Of course, Meltdown Monday arrived with numbers never before witnessed. The daily Arms of 14.07! The 10–A registered 3.03, the 10–O was 1.61, the 25–A hit 1.79, and the 25–O was 1.14—buy signals of a lifetime. Unfortunately, the damage had been done and there would be reverberations, especially in the over-the-counter stocks, until they bottomed on December 4, 1987. For the eight weeks after the crash, the Arms indexes were so distorted that they continued to give buy signals almost every day. On December 4, the series read 1.36, 1.02, 1.36, and 1.00—a strong short-term buy signal.

The Iceberg and the *Titanic*

For those who have intimations of destiny, the story of the iceberg and the *Titanic* must hold an ironic fascination. As the plans for the great ship took form, the great

---

[2] Peter Eliades, "Buying Opportunity? That's What This Technical Indicator Said," *Barron's*, September 21, 1987, p. 73.

ice floe that would give birth to that iceberg was moving inexorably toward the ocean. As the *Titanic* was being provisioned for its gala maiden voyage, the iceberg was breaking off from its glacier and being launched to venture forth on the North Atlantic. In spite of all the preparation for the safest ship ever built—it was "unsinkable"—and a record passage, unexpected disaster befell these two wondrous objects, which had been set in motion independent of each other.

The Crash of '87 reminds me of the story of the iceberg and the *Titanic*. Events and conditions were set in motion that had the promise of a record-breaking excursion and the minimized potential for a devastating collision. The "unseen" conditions for the Crash were the New York Stock Exchange, with its programmed trading of stocks for risk arbitrageurs and portfolio insurers, and Chicago with its promotion of derivative instruments such as the S&P 500 futures contracts. This complex story reaches back years. Traditional practices and attitudes were modified in a cauldron of greed under the aegis of barely regulated free markets. Risk arbitrageurs and portfolio insurance hacks became the darlings of Wall Street because of the alleged safety and profits they generated. To get anywhere near the full flavor of the Crash of '87, I strongly recommend a study of the fascinating, informative, and readable book *Black Monday* by Tim Metz.

Metz narrates the events and actions of several key players in the years leading up to the debacle. Much of his information comes from the Brady Commission task-force report and the "presumably exhaustive, 874-page Securities and Exchange Commission's study of the crash."[3] Metz paints a clear picture of markets out of control and the efforts to stabilize them, even if existing rules and practices had to be bent or ignored.

The Crash of '87 was a setup, if unintentional and without collusion. One of the problems of putting historical events into perspective is deciding upon how far back to set the scene. A case could be made that Black Monday, October 19, 1987, was an offspring of the famous Black Tuesday, October 29, 1929. Actually, we would have to go back at least one more day, as the Black Monday of its time, October 28, 1929, was the greatest one-day plunge in stock exchange history— until 58 years later—resulting in a then-devastating crash of 12.8 percent. The reason why Black Tuesday (October 29, 1929) is celebrated as the Crash of '29 (the Dow tumbled 11.7 percent that day) is that 16.4 million shares were traded—an all-time record volume, not to be witnessed again for the next 35 years.

Although it would be intrinsically interesting, reviewing the past six decades of stock market history would not necessarily tell us what to expect in the next six decades or even the next six months. One fact is clear: The stock market was a significantly different institution before 1982 than after. When we look back to '80

---

[3] Tim Metz, *Black Monday* (New York: William Morrow & Co., 1988), p. 63.

and '81, we see average daily volumes in the 30–50 million share range. A review of the shares traded and their turnover rates for the New York Stock Exchange shows a 50 percent increase in turnover and a fourfold increase in trading between 1981 and 1988 (see Table 6–3).

Crudely observed, the trading volume for 1982 was about 39 percent over 1981, while the turnover percentage increased about 30 percent for '82. However, by 1984, trading volume almost doubled that of 1981; it redoubled by 1987. Along the way, turnover percentage more than doubled from 33 percent in '81 to 73 percent in '87. Most of this increasing activity was attributable to institutional trading, involving increasing turnover rates due to market-timing techniques augmented by risk arbitrage and portfolio insurance practices, according to Metz.

From 1982 through September 1987, assets in mutual funds grew to more than $827 billion, almost tripling for the period. During the same time, mutual funds invested $233 billion in stocks, more than a 400 percent increase since the end of '82. About 800 U.S. institutions held portfolios of stocks greater than $100 million by the end of '86. According to Amen & Associates (Greenwich, Connecticut), by 1987 almost 40 percent (more than $500 billion) of assets under management by 786 of the largest institutions were placed in index funds, funds that mirror the stocks in the index.

In April 1982, the Chicago Mercantile Exchange (CME) introduced the S&P 500 futures contract, a metaphorical iceberg if ever there was one. The next year saw the introduction of other index future contracts and stock index options, different forms of derivatives. There had been option trading before, but never anything approaching the scale of these products. Thus the era of derivative instruments began, a tail that would come to wag the dog, the New York Stock Exchange.

Table 6-3. Trading Volumes and Turnover Percentage, NYSE (in millions)

Year	Shares Traded	Average Shares Listed	Percent Turnover
1981	11,853.7	36,003.5	33%
1982	16,458.0	38,907.0	42
1983	21,589.6	42,316.9	51
1984	23,671.0	47,104.8	49
1985	27,510.7	50,759.4	54
1986	35,680.0	56,023.8	64
1987	47,801.3	65,711.4	73
1988	40,849.5	76,093.0	55

Source: Adapted from Phyllis S. Pierce, *Dow Jones Investors Handbook of 1989* (Homewood, IL: Dow Jones-Irwin, 1989), p. 79.

In *Black Monday*, Metz points out:

> Volume of all stock index futures contracts in 1986 would reach
> 26.5 million contracts, more than quadruple the 1982 level. Index
> options trading would grow almost tenfold from 1983 through 1986.
> And, reflecting the relentless advance of institutional trading, the
> NYSE block trades of 5,000 or more shares accounted for 49.9 per-
> cent of the total volume of 1986, up from 41 percent in 1982.[4]

Arbitrage is the noble art of profiting from differences in prices for the same
object in different places, or from equivalent items with divergent values over time.
It happens that a "basket of S&P 500 stocks" and an equal representation of S&P
500 futures have divergences in value because they are traded in different markets
with different trading objectives and costs. We do not want to get bogged down in
the fine points of programmed trading, but it is worth understanding the general
practice, if only to see how insidious and indifferent to investing values it is.

The S&P 500 Index is a weighted index of 500 stocks, most listed on the NYSE.
The S&P 500 futures contracts are bets on where the S&P 500 Index will be during
the life of the future's contract. It happens that if the S&P 500 futures price varies a
certain amount, say 75 basis points (0.75 percent), from "fair value" of the S&P 500
Index, then it can be profitable for an institution to buy $10 to $20 million of one and
sell an equivalent amount of the other to lock in the difference. As Metz puts it:

> Therefore, if the futures price spikes to, say, 171.75, or a premium
> of 1.75 points over the index itself, then look for the index arbi-
> trageur to sell futures in Chicago and buy stocks in New York. Or if
> it drops to 168.25 or less, look for buying in Chicago and program
> selling on the NYSE. Assuming the full-point fair-value estimate
> does in fact reflect all the costs of such trades, the index arb's profit
> is a bit over $44,000 on a $10 million position. That may not seem
> eye-popping, but what if the arb could do that every day? A
> $44,000-a-day return over 250 trading days is more than $11 mil-
> lion, or a low-risk return on investment above 110 percent of the
> $10 million of capital being risked.[5]

Obviously, an institution would not need to program trade every day. Every
other day or even once a week would provide a handsome return, as their capital
draws interest while resting between trades. Of course, such action requires sufficient
disparity between the futures and the cash price, but this occurs with some frequency.

---

[4] Metz, *Black Monday*, p. 63.

[5] Metz, *Black Monday*, pp. 73–74.

Consider that the Brady Commission found that U.S. corporations purchased $274.3 billion more in shares than they issued between the end of 1983 through June 1987. As the volume of trading was multiplying, significant net amounts of stock were being withdrawn from trading through mergers, acquisitions, buyouts, and buybacks. This reduction of shares outstanding, which continued through 1988 and 1989, is considered to be a long-term positive for higher stock prices, based on the classical economics of a reduced supply meeting increasingly available funds for investing in stocks. For some participants, the stock buyout/buyback trend was a strong reason for buying or holding stock positions as the market advanced and corporations were being bought out left and right.

In a sense, the decreasing amount of shares available for trading was more than compensated for by the increasing number of futures and index option contracts being traded. The nearly risk-free profits from programmed trading, and the sense of security gained from insurance hedging, began to increase stock-market volatility, first seen in the market break of September 11, 1986. On that day the DJIA lost 86.61 points, a record point fall for one day and a percentage decline not seen for decades. There was also record trading volume of 237.6 million shares. The next day the DJIA dropped another 34.17 on another record volume day of 240.5 million shares traded.

The press correctly blamed programmed trading for the dramatic drops with record volume for September 11 and September 12, but neither the SEC nor the markets admitted to that cause or did anything about it. The SEC blamed investor's fears of higher interest rates for the September '86 break, although they conceded that programmed trading may have reduced the time period in which investors adjusted to those fears. In fact, institutions, the stock exchange, and the SEC seemed to support programmed trading and portfolio insurance, both of which grew in size and frequency. Why not? They were money-makers (profit centers) for all concerned.

In August '87, portfolio insurance assets under management grew to more than $60 billion—with some estimates as high as $90 billion—from a 1984 level of a mere $200 million in assets. Contributing to the growth of programmed trading and portfolio insurance was (and is) the New York Stock Exchange's Designated Order Turnaround (DOT) system. The DOT system was implemented in 1976 to provide specialists with an efficient way to complete small orders (under 200 shares), thus permitting floor traders more time to work on bigger orders. The NYSE began lifting the size limit to 599 shares, then 1,099 shares, and by October 1987 to 2,099. By 1984 the exchange made programmed trading easy by modifying the DOT system so that groups of stocks can be traded instead of one at a time.

When more stocks are traded on the exchange, traders, brokers, and specialists all benefit from increased trading commissions. However, this increase in programmed trading and portfolio insurance can exceed stock specialists' liquidity capabilities. As Metz puts it:

> Their buy programs in New York will send the stock market soaring and the portfolio insurers scampering back into the pit to trigger the whole mutually reinforcing cycle again and again. This year alone, the Dow will rise nearly 850 points, or 43.5 percent, to its August 25 peak.[6]

Some people have said—without really thinking it through, I believe—that the bull market (or rally) of '85 to '87 was merely driven by derivative instruments, which permitted programmed trading and portfolio insurance hedging to drive prices higher. Their argument is that there wasn't much outcry when buy programs were pushing up the DJIA, and therefore one should not be critical when these same programs—only this time sell programs—pushed the DJIA down.

The stock market is a very complex process involving hundreds of thousands of competing forces. From my point of view, programmed and portfolio insurance trading certainly increased the market's volatility (and programmed trading continues to do so), with sharp advances and declines. Still, both the fundamental values of corporations and their earning potentials supported the great advances made during this market cycle. Corporate growth, augmented by the growth of money supply and declining interest rates, essentially fueled the advance. That is why, after the unprecedented Crash of '87, the overall market was able to begin advancing for the next two and one-half years, regaining all losses, on a total return basis, that had been generated by the crash.

After all is said and done, programmed trading only intensified the swings and increased the turnover rate. The reason I believe the market could have gone to DJIA 2700 in '87, with or without programmed trading, is because the Dow earnings were projected to be over $200 for '88, and a price/earnings multiple slightly below the long-term average 13.5 would see the DJIA at 2700. With even higher earnings projected for '89—assuming the economic environment, including Federal Reserve policy, was not hostile—the DJIA could easily trade at 18 times earnings, or something well over 3600.

The *Titanic* and the iceberg analogy echoes the realization that a sequence of events that didn't have to happen resulted in a great tragedy. Aside from design flaws in the ship (including the insufficiency of lifeboats), there were questions about the radio room being too busy with congratulatory cables to pay enough attention to iceberg warnings, about the speed of the ship in such dangerous waters, and about the lookout procedures.

---

[6] Metz, *Black Monday*, p. 86.

We can see design flaws in the markets—the relationships between Chicago and New York—that permitted vicious cycle waves of panic selling, leading to the near-sinking of the New York Stock Exchange. With the benefit of hindsight, we can also witness seemingly independent events, that led to that inexorable outcome.

In the weeks and days preceding the Crash of '87, an almost unbelievable series of events were unleashed against the normative mode of stock investing. Alan Greenspan, newly appointed Federal Reserve Board (FRB) Chairman, led his fellows to raise the discount rate by 1/2 percent (to 6 percent) just before Labor Day, signaling higher interest rates and increasing the attractiveness of bonds over stocks. About October 9, rumors begin circulating that the House Ways and Means Committee was crafting a bill to eliminate the tax benefits permitted to those doing deals with debt-financed leveraged buyouts. By October 13, these rumors were confirmed, as takeover candidates (a few of which crashed 45 percent on Meltdown Monday) had fallen 5 percent in the previous days.

The next day, Wednesday, October 14, the U.S. balance of trade deficit was announced as $15.7 billion—more than $1 billion above consensus estimates. The trade-deficit shocker led to 30-year Treasury bonds yielding over 10 percent for the first time in 23 months. These events drove the DJIA to a record 95-point loss on not very impressive volume of 207 million shares. According to the Brady Commission study, portfolio insurers sold about $250 million in S&P 500 contracts, while index arbitrageurs used $1.4 billion worth of stocks in programmed selling, one sixth of the exchange's total trading.

Adding fuel to the fire the next day, Thursday, October 15, Chemical Bank raised its prime rate 1/2 percent (to 9 3/4 percent). Already troubled by Secretary of the Treasury James Baker's public and disdainful argument with German financial leaders, stock-market participants were further alarmed when the Administration announced it had no plans to further reduce the budget deficit. Then, as if swamping a listing ship, Friday the 16th began with news of an Iranian attack on an American-protected oil tanker and an emergency meeting of national security officers and President Reagan to determine a probable military response.

Several market analysts had announced that below 2400 was a buying opportunity, and chartist traders thought the 2280–2300 should be as far as a correction would go. Some of these technicians acted on their signals and stepped into the market only to get creamed by programmed selling that in the final 90 minutes drove the DJIA to 2246.74, down a record 108.35 points. The SEC found out later that portfolio insurers sold more than 9,000 S&P 500 contracts worth around $1.3 billion, plus at least another $151 million worth of stock in New York. Keeping up their end of the strategy, index arbitrageurs completed sell programs worth some $1.37 billion.

As chance would have it, I was in Boston on Friday the 16th, and as I dropped into a brokerage office just after the close, I heard several interested onlookers mention in relieved tones that the market had come back on the close. Indeed, in the final 10 minutes the DJIA recovered 22 points, giving hope for a bounce-back rally the following Monday. The SEC findings were that, in the final half-hour, program traders did 43 percent of the NYSE's total volume.

Metz writes that Friday's massacre should have been far worse, as portfolio insurers should have sold many more contracts during the week than they did, based upon their formulas. He adds, "Among insiders there is no question that the market will plunge on the coming Monday."[7]

Summing Up the Crash of '87

Many philosophers have written that we are all fatalists about the past, meaning that once an event has occurred it usually seems obvious that it was bound to happen. From the vantage point of hindsight, the Crash of '87 seems inevitable. From the remembrance of daily events leading up to the crash, its inevitability was not at all clear, and subsequent events have confirmed that the crash was a technical accident rather than a fundamental economic signal. In the almost eight years that have passed since Meltdown Monday, the principal concerns have been a too robust economy threatening an intolerable level of inflation.

In response to the Crash, the pessimistic consensus called for a recession beginning in the last quarter of '87—and thereafter each subsequent quarter of '88 and '89—a consensus that had given way in the Spring of '89 to concerns of too much optimism and therefore the imminent likelihood of economic boom, inflation, and a subsequent major bear market. Due to the economic slowdown by late June 1989, this consensus flipped again to dire threats of recession and falling profits. Well, sooner or later there will be significant market corrections and economic recessions, but it will be hard to blame either on the Crash of '87.

A recession in 1990 and a sharp market selloff from July 17 through early October 1990 did occur, the principal reasons for which were Federal Reserve tightening and higher interest rates.

In 1989, I wrote that the next time the major averages are trading near or above 20 times earnings, yielding 3 percent or less in dividends and trading above 2.2 times book value, we should certainly be prepared for a significant and probably severe stock market decline. These historically dangerous fundamental considerations should be considered in terms of the marketwide technical conditions of the time. One lesson learned from the Crash of '87 is to remember that some technical indicators give off buy signals as the market declines and becomes oversold, while others warn of the likelihood of further weakness. Penetration of 150- and

---

[7] Metz, *Black Monday*, p. 91.

200-day moving averages in both the DJIA and NYSE Composite Index, as well as new 52-week lows becoming greater than new 52-week highs, augment the storm signals of the too-high fundamental criteria.

To all this we must factor in Federal Reserve Board policy and the general economy. We should avoid knee-jerk reactions, such as comparing 1929 to 1987 when their economies were significantly different, trending in opposite directions, and their stock, bond, and derivatives' markets were not comparable. Having learned to recognize dangerous waters and guard against icebergs like those of October '87, and gained perspective from Meltdown Monday and Turnaround Tuesday, we are prepared to react logically to such a market "break" and take advantage of the once-in-a-decade values created by such a panic. We need not have been heroic and bought at the bottom in October, but we could have been logical and bought blue chips after the retest of October 26 and bought secondary stocks after the bottoming confirmation of December 4.

The Selloff of 1990

It almost grieves me to add this section to this revised edition. In 1987, TPS Portfolio lost 55.65 percent; in 1990 TPS Portfolio lost 60.62 percent. The Selloff of '90 was actually more difficult than that of the Crash or '87. What happened?

Again, we were at a juncture in the stock market. The DJIA was making all-time new highs, although not that much more than in August '87, almost three years earlier. The defining moment that sticks in my memory is the market action of July 16 and 17, 1990.

On Friday, July 13, the DJIA closed at 2980.20, up 10.40 on 259,302 shares traded with 954 advances to 619 declines and 124 million shares up to 68 million shares down. There were 159 new 52-week highs to 37 new lows, a relatively strong day (and week). The following Monday, July 16, the DJIA made an all-time new high of 2999.75 with a gain of 19.55 points, on modest breadth (A/D 867/678, 86 million shares up/45 million shares down, and 102 new highs to 37 new lows. Then, even with concerns about DJIA's struggling in 1990 and its modest new high—only 10.2 percent (277.33 points) above its August 25, 1987, high of almost three years earlier—we watched the trading on the next day. Tuesday, July 17, saw the DJIA closed unchanged at 2999.75, a rare occurrence.

Alas, there were only 641 advances to 877 declines and 61 million shares up to 101 million shares down, with only 77 new highs to 50 new lows. Shades of August 26, 1987, the day after a new DJIA high, which generated only 683 advances to 897 declines and 76 million shares up to 110 million shares down. I distinctly remember thinking, this is an "exhaustion top" signal, and the market is likely to decline after it, sooner or later.

It didn't take very long for my premonition to be fulfilled. From the high of 2999.75 on July 16–17, the DJIA dropped to 2365.10 on October 11, 1990, a 634.65-point (21.2 percent) decline in just under three months. Worse yet, the Russell 2000 Index of smaller capitalization stocks declined 29.4 percent (from 170.03 to 120.02) during the same period. TPS Portfolio was heavily weighted in small-cap stocks.

To show what I was thinking I quote from *The Prudent Speculator* newsletter dated July 19, 1990, which had gone to the printer after the market day of July 17:

> New Dow highs since January 3rd's have led to selloffs, so we should be extra careful about how the market behaves at this time. But July 16's new highs were made with more strength and with only modestly overbought readings, which suggests the advance could continue without a significant correction. The Weekend Technical Review is a summary of some indicators we watch daily and weekly. On balance it is positive and suggests the uptrend is likely to continue, albeit after a pause or two.[8]

In a black humor sense, my analysis was correct, especially the part, "the uptrend is likely to continue, albeit after a pause or two." Some pause, and yet, here we are in 1995 with the Dow having broken above 4700 and . . .

In reviewing the July 19 *TPS* issue, I am struck by how optimistically I interpreted the technical data. The following are 12 items I reviewed at that time:

1. NYCI: concerned that 100-, 150-, and 200-MAs (moving averages) are 5.39 percent, 5.77 percent, and 5.55 percent below Friday's all-time high close of 200.33.

2. DJIA: concerned that 25-, 50-, 100-, 150-, and 200-MAs are 2.76 percent, 4.07 percent, 7.33 percent, 8.61 percent, and 9.29 percent, respectively, below all-time high close of 2980.20.

3. ARMS: relieved that 4Arms (4-day Arms/Trin Index) is 0.85, while 25 Arms is 1.02 even after 90-point DJIA advance.

4. OPEN ARMS: satisfied that all OArms are above 0.85.

5. A/D: Net 1738 advances since 6/26 low is OK, but no 1000-advances day since then is a negative.

6. ADOBV: breadth and up volume positive since 6/26 low.

7. HILOW: Happy to see 159 new 52-week highs on 7/13—most since the 171 of 8/9/89—and a nice progression since 7/10. Unfortunately, the

---

[8] *The Prudent Speculator*, July 19, 1990, p. 2.

Logic High-Low registered .0630 due to 138 weekly new lows, 224 weekly new highs, and 2,192 issues traded.

8. HL-OEX: All momentum readings positive, put/call indications slightly positive.

9. 20BANDS: All closes above bands, with 2 standard deviations at low, buy-level readings. This pattern looks even better than the 5/11–5/15 "overboughtness" that occurred only halfway into May's strong rally. Very encouraging.

10. 30BANDS: Similar pattern to 20BANDS.

11. S&P: The S&P 100 and 500 comparisons are slightly concerning, especially with the 100's close of 6.59 percent and the 500's close of 7.58 percent above their 200MAs.

12. INDEX: The 45-week MA of the S&P 500 (344.90) is nicely rising and well below the weekly S&P 500 (367.31).[9]

Obviously (at least in hindsight) there were many negative caveats about the market's technical condition—and other potential problems: ("We go to the printer after hearing that the Consumer Price Index was up 0.5 percent, but before Alan Greenspan's testimony to Congress today.) Either or both of these elements could affect the market for a little while." Apparently they contributed to the market's swift and sharp decline over the following three months.

Now that I reread the Weekend Technical Review for July 13, 1990, and other comments in the newsletter, I wonder how I could have been so bullish and sanguine. With the NYCI (NYSE's Composite Index) and DJIA *below* their long-term moving averages, the normal interpretation is bear market. The ARMs indexes were closer to overboughtness than to neutrality or oversoldness. Norm Fosback's High-Low Logic index has yielded good trend reversal signals in the past and since 1990, so there was a strong red flag. I probably misinterpreted the Bollinger Bands (20BANDS), as closes above the bands indicate likely overboughtness. Even the S&P 100 and 500 closes over 6.5 percent above their 200MAs could indicate vulnerability, although those percentages get much higher in strong bull markets.

Next time there is an all-time new DJIA high with so many negatives including an interest and inflation rate trend that is not down or at least stabilized, I want to err on the side of caution by hedging portfolios with OEX stock index put options, perhaps 2 to 4 percent out of the money, with at least two but preferably six weeks to run. Such insurance hedges can be accomplished for 1 to 2 percent or so of the portfolio's value and, if past experience is any criterion, represent very worthwhile expenses.

---

[9] *The Prudent Speculator*, July 19, 1990, p. 2.

Summary

What can we learn from the Crash of '87 and the Selloff of '90? Much of the answer to that question has been given in the paragraphs above. With the hindsight of almost eight years from the former and five years from the latter, we learn that these crashes weren't the end of the financial world, or even of an economic era. By mid-1995 all major indexes had recovered all their crashes' losses on a total return basis and all have gone on to make all-time new highs. That's not to say that everyone was restored to pre-crash wealth. Those who bailed out and "locked in their losses" and those who reduced their exposures greatly but didn't return to the market vigorously, may still be trying to make up all the losses they suffered during periods of greater exposure.

As we have pointed out in reviewing the returns of various financial instruments, we should be aware of real (inflation adjusted returns) rather than nominal returns. The summer 1995 dollar buys significantly less than did the summer 1990 dollar or the summer 1987 dollar.

Still, compared to the investors who sold out during or just after the crashes—locking in their losses and not participating in the subsequent advances—the long-term shareholders need hardly have been highly disturbed by the traumatic events. And if they had the wherewithal, foresight, and intestinal fortitude to pick up some more bargains deep in the crashes or shortly thereafter, they could be holding significant unrealized gains overall.

My portfolio was badly damaged by the Crash of '87 and Selloff of '90. I had the double misfortune of being fully margined with a preponderance of over-the-counter, secondary stocks. Many of my margined stocks were driven below $5 per share, making them unmarginable, which radically reduced the equity supporting the debit balance (margin loan value), thus creating large minimum maintenance calls (see Chapter 5). I had to sell large amounts of stocks at just about their market-cycle lows, and so did not have many of them working in my favor in the subsequent market advance. Even so, the total returns for over 18 years, including the two crashes, have significantly surpassed those of the major market averages.

Some friends suggest I should not write about my setbacks during the Crash of '87 and the Selloff of '90, because too many people seem to focus on those events, on the short-term negatives rather than the long-term positives. Many people equate the use of margin with gambling. I have been called a "river-boat gambler" by one allegedly conservative investment advisor, who has held very low stock positions since 1986. All I can do is remind readers that my view of the use of leverage is that of a businessperson employing borrowed funds to enhance my business. If borrowing to open another carefully considered branch store, or taking advantage of improving one's inventory at bargain prices is gambling, then so be it. But I believe that what I am following is the same strategy employed when great corporations borrow—raise cash through the sale of bonds, commercial paper, or bank loans—to expand their plants or services.

As is true for anyone who borrows, we must be careful not to borrow more than we can likely repay, and we must guard against conditions changing that would cause us to make forced liquidations during market lows. Having experienced this phenomenon twice is no reason to cease being logical and businesslike, even as one takes greater precautions against becoming overextended. "Once bitten, twice shy" is O.K. as a guideline; "If you fall off a horse, get right back on" is a better motto for learning from experience and overcoming adversity in life and stock market.

7

18 Years and Counting

As long as I can remember, life has always seemed a little unreal to me, as if I were participating in a play which later I could hardly believe happened. And so it is with my role as an investment adviser and stock speculator. Providence, in the form of a couple friends, led me as a relatively penniless, aging graduate student, to buy a few shares of stock with a few hundred dollars, surplus funds from my GI Bill and meager part-time earnings.

I was a 38-year-old UCLA grad student studying philosophy of education when I had several practical and serendipitous conversations about the stock market with my fellow teaching assistant, Tom Haldi (now Dr. Haldi). All this led to my Ph.D. sponsor, Professor George Kneller, a veteran of three decades in the stock market, encouraging me to open an account. Kneller sent me to one of his bright young brokers, Peter Palmer, at the old Francis I. duPont office in Beverly Hills. There I opened a pathetically small account with a few hundred dollars that was burning a proverbial hole in my pocket.

I can hardly believe how ignorant I was about the stock market at the age of 38, even though I had owned two businesses, had worked for several major corporations since I turned 18, and had earned two master's degrees. I was quite naive when Mr. Palmer put me into the old Enterprise Fund, saying it had doubled in each of the past two years and implying—or did I just imagine he said?—that it would likely double yet again during the next 12 months. My first purchase was $300 worth of Enterprise Fund (22.239 shares) on December 12, 1968. It turned out that in 1969 the old Enterprise Fund made a "round trip," and instead of doubling it lost a significant portion of its net asset value.

185

Next, Peter said something like, "Let's buy some Whittaker [WKR]; it's at 27, down from 37, and we should get it because we may never see this price again." That sounded good to me, so I bought 30 shares at $25 per in June 1969. Peter was right, I never saw that price again while I owned it. Whittaker continued to decline to 1 1/8 by December 1984. Now Peter had my full attention.

Thus began the Whittaker Saga and my dogged determination to learn this stock game. By November, convinced that Whittaker wouldn't go much lower, I bought another 30 shares $19.75, and another 20 shares just before Christmas for $15.625. By September 8, 1970, I was able to buy another 100 shares of Whittaker at $7.375. Whittaker was probably at fair value when I bought my next 20 shares at $6.75 on December 22, 1970. WKR must have rallied a bit because I bought another 100 shares on April 2, 1971 at $10.75. Nothing if not persistent, I bought another 100 shares of WKR on June 30, 1972, for $8.75 and still another 100 shares on September 14, 1972 at $7.625. On May 24, 1973 (I cannot remember why) I sold my supply of WKR for $1,007.33, taking a long-term capital loss of $2,683.50.

Selling Whittaker in May of '73 left me with no lasting lesson. Three months later, I could not resist buying 300 shares of WKR at $3 on August 29, 1973, and then another 200 shares at $2.50 on December 4, 1973. One more time, I picked up my final 100 shares of WKR on February 26, 1974, at $2.50. I had accumulated 800 shares since having sold out my earlier positions. By November of '74, just at the end of the great bear market of '73–'74, I sold out again, first 400 shares for $602.71 on November 19, 1974, creating another long-term capital loss of $1,101.95, and then on November 25, 1974, the final 400 shares for $602.72, again creating a long-term capital loss of $547.16.

The irony of this series of Whittaker trades is that I bought overvalued shares at the beginning, was impatient, and sold them when they were undervalued. I then bought very undervalued shares, was impatient, and sold them when they were more undervalued, just at the end of a great bear market, which was followed by a great bull market. At that time, I did not know the meaning of the terms "bull" and "bear markets," or for that matter "market timing."

By May of '81, Whittaker traded for more than $50 per share. The 800 shares of WKR I sold in November 1974, which had cost $2,854.54, would have been worth $40,000.00—a long-term capital gain of $37,145.46 or 1,300 percent, not counting dividends or margin leverage—a compounded annual gain of 67 percent per annum for the 6.5-year holding period. Ah, paying those kinds of dues—having taken the repeated losses and missing the great gains—did much to develop my patience as a stock speculator.

Somehow, instead of becoming discouraged at what happened to my initial "investments" in '69 through '74, I became intrigued and fascinated. I still felt sheepish and a bit of an impostor entering the august and beautifully appointed offices of

Francis I. duPont in Beverly Hills, my old-line prestigious "wire-house" (a.k.a. full-service) brokerage. I would grab all the research reports available in the bins lining the reception area, guilty that I only had a few hundred bucks to throw at the market, rather than the thousands and tens of thousands I presumed their average client had.

Slowly and unsurely I began to acquire the lingo and read a couple of important books that fortunately made a lot of sense to me, especially Ben Graham's *The Intelligent Investor*[1]. Somehow I managed to escape in these formative years the scourge of chart reading and technical analysis, although in recent years I've become fascinated with technical analysis and wonder if chart reading can be far behind. (It can.)

And so it went, this vague recollection, as I studied philosophy, psychology, history, passed my orals, and began writing my dissertation on "The Concept of Consciousness in Higher Education," all the while defecting intellectually to the seductress stock market. After several years of trying to serve two muses, the challenge of stock speculation overwhelmed the challenge of the classroom. Graduate studies, especially many of the courses in philosophy, logic and linguistics, and teaching at the university level, set the stage for what I've learned and done in speculating and as an investment adviser.

The teaching jobs at UCLA, Cal State University L.A.; the two summers spent as an associate professor at Bloomsburg State College; several other positions at colleges and universities (part-time, "adjunct assistant professor"); the hundreds of interesting classroom encounters—all seem like a lifetime ago, a different life. On the other hand, I have for more than 18 years published my newsletter (over 346 issues of *The Prudent Speculator*) and have amassed 25 years' worth of trade confirmation slips; yet, in contrast to my perception of my academic years, I have the sense that I've been at this only a few years. Maybe that's what happens when one is having fun (most of the time).

I'm still studying new books and old facts to try to learn more about the mechanics of the stock market and consolidate what I think I know about investing. In fact, one of the reasons for writing, and now revising, this book is to gather together many of the bits and pieces of the past 25 years, focusing them into a recognizable and heuristic tableau, reinforce my own learning and behavior—and to help you.

To the end of reviewing actual events in the expectation that what is past is prologue, at least to a meaningful degree, I embark on reviewing the 18+ years of publishing *The Prudent Speculator*. I could not imagine 18 years ago that I would be still at it today. Actually, the advisory letter originally was supposed to be a kind of course, which readers would complete in two or three years and thereafter be sufficiently knowledgeable to succeed on their own. I am an advocate of the

---

[1] Benjamin Graham, *The Intelligent Investor*, 4th rev. ed., (NY: Harper & Row, 1973).

Tao Teh King of Lao Tzu, a tenet of which is, "In teaching, he teaches, not by describing and pointing out differences, but by example."[2] I am a believer in the emphasis on learning as opposed to teaching, eloquently exemplified in Carl R. Rogers' *Freedom to Learn.*[3]

By sharing my experiences, learning, and actions—especially if they turn out to be somewhat successful—I hope to facilitate your education in the stock market. A distillation of the printed record might better speak for itself, and so we begin with the first issue of *TPS.* As there are over 346 issues of *TPS,* I can sample briefly only a few of them.

This chapter is a history, the record of a learning curve, with successes and failures along the way. Most of the stocks mentioned will probably not mean much to you, but the idea of having some historic awareness of the market and a system of dealing with it is very important to successful future investing. One of the average investor's shortcomings is lack of background and no memory of stock market gyrations. Philosophically, spiritually, and psychologically we may want to live in the now, but as investors/speculators we want to avoid making the errors of the past if we can. Highly applicable is Santayana's famous admonition, "Those who cannot remember the past are condemned to repeat it."

The First Year: 1977

For the first year—actually nine months, or 22 issues—of publication I am going to review from each issue my thinking at the time and how my advisory letter and stock portfolio developed. This would require too much detail to carry through for the following 17 years, so I will merely summarize some of the most noteworthy events and recommendations of subsequent years.

I am reminded of term papers turned in for college assignments as I look at *TPS 1,* dated March 12, 1977. Typed with a manual typewriter and photocopied on one side of the sheets, this "gem" was sent to fewer than 100 friends and acquaintances. A few paragraphs set the spartan stage, which hasn't changed all that much in 18 years.

> Welcome to the *Pinchpenny Speculator* (PS), dedicated to the small speculator. I will express my experience and thinking about "playing" with stocks for fun and profit. My essential commitment is with New York Stock Exchange common stocks. I will take an irreverent view and tone to such goings on, attempting to penetrate mystifications and obfuscations created by jargon and semantics.

[2] Lao Tzu, *Tao Teh King,* Interpreted as *Nature and Intelligence* by Archie J. Bahm, 2d ed., (Albuquerque, NM: World Books, 1986), p. 12.

[3] Carl R. Rogers, *Freedom to Learn,* (Columbus, OH: Charles E. Merrill Publishing Company, 1969).

For example, "playing" is a reasonable term denoting what I and others do when we involve ourselves in buying, selling, and talking about the "market" and stocks. The word investing is frequently used to hide or mask the play of speculating with stocks.

. . . After several years of helter-skelter buying and selling, I learned that successful speculating is more a matter of character than mathematics, analysis, or luck. Obviously the latter are required, but the great gains and losses seem to occur in consequence to individual psychology. This has been my experience; perhaps you recognize it also.

. . . Essentially, the PS method is to "buy low and sell high." Low refers to "undervalued" (in the market place) stocks, and high refers to fully or overvalued stocks. These valuations are based upon historical, current, and projected: 1) tangible book value; 2) net working capital; 3) price/earnings ratio; 4) earnings; 5) dividends and dividend policy; 6) price; 7) earned on net-worth percentage; 8) other special considerations unique to the company being analyzed (e.g., management, products, cultural trends); 9) stock market climate; and 10) the individual's needs, capacities, and portfolio. I include items 9) and 10) in the notion of valuation because it is silly to consider any equity independently of them. Thus, any "recommended" stock is in an individual- and market-dependent context.

Pages 3 and 4 of the initial letter review the record of all my sales of common stocks for 1976, Table 7–1, and my portfolio as of March 11, 1977, displayed in Table 7–2.

I thought I was pretty clever back in '77, as I boasted that all sales in '76 resulted in long-term (then six months) capital gains, having been held from 9 to

Table 7–1. Sales of Common Stocks for 1976

Sold	Shares Issue	Sale Net	Cost Net	Gain/Loss	Bought
1/12/76	100 Western Union	1,602.19	1,092.44	509.75	1/ 7/75
2/10/76	100 Garfinkle-Brks	1,450.60	1,153.43	297.17	5/28/75
5/ 5/76	100 Avnet Inc.	1,672.74	752.50	920.24	5/28/75
7/27/76	100 Boeing Arcrft	3,976.86	2,056.69	1,920.17	3/ 4/75
9/29/76	100 Western Union	1,980.23	1,257.38	722.85	2/14/75
10/ 7/76	100 Consumers Pwr.	2,164.72	1,406.93	757.79	5/ 9/75
		$12,847.34	$7,719.37	$5,127.97	

19 months. I also pointed out that the gains amounted to 66.43 percent net, since my portfolio was fully margined for the entire period

> ... so the gain on invested capital amounted to more than 132 percent. I say more than for two reasons: the dividends received were more than the margin interest paid, and some of the stock was bought with surplus in the margin account, that is, leveraged with increases in market values. I must say that 1976 was an "easy" year in which to profit from the terrible declines of '73 and '74, the opportunity of a decade!

Oh man, was I smug. With the proceeds from the brilliant trade in Boeing I bought a brand-new Honda 550-4 motorcycle, which at the time cost just about the equivalent of the Boeing profits ($2,000). I didn't realize until a while later that the motorcycle cost me about five times what I paid for it by not holding Boeing, as Boeing went on to split twice and reach the equivalent of $120 per share a couple years later. Score another one for the long-term holding of undervalued, growing corporations.

On page 4 of the first issue, I began a tradition of displaying my personal, actual ("model" TPS) portfolio. Not only would the triumphs be shown and trumpeted, but the failures would also be highlighted in an effort to learn from sometimes painful trial and error. Table 7–2 shows my portfolio as of March 11, 1977. The portfolio was fully margined, with equity actually at $8,006. "For the 10 weeks in

Table 7–2. TPS Portfolio at March 11, 1977

Date BOT	Issue (in 100-share lots)	BOT at	3/11/77	+ / –
9/28/76	American Medical Int'l	11 1/2	12 1/2	+ 1
10/ 7/76	American Seating	10	11 1/4	+ 1 1/4
3/10/74	Chemitron Corp.	30	33 5/8	+ 3 5/8
9/22/76	Cluett, Peabody & Co.	8 1/4	9 1/4	+ 1
9/22/76	Dan River	8 7/8	8 1/2	– 3/8
1/17/77	Marathon Manufacturing	14	13 1/8	– 7/8
9/29/76	McNeill Corp.	12 1/4	11 7/8	– 3/8
9/29/76	Phillips-Van Heusen	10 1/4	10 5/8	+ 3/8
10/ 7/76	Triangle Industries	10 1/8	9 1/4	– 7/8
3/31/75	United Financial of CA	7 3/8	11 3/4	+ 4 3/8
9/ 8/76	United Financial of CA	11 1/8	11 3/4	+ 5/8
9/13/76	Western Pacific Ind's	11 1/2	18 1/2	+ 7
		$14,525.00	$16,200.00	$1,675.00

1977, the portfolio has a 'paper profit' of $575 or 48 cents per share, while the Dow Jones Industrial Average has declined 56.96 points (947.72) and the Average Price per Share of Common has declined $1.91 on the New York Stock Exchange."

To look at the March 11, 1977, portfolio can be shocking if one thinks about the corporations and their stocks that are no longer with us, or corporations so changed as to be for all practical purposes different entities. By 1989, just 12 "short years," American Seating, Chemitron, Cluett, Peabody & Co., Dan River, Marathon Manufacturing, McNeill Corp., United Financial of California, Triangle Industries, and Western Pacific Industries no longer exist as independent corporations—9 out of 11 gone! American Medical International and Phillips-Van Heusen are still listed, but they too are under threat of being bought out or "restructured."

TPS 2 (March 26, 1977) featured a review on tangible book value (TBV) and quoted the 1971 *NASD Training Guide* "Because investors place greater importance on the earning power of a corporation, book value and market value per share are usually not related."[4] Of course, some investors focus on book value or asset plays in their stock selection. Phillips-Van Heusen (PVH) and Dan River Inc. (DML) were recommended. PVH at 10 3/8 was trading for "less than half its TBV and for less than net working capital" with a P/E of 8 and a dividend yield of 5.78 percent. DML traded for P/E 5 and 40 percent of TBV. Hard to find those kinds of bargains for many years now.

Net working capital (NWC)—sometimes called net liquidating value—was the featured topic of *TPS 3* (April 9, 1977). You could find many corporations in those days trading for less per share than the difference between current assets and all liabilities, one of Benjamin Graham's favorite buy criteria. Still:

> It is important to note that a company can prosper with a negative NWC, and its stock may be an attractive purchase based upon other criteria. Western Pacific Industries (WPI), with a TBV of some $50.00 per share and a negative NWC, is an example. WPI advanced from 6 to 18 7/8 during the recent 15 months.

Who could have known that WPI would go on to be bought out for $163 per share in cash, after paying a $23 return of equity "dividend" per share on December 31, 1979?

Hughes & Hatcher, Inc. (HGH) at 7 and Kroehler Manufacturing Co. (KFM) at 14 1/8 were recommended on April 9, 1977. Both traded for less than half their TBVs and about 2/3 their NWCs.

By *TPS 4* (April 23, 1977), the P/E ratio was assayed, with a degree of breathless amazement.

---

[4] 1971 *NASD Training Guide*, p. 19.

On April 15, 1977, the P/E for Dow Jones Industrials was 9.8, compared to 13.0 on April 15, 1976 and 8.2 on April 15, 1975. These figures show quite a variation over just a 24-month period. Furthermore,
the P/Es of DJIA[-type] stocks currently range from 4 for Chrysler to
26 for Eastman Kodak.

Reviewing further, I find that:

P/E can be a tricky figure. For example, the P/E for Lowenstein &
Sons (LST) was 21 at the week ending February 25, 1977. During the
next week, LST's P/E became 5, when it reported annual earnings of
$2.50 a share for 1976, versus a deficit for the same period 1975. On
the other hand, Triangle Industries' P/E of 18 became zero during
October, 1976, when its nine-months' *earnings* were published.

The recommended stocks for April 23, 1977, were American Medical
International, Inc. (AMI) at 13 1/4, around its book value with a P/E of 8, and
United Financial of California (UFL) at 14 5/8, at 75 percent of TBV and P/E 5.

TPS 5 (May 7, 1977) dealt with earnings and the unexpected buyout bid for
dull-trading Hughes & Hatcher (HGH), recommended four weeks earlier, which
jumped its price from 7 to 10 3/4 (54 percent). I quoted my favorite mentor,
Benjamin Graham: "Don't take a single year's earnings seriously . . . If you do pay
attention to short-term earnings, look out for booby traps in the per-share figure."
Marathon Manufacturing Co. (MTM) at 16 1/4, 60 percent of TBV and P/E 5, and
McNeil Corp. (MME) at 12 1/8, 50 percent of TBV and P/E 6, were the recommended stocks for May 7, 1977.

"Dividends and Dividend Policy" was the essay for *TPS 6* (May 21, 1977),
using non dividend-paying Western Pacific Industries (WPI) as a high-appreciation
example compared to high-dividend-paying Western Union Corp. (WU), with a
dividend yield of 7.8 percent, as a low-total-return example. In conclusion:

An important argument is made that a good yield puts a floor under
the market price of a stock, however, when all is said and done, The
Pinchpenny Speculator looks principally for stocks he hopes will
appreciate significantly, and lets whatever incidental dividends
accrue balance the ravages of his margin interest.

By May 21, 1977, Wurlitzer Co. (WUR) at 8 3/4, 50 percent of TBV and P/E
5, and Triangle Industries, Inc. (TRI) at 9 1/2, about 40 percent of TBV and P/E
negative, made the recommended page.

TPS 7 (June 4, 1977) celebrated "our first quarter" and espoused the speculation strategy of the margin account, touching on some of the basics revealed in

Chapter 5. TPS Portfolio was updated, noting that American Seating (AMZ) was tendered for $15.00 per share net on May 20, 1977. "This year's gain (so far) of 10 percent is modest, but delightful, when compared to the other averages, which show a loss of 8–9 percent . . ."

By June I was aware that recommending two stocks an issue did not nearly represent the population of recommendable stocks I'd been discovering. I was becoming frustrated that some formerly recommendable stocks had already advanced in price too far to be currently recommended. So I listed 71 "closely followed stocks" that "are not all recommended at this time!" Still, I believed "many of them [are] appropriate commitments, depending upon the individual's situation."

TPS 8 (June 18, 1977) was rather upbeat:

> Take Friday the 17th, for example. I was delighted that the market traded almost 22 million shares and though the DJIA was unchanged on Friday the 17th, the average share of common gained five cents . . . The DJIA continues to mask market appreciation as the broader averages show greater increases, especially among the so-called secondary stocks.

The essay was on price, mostly in relationship to fundamentals. Salant Corp. (SLT) at 7 1/8 and Faberge, Inc. at 8 5/8, were recommended stocks.

"Serendipity" was the title of a paragraph in *TPS 9* (July 2, 1977):

> I was talking to a wave theorist the other day, a market watcher who claims to follow apparent (chartable or graphable) wave actions based upon price and volume, etc. He suggested that the smaller capitalized and lesser-traded stocks may avoid the consequences or implications of wave theory. I thought to myself, well, these stocks just don't make sufficient waves! But they do often get results nonetheless, and sometimes counter to the apparent trend. And I was pleased to read in the current issue of *Forbes* that people who are too concerned with the 'market' and where it is going, often miss good opportunities present in individual stocks.

The essay for July 2, 1977 reviewed earned on net worth (ENW). The two recommended stocks were Spring Mills, Inc. (SMI) at 12 1/4 and Gibraltar Financial Corp. of California (GFC) at 10 3/8. I suggested readers regard "the pinchpenny angle" when checking out ENW. For instance, SMI for '76 had net income of $15.1 million and net worth of $284.4 million, for an ENW of 5.3 percent. "However, SMI's net worth, which was about $32.80 per share, could have been purchased at Friday's close for $14.25." This works out to an earned on net worth cost to stock purchasers of 12.23 percent. "The astute speculator will look for these relationships, which are not immediately apparent in the published ENW percent."

"A funny thing happened to the NYSE on the way to the Bastille Day rally— New York City had an energy knockout which kept the Exchange dark." Thus began *TPS 10* (July 16, 1977), which spent two full pages (out of the four published then) on "some reflections on the individual and the market." The essay called for trying to get our thinking straight about stocks and the market and took a swipe at the system (this theme is reiterated more forcefully in Chapter 8):

> I do not like stock brokerage houses nor the role of account executives, because I believe there is an essential conflict of interest in their functions. The account executive generally works on commission and only makes a living if he can have customers who trade stocks, bonds, and options. He cannot say, "The market looks blah; why don't you go to Europe for a year and forget it!" He would be out of business.

Cluett, Peabody & Co., Inc (CLU) at 11 and Franklin Mint Corp. (FM) at 11 1/8 were the recommended stocks on July 16, 1977.

The market tumbled a bit in the fortnight preceding July 30, 1977, when *TPS 11* was published:

> On Wednesday occurred something akin to panic selling, as the DJIA dropped 19.75 points, ending down 33.35 for the week, making a new 18-month low. The heavy, across-the-board declines have been attributed to the tremendous trade deficits (estimated at possibly 25 billion dollars this year); the poor showing of steel companies, with the second largest, Bethlehem Steel, cutting its dividend; a surprising jump in the money supply; and the second monthly decline in leading economic indicators.
>
> Meanwhile, second-quarter earnings are generally good, inflation seems under control, unemployment is steady, and stocks are historically cheap. Not to panic, a time to pick up more bargains at even better prices. TPS recommends purchase and accumulation of underpriced, recommended issues.

The essay for June 30, 1977, was entitled "The Individual's Psychology," and began:

> As an investment adviser, I am often disappointed when individuals tell me they are not interested in the stock market because they "took a bath" or "lost my shirt" a few years ago. As a speculator, I

am secretly pleased that there are so many such people because they contribute to the recurring opportunities in undervalued stocks. It's *dejá vu*, all over again, as Yogi Berra is said to have said. [I might write the same sentence in a current edition of *TPS*, except for the scars remaining from '87 and '90.] I cited the example of Consolidated Edison (ED), the NYC utility that traded between $6-$8 per share during the last eight months of '74 after its directors omitted the June dividend. "Today [July 30, 1977], ED trades at 23 5/8 and pays a $2 dividend, a yield of 25 percent to 33 percent annually, based on the fall and winter of '74 price."

In the summer of 1995, the 52-week trading range for Consolidated Edison was $23.00 to $31.375 with a dividend of $2.04. While ED was a great buy in '74 because of its omitted-dividend price, it hasn't been a good buy since 1987. ED is an example of why we have a general disposition against utility stocks, which are vulnerable to dividend cuts and rarely have substantial growth rates or price appreciations unless there has been a traumatic market crash.

The recommended stocks for July 30, 1977, were Zale Corporation (ZAL) at 14 3/4 and Morse Shoe, Inc. (MRS) at 10 3/8.

By August 13, 1977—and *TPS 12*—I am still marveling at the average daily volume during the summer decline of less than 19 million shares and how encouraging it is "that there is little apparent rush to sell large amounts of stock at lower prices." I am still exploring "Some psychological aspects of speculation, especially the toos, too much procrastination or too little patience." Again, Western Pacific Industries (WPI) is cited as having traded between 6 and 10 3/4 in '74, between 6 and 8 3/4 in '75, between 6 and 14 7/8 in '76, and between 14 and 23 7/8 so far this year:

Clearly one might have stuck with WPI through '74 and '75, at whatever purchase price, and see it more than double or triple in value two or three years later . . . It is still selling for only four times earnings and looking good otherwise . . . so even though the stock has doubled in price since last September [1976] when it was bought for 11 1/2—it sold for 9 1/2 on October 15! [1976]—it may well double again in the next year or so, and should be held in spite of the 15 percent retrenchment suffered during the recent three weeks.

Western Pacific Industries, Inc. (WPI) at 20 3/4 and Dean Witter Organization, Inc. (DW) at 12 1/2, were the two stocks recommended in *TPS* as of August 13, 1977. Ironically, we noted that DW is a holding company, which has never had an unprofitable year since its founding in 1924. Later, Dean Witter became Dean Witter Reynolds, still later it was acquired by Sears Roebuck at a handsome profit for longtime DW stock owners.

To paraphrase an old vaudeville joke, "How come you never ask me about the market?" inquired the speculator to his friend. "So, how's the market?" "Don't ask!" This was the mood when *TPS 13* (August 27, 1977) was published. The theme for this issue was "Some thoughts on when to sell a stock"; it included such gems as, "In order to determine when to sell a stock, consider the reasons for which it was bought." Of course, that was a takeoff of Gerald M. Loeb's notion of "The Ruling Reason" for buying and owning a stock, the violation of which should lead to the immediate sale of the stock. The ruling reason could be a level or trend of profitability or asset valuation which, if broken or diminished, should lead to exiting that position.

In *TPS 13* the 20 stocks recommended during the first six months were reviewed. Happily, the overall recommendations appreciated 2.03 percent during a period in which the DJIA declined 7.19 percent and the New York Stock Exchange Composite Index lost 2.45 percent.

TPS 14 (September 10, 1977) mentions watching *Wall $treet Week* and being:

> . . . struck again with the wisdom of the venerable and sanguine Philip Carret, who offered as his major single piece of advice to the investor, "Patience." If one has made a good stock selection, he should be unaffected by transitory market conditions or fluctuations in the price of the stock—trading frequently is not the way to consistently make money in the market, although there are no doubt traders who do. Of course, if one discovers an error in his selection, or conditions alter radically, he must be prepared to accept change and act accordingly.

The essay for *TPS 14*, "A Game Plan, or Two," was based on one of those tables I love, showing 10 years of compounded annual returns. The recommended stocks were Armstrong Rubber (ARM) at 28, Avco Corp. (AV) at 15 1/8, and Sterchi Bros. Store (SBI) at 9, each without any fundamental criteria because page 4 was used to review TPS Portfolio. It showed additions of Marathon Mfg. (MTM), Morse Shoe (MRS), and Zale (ZAL) to the tender of American Seating (AMZ), and the sales of Chemitron (CTN), Triangle Industries (TRI), and United Financial (UFL). Alas, I reported:

> Chemitron (CTN) was sold the day before the first Crane Co. tender offer was made . . . CTN closed yesterday at 48 1/2. My impatience cost some $2,000 on one stock in one month, after owning CTN patiently for some 29 months. I didn't have an inkling of the takeover bid, however, the numbers indicated that CTN was a good stock to

own at $30.00 a share on August 1, 1977. I present this information in all candor that readers, clients, and I may learn from my experience. The American Seating was a tender offer by the company itself; it seemed wise to take the 100 percent (margined) profit. I sold Triangle Industries and United Financial (100 shares each) to obtain funds.

The broad market and DJIA stocks were still declining by September 24, 1977, when *TPS 15* opened with:

> "If you can keep your head when all about you are losing theirs . . ." you may not know what they know. But then, they may not realize what you have either. It is trying to watch the general averages declining all year long and keep shouting that they are only telling half the truth. Look at the new highs (e.g., United Financial, UFL, closed Friday at a new high, 16 5/8, up 38.5 percent this year) . . .

The first one-page essay for September 24, 1977, was "Lifestyle and Speculating," still another attempt to show that "speculator" was a more honest term than "investor" and was not to be associated with gambling or other pejoratives. The second one-page essay, "The Art Is Learning from Experience," reviewed my Whittaker Corp. (WKR) experience, but extended it to a missed Act II, because I had quit after Act I:

> WKR worked its way to $1.125 per share by December, '74. Did I know that WKR had a book value about $5.00 per share, paid no dividend, sold for over 16 times earnings, and had a negative net working capital? I do not remember even being aware of those kinds of facts when I started buying the stock. All I knew is that WKR had sold for higher prices, was a "bargain," and was recommended by a man who was recommended to me by a man who made a lot of money in the market during the '60s.
>
> Nor was I aware that by December '74, WKR was selling for three times earnings and only 20 percent of book value, making it a good speculation near the bottom of a great and exhausted bear market. As hindsight shows, WKR tripled in market value between December 1974 and May 1975, about five months, to $4.625 per share. I was only "aware" in December 1974 that I had bought and sold WKR at ever-decreasing prices (e.g., 3.50 on May 24, 1973; 1.625 on November 25, 1974), and would not go near the stock again because I had been "burnt" so much already. So I was emotionally blocked from having perspective about profiting, no matter

what the numbers suggested. I see a lot of that kind of thinking and acting still going on, as people who took big losses in the early '70s and missed out on the big gains since then are still unable to recognize fundamental values in the market.

The three recommendations mentioned in the previous issue were detailed as recommendations on September 24, 1977: Armstrong Rubber Co. (ARM) at 26 1/8, Avco Corporation (AV) at 15, and Sterchie Brothers Stores, Inc. (SBI) at 9. It was startling to see that ARM traded with a P/E of 3.46 and for less than 50 percent of tangible book value, while AV's P/E was 2.62 and traded for less than TBV, and SBI with a P/E of 6.56 traded for less than net working capital. Those were the days.

"The Market versus the Stock" was the theme for *TPS 16* (October 8, 1977), expanding on the maxim, "This is a market of stocks, and not a stock market." I noted that while the DJIA hit 21-month lows, 79 stocks made new 52-week highs during the week ended September 30, 1977:

> The reasons I cannot predict what The Market will do are the same reasons that are given every day by market commentators (post hoc) as to why the market advanced, was unchanged, or declined. Example: Friday morning (October 7, 1977) the pre-opening news was: 1) major banks raised their prime rate to 7 1/2 percent, bearish; 2) unemployment figures showed a decline from 7.1 percent to 6.9 percent, bullish; 3) wholesale prices rose 0.5 percent for the reported month, bearish; and 4) the money supply M1 decreased 1.2 billion, bullish [?]. Meanwhile, the Fed is "tightening up," short-term interest rates are rising—bearish. However, construction and consumer credit is up—bullish. Thus, the economy is a) doing well, b) merely getting by, c) pretty shaky. Take your pick. The market opened nicely up, then settled back. It closed off 1 cent, APSC [Average Price per Share Common], virtually unchanged for the day, although many stocks took gains and losses. Who knows what it will do next week?

Rockower Brothers Inc. (ROC) at 11 1/2 with a P/E of 5.18 and Pier 1 Imports, Inc. (PIR) at 6 1/8 with a P/E of 4.94 were the recommended stocks for October 8, 1977.

Another tough fortnight was the message in *TPS 17* (October 22, 1977), with Citibank raising its prime rate to 7 3/4 percent and *The Wall Street Journal* headline "Consumer Confidence Found at 15-Month Low." The essay pointed out the glories of the earnings-to-price ratio, or how much in earnings you would get per dollar's worth of stock. The recommended stocks were Allis-Chalmers Corp. (AH) at 23 5/8 with a

P/E of 4.75, trading for about 50 percent of TBV, and Cooper Tire & Rubber Co. (CTB) at 12 3/8 with a P/E of 2.64, trading for about half of TBV and 2/3 of NWC!

By *TPS 18* (November 5, 1977), the question was, had the market bottomed on November 2 at DJIA 800.85? The essay "A Technique within an Approach within a Game within the System," attempted to describe the desirability of focusing on one kind of stock selection augmented by using margin as a form of being in business. The recommended stocks were Oxford Industries, Inc. (OXM) at 9 5/8 with a P/E of 2.38, trading at less than 50 percent of TBV and 2/3 of NWC, and Zayre Corp. (ZY) at 6 3/4 with a P/E of 3.48, trading at less than NWC and less than 30 percent of TBV. Prophetically, I wrote, "The ruling reason for speculating with ZY is that it could be selling for four to six times its current price if it continues to improve as a business and the market climate turns bullish." Zayre's stock appreciated over 2,400 percent between November 5, 1977 (adjusted cost basis $0.959 per share) and April 1988, when we closed out the original recommendation at $24.00 per share.

"Finally, the summer rally, and just in time!" was the lead sentence in *TPS 19* (November 19, 1977):

> True, it seems to have lasted only six trading days (Nov. 4–11), but what a week the penultimate one was, including two days of 30-plus-million share days. For those six days, the DJIA gained 43.22 . . . far and away the largest advance of the year. I'm not sure how many (if any) readers were amused at a summer rally in November, but a quick 5 percent market gain is almost always satisfying. The little essays were "The market as an Animal" (bull, bear or pig), "The Market as a Condition," (undervalued, valued, or overvalued), and "Important to Keep Invested in Undervalued Markets" because "For TPS, the week of Nov. 7–11 alone added one-third again as much appreciation earned during the previous 44 weeks of this calendar year."

The recommended stocks for November 19, 1977, were Budd Company (BF) at 23 5/8 with a P/E of 3.87 and International Harvester Co. (HR) at 29 1/8 with a P/E of 4.85. The former International Harvester—now renamed Navistar International (NAV)—never worked out well.

The following fortnight saw the DJIA lose 1.41 percent, while TPS Portfolio gained 5.71 percent. The essay in *TPS 20* (December 3, 1977), "Buy 'at market',," pointed out the penny-wise but pound-foolish attempt to save a few dimes on the cost basis while missing a position that advances several dollars. The recommended stocks were Magic Chef, Inc. (MGC) at 9 5/8 with a P/E of 5.12 and Eastern Air Lines, Inc. (EAL) at 6 1/4 with a P/E of 5.10. For the first time, I began listing goal prices: $18–$25 for MGC and $18–$27 for EAL. It's interesting to see that MGC did well enough—advancing to $73 (658 percent) on May 23, 1986, before being bought out by Maytag Corp. (MYG) on June 2, 1986, for 1.671 shares of MYG—as if to compensate for how poorly EAL performed before it went belly up.

TPS 21 (December 17, 1977) reported on a negative market during the first two weeks. The theme article was "The Stock Market Waltz Is Rarely in Three-quarter Time," based on the Spanish proverb, "With patience, everything is possible." The recommended stocks were Cummins Engine Company (CUM) at 38 3/8 with a P/E 4.21 and a goal of $86+ and Elixir Industries (EXR) at 4 7/8 with a P/E of 4.78 and a goal of $11–$14.

The final issue for the year, *TPS 22*, was dated December 31, 1977, and reported on a small Santa Claus rally. For the year, TPS Portfolio gained 38.71 percent in appreciation with an estimated margined gain of over 77 percent, while the nominal DJIA declined 17.27 percent. The "total reinvested percent change" for the DJIA for 1977 (full year) was –12.84 percent according to Lipper Analytical Securities Corporation. The nominal NYSE Composite Index dropped 9.30 percent. There is a small disparity with the audited figures for TPS Portfolio (see Table I-1) because they date from March 11, 1977, not for the whole year. "The Recent Year" was reviewed in a few paragraphs pointing out the strong advances for the American Stock Exchange and NASDAQ Composite.

For "The Upcoming Year" my advice was: "BUY! The rally so many of us expected for January '77, which did not occur, and the many who do not believe a rally will happen in January '78, combine to make a metaphysical irony too great to resist." TPS Portfolio—which was fully margined all year—was displayed and reviewed. Based on an equity value of $7,158.61 on December 31, 1976 and a $5,125 appreciation, the gain was 71.59 percent; however, during the year $2,816.16 was withdrawn for living expenses. The 35 stocks that had been recommended during 1977 were reviewed, showing a market appreciation of 7.38 percent, not annualized for time held.

All in all a very good year for TPS Portfolio, especially in comparison with the DJIA and NYSE Composite Index. I didn't keep subscription records, but I doubt that there were over 30 paid subscribers and perhaps another 45 copies sent to other newsletter writers or very important people. Still, I was getting into the swing of things and looking forward to another good year.

The Beginnings of a Track Record: 1978

Some investment books are entertaining, with delightful anecdotes and colorful stories of smart moves that do not actually help the reader make smart moves in the future. Others are academic treatises, replete with charts, tables, and statistical analysis, which tend to overwhelm all but the highly trained and math-addicted buffs. I am trying to tread a middle ground, with real examples and learning experiences that are recognizable and useful to the nonspecialist financial or stock-market student.

Still, investing and speculating in stocks is very much an activity of bookkeeping and number-crunching. Plowing through tabular and technical data in order to gain perspective and insight is a chore well worth undertaking. The Appendixes list all stocks recommended by *The Prudent Speculator* (*TPS*) in its 18+ years, from 1977 through the first six months of 1995. Those that have been closed out through recommended sale, buyout, or merger appear in Appendix C; those that were still "holds" or currently recommended, that is, not closed out at the publication deadline, appear in Appendix B.

I have not gone into extended analysis of the total return of all TPS recommended stocks, dividends included, per period of recommendation, because I feel this would be relatively meaningless, with a large number of caveats that could become very confusing. For instance, almost all of the stocks were recommended more than once at both higher and lower prices than their original recommendation. A large number of the stocks were bought out, mostly for cash. Others gave the choice of accepting their common stock completely or partially, or preferred stocks and bonds.

What I believe will prove instructive to the reader is the performance of a list of the stocks recommended at year's end (taken from that year's final issue of *TPS*) during the following year. We can, if interested, compare these opening-year recommendations with subsequent recommendations and the final disposition of the stocks in question. We can also see how, year after year, certain patterns tend to recur, which generally lead to better-than-market returns over multiyear holding periods. Numbers after names represent stock splits (e.g., Marathon Manufacturing 3:2 equals 3-for-2 shares).

In Table 7–3, which lists stock recommendations for 1977, I've used the original TPS Portfolio at the time of the first issue of *TPS*.

Notice that the 11 positions are all in so-called secondary stocks, with no very large-capitalization, blue-chip stocks owned. Inadvertently, though I would love to claim it was by design, I had selected stocks in that segment of the market for 1977. We have noted elsewhere that the "total reinvested percent change" for the DJIA for 1977 (full year) was –12.84 percent, according to Lipper Analytical Securities Corporation. The equivalent total return with dividends reinvested for the S&P 500 was –7.2 percent, while for "small-company stocks" it was +25.4 percent, according to Ibbotson Associates' *Stocks, Bonds, Bills, and Inflation 1995 Yearbook* (*SBBI*). All subsequent performance quotes for Common Stocks (S&P 500) and Small Company Stocks (representing very small-capitalization stocks) are taken from *SBBI*.

Obviously, with the 27.66 percent market appreciation for TPS Portfolio for some nine months of '77, my portfolio's stocks outperformed the major averages and, with the leverage of margin (including dividend income and margin loan

Table 7–3. Stock "Recommendations" for 1977

(Original Price, Split-Adjusted Year-End Values)

Symbol	Corporation	3/11/77	12/31/77	%Change
AMI	American Medical International	12.500	19.500	56.00
AMZ	American Seating	11.250	13.750	22.22
CTN	Chemitron (Allegheny Ludlum)	33.625	47.500	41.26
CLU	Cluett, Peabody	9.250	10.625	14.86
DML	Dan River	8.500	11.625	36.76
MTM	Marathon Manufacturing 3:2	13.125	25.125	91.43
MME	McNeill Corp.	11.875	12.125	2.11
PVH	Phillips Van-Heusen	10.625	9.250	−12.94
TRI	Triangle Industries	9.250	7.250	−21.62
UFL	United Financial of California	11.750	16.500	40.43
WPI	Western Pacific Industries	18.500	24.750	33.78
	Averages:	13.695	18.000	27.66

expense), the actual audited rate of return was +70.28 percent. If you review much of the stock-market commentary for 1977 you will find that the year was considered a difficult period, but of course, that was mostly true of the large-capitalization portion of the stock-market. The old *cliché* "A market of stocks, not a stock market" can be seen as important and meaningful in '77.

1978—Another Tough Market Year

The tremendous gains of '75 and '76—following '73 and '74, the worst market period since the '30s—were still being corrected in '78. We note that the DJIA made a total return of only +2.81 percent, while the S&P 500 did a bit better with +6.6 percent, both well below their 63-year average returns. Simultaneously, very-small-capitalization stocks continued to prosper, with a total return of +23.5 percent. The market was jarred in October with the first of its "October Massacres," a sharp and swift selloff that was repaired over the succeeding months.

Table 7-4. Stocks Recommended for 1978

(Original Price, Split-Adjusted Year-End Values)

Symbol	Corporation	12/31/77	12/31/78	%Change
AH	Allis Chalmers	24.750	29.000	17.17
ARM	Armstrong Rubber	23.375	24.500	4.81
CCF	Cook United 6%	2.875	3.710	29.04
CLU	Cluett, Peabody	10.625	10.875	2.35
CP	Canadian Pacific	15.625	21.500	37.60
CTB	Cooper Tire & Rubber	13.625	10.125	−25.69
CUM	Cummins Engine	38.125	33.250	−12.79
DWR	Dean Witter Reynolds	12.000	10.500	−12.50
EAL	Eastern Airlines	6.125	8.500	38.78
EXR	Elixir Industries	4.875	4.250	−12.82
GFC	Gibraltar Financial 3:2	11.000	15.375	39.77
GR	B.F. Goodrich	21.000	17.375	−17.26
HR	International Harvester	30.250	36.250	19.83
HSM	Hart, Schaffner, & Marx	11.875	11.250	−5.26
HZ	Hazeltine Corp.	10.375	12.250	18.07
ICA	Imperial Corporation of America	15.875	16.125	1.57
JOL	Jonathan Logan	12.625	11.875	−5.94
MG	Monogram Industries	14.875	24.750	66.39
MGC	Magic Chef	9.375	10.125	8.00
MRX	Memorex Corp.	31.750	29.375	−7.48
OXM	Oxford Industries	10.500	9.375	−10.71
PIR	Pier 1 Imports	5.250	8.000	52.38
RAY	Raybestos-Manhattan 10%	31.125	32.175	3.37
SLT	Salant Corp.	6.750	5.750	−14.81
SMC	Smith (A.O.) Corp.	13.875	18.250	31.53
UFL	United Financial of California	16.500	19.500	18.18
WPI	Western Pacific Industries	24.750	34.375	38.89
YES	Yates Industries	11.000	18.125	64.77
ZAL	Zale Corp.	15.625	16.000	2.40
ZY	Zayre Corp.	8.500	10.125	19.12
	Averages:	15.496	17.088	12.96

There were 30 stocks being recommended in *TPS* as '77 drew to a close (these form the recommendations for '78) including three in TPS Portfolio. This batch (see Table 7–4) was to garner a market appreciation of only 12.96 percent (not including dividends or reinvestment), performing far better than the big-cap stocks but only about half as well as the small-company stocks. The three stocks still recommended from 1977's list (Table 7–3) all showed gains, early evidence of an important pattern now known as time diversification (see Chapter 3).

Also worthy of note are the losses registered in several stocks that went on to become big winners over the years. Cooper Tire and Rubber, Dean Witter Reynolds, and Elixir Industries are examples of this pattern. Of course, some winners in '78 turned sour in succeeding years, such as Gibraltar Financial, while many other stocks that showed little appreciation in their first year of recommendation provided handsome total returns in the months and years to come.

1979—A Solid Stock-Market Year

In summarizing these years, I am not going to detail greatly the concerns that plagued the stock market or the happy news that supported stock prices. We observed some of these "news" items in detailing 1977, hopefully showing how unpredictable and misleading they could be. Many of these news items and concerns are perennial, such as interest and inflation rates, world conditions, the effects of governmental actions (actual or anticipated), and the strength of the business cycle. They are not unlike those being feverishly analyzed in the media in 1995. These 18+ year-by-year snapshots support the idea that the stock market is only a vehicle to allow anxious people to sell undervalued corporations to astute and disciplined speculators, and in turn to allow fully valued stocks to be given back to greedy investors during periods of market euphoria.

The 34 opening recommendations for 1979 (Table 7–5) begin to show some cumulative effects of long-term investing in widely diversified portfolios. With 14 stocks carried over from 1978's list, and United Financial of California (UFL) recommended for the third year (still undervalued by 50 percent or more according to our analysis), one begins to get a glimmer of what *long term* means in operational terms. In those days (1979) of negativism toward both the market and many industry groups (for example savings and loan companies)—which paralleled similar appraisals during the high interest-rate periods of the early '70s—we see how some S&Ls overcame difficult periods and provided handsome market price gains. UFL appreciated a handsome 40.43 percent in '77, a satisfying 18.18 percent (split-adjusted) in '78, and then a terrific 113.14 percent (split-adjusted) in '79, being bought out for cash by National Steel.

Table 7-5. Stocks Recommended for 1979

(Original Price, Split-Adjusted Year-End Values)

Symbol	Corporation	12/31/78	12/31/79	%Change
ARM	Armstrong Rubber	24.500	18.250	−25.51
AV	Avco Corp.	22.875	27.750	21.31
CAL	Continental Airlines	8.750	10.000	14.29
CNV	City Investing	13.625	18.000	32.11
CPS	Columbia Pictures	22.375	34.125	52.51
CRO	Chromalloy American	15.500	23.000	48.39
CTB	Cooper Tire & Rubber	10.125	11.875	17.28
CUM	Cummins Engine	33.250	31.000	−6.77
DWR	Dean Witter Reynolds	10.500	11.000	4.76
EAL	Eastern Airlines	8.500	7.750	−8.82
EXR	Elixir Industries	4.250	4.875	14.71
FBG	Faberge Inc.	8.250	11.250	36.36
FLX	Flexi-Van Corp.	14.625	14.125	−3.42
FWF	Far Western Financial	11.875	12.625	6.32
GDV	General Development	7.000	11.500	64.29
GFC	Gibraltar Financial	10.250	11.250	9.76
GDW	Golden West Financial	11.750	16.000	36.17
GR	B.F. Goodrich	17.375	19.625	12.95
GW	Gulf + Western	14.125	18.500	30.97
HSM	Hart, Schaffner, & Marx	11.250	11.875	5.56
ICA	Imperial Corporation of America	16.125	25.500	58.14
IU	IU International	10.250	11.125	8.54
NPH	North American Phillips	25.375	26.750	5.42
OXM	Oxford Industries	9.375	10.750	14.67
SHA	Shapell Industries	22.750	40.625	78.57
SHP	Stop & Shop Industries	16.250	15.625	−3.85
SMC	Smith (A.O.) Corp.	18.250	17.000	−6.85
SMI	Spring Mills	14.750	18.750	27.12
UFL	United Financial of California 5:4	19.500	41.563	113.14
WIX	Wickes Corp.	10.500	16.750	59.52
WNT	Washington National	23.250	25.500	9.68
Z	F.W. Woolworth	19.375	25.125	29.68
ZAL	Zale Corp.	16.000	20.250	26.56
ZY	Zayre Corp.	10.125	10.875	7.41
	Averages:	15.077	18.546	23.26

Table 7–6. Stocks Recommended for 1980

(Original Price Split-Adjusted Year-End Values)

Symbol	Corporation	12/31/79	12/31/80	% Change
AR	Asarco Inc.	37.375	43.250	15.72
AV	Avco Corp.	27.750	29.000	4.50
BG	Brown Group	25.500	31.000	21.57
CP	Canadian Pacific	33.875	36.375	7.38
CHD	Chelsea Industries	10.625	7.500	−29.41
CNV	City Investing	18.000	21.500	19.44
CLU	Cluett, Peabody	9.750	9.500	−2.56
ETN	Eaton Corp.	25.625	28.500	11.22
FMC	FMC Corp.	26.000	30.500	17.31
FCA	Fabri-Centers of America	5.125	8.375	63.41
FLX	Flexi-Van Corp.	14.125	20.250	43.36
FM	Franklin Mint	9.625	25.000	59.74
FQA	Fuqua Industries	18.500	14.500	−21.62
GDV	General Development	11.500	13.875	20.65
GR	B.F. Goodrich	19.625	24.875	26.75
GOR	Gordon Jewelry	23.375	19.125	−18.18
GW	Gulf + Western 5:4	18.500	19.844	7.26
HSM	Hart, Schaffner & Marx	11.875	14.250	20.00
HR	International Harvester	39.125	25.625	−34.50
KCC	Kaiser Cement	26.625	25.000	−6.10
KOE	Koehring Company	20.000	37.000	85.00
LES	Leslie Fay	6.625	8.875	33.96
MGC	Magic Chef	8.375	8.000	−4.48
MHT	Manhattan Industries 4%	6.875	7.410	7.78
MRX	Memorex Corp.	17.875	12.750	−28.67
MG	Monogram Industries	39.000	40.000	2.56
MRS	Morse Shoe	13.500	22.250	64.81
NPH	North American Phillips	26.750	38.125	42.52
OXM	Oxford Industries	10.750	12.125	12.79
PN	Pan American Corp.	6.000	4.250	−29.17
PHL	Phillips Industries	5.500	7.125	29.55
PVH	Phillips-Van Heusen	14.125	10.875	−23.01
RAY	Raybestos-Manhattan	22.375	29.375	31.28
SVN	Sav-On-Drugs (Jewel)	9.875	19.000	92.41
SCI	Seaboard Coast Line (Chessie)	29.375	52.375	78.30
SHC	Shaklee Corp.	15.125	29.000	91.74

Table 7–6. Stocks Recommended for 1980 (cont.)

	(*Original Price Split-Adjusted Year-End Values*)			
Symbol	**Corporation**	**12/31/79**	**12/31/80**	**%Change**
SMC	Smith, A.O.	17.000	13.750	–19.12
SMI	Spring Mills	18.750	17.375	–7.33
SHP	Stop & Shop Companies	15.625	15.250	–2.40
SMB	Sunbeam Corp.	17.625	16.750	–4.96
TRI	Triangle Industries	8.125	11.750	44.62
USG	U.S. Gypsum	31.500	33.000	4.76
USL	U.S. Leasing	14.875	27.000	81.51
WRC	Warnaco Industries	11.625	15.625	34.41
WNT	Washington National	25.500	38.000	49.02
WH	White Motor	5.875	3.500	–40.43
WIX	Wickes Corp.	16.750	3.500	–19.40
WWW	Wolverine World Wide	13.250	21.000	58.49
Z	F.W. Woolworth	25.125	24.750	–1.49
ZAL	Zale Corp.	20.250	27.625	36.42
ZY	Zayre Corp.	10.875	21.250	95.40
	Averages:	17.988	21.304	22.02

Western Pacific Industries (WPI) was trading above its recommendable buy level by December 31, 1978; but another interesting position, Stop & Shop Industries (SHP), saw its stock lose 3.85 percent during a positive market year. Meanwhile, Zayre (ZY), a repeat from '78 during which it gained 19.2 percent, was only up 7.41 percent for '79. You might notice a stock that interested you during this period, perhaps Gulf + Western (GW) with a 30.97 percent appreciation. GW became part of Paramount Communications, which was bought by Viacom, Inc. in 1994.

For '79 the DJIA registered a total return of +10.68 percent, while the S&P 500 was considerably better at 18.4 percent. Small Company Stocks scored an amazing 43.5 percent total return. Our list managed a satisfying 23.26 percent market appreciation (not including dividends or cash/buying power reinvested). TPS Portfolio's margined total return was 63.46 percent for 1979.

1980—Good Year for Stocks

With the DJIA showing a total reinvested return of +22.13 percent, the S&P 500 registering 32.4 percent, and the small-company total return at +39.9 percent, I could almost be embarrassed by the 22.02 percent market appreciation (not including dividends or reinvested proceeds) indicated for 1980's recommended list (see Table 7–6). Actually, my margined portfolio (see Table I–2) only managed a 15.69 percent total return, which could be of concern, given that a fully margined "unmanaged" portfolio of the stocks in TPS Portfolio "should" have produced about a 35 percent margined return. There was another October Massacre in '80, so aggressive portfolios buying stocks heavily just before the big correction would show decreased annual performance.

By the end of 1979, many stocks met our criteria as buy candidates—51 in Table 7–6. About this time, a couple subscribers began to complain that they didn't know where to begin selecting a single stock or a few stocks from such extensive recommendations. I was quite sympathetic to their plight in that I also couldn't afford to buy nearly all the recommendable stocks myself. But it was important to display all the undervalued stocks of which we were aware. I made suggestions that they select stocks to meet their individual portfolio configuration, especially diversifying among industry groups, or emphasizing low P/E, low P/BV, and low-priced stocks.

Fourteen of the recommendations were holds or repeats from 1979's list and another eight were holds recommended for '77 or '78. Actually, 51 stocks would not be too many to own in a portfolio of $200,000 or more, which means that each position would represent about $4,000, or 2 percent of the portfolio.

I've noticed that some investors with a couple hundred thousand dollars or more would consider it beneath their dignity to buy fewer than 100 shares (round lots) of any stock, lest they be thought of as odd lotters or amateurs. There is nothing wrong with buying 35 or 53 shares of a high-priced, undervalued stock if that amount approximates the average dollar position in the portfolio. I have often held over 100 positions in my portfolio, happy to have less than 1 to 2 percent in any given stock, however many shares that was. When the bad positions bomb, only a percent or two or fraction thereof is given up, while a good position gaining many times its cost has a significant cumulative effect on one's total return, especially if the portfolio is heavily leveraged (margined).

Apparently the big winner for 1980 was Franklin Mint (FM), up 159.74 percent, although several other recommended stocks advanced handsomely. We see that Zayre Corp (ZY), after only gaining 7.41 percent in '79, was able to almost double (95.40 percent) in its third recommended year. Alas, Zayre advanced beyond our recommendation level—while remaining a strong hold—and was able to appreciate 2,402.61 percent before it was closed out in April 1988. Although ZY's originally recommended price was $8.50 in late '77, due to several splits, its cost-adjusted price became 96 cents (0.959) per share by the time it was closed out at $24.00 per share. When comparing historical prices, we must remember to check for splits, stock dividends, and returns of capital over the years.

It would not be fruitful for me to try to analyze each of the hundreds of recommended stocks for the past 18 years, or to comment on their particular performance. As you can imagine, each company and its stock has its own unique story in a fickle, seemingly irrational, and rarely efficient market. As I gaze at the recommendations for 1980, I see little gems such as Magic Chef (MGC), which lost

Table 7-7. Stocks Recommended for 1981

(Original Price, Split-Adjusted Year-End Values)

Symbol	Corporation	12/31/80	12/31/81	%Change
AFL	American Family	7.500	7.625	1.67
AR	Asarco	43.250	25.750	−40.46
BG	Brown Group 3:2	31.000	42.563	37.30
CP	Canadian Pacific	36.375	35.125	−3.44
CPH	Capital Holding	17.750	22.250	25.35
CEC	Ceco Corp.	16.875	19.250	14.07
CNV	City Investing	21.500	22.750	5.81
CLU	Cluett, Peabody	9.500	15.000	57.89
CPG	Colonial Penn	16.250	15.000	−7.69
CNK	Crompton & Knowles 3:2	19.500	25.500	30.77
FLX	Dan River	14.750	13.375	−9.32
DSO	DeSoto Inc.	12.500	17.000	36.00
FQA	Fuqua Industries	14.500	21.250	46.55
GOR	Gordon Jewelry 3:2	19.125	25.500	33.33
GW	Gulf + Western	15.875	15.875	0.00
HML	Hammermill Paper	27.000	27.750	2.78
INB	Industrial National	19.750	26.875	36.08
INA	INA Corp.	40.500	44.125	8.95
IU	IU International	17.500	13.750	−21.43
KT	Katy Industries	14.875	10.750	−27.73
LES	Leslie Fay	8.875	13.875	56.34
LEV	Levitz Furniture	24.500	34.500	40.82
NAC	National Can	22.500	21.250	−5.56
OI	Owens-Illinois	25.500	29.625	16.18

Table 7-7. Stocks Recommended for 1981 (cont.)

(Original Price, Split-Adjusted Year-End Values)

Symbol	Corporation	12/31/80	12/31/81	%Change
PCF	PennCorp Financial	7.125	5.625	–21.05
PVH	Phillips-Van Heusen	10.875	15.750	44.83
PII	Pueblo International	3.625	3.625	0.00
RVB	Revere Copper & Brass	16.250	14.750	–9.23
SLF	Scot Lad Foods	5.125	4.000	–21.95
SHP	Stop & Shop Companies	15.250	22.000	44.26
SMB	Sunbeam (Allegheny International)	16.750	27.750	65.67
TA	Transamerica	18.750	23.375	24.67
UK	Union Carbide	50.250	51.375	2.24
WRC	Warnaco Industries	15.625	27.000	72.80
Z	F.W. Woolworth	24.750	18.000	–27.27
ZAL	Zale Corp.	27.625	21.000	–23.98
	Averages:	19.701	31.682	13.48

4.48 percent in market price that year, then advanced nicely over the years (as mentioned above), and which I still hold in the form of Maytag Corp. (MYG) shares, the appliance manufacturer that acquired Magic Chef.

1981—The Pause before the Next Leg Up

After a strong 1980, 1981 was a bit of a downer according to the major averages, with the DJIA declining 3.65 percent and the S&P 500 managing a total return of –4.9 percent. Meanwhile, the Small Company Stocks' total return registered a much better 13.9 percent gain. When we review *TPS*-recommended stocks at year-end '81 (Table 7–7), we see that they appreciated 13.48 percent without dividends included or reinvested, just a tad better (factoring in dividends) than the Small Company Stocks' performance.

Even in a down year, at least according to the DJIA and S&P 500, it is quite possible to obtain a positive return through decent stock selection and a well-balanced portfolio. On the other hand, some years are very large-capitalization (blue-chip) stock years, outperforming mid-capitalization and Small Company Stocks' performances. TPS Portfolio actually lost 0.74 percent in its margined condition in

'81, although a hypothetically unmargined TPS Portfolio would have gained 17.28 percent. The apparent disparities among these figures is understandable. TPS Portfolio in 1981 represented mostly undervalued stocks that had been held for several years with many appreciating strongly, such as Cluett, Peabody (CLU), Fuqua Industries (FQA), and Stop & Shop (SHP). The margined loss developed through the purchase of additional undervalued stocks that generally remained out of favor during 1981 and dragged down the overall performance.

Meanwhile, we see that, of the 36 recommendations for 1981, 13 were also recommended for 1980 and 9 had been recommended in previous years. One-third of the recommendations declined in 1981, although over longer periods of time our experience is that about 25 percent of all recommended stocks fail to advance (see Appendix C). As a large majority tend to advance over time, and winning stocks usually win much more than losing stocks lose, the average multiyear gains accumulate nicely, in spite of October Massacres and Meltdowns.

Late 1982—The Great Bull Market Begins a Big Leap Forward

Many market historians count the great bull market of '82 to '87 as beginning on August 12, 1982, with the DJIA closing at 776.92 (easily remembered as "777"), a two-year low. Just seven years later (at the initial writing of this book), it hardly seemed possible that conditions felt so bad in the summer of '82, yet the market advanced so forcefully over the next five years—almost 2,000 points on the DJIA! In 1995, the large-capitalization indexes' two-year decline of '81 and '82 is a faint memory; if anything, many of today's investors and professionals are unaware of that bit of market history.

In *IPS 137* (August 5, 1982), under "Current Approaches," I wrote: "BOLD SPECULATORS can hold 150 percent (margined) positions, given the currently oversold market conditions and the extreme undervaluations of selected common stocks." Under "Recent Stock Market Activity and Outlook" I wrote:

> Suicide is not the answer, patience is. I am taking my lumps this year for a variety of reasons, many of which have little to do with speculating in the stock market, such as using capital funds for personal reasons. When one considers how well the stock market is bound to do over the next few years, this period of adjustment (bottoming) in this current market cycle will seem relatively trivial.

From the December 31, 1981, DJIA close of 875.00 to the August 12, 1982, DJIA close of 776.92, the Dow Jones Industrial Average only declined 11.2 percent. Thereafter, the DJIA advanced to close on December 31, 1982, at 1046.54, a gain of 34.7 percent for the four and one-half months, resulting in a 19.6 percent

Table 7–8. Recommended Stocks for 1982

(Original Price, Split-Adjusted Year-End Values)

Symbol	Corporation	12/31/81	12/31/82	% Change
ARE	Amerace Corp.	17.000	8.250	7.35
AMZ	American Seating	13.375	29.125	117.76
ASR	Amstar Corp.	25.875	25.125	−2.90
ARM	Armstrong Rubber 2:1	32.750	61.000	86.26
BNK	Bangor Punta	18.875	18.500	−1.99
CIL	Continental Illinois	33.125	20.375	−38.49
CTB	Cooper Tire & Rubber	14.500	36.750	153.45
CNK	Crompton & Knowles	17.000	19.375	13.97
DSO	DeSoto Inc.	12.250	24.250	97.96
DYN	Dynalectron Corp.	9.000	10.875	20.83
FWB	First Wisconsin	30.375	30.250	−0.41
GOR	Gordon Jewelry	17.000	18.375	8.09
GW	Gulf + Western	15.875	16.750	5.51
INB	Industrial National	26.875	28.375	5.58
KT	Katy Industries	10.750	12.125	12.79
LTV	LTV Corp.	16.375	1.375	−30.53
MGC	Magic Chef	9.000	20.750	130.56
MHT	Manhattan Industries 4%	12.125	14.040	15.79
MGU	Michigan Sugar	15.000	19.000	26.67
MOB	Mobil Corp.	24.125	25.125	4.15
MWK	Mohawk Rubber	15.375	24.125	56.91
NOM	Natomas Co.	24.000	16.250	−32.29
OXY	Occidental Petroleum	23.000	19.750	−14.13
OM	Outboard Marine	20.000	28.875	44.38
OSG	Overseas Shipping	16.250	15.250	−6.15
OI	Owens-Illinois	29.625	28.250	−4.64
PII	Pueblo International	3.625	8.500	134.48
PRN	Puerto Rican Cement	3.375	3.500	3.70
RCI	Reichold Chemical	11.375	19.000	67.03
RS	Republic Steel	24.500	15.625	−36.22
RD	Royal Dutch Petroleum	34.875	34.625	−0.72

Table 7-8. Recommended Stocks for 1982 (cont.)

(Original Price, Split-Adjusted Year-End Values)

Symbol	Corporation	12/31/81	12/31/82	% Change
SLF	Scot Lad Foods	4.000	4.625	5.63
SCN	Sea Containers	21.000	23.500	11.90
VO	Seagram Company Ltd.	57.625	73.750	27.98
SHW	Sherwin Williams	22.000	4.000	100.00
SMI	Spring Mills	23.500	38.625	64.36
TK	Technicolor Inc.	14.625	22.625	54.70
TX	Texaco Inc.	33.000	31.125	−5.68
TYC	Tyco Labs	12.375	17.500	41.41
X	U.S. Steel	29.875	21.000	−29.71
WWW	Wolverine World Wide	14.000	20.875	49.11
	Averages:	19.738	23.687	28.65

gain for the year! These 1982 results are a strong argument against market suicide during a cycle low.

By the end of 1981, there were 41 recommended stocks for 1982, with 7 holdovers from '81 and eight from prior years (see Table 7–8). The overall list managed a market-price appreciation of 28.65 percent, not including dividends or reinvestment. This compares very favorably with the S&P 500's total return of 21.4 percent; it is just a tad better than the DJIA's reinvested return of 27.20 percent and the Small Company Stocks' total return of 28.0 percent. Of course, if 1982's recommendations had been margined, they would have likely gained 50 to 90 percent or more depending upon what stocks were bought during the year with increasing buying power based on increasing equity.

During turbulent 1982, we see 13 of the recommended stocks decline in market price (just under one-third of the total number recommended) losing from 0.41 percent to 38.49 percent, while the remaining 28 advance from 3.7 percent to 153.45 percent, not counting dividends. Again, there are many sagas associated with these stocks ranging from the continuous three-year recommendation of Cooper Tire (CTB, up +153.45 percent) to the emergence of lowly Puerto Rican Cement (PRN) which, by 1989, was up over 1,200 percent.

If you are really curious about the total performance of any of these stocks, the lists of all formerly recommended stocks in Appendix B, and all formerly recommended stocks closed out in Appendix C, include their dispositions as of June

Table 7-9. Stocks Recommended for 1983

(Original Price, Split-Adjusted Year-End Values)

Symbol	Corporation	12/31/82	12/31/83	%Change
BK	Bank of New York 2:1	49.750	65.500	31.66
CIL	Continental Illinois	20.375	21.875	7.36
DYN	Dynalectron Corp.	10.875	12.500	14.94
FHR	Fisher Foods	8.125	10.000	23.08
FLT	Fleet Financial Group	34.500	47.750	38.41
GBS	General Bancshares	20.000	37.750	88.75
GLM	Global Marine	9.250	7.875	−14.86
KAB	Kaneb Services	15.000	14.375	−4.17
KT	Katy Industries	12.125	30.125	148.45
KEN	Kenai Corp.	5.375	4.000	−25.58
MHT	Manhattan Industries 4%	13.500	24.875	84.26
MM	Marine Midland	18.750	24.750	32.00
MCN	MidCon Corp.	25.750	35.000	35.92
NBD	NBD Bancorp	30.250	45.875	51.65
NOM	Natomas (Diamond Shamrock)	16.250	25.593	57.50
PSA	PSA Inc.	30.625	21.750	−28.98
PRN	Puerto Rican Cement	3.500	8.750	150.00
RD	Royal Dutch Petroleum	34.625	45.000	29.96
SCN	SeaCo Inc.	23.500	26.250	11.70
TOS	Tosco Corp.	11.125	5.000	−55.06
UER	United Energy Resources	<u>27.125</u>	<u>24.875</u>	<u>−8.29</u>
	Averages:	20.018	25.689	31.84

1995. Remember, the market price gains do not include dividends, proceeds reinvested, or the powerful effects of margin leverage. They are not total return performances, and therefore understate the actual gains obtained by shareholders.

1983—One Good Year Deserves Another

The explosive year-end rally of 1982 carried on through 1983, with the DJIA registering a 26.06 percent reinvested return, about 1 percent less than for 1982. The S&P 500 showed a total return of 21.4 percent, and the Small Company Stocks gained a fantastic 39.7 percent. It was a great time to be fully invested and leveraged (margined), though undoubtedly some investors probably lost money in '83 by being in the wrong stocks or trading the market (or a specific industry) counter to its trend. My TPS Portfolio showed a margined total return of +117.74 percent, or a hypothetical cash account (unmargined) market-price appreciation of 45.44 percent (not counting dividends).

After 1982's fall and winter rally, there were fewer undervalued stocks to recommend, so the Table 7–9 shows only 21 stocks.

Of the 21 recommended stocks for 1983, eight are carryovers from 1982's list. The 31.84 percent market-price appreciation compares very favorably with the major averages mentioned above, but looks anemic compared to TPS Portfolio's margined total return, or even with the hypothetical cash-price appreciation return. These differences, I submit, are due to the long-held and maturing nature of TPS Portfolio's undervalued stock positions, which tend to do better after a year or two than when they are selected during out-of-favor periods when they are severely underpriced.

The greatest gainer for 1983, Puerto Rican Cement (PRN), up 150 percent, did not make the 1984 recommended list because it had risen to more than 50 percent of its then goal price. PRN attained the status of a long-term hold but, as we know now, did continue to advance another 400 percent from its 1983 closing price into mid-1989. PRN is still a hold in 1995, although near its goal price at this writing, which has continued to rise during the years (see Goal Prices in Appendix B). Tosco Corp. (TOS), which I had the misfortune to recommend on *Wall Street Week* in September 1983 around $10 per share, has taken a long time to recover from its tumble, but began to show signs of improving in market value by 1989. By 1995, Tosco had traded as high as $36.50 per share, not an outstanding winner but not the terrible loser it seemed to be for several years.

1984—A Hangover Year

The tremendous gains of late '82 and '83 actually petered out on November 29, 1983, when the DJIA made a closing high of 1287.20. With the DJIA opening at 1252.74 for 1984, its high for the year was made January 6 at 1286.64, with the yearly low at 1086.57 on July 24, and a close of 1211.57, off 3.74 percent for the year. The "total reinvested percent change" for '84, according to Lipper Analytical Securities Corporation, was +1.35 percent, gained by accounting for reinvested dividends. For 1984, *SBBI* shows the S&P 500 total return +6.3 percent, while their Small Company Total Return registered –6.7 percent, reversing the trend of smaller-capitalization stocks outperforming larger-cap stocks.

TPS Portfolio came up with a loss of –12.71 percent in its actual margined account, but as a hypothetical cash account would have earned +2.14 percent plus

Table 7–10. Stocks Recommended for 1984

(Original Price, Split-Adjusted Year-End Values)

Symbol	Corporation	12/31/83	12/31/84	%Change
C	Chrysler Corp.	27.625	32.000	15.84
F	Ford Motor	42.375	45.625	7.67
FWB	First Wisconsin	20.375	24.750	21.47
GFC	Gibraltar Financial	10.375	9.500	−8.43
MM	Marine Midland	24.750	28.500	15.15
PGT	Pacific Gas Transmission "A"	16.625	20.000	20.30
RD	Royal Dutch Petroleum	45.000	49.375	9.72
SMP	Standard Motor Products	18.375	13.250	−27.89
TSO	Tesoro Petroleum	14.000	10.000	−24.53
WKT	Wayne-Gossard	13.375	9.625	−28.04
	Averages:	23.288	24.263	0.13

dividends. Because of the magnificent advances during 1982–83, there were only 10 stocks to recommend at year-end for 1984 (see Table 7–10). These managed to appreciate a scant 0.13 percent in market value, excluding dividends, not keeping up with the S&P 500's results but avoiding the small cap's underperformance. The 1984 recommended list contains several large-cap stocks including Chrysler, Ford, and Royal Dutch Petroleum, nice gainers in a mediocre year.

1985—Making Up for 1984's Pause

When the DJIA closed at 1211.57 on December 31, 1984, it sported a P/E ratio of 10.7. This ratio was based on the 30 DJIA stocks having earned $113.58 for 1984, actually a handsome increase over 1983's earnings of $72.45. Ironically, in 1985 the DJIA stocks earned only $96.11, a 15.4 percent drop from 1984, but the DJIA closed at 1546.67—335 points higher for the year—resulting in a P/E ratio of 16.1! Next time someone tells you stocks cannot advance during a year of declining profits, point to 1985.

If nothing else, the DJIA relationship between 1984 and 1985 shows that you can't count on lower earnings alone keeping the market from rising. If general or specific conditions are perceived to be improving, so that the following year's earnings, interest rates, inflation, the dollar, or what have you, look to be better, then the anticipating market will make its own adjustments.

Table 7-11. Stocks Recommended for 1985

(Original Price, Split-Adjusted Year-End Values)

Symbol	Corporation	12/31/84	12/31/85	% Change
ANT	Anthony Industries 5%	12.750	15.356	20.44
ABZ	Arkansas Best	15.875	29.125	83.46
CAL	CalFed Inc.	16.000	27.375	71.09
C	Chrysler Corp.	32.000	46.625	45.70
CBU	Commodore International	16.375	10.625	−35.11
CUB	Cubic Corp.	15.625	22.375	43.20
CUM	Cummins Engine	77.625	72.000	−7.25
DBRSY	DeBeers Consolidated	4.125	4.719	14.40
DUCK	Duckwall–Alco (LBO)	13.500	17.750	31.48
EFG	Equitec Financial Group	10.375	9.625	−7.23
FRA	Farah Manufacturing Co.	19.375	21.125	9.03
FBT	First City Banc Texas	14.625	12.875	−11.97
FFHC	1st Financial Corp 2:1	18.000	35.000	94.44
F	Ford Motor	45.625	58.000	27.12
GRX	General Refractories	8.250	11.375	37.88
GLEN	Glendale Federal	8.875	17.500	97.18
GDW	Golden West Financial 3:2	23.750	46.500	95.79
GRR	G.R.I. Corp.	4.500	4.125	−8.33
HR	International Harvester	8.125	8.500	4.62
ITT	ITT Corp.	29.375	38.000	29.36
KZ	Kysor Industrial	16.625	22.125	33.08
MGC	Magic Chef	35.375	52.875	49.47
MXM	MAXXAM Group	12.750	11.000	−13.73
MSL	Mercury Saving & Loan 6%	6.125	11.395	86.04
MODI	Modine Manufacturing 5:2	35.750	58.125	62.59
PN	Pan Am Corp.	4.625	7.750	67.57
PRN	Puerto Rican Cement	6.875	8.125	18.18
RADC	Radice Corp. "A"	8.750	14.625	67.14
RBSN	Robeson Industries 10%	6.000	5.775	−3.75
ROP	Roper Corp.	14.625	15.875	8.55
RD	Royal Dutch Petroleum	49.375	63.000	27.59
SCR	Sea Container Ltd.	29.500	30.500	3.39

Table 7–11. Stocks Recommended for 1985 (cont.)

(Original Price, Split-Adjusted Year-End Values)

Symbol	Corporation	12/31/84	12/31/85	%Change
SC	Shell Transport & Trading	30.500	38.750	27.05
SM	Southmark Corp. 10%	6.750	10.725	58.89
TCL	Transcon Inc.	8.250	7.875	–4.55
U	US Air Group	33.250	34.375	3.38
YNK	Yankee Oil	5.500	6.625	20.45
	Averages:	11.288	17.788	30.99

Because of the droopy market action of '84, and the increasing fundamental stock values, we found 37 stocks to recommend for 1985 (Table 7–11). Of this group only three were holdovers from '84, although another five had been recommended in prior years. To show how strong '85 was, only 8 of 37 on this recommended list failed to show a price gain, 22 percent "first-year losers" versus our first-year "average" of 33 percent or more. The average gain of the recommended list for '85 was 30.99 percent, not including dividends or reinvestment. This gain compares with the DJIA total invested percent change of 33.62 percent (actual DJIA nominal points gained 27.66 percent). The S&P 500's total return was 32.2 percent, while the Small Company Stocks' total return was "only" 24.7 percent, continuing the current trend of small-cap stocks underperforming large-cap stocks for the while.

While the hypothetical unmargined TPS Portfolio only managed a 23.41 percent gain, not counting dividends for '85, the actual, margined account recorded a 50.72 percent total return. A nice performance goal is 15 to 18 percent per year, compounded, so any time portfolio performance or the major averages exceed that 15 percent you would have to say you were having a good year. Fortunately and unfortunately, many of the years between '82 and '87 far exceeded 15 percent, thus unduly raising expectations for higher systematic stock-market profits. Perhaps the rich years of this secular bull market—from December '74 through August '87 (if indeed the Crash of '87 was more than just a "normal" 36 percent bear market correction)—have led individual investors to expect too much, become disappointed too easily, and try too hard to find higher returns in highly speculative options and futures contracts.

At any rate, 1985 was undoubtedly another leg, so to speak, of the great bull market that began from very undervalued and soldout levels in October or

December 1974, and was renewed in August 1982. Some of the stocks on the '85 recommended list, such as First City Banc of Texas, Roper Corp., and Arkansas Best, are gone because of buyouts or bankruptcies. Others have yet to retrieve their originally recommended price, while some have made a comeback, such as Commodore International (CBU) reversing its '85 loss to sell at a small profit before floundering again and going belly up.

Table 7-12. Stocks Recommended for 1986

(Original Price, Split-Adjusted Year-End Values)

Symbol	Corporation	12/31/85	12/31/86	%Change
ACF	AirCal	7.500	14.500	93.33
AINC	American Income Life	10.625	14.500	36.47
AFS	Amfesco	1.375	2.000	45.45
AZP	AZP Group	27.250	28.375	4.13
CAL	CalFed Inc.	27.375	33.500	22.37
CARG	Carriage Industries	7.750	7.500	−3.23
C	Chrysler Corp. 3:2	31.083	37.000	19.04
DBRSY	DeBeers Consolidated	4.750	7.500	57.89
FWF	Far West Financial 3:1	16.583	13.875	−16.33
FFOM	1st Fed Savings & Loan Michigan	16.125	2.875	41.86
F	Ford Motor 3:2	38.667	56.250	45.47
GDF	General Defense (Clabir)	12.875	15.865	23.22
GDV	General Development	15.500	17.500	12.90
GFC	Gibraltar Financial	10.625	10.750	1.18
GDW	Golden West Financial	31.000	34.875	12.50
HERE	Heritage Entertainment	2.625	7.375	180.95
HFD	Home Federal Savings & Loan	26.500	26.375	−0.47
MXM	MAXXAM Group	11.000	8.750	−20.45
PLM	PLM Financial	5.250	6.500	23.81
SCR	Sea Containers	30.500	13.625	−55.33
SC	Shell Transport & Trading	38.750	58.500	50.97
SHG	Sheller Globe (LBO)	30.500	46.650	52.95
SM	Southmark Corp. 15%	8.478	8.375	−1.21
TKA	Tonka Corp. 3:2	18.333	19.875	8.41
TUR	Turner Corp.	25.750	20.625	−19.90
WLC	Wellco Enterprises 2:1	<u>7.938</u>	<u>13.750</u>	<u>73.22</u>
	Averages:	17.873	21.049	23.60

1986—Riding 1985's Momentum

With 1986, we are getting into "current history" concerning the stock market, especially as '86 set up the great advance that carried through the first three quarters of '87. After advancing so strongly in '85, there were only 26 stocks to recommend at year-end '85. Old stalwarts such as Chrysler, Ford, Sea Containers, and Shell Transport (40 percent of the Royal Dutch Petroleum complex) continued to be recommended. Savings and loans began to reflect a larger portion of the list (unfortunately).

The 26 stocks recommended for 1986 (displayed in Table 7–12) show a market price gain of 23.60 percent, not counting dividends or reinvestment. This handsome return about equals the DJIA total dividend reinvested return of 27.25 percent. The S&P 500 total return for '86 is reported at 18.5 percent, while the Small Company Stocks' total return is a measly 6.9 percent.

Thus continued the trend of large-cap stocks outperforming small-cap stocks. Even more important, the DJIA became the premiere performing average, due to programmed trading and the emphasis on such derivative instruments as those based on the Major Market Index (MMI, an index of 20 stocks designed to emulate the DJIA), the S&P 500, and S&P 100 index futures and options contracts.

1987—1986's Momentum Continues, for a While

In Chapter 6, "The Crash of '87 and the Selloff of '90," 1987 is dealt with in some detail, but it's still part of the recommended stocks series and each year's performance, so we continue with the 1986's year-end recommendations in Table 7–13.

While 1987 was a traumatic experience for many market participants, especially those of us who were fully invested and on margin, conservative investors who emphasized owning the DJIA or equivalent stocks did not have that bad a time of it, according to the major indexes. Large-capitalization common stocks, as represented by the S&P 500, actually had a 5.2 percent total return, slightly outdone by the DJIA's total reinvested gain of 5.55 percent. Not so for Small Company Stocks—they lost 9.3 percent on a total return basis, continuing their multiyear out-of-favor trend.

Obviously, our recommendations fared badly in 1987, significantly underperforming the major market averages. It was a difficult year for secondary stocks in general, and especially bad for out-of-favor undervalued stocks, which underperformed during the months before the Crash and then were doubly trounced during October and November, not bottoming out until the first week in December. The reinvestment of proceeds from Roper Corp. and Triangle Industries could have further enhanced the total returns of the stocks recommended for 1988.

Table 7-13. Stocks Recommended for 1987

(Original Price, Split-Adjusted Year-End Values)

Symbol	Corporation	12/31/86	12/31/87	% Change
ARAI	Allied Research	5.375	3.500	−34.88
AFC.A	American Fructose	12.750	6.250	−50.98
ANT	Anthony Industries	10.875	11.875	9.20
CAL	CalFed, Inc.	33.500	21.750	−35.07
C	Chrysler Corp. 3:2	24.667	22.125	−10.31
DBRSY	DeBeers Consolidated	7.500	9.375	25.00
ELCN	Elco Industries	16.750	24.250	44.78
FWF	Far West Financial	13.875	9.875	−28.83
FIN	Financial Corp. of America	7.500	1.125	−85.00
FFOM	1st Federal Savings & Loan Michigan	22.875	9.000	−60.66
FFHC	1st Financial Corp.	17.250	12.750	−26.09
F	Ford Motor	56.250	75.375	34.00
GEMH	Gemcraft, Inc.	7.000	0.875	−87.50
GDV	General Development	17.500	10.875	−37.86
GFC	Gibraltar Financial	10.750	3.500	−67.44
GDW	Golden West Financial	34.875	25.000	−28.32
GTA	Great American 1st	17.500	12.625	−27.86
HHH	Heritage Entertainment	7.375	3.125	−57.36
HFD	Home Federal S&L	26.375	20.750	−21.33
HUM	Humana Corp.	19.125	19.250	0.65
ICA	Imperial Corp. of America	13.221	7.500	−43.27
JII	Johnston Industries	13.875	18.500	33.33
LK	Lockheed Corp.	50.125	34.375	−31.42
MSL	Mercury Savings	10.625	5.875	−44.71
NTK	Nortek Corp.	13.000	7.000	−46.15
PFIN.A	P&F Industries	4.000	2.250	−43.75
RI	Radice Corp.	9.250	0.938	−89.86
RIHL	Richton International	4.125	3.250	−21.21
SM	Southmark Corp.	8.375	4.625	−44.78
TKA	Tonka Corporation	19.875	8.875	−55.35
TCL	Transcon Inc.	8.125	2.750	−66.15
TUR	Turner Corp.	20.625	16.125	−21.82
WLC	Wellco Enterprises	13.750	12.125	−11.82
WILF	Wilson Foods	9.000	7.625	−15.28
	Averages:	16.695	12.796	−30.83

1988—Year of Recovery

Many people threw in the towel, the sink, and all their stocks after the Crash of '87. This was particularly ironic as history shows time and again that, after a terrible selloff, the market usually recovers at least 50 percent, as it did in early 1930 following the 1929 Crash.

Many of the gurus who had anticipated a selloff—and many who didn't, but quickly joined the bearish camp—were convinced that the worst was yet to come. They predicted recessions, depressions, much lower market prices, and perhaps a breakdown of the world economic system. They certainly urged readers and listeners to stay out of the market, especially with the handsome, so-called "risk-free" returns on U.S. Government bills, notes, and bonds. They also missed the significant rebound in 1988 and 1989, because these risk-free investments turned out to carry a considerable negative "opportunity risk"—the risk and actuality of not participating in the historically and potentially greater gains from common-stock appreciation.

For 1988, S&P 500 common stocks earned a total return of 16.8 percent, just a bit better than the DJIA's total reinvested gain of 16.21 percent. Finally, after several years in the doldrums, Small Company Stocks accelerated to a total return gain of 22.9 percent, or 36.3 percent more than their larger-cap cousins.

The list of recommended stocks in *TPS* was the largest in its history at the end of 1987, amounting to 99 (see Table 7–14), yet gaining 18.55 percent on average for the year, not counting dividends or reinvestments—comparable to the Small Company Stocks' performance. Several previously recommended stocks were bought out, such as Stop & Shop (SHP), Mohasco Corp. (MOH), USG Corp. (USG), and Arkansas Best (ABZ), as well as Roper Corp. (ROP) and Triangle Industries (TRI).

1989—Another Split Market Year

On June 30, 1989, the DJIA closed at 2440.06, dropping a sharp 91.81 points for the week ending June 30—still up 12.52 percent for the six months, not counting dividends. By September 1, the DJIA advanced to 2752.09, up 26.91 percent for the year to date. On December 29, the last trading day of 1989, the DJIA closed at 2753.20, compared to December 30, 1988's close of 2168.57, up 584.63 points or 26.95 percent (not counting dividends) for the year.

The recommended stocks at year-end 1988 represent a continuation of undervaluation from the Crash of '87. Although the margined TPS Portfolio gained 20.69 percent for 1989 (16.76 percent as a hypothetical cash account, not counting dividends), the 46 stocks recommended for '89 managed only a minuscule gain of 0.9 percent, plus dividends. The S&P 500 total return was 31.49 percent, while Small Company Stocks came up with a total return of 10.18 percent.

Table 7–14. Stocks Recommended for 1988

(Original Price, Split-Adjusted Year-End Values)

Symbol	Corporation	12/31/87	12/31/88	%Change
AEPI	AEP Industries	8.250	12.750	54.55
AFC.A	American Fructose "A"	6.250	9.500	52.00
AIIC	American Integrity	2.875	1.188	−58.70
AINC	American Income Life	9.750	17.625	80.77
ARAI	Allied Research	3.500	2.500	−28.57
APK	Apple Bank	25.250	30.750	21.78
ARV	Arvin Industries	19.250	19.375	0.65
ARX	ARX Inc.	6.875	6.375	−7.27
C	Chrysler Corp.	22.125	25.750	16.38
CAL	Calfed Inc.	21.750	22.000	1.15
CCI	Citicorp	18.625	25.875	38.93
CCTC	CCT Corp.	6.500	2.500	−61.54
CFG	Copelco Financial	5.000	8.750	75.00
CGE	Carriage Industries	4.375	5.250	20.00
CHCR	Chancellor Corp.	7.500	6.000	−20.00
CI	CIGNA Corp.	43.875	47.125	7.41
CIS	Concord Fabric	3.813	3.125	−18.03
COFD	Collective Federal S&L	8.750	7.375	−15.71
CSA	Coast S&L	16.000	14.750	−7.81
DHTK	DH Technologies	4.750	5.625	18.42
DPT	Datapoint	4.625	4.500	−2.70
DSL	Downey S&L	11.500	15.375	33.70
EFG	Equitec Financial Group	5.750	3.000	−47.83
ELK	Elcor Corp.	6.000	8.750	45.83
ENVR	Envirodyne	16.500	31.250	89.39
ESCA	Escalade Corp.	8.250	9.000	9.09
EXC	Excel Industries	5.909	12.000	103.08
F	Ford Motor	37.688	50.500	33.99
FBC	First Boston	24.875	52.625	111.56
FED	First Federal Financial	11.800	13.875	17.58
FFHC	First Financial Wisconsin	12.750	14.000	9.80
FG	USF&G Corp.	28.375	28.500	0.44
FNB	First Chicago	18.875	29.625	56.95
FWF	Far West Financial	9.875	7.875	−20.25
GD	General Dynamics	48.750	50.750	4.10
GDV	General Development	10.875	12.625	16.09
GDW	Golden West Financial	25.000	31.375	25.50

Table 7-14. Stocks Recommended for 1988 (cont.)

(Original Price, Split-Adjusted Year-End Values)

Symbol	Corporation	12/31/87	12/31/88	%Change
GDYN	Geo Dynamics	8.000	9.750	21.88
GLN	GlenFed Inc.	22.000	19.625	−10.80
GNT	Greentree Acceptance	15.125	10.375	−31.40
GRR	GRI Corp.	4.875	9.625	97.44
GTA	Great American 1st	12.625	11.250	−10.89
GXY	Galaxy Carpets	11.500	14.375	25.00
HEI	Heico Corp.	16.375	18.250	1.45
HELE	Helen of Troy	6.875	15.625	27.27
HFD	Home Federal S&L San Diego	20.750	24.875	19.88
HME	Home Group Inc.	12.000	11.000	−8.33
HOF	Hoffman Industries	2.750	5.625	104.55
HTHR	Hawthorne S&L	16.750	22.000	31.34
HYDE	Hyde Athletic	7.000	8.875	26.79
FWES	First West Financial	6.125	6.250	2.04
ICH	ICH Corp.	7.750	4.750	−38.71
IRE	Integrated Resources	16.500	13.875	−15.91
ITT	ITT Corp.	44.500	50.375	13.20
JII	Johnston Industries	18.500	16.375	−11.49
KB	Kaufman & Broad	14.500	13.500	−6.90
KLM	KLM Royal Dutch	15.750	21.000	33.33
LADF	LADD Furniture	14.000	13.750	−1.79
LEN	Lennar Corp.	16.625	17.625	6.02
LK	Lockheed Corp.	34.375	41.250	20.00
LNDL	Lindal Cedar Homes	5.165	8.750	69.40
MRI.A	McRae Industries	6.000	5.500	−8.33
NTK	Nortek Corp.	7.000	9.125	30.36
NUVI	NuVision Inc.	6.250	8.125	30.00
PFINA	P&F Industries	2.250	2.000	−11.11
PGI	Ply Gem Industries	11.000	11.875	7.95
PLM.B	PLM Financial "B"	5.125	5.875	14.63
PMSI	Prime Medical Services	1.875	0.875	−53.33

Table 7-14. Stocks Recommended for 1988 (cont.)

(Original Price, Split-Adjusted Year-End Values)

Symbol	Corporation	12/31/87	12/31/88	%Change
PNRE	Pan Atlantic Insurance	7.000	6.250	–10.71
RAY	Raytech Corp.	7.125	2.875	–59.65
RBSN	Robeson Industries	1.063	1.500	41.18
RGB	R.G. Barry	6.250	5.500	–12.00
RIHL	Richton International	3.250	2.500	–23.08
RLI	RLI Corp.	9.625	7.625	–20.78
ROP	Roper Corp.	15.500	54.000	248.39
RTN	Raytheon	66.625	67.000	0.56
S	Sears, Roebuck	33.500	40.875	22.01
SBIG	Seibels Bruce	11.250	11.375	1.11
SBOS	Boston Bancorp	17.750	15.375	–13.38
SCR	Sea Containers	17.500	0.125	72.14
SIA	Signal Apparel	6.000	4.750	–20.83
SM	Southmark Corp.	4.625	1.625	–64.86
SMC.A	Smith A.O. "A"	13.875	16.500	18.92
SP	Spelling Productions	4.625	6.375	37.84
SPF	Standard Pacific	8.000	12.000	50.00
SUPD	Supradur Companies	6.250	12.500	100.00
TGR	Tiger International	11.000	19.750	79.55
THMP	Thermal Industries	6.250	4.750	–24.00
TMK	Torchmark	24.500	30.500	24.49
TRI	Triangle Industries	26.750	32.625	21.96
TSOF	TSO Financial	3.125	4.375	40.00
TT	TransTechnology	17.750	17.750	0.00
TUR	Turner Corp.	16.125	16.750	3.88
USH	USLIFE Corp.	28.500	34.875	22.37
VFC	VF Corp.	24.500	28.750	17.35
WDC	Western Digital	16.250	14.750	–9.23
WLC	Wellco Enterprises	12.125	15.250	25.77
WLD	Weldotron	4.625	7.250	56.76
ZY	Zayre Corp.	14.000	24.000	71.43
	Averages:	13.815	16.485	19.33

Table 7-15. Stocks Recommended for 1989

(Original Price, Split-Adjusted Year-End Values)

Symbol	Corporation	12/30/88	12/29/89	%Change
AFC.A	American Fructose "A"	9.500	22.750	139.47
ALWC	Williams (AL)	14.500	23.730	61.17*
BAC	BankAmerica Corp.	17.625	26.750	51.73
BS	Bethlehem Steel	23.250	18.500	−20.43
BVFS	Bay View Federal	17.875	20.500	14.66
C	Chrysler Corp.	25.750	19.000	−28.97
CAL	CalFed Inc.	22.000	20.375	−7.39
CCI	Citicorp	25.875	28.875	11.59
CCTC	CCT Corp.	2.500	0.750	−70.00
COFD	Collective Bancorp	7.375	7.500	1.69
CSA	Coast Saving & Loan	14.750	11.750	−20.34
DAL	Delta Airlines	50.125	68.250	36.16
F	Ford Motor	50.500	43.625	−13.61
FBO	Federal Paper Board	20.250	25.750	27.16
FED	First Federal Financial	13.875	21.000	51.35
FFA	FirstFed America	15.500	33.250	114.52
FNB	First Chicago	29.625	37.125	25.32
FWES	First Western Financial	6.250	5.250	−16.00
FWF	Far West Financial	7.875	6.500	−17.46
GD	General Dynamics	50.750	44.875	−11.14
GDV	General Development	12.625	0.750	−22.77
GLN	GlenFed Inc.	19.625	16.250	−17.20
GTA	Great America 1st	11.250	6.875	−38.89
HME	Home Group (Ambase)	11.000	12.500	13.64
HOC	Holly Corp.	19.500	25.875	107.00
HTHR	Hawthorne Financial	22.000	27.500	25.00
ICA	Imperial Corporation of America	9.125	0.938	−89.73
INDB	Independent Bank Corp.	10.750	7.750	−27.91
IRE	Integrated Resources	13.875	0.250	−98.20
JII	Johnston Industries 3:2	16.375	10.750	−1.53
LEN	Lennar Corp.	17.625	19.500	10.64
LK	Lockheed Corp.	41.250	39.000	−5.45
LMS	Lamson & Sessions	12.875	9.500	−26.21
LNDL	Lindal Cedar Homes 10%	8.750	5.500	−30.86
MRI.A	McRae Industries Cl A	5.500	4.875	−11.36

Table 7–15. Stocks Recommended for 1989 (cont.)

(Original Price, Split-Adjusted Year-End Values)

Symbol	Corporation	12/30/88	12/29/89	%Change
PGI	Ply Gem Industries	11.875	11.250	–5.26
RBSN	Robeson Industries	1.500	1.438	–4.17
RLI	RLI Corp.	7.625	8.500	11.48
SBOS	Boston Bancorp	15.375	16.250	5.66
SPF	Standard Pacific	12.000	14.375	19.79
STO	Stone Container	32.000	23.875	–25.39
SUPD	Supradur Companies	12.500	10.500	–16.00
UAC	Unicorp America (Lincorp)	5.750	2.000	–65.22
UK	Union Carbide	15.480	23.250	60.53
WDC	Western Digital	14.750	8.375	–43.22
WLC	Wellco Enterprises	15.250	13.125	–13.93
	Averages:	17.655	17.728	0.87

* A.L. Williams was bought out by Primerica (PA) for 0.82 share of PA.

By May 19, 1989, only 15 stocks were recommendable—compared to the 46 (Table 7–15) at year-end '88, which indicates that the market was getting close to a top, at least in terms of fundamental valuations. Of course, there are usually hundreds of stocks that range from "somewhat" to almost 50 percent undervalued and are strong holds or buys in other systems that do not require a 50 percent or less of goal price to buy. And, with every correction of any magnitude, many stocks drop into the buy level through lower prices, just as other stocks become candidates by reporting higher earnings and improved fundamentals as their prices remain fairly stable.

1990—My Worst Year (So Far)

Have you ever had a year in which you felt you shouldn't have gotten up most mornings? I can hardly believe what happened to me in 1990. It was worse than 1987, although curiously not as painful because there was far less hoopla about the market crashing. Of our 30 recommended undervalued positions, only two had a positive return (see Table 7–16). The precipitating causes for the mid-July to mid-October 1990 selloff were many, including the budget deficit, the savings & loan bailout, inflation control, higher interest rates abroad, but especially higher interest rates at home and the recession of 1990.

Table 7-16. Stocks Recommended for 1990

(Original Price, Split-Adjusted Year-End Values)

Symbol	Corporation	12/29/89	12/31/90	%Change
AMX	Alumax	23.000	21.125	−8.15
ABC	Ambase Corp.	12.250	0.313	−97.45
BK	Bank of New York	40.250	17.750	−55.90
BS	Bethlehem Steel	18.500	14.750	−20.27
SBOS	Boston Bancorp	16.250	13.500	−16.92
CANX	Cannon Express	5.250	6.375	21.43
CASC	Cascade International	2.810	2.875	2.22
C	Chrysler Corp.	19.000	12.625	−33.55
CCI	Citicorp	28.875	12.625	−56.28
CSA	Coast Saving & Loan	11.750	2.375	−79.79
COFD	Collective Bancorp	7.500	6.750	−10.00
CIS	Concord Fabrics	4.875	4.000	−17.95
CIL	Continental Bank	19.875	8.875	−55.35
COS	Copperweld Corp.*	12.250	17.000	38.78
FWF	Far West Financial+	6.500	1.750	−73.08
FBO	Federal Paper Board	25.750	18.375	−28.64
FNB	First Chicago	37.125	16.500	−55.66
F	Ford Motor Co.	43.625	26.625	−38.97
HTHR	Hawthorne S&L	27.500	12.750	−53.64
HFD	HomeFed Corp.	31.875	5.000	−84.31
N	Inco Ltd.	26.875	25.375	−5.58
INDB	Independent Bank Corp	7.750	3.000	−61.29
IDCC	Intek Diversified	1.688	0.313	−81.48
KBH	Kaufman & Broad Home	13.625	9.250	−32.11
MCU	Magma Copper Co.	5.125	4.625	−9.76
RLM	Reynolds Metals	53.625	57.000	6.29
SGAT	Seagate Technologies	15.000	11.750	−21.67
SPF	Standard Pacific	14.375	5.875	−59.13
SUPD	Supradur Companies	10.500	3.250	−69.05
WFC	Wells Fargo	<u>74.125</u>	<u>57.875</u>	<u>−21.92</u>
	Averages	9.818	6.287	−35.97

* Copperweld bought out for $17.00 cash 8/90.
+ Far Western Financial closed out at $1.75 7/90.

In *TPS 274* (June 28, 1990), I quoted Stephen Quickel, editor of *US Investment Report*, praising the Federal Reserve for "doing a very good job of managing its Soft Landing—of slowing economic growth to check inflation without causing a recession." Quickle wrote:

> The Fed's inflation fight should send bond yields as low as 7 to 7.5 percent within 12 months. Stock should rise to a 3000-plus Dow, perhaps even 3400, as corporate earnings rebound and institutions commit their huge cash reserves.[5]

Several successful newsletter editors were bullish in June 1990 around DJIA 2860, commenting that a soft economy would prompt further easing by the Federal Reserve, reviving depressed corporate profits. [Much of mid-1990's commentary could apply to mid-1995 without missing a beat.]

The clincher to the sharp, swift bear market of 1990 was the invasion of Kuwait by Saddam Hussein's Iraq, which led to a panic stock-market selloff, due to increasing crude oil prices and inflation fears. It did not help that the Federal Reserve stood aside on lower interest rates and monetary easing.

1991—Thank Goodness

Yet again, after a bad year a good year or two or three. The 51 stocks recommended in *TPS* at year-end 1990 gained an average 49.6 percent, not counting dividends, reinvestment of proceeds, or any use of leverage (see Table 7–17). Margined TPS Portfolio had a total return of 69.58 percent (hypothetical cash account of 31.03 percent), Small Company Stocks had a total return of 44.63 percent. Large Company Stocks (S&P 500) gained a total return of 26.31 percent. All in all, 1991 was a very satisfying year.

1992—A Continuation of 1991

As if the one good year 1991 wasn't enough to make up for the trauma of 1990, the stock market continued its very strong rally through 1992. Due to the many advances beyond our buy limits in 1991, the reduced list of 20 recommendations at year-end 1991—from the previous year's 51—were able to gain an even greater 55.8 percent market appreciation than the 49.6 percent of 1991 (see Table 7–18). TPS Portfolio managed a total return of 62.25 percent; the S&P 500 total return was 4.46 percent; the Small Company Stocks had a total return of 23.35 percent.

---

[5] Stephen Quickel, *US Investment Report*, (25 Fifth Avenue, Suite 4–C, New York, NY 10003), June 27, 1991.

Table 7-17. Stocks Recommended for 1991

(Original Price, Split–Adjusted Year–End Values)

Symbol	Corporation	12/30/90	12/31/91	%Change
ARI	ARI Holdings	10.000	16.000	60.00
ABIG	American Bankers	8.750	20.500	134.29
APFC	American Pacific	9.000	18.000	100.00
ARTG	Artistic Greetings	3.000	14.375	379.17
BAC	Bank of America	23.200	35.875	54.62
BK	Bank of New York	17.750	30.875	73.94
BOF	Bank of San Francisco	4.750	3.125	−34.21
BVFS	Bay View Capital	14.125	21.000	48.67
BCO	Blessings Corp.	11.750	19.000	61.70
BRO	Broad	5.500	19.750	259.09
CAL	California Federal Bank "A"	4.375	2.250	−48.57
CMIC	California Microwave	7.125	18.250	156.14
CATA	Capitol Transamerica	11.800	28.250	139.41
KOSM	Cascade International	2.710	0.000	−100.00
CHPS	Chips & Technologies	7.250	7.750	6.90
CLE	Claire's Stores	9.750	8.375	−14.10
CIS	Concord Fabrics	4.000	3.750	−6.25
DSPT	DSP Technology	1.000	3.000	200.00
FNB	First Chicago	16.500	24.625	49.24
FED	First Fed Financial	13.100	22.375	70.80
FFHC	First Financial Corp.	11.000	23.250	111.37
FFOM	FirstFed Michigan	10.625	13.375	25.88
F	Ford Motor Co.	26.625	28.125	5.63
GRR	GRI Corp.	2.875	1.125	−60.87
GLN	Glendale Federal	6.375	4.625	−27.45
GVF	Golden Valley Micro	10.000	24.625	146.25
GNT	Green Tree Acceptance	10.875	39.000	258.62
HGIC	Harleysville Group	15.000	21.250	41.67
HRS	Harris Corp.	19.875	26.875	35.22
HIB	Hibernia Cp. "A"	6.625	2.750	−58.49
HFD	HomeFed Corp.	5.000	0.313	−93.75
HI	Household International	32.875	51.250	55.89
MXM	MAXXAM Inc.	31.125	29.375	−5.62
MCU	Magma Copper Co.	4.625	5.875	27.03
MLLE	Martin Lawrence	2.875	1.875	−34.78
MRI.A	McRae Inds Class A shares	4.875	5.375	10.26
PD	Phelps Dodge	56.625	67.000	18.32
PVH	Phillips–Van Heusen	7.313	16.750	129.06
RAVN	Raven Industries	10.125	20.250	100.00
SSI	Safecard Services	6.500	9.750	50.00

Table 7-17. Stocks Recommended for 1991 (cont.)

Symbol	Corporation	12/30/90	12/31/91	%Change
	(Original Price, Split–Adjusted Year–End Values)			
SCR.A	Sea Containers	20.625	22.250	7.88
SIF	Sifco Industries	7.250	6.000	–17.24
SMC.A	Smith, A.O. Class A shares	16.000	19.625	22.66
SPF	Standard Pacific	5.875	10.750	83.98
STO	Stone Container	11.500	25.875	125.00
SFY	Swift Energy	10.375	6.000	–42.17
TOS	Tosco Corp.	15.000	25.625	70.83
VAT	Varity Corp.	20.000	13.125	–34.37
VSH	Vishay Intertechnology	13.330	18.000	35.00
WFC	Wells Fargo	57.875	58.000	0.22
WDC	Western Digital	4.875	2.625	–46.15
	Averages	6.893	10.313	49.61

Table 7-18. Stocks Recommended for 1992

Symbol	Corporation	12/31/91	12/31/92	%Change
	(Original Price, Split–Adjusted Year–End Values)			
ASTA	AST Research	16.750	21.000	25.37
AIIC	American Integrity Inc.	3.875	1.625	–58.07
CAL	California Federal Bank "A"	2.250	2.875	27.76
C	Chrysler Corp.	11.750	32.000	172.32
CSTL	Constellation	2.000	5.250	162.50
DSPT	DSP Technology	3.000	6.625	120.81
FFOM	FirstFed Michigan	13.390	23.125	72.74
GLN	Glendale Federal	4.625	2.625	–43.25
IRDV	International R & D Corp.	3.500	2.875	–17.86
MXM	MAXXAM Inc.	29.410	27.500	–6.50
MCU	Magma Copper Co.	5.875	13.375	127.64
PNRL	Penril Datacomm	6.500	5.250	–19.25
PD	Phelps Dodge	33.563	48.500	44.53
POLK	Polk Audio Inc.	4.750	8.375	76.29
QUIK	Quiksilver	6.875	6.000	–12.76
SEVN	Sevenson Environment	9.000	13.000	44.43
SFY	Swift Energy	6.000	9.125	52.02
UFN	Unicare Financial	9.513	12.000	26.24
VAT	Varity Corp.	13.140	25.250	92.15
WDC	Western Digital	2.625	8.625	228.53
	Averages	5.207	8.112	55.78

Table 7-19. Stocks Recommended for 1993

(Original Price, Split-Adjusted Year-End Values)

Symbol	Corporation	12/31/92	12/31/93	% Change
AIIC	American Integrity Inc.	1.625	0.000	-100.00
ATVC	American Travellers	7.625	12.000	57.38
CBU	Commodore International	7.125	3.000	-57.89
GB	Guardian Bancorp	6.000	2.250	-62.50
IPLSA	IPL Systems	11.750	9.000	-23.40
KLM	KLM	13.875	21.000	51.35
MXM	MAXXAM Inc.	27.500	36.750	33.64
PFINA	P & F Inds "A"	1.250	1.750	40.00
RJF	Raymond James 3:2	14.925	16.625	11.45
	Averages	4.255	4.018	-5.57

Note that the big losses of 1990's recommended stocks and my TPS Portfolio were more than made up by the big gains in '91 and '92. That is not to say the performance for these three years was good on balance: a mere 8.35 percent overall return for three full years. Still, it's nice to be in the black in such a short time after such a huge setback.

1993—A Mixed Year

There were few deeply undervalued recommendable stocks for 1993. The nine we found contained four losers and only managed an average market loss of –5.6 percent, not counting dividends (see Table 7–19). TPS Portfolio gained a 41 percent total return (20.17 percent market appreciation as an hypothetical cash account). There was a certain embarrassment in doing so well in my margined portfolio while new subscribers may have done poorly (in the short term) with our currently recommended stocks. Meanwhile, Small Company Stocks had a total return of 20.98 percent, while S&P 500 stocks' total return was only 7.06 percent, a sub-average year.

1994—A Curiously Difficult Year, for Most

January started the year off well, but the first of six interest rate increases by the Federal Reserve, beginning on February 4, not only took the bloom off the rose but many of its petals as well, leaving mostly thorns. It was a horrendous year for U.S. Treasury bonds and a terrible year for the Dow Jones utilities, auto stocks, and sev-

Table 7-20. Stocks Recommended for 1994

(Original Price, Split-Adjusted Year-End Values)

Symbol	Corporation	12/31/93	12/30/94	% Change
ECOL	American Ecology	8.500	7.250	−14.71
ARTG	Artistic Greetings	5.625	3.000	−46.67
BSC	Bear Stearns	20.830	15.375	−26.20
BELF	Bel Fuse	8.500	8.250	−2.94
CBEX	Cambex Corp.	4.125	3.375	−18.18
DSPT	DSP Technology	3.125	5.250	68.00
GNA	Gainsco	8.280	8.250	−0.32
GB	Guardian Bancorp	2.250	0.625	−72.22
HNSI	Home Nutritional*	4.500	7.850	74.44
HYDEB	Hyde Athletic "B"	5.500	4.750	−13.64
IASG	International Airline Support	3.000	0.090	−96.87
NWLIA	National Western	44.500	34.750	−21.91
RJF	Raymond James	16.625	14.000	−15.79
STJM	St. Jude Medica	26.500	39.750	50.00
SYN	Syntex Corporation⁺	15.875	24.000	51.18
UTMD	Utah Medical	7.875	8.500	7.94
	Averages	6.067	5.771	−4.87

* Home Nutritional was bought out for cash in April 1994 by W.R. Grace.

⁺ Syntex Corporation was bought out for cash in September 1994 by Roche Holdings.

eral other sectors. After the dust had settled, the 16 recommended stocks for 1994 had a market price decline of −4.9 percent, excluding dividends (see Table 7–20). TPS Portfolio lost 12.91 percent, with its hypothetical cash account down 2.73 percent, excluding dividends. Ironically, the S&P 500 had a minuscule total return of 1.31 percent, while Small Company Stocks had a total return of 3.11 percent.

1995—In Progress

For a whole slew of reasons (precedents), 1995 should be a strong up year. Obviously, anything can happen. Wars, governmental interference, Federal Reserve miscalculation, whatever, could drive the market down. As this book goes to press, the 42 stocks recommended for 1995 had gained an average of 29.63 per-

Table 7-21. Stocks Recommended for 1995

	(Original Price, Split-Adjusted Year-End Values)			
Symbol	**Corporation**	**12/30/94**	**6/30/95**	**% Change**
AKLM	Acclaim Entertainment	14.375	18.438	28.26
ECOL	American Ecology	7.250	5.000	−31.03
APFC	American Pacific	7.000	4.750	−32.14
AMRC	American Recreation Centers	5.000	7.250	45.00
AMSWA	American Software	3.000	5.125	70.83
ARTG	Artistic Greetings	3.000	3.500	16.67
BGSS	BGS Systems	22.000	32.750	48.86
BSC	Bear Stearns	14.643	21.375	45.98
SBOS	Boston Bancorp	29.125	42.500	45.92
CBEX	Cambex Corp.	3.375	10.625	214.81
C	Chrysler Corp.	49.000	47.875	−2.30
PAR	CoastCast Corp.	11.750	10.875	−7.45
COFD	Collective Bancorp	19.677	20.250	2.91
CIS	Concord Fabrics	7.125	6.063	−14.91
CNR	Conner Peripherals	9.500	12.375	30.26
CRFT	Craftmade International	4.625	8.000	72.97
DWD	Dean Witter, Discover	33.875	47.000	38.75
FFHC	First Financial Corp.	13.750	17.500	27.27
F	Ford Motor Co.	27.875	29.750	6.71
GNA	Gainsco	8.250	9.938	26.48
GM	General Motors	42.125	46.875	11.28
GB	Guardian Bancorp	0.625	0.000	−100.00
HYDEB	Hyde Athletic "B"	4.750	4.375	−7.89
IPLSA	IPL Systems	2.500	6.313	152.52
IRDV	International R & D Corp.	1.375	0.750	−45.45
IFG	Inter–Regional	22.500	29.500	31.11
LSKI	Liuski International	4.125	4.625	12.12
LUR	Luria & Sons Inc.	5.875	7.250	23.40
MCH	MedChem Products	4.625	8.625	86.49
NWLIA	National Western	34.750	43.250	24.46
PATK	Patrick Industries	12.500	11.250	−10.00
PNRL	Penril Datacomm	2.500	4.500	80.00
PFS	Pioneer Financial	9.000	14.750	63.89

Table 7–21. Stocks Recommended for 1995 (cont.)

Symbol	Corporation	*(Original Price, Split-Adjusted 6-Months Values)* 12/30/94	6/30/95	%Change
QNTM	Quantum Corp.	15.125	22.875	51.24
RJF	Raymond James	14.000	19.375	38.39
SB	Salomon Inc.	37.500	40.125	7.00
SCR.A	Sea Containers	13.250	16.750	26.42
TXHI	THT Inc.	1.000	1.438	43.80
TSNG	Tseng Labs	5.875	8.750	48.94
TTI	Tyco Toys	5.625	6.875	22.22
UIC	United Industrial	4.875	7.125	46.15
WDC	Western Digital	<u>16.750</u>	<u>17.500</u>	<u>4.48</u>
	Averages	4.853	6.291	29.63

cent (see Table 7–21). This compares favorably with the S&P 500's nominal gain of 22.57 percent and the Russell 2000 Index of smaller capitalization stocks' nominal gain of 19.52 percent. Meanwhile, TPS Portfolio is up 51.85 percent as of June 30, 1995. I expect prices and gains to be even higher by year-end, although there may be a strong correction or two along the way.

Summary

This chapter does not need a summary section so much as an epilogue. For example, overnight, market psychology flipped—on June 27, 1989, with the release of the leading economic indicators down 1.2 percent—from a belief in a "soft landing" with reduced growth to a substantial fear of a "hard-landing" recession. From a scenario that would permit decreasing interest and inflation rates with continued slow economic growth, the script was rewritten to include a recession in progress or just around the corner, with corporate earnings about to tank. Time will tell, but we know that markets advance smartly from about the middle of a recession in anticipation of the next up cycle.

Although written in the summer of '89, the preceding paragraph could be written almost verbatim in the summer of '95. Can you spell "soft landing?" Some analysts are concerned that the next problem facing the market after 1995 is not inflation but deflation and recession. Presently, I expect both 1995 and 1996 to be good years for the stock market, but as with all market expectations, my outlook is subject to rapid change. In late June 1995, I am concerned that the Federal Reserve will wait too long to lower short-term interest rates and loosen the money supply, thus allowing the economy to slip into recession, not unlike 1990.

I hope the spartan but consistent review of each year's recommendations and outcomes was a window into the hurly-burly of actually investing/speculating in the stock market. True, I am not proud of my terrible losses of 1987 and 1990, but I am proud that I stuck it out and prospered in the process. As pointed out elsewhere, the total return for TPS Portfolio for the past 18.25 years is 22.92 percent compounded annually, including the two big setbacks. There is every reason to believe that I or my associate John Buckingham can do that well—or better if we guard against swift and sharp corrections (selloffs, bear markets)—for the next 18 years. Of course, past performance is no guarantee of future performance or profitability.

In updating and reviewing this chapter, I noticed that from 1977 through 1989 the average cost of a recommended share was double-digit, ranging from $11.29 in 1985 to $23.29 in 1984. However, beginning in 1990 the average cost of recommended shares was in single digits, ranging from $4.26 in 1993 to $9.82 in 1990. The overall average initial price for 18 years is $13.65 per share, although from '77 through '89 the average was $17.10 compared to the '90 through '95 average of $6.18. I find this odd, but do not know what it might mean or portend. Intuitively, I would think that stocks were getting higher priced all the time, in keeping with higher index numbers and the effect of inflation on dollar-denominated items. Or perhaps our methodology is just finding more out-of-favor stocks in the lower price ranges.

By the way, studies have shown that low-priced stocks tend to appreciate more than high-priced stocks on average. Most of the stocks we recommend are in the low-priced category, which may help to account for their superior average performance.

Still, the process continues year after year, each year having its crisis or two, and yet over decade-length periods the market—or well-selected stocks—rise on average. After so many years, so many trend changes, it seems silly to get concerned over daily, weekly, monthly, or even yearly fluctuations in the market. Just become "partners" with a large number of corporations when their stocks are undervalued—especially when conditions look pretty bad—and benefit over the years by their long-term growth (on average) until euphoria whistles in your ear to take profits and reduce exposure. You might even consider selling all but your core holdings when conditions look great and then taking a long vacation until they look terrible.

8

Potpourri—A Stock Marketeer's Stew

This is a catch-all chapter, but it is not just a compendium of afterthoughts or minor miscellaneous subjects. It includes important ideas that are not chapters in themselves, yet have been helpful to me and are worthy of your consideration. Some ideas are taken from the better essays of 18 years' worth of *The Prudent Speculator* newsletter. Some are my favorite studies which point out important advantages and strategies for speculating in stocks. Some are partially reviewed elsewhere but deserve more repeated and specific emphasis, such as the following topic.

The Stockbroker Is Not Your Friend

In my 26 years of speculating and my 18 years as a money manager, I have known a few good registered representatives—also known as account executives, vice presidents, financial consultants, first vice presidents, senior vice presidents, investment representatives, but generally called *stockbrokers* or *brokers* by the investing public. For the most part, though, I have been disillusioned and disappointed with brokers and brokerage houses.

In Chapter 5, I reviewed some of the questionable practices brokers use in relation to margin accounts and their maintenance levels. Anyone using a margined account must be clear on what could happen in a crunch. For years, you might have a wonderful, relatively conflict-free relationship with your broker, only to be abused during a period of chaos in a sharp market selloff. I wrote about the subject of brokers for the March 28, 1984, edition of *The Prudent Speculator*, and nothing much in my experience since then has changed that opinion. In fact, during the Crash of '87, several brokers and brokerage houses behaved worse than I ever thought likely.

237

At the risk of offending "the brokerage industry," but in the service of my most needful readers, let me state that the small investor ought not to think of his or her broker (account executive) as a friend, fiduciary, or investment counsel. While not necessarily one's adversary, the broker's business practices and self-serving needs are sometimes antagonistic to the investor's interests. With a few notable exceptions, the typical account executive has not the time, talent, nor expertise to pick stocks, time markets, or manage portfolios.

Essentially, the typical account executive is a telephone-order taker and "product" salesperson. The full-service broker generally works strictly for commission income, the percentage of which increases as gross commissions are generated (except in most discount brokerages). Thus, no trades mean no new shoes for the kids and no new toys for the parents. A registered representative may be on the phone 100 to 200 or more times during a long working day—perhaps from 6:30 A.M. to 6:30 P.M. on the West Coast—often prospecting by making "cold calls" in a frantic effort to build up a "book" of customers, otherwise canvassing active and inactive clients in an effort to induce trades or sell brokerage-sponsored products, such as annuities or limited partnerships.

The account executive is given canned research, which may be out-of-date or inappropriate for a given client's portfolio. The client rarely has the time, skill, or documentation to analyze the brokerage's recommendations. The account executive is often told to sell new issues and secondary distributions, with the infamous prevarication, "And there's no commission when you buy this stock." The "no commission" ploy is an egregious dissembling as the "commission" is factored into the net price of the stock or product, usually at a much higher amount paid to the broker than a normal trading commission would amount to. With apologies to those few good brokers I have known, investors might better think of account executives as competitors rather than allies.

The realities of the system work against the benefit of the small investor. It takes no more time to write a trading ticket order for 500 shares of a $50 stock than for 100 shares of a $9 stock. On the latter, the brokerage house makes its minimum commission, often crying all the way to the bank that it costs more to service that transaction than it makes. And the account executive gets his 25 to 40 percent, a paltry $10–$20, perhaps (but sometimes a minimum cutoff with nothing on small trades) for the small placement, while the larger item—the $25,000 ticket—may bring in several hundred dollars in commissions, even though the percentage rate is smaller than for the $900 trade.

In whom is the account executive and his or her boss, the branch manager, going to be interested, given their druthers—the $900 investor or the $25,000 trader? An extreme example perhaps, but I have seen the principle applied—in both directions over the years—to myself and to many others. The big, active investor gets attention and service; the small fry gets tolerance, perhaps. But don't blame only the broker for this. Think of your own business or activity. Do you want to deal with and spend much time on people who usually do not know the score and clearly cannot contribute much to your well being? There is a lot of lip service about goodwill and developing the little investor into the big client over the years, but time and reality intrude and take their toll.

Discount brokerages are not always a relief from the "better service for the VIP" syndrome. They are sometimes manned with burnt-out or beginning registered reps who cannot or will not compete in the full-service brokerage business jungle. For your discount, you may get long waits on the telephone, no advice (probably a blessing), and the run-around when something goes wrong. And many things can go wrong with all brokers. If Las Vegas or Atlantic City operated like most brokerage houses, they would be out of business within one year. As history shows, many brokerage houses have not survived deregulation, slack markets, the Crash of '87, or recent trading scandals, either closing their doors or saving face with timely (shotgun) mergers.

Perhaps I paint too strong a picture. If I overstate, it is in the hope that you will be saved from placing unwarranted trust in the brokerage industry. Many brokerages are shameless. Many will issue checks on out-of-state banks—in spite of the scandals associated with such float strategies—often causing the small investor delays in clearing the check. This scheme gives the brokerage house a float of two or three extra days, earning interest on your funds. You must be prepared to defend yourself against your broker and be willing to ferret out the few who can and will give you the kind of service you need and deserve.

Few novices know about *negotiated commissions*, a phrase many account executives abhor. Savvy investors with accounts of $100,000 or more regularly obtain 25 to 50 percent commission reductions from full-service brokerages, based sometimes upon trading frequency. Even small investors may be able to obtain a discount from a full-service brokerage if they press their case. Most everything in the financial community is negotiable, and there is still considerable competition, although the industry has closed ranks on certain subjects such as arbitration versus court trials. It helps to be aware of all these considerations (and those detailed in Chapter 5) in selecting a brokerage house and an account executive. And you might consider one more truism: one usually gets what one pays for. Free advice is usually worth what it costs, while expensive investment advice is often overpriced.

It's Only Money—Or Is It?

One of the small comforts of investing in stocks and not doing well (which is to say, losing) is the cheerful little rationalization, "It's only money."

Of course, we should not speculate with money we cannot afford to lose, especially for the short term. A person I knew who was looking to buy a house in the fall of '87 with money he had accumulated through the spring of '87, decided to get on the booming stock market bandwagon for just six months in order to enhance his down payment. After October, his funds were insufficient for a minimum down payment, and to add insult to injury he also had to forfeit a substantial option deposit on the house of his choice.

For approximately four months I studied gaming in Las Vegas, especially the craps and 21 tables. The sagest thing I ever heard in Vegas was: "There are two kind of players, those who make money bets and those who make mental bets. If you bet money, that's all you can lose; but if you make mental bets you can lose your mind."

We should not make investing in the stock market a test of our worth as human beings, win or lose. If we have a good day in the market, that doesn't make us any brighter, wiser, or even kinder, although it's easier for most people to be kinder after a good day than a bad one. If we have a good year in the market, we may not be more interesting, warm, intelligent, or loving than before, although a good year may be interesting in a limited way, and we may feel more generous and loving than we would after a bad year.

It is this reinforcement of high self-esteem that "winning" may give, and the opposite reinforcement of low self-esteem that "losing" may engender that makes speculating in stocks such a dangerous enterprise. If it were only money at stake, that would be bad enough, but for some it may be a question of mental health. And I'm not even talking about compulsive gamblers or other neurotics who have a need to "keep up with the Joneses" or who are punishing themselves by losing in that sophisticated casino (for them) called the stock market.

There is considerable danger that success in speculation could turn you into a tunnel-visioned, self-deluded, insular person. You spend more and more time studying corporations, the market, the economy, newsletters, and government regulators. You find satisfaction only in conversations about the market, especially those in which your savvy is displayed. It is very easy, especially for those who meet with the winning ways of a bull market, to become stock-market junkies, paying dearly for their initial good fortune over and over again in bear markets. Early or big success often leads to unrealistic expectations and frustration with historically reasonable, or even somewhat better than average, returns.

Paper Trading Is Not Actual Trading

People who trade so well in their imaginations or on paper usually do less well when real dollars are involved in real time. One can easily forget a bad trade one would have made while recalling another trade that would have turned out great. One can remember a low entry price, perhaps lower than it actually was at the time that the purchase of the stock was feasible. What about the mental effect of seeing a price higher than one would have been likely to realize, trapped in the optimism (or greed) of a roaring blowoff that quickly collapsed?

When "paper trading," one can easily ignore trading commission expenses; after all, they may "only" amount to 1 or 2 percent of the transaction. Ah, but every position involves at least two trades, buying and selling, so that turning over the portfolio two or three times a year involves perhaps 8 to 12 percent in commissions. Considering that long-term, common-stock total returns range from 10.2 to 12.2 percent (depending upon the stocks being studied), it would be very easy to spin one's wheels by paying as much for the privilege of trading as one might expect to gain as an average annual return. Furthermore, that 10.2 to 12.2 percent per year total return includes dividends (amounting on average to half of the total return), many of which would not be received in a heavily traded portfolio.

Sometimes when people are practicing, clocking, back checking, or trying other forms of paper trading, there is a tendency to fix on the closing or average price of a stock for that day's "trade." In reality, one often pays a bit more, due to buying at the asking price, or receives a bit less, due to selling at the bid price, than the closing or average price for a day. These eighths or quarters (or more) of additional costs and reduced proceeds can alter your "paper" profit percentage significantly.

Say you bought a stock intraday for $10.25 that closed at $10.00, and sold another stock intraday for $9.75 that closed at $10 per share. The effect of these two trades—not unlike buying and selling the same stock—cost you 2.5 percent each way compared to the closing prices (plus another 2 percent or so in commissions). If this occurs often, or if the differences turn out to be even greater, say 3/8 or 1/2 of a point, real-time results would vary from the paper trading results by several percent, depending upon the number of trades and varying executions. It is not surprising that many an investor cannot seem to match real performance to simulated or paper performance. This is especially true of those who like to trade frequently.

The Perfect Is the Enemy of the Good

Whoever said, "The perfect is the enemy of the good," could have been talking about the stock market. Many investors who have done rather well in the market still tend to be dissatisfied because they read of those few who have done spectacularly well—often for only a short period of time. The conviction that the returns are always greener in another system makes some investors discontented and impatient. Worse results often follow, as they shift to last year's hot strategy rather than sticking with their own long-time, "adequate," or better-than-average strategy.

There is a saying (mine, but it doesn't seem to have caught on yet) that almost every mistake leads to another mistake. If I buy "too early" and the undervalued stock in question declines, that is not necessarily a mistake. But if I turn around and sell that declining stock, even though it may be a better buy candidate because of its lower market price, that is a mistake. Later, when the stock I was impatient with has advanced nicely, I may well "chase it," buying a fully- or overvalued stock that is unlikely to generate a handsome return, and that is a mistake.

Deviating from one's game plan is usually a mistake. For every happy windfall there probably will be several disappointments, causing overall poor performance.

The Hulbert Financial Digest

I have been a supporter of *The Hulbert Financial Digest* (*HFD*)[1] since it began publishing in 1980 with the purpose of bringing objectivity to the performance claims of newsletters. As soon as I heard of *HFD*'s launch, I began a courtesy exchange subscription with it. As chance would have it, *HFD* began following *TPS* in its performance rankings at the beginning of 1983. Happily, *TPS* was the best-performing newsletter *HFD* followed for each of the four quarters and the year of 1983. This brought a tremendous amount of recognition and publicity, with Dan Dorfman's column each quarter on newsletters noting *TPS*'s top performance, *Barron's* feature articles highlighting *TPS*, *Money* magazine doing a profile of me, and *Wall $treet Week* inviting me to be their program guest in September 1983.

Other interviews, articles, and TV appearances followed, including a profile in *Fortune* and a weekly "spot" on the Financial News Network (the old FNN, since merged into CNBC), during which I developed a camaraderie with anchors Bill Griffeth, Ron Insana, and Sue Herrera. All the while, the superior performance of *TPS* was being displayed in *HFD*. Literally, being monitored by Mark Hulbert was the making of *The Prudent Speculator*, both as a newsletter and a money management company. We did very little advertising and mostly prospered by word of mouth.

Mark Hulbert is personally likable because of his intelligence and sincerity. We would sometimes meet in passing at an investment seminar and find time for a chat not only about the stock market but about philosophy in general and one of our favorite philosophers, David Hume.

Even when *TPS* was reported as the second worst-performing newsletter (in 1987) my admiration and respect for Mark Hulbert continued. After all, he was reporting the reality of the situation, albeit very negatively, and I was sure that he would report future, positive realities as he had in the past.

---

[1] Mark Hulbert, *The Hulbert Financial Digest*, 316 Commerce Street, Alexandria, VA 22314.

Somewhere along the way Mark Hulbert began to focus on risk and risk-adjusted performance, perhaps emphasizing it over total return gains. An example of this selected emphasis is his column entitled "Measuring the market mavens," in the January 30, 1995, issue of *Forbes*, pp. 128–30, wherein he reviewed newsletter performance between August 1987 and November 1994. Those few letters on the "Honor Roll," with compounded annual gains of 8.9 to 12.2 percent, were not the best-performing newsletters overall, but only those that did well in both up and down markets—a form of risk-adjusted results. The two non-Honor Roll best-performing letters, up 15.5 and 19.3 percent compounded annually, did not do well in down markets. I wrote to the editor of *Forbes* asking if he would rather have had the Honor Roll performance or the best-performing newsletters' gains. I never received an answer.

In late April 1995, I received a personal letter from *The Hulbert Financial Digest* stating that since *TPS* was the second-best-performing total return newsletter for the past three years (to March 31, 1995), they would like to include a two-issue trial of *TPS* as a free premium in their subscription renewal package (their promotional arrangement, to which I had agreed previously). I was delighted at this news—not only the recognition of our performance but the additional exposure of our newsletter to renewing *HFD* subscribers. (*HFD* notes that they do not endorse nor recommend newsletters.)

A few days later, I received the April 17, 1995, issue of *The Hulbert Financial Digest*. On page 8, in a table titled "The Top Performers Through 3/31/95," *The Prudent Speculator* is ranked number 4 with a 14.75-year gain of +714.4 percent, which is 15.3 percent compounded annually. All five top-ranked letters were compared to the Wilshire 5000 total return of +614.2 percent (14.3 percent compounded annually). So far so good.

Page 3 of the *HFD* is a profile of *The Prudent Speculator,* with about half a page of commentary. After two paragraphs of description, Hulbert mentions:

> There are some discrepancies between Frank's actual performance and what *HFD* reports, however. One source of these discrepancies is the margin level in the portfolio the *HFD* constructs. As an ongoing portfolio, Frank need keep the equity value of his personal portfolio no higher than the 30 percent maintenance level. And for much of the last 15 years, in fact, Frank has stayed close to that 30 percent level. In contrast, the *HFD* starts out each year with Frank's portfolio at the 50 percent margin level (since a new subscriber would not be able to leverage his portfolio as much as Frank's is).[2]

---

[2] *Hulbert Financial Digest*, April 17, 1995, p. 3.

There are some discrepancies in the above quotation. While I have tried to use "margin to the hilt," my portfolio has not been "close to" its 30 percent mainte- nance level for most of the past 15 years. In fact, with my account currently (and for the past few years) at Charles Schwab, I must keep a 35 percent minimum maintenance-equity level, and at this writing (June 20, 1995), TPS Portfolio is at a 50 percent equity level. I would guesstimate that for the past 15 years, TPS Portfolio may have averaged a 40 percent equity level, although there were periods when it was between 30 and 35 percent equity. Recall that at 40 percent equity or 60 percent leveraged, a 20 percent gain in market value equals a 50 percent gain in equity (less margin interest, plus dividends).

While a subscriber to *TPS* could only be at 50 percent equity at the initiation of a margined portfolio, that equity would soon decline as margin interest was deb- ited to the account, unless the market advanced nicely. Dividend income would help raise one's equity, but could be withdrawn or spent on buying more stocks with 50 percent equity, possibly driving equity below 50 percent, again unless the market advanced nicely. Sooner or later, with a normal declining fluctuation, the fully margined portfolio could easily be at less than 50 percent maintenance. For more on this potentially confusing relationship, see Chapter 5.

Hulbert goes on to say that:

> You should keep this [using margin] in mind when interpreting the fact that Frank only slightly outperformed the market over these 15 years. On a risk-adjusted basis, in fact, his long-term return is well below the market's.
>
> Why should you care that Frank's risk-adjusted performance is below the market's? For at least two reasons. First, it indicates to you that, if you had been willing to leverage your portfolio as much as Frank's, you could have performed even better by simply using an index fund. In fact, *HFD* calculates that had you done so, you would have achieved an 18.4 percent compound return since 1980—more than 3 percent better.[3]

Again, Hulbert, while emphasizing risk-adjusted performance, emphasizes the fact (according to *HFD*'s accounting) that TPS Portfolio "only slightly outper- formed the market over these 15 years." He does not mention that only a handful of letters have outperformed the market over the past 15 years. And his comment about leveraging an index fund (which one?) doesn't mention that index funds were not leverageable 15 years ago. Charles Schwab started its Fund Marketplace in 1984 with 140 no-load funds. I understand that since that time only mutual

---

[3] *Hulbert Financial Digest*, April 17, 1995, p. 3.

funds that have agreements with brokerages to market them were able to be held in a margin account. I did not find the $9+ billion Vanguard Index 500 nor the Fidelity Market Index funds in Schwab's Fourth Quarter 1994 *Performance Guide*. I'm informed that these index funds are not marginable today.

The appearance of short-term, erratic returns versus the reality of long-term, relatively consistent gains has often been the subject of editorial comment in *The Hulbert Financial Digest*. Not only does the *HFD* report on the performance of a large number of newsletter portfolios, it also reviews investing strategies and historical comparisons worthy of consideration. On the other hand, for some years now, Hulbert has emphasized risk-adjusted performance, generally based on portfolio and market volatility. I disagree strongly with the academic concept of risk based on price volatility, especially for investments taken for the long term and as a total, diversified system. Such risk analysis does not consider the upside volatility of undervalued stocks sold at fair value, thus missing much of the downside volatility, on average.

Perhaps the greatest service the *HFD* performs is to explode false and outrageous performance claims while bringing reasonable and realistic expectations to its readers' attention.

Unfortunately, even Hulbert cannot keep newsletters from advertising that they are No. 1 according to *The Hulbert Financial Digest*. Unscrupulous advertisers will call themselves No. 1, even if they had only received that evaluation for a month or two, years ago, and some give themselves a high *HFD* rating that they never received in the publication. By the way, *HFD* calculates that *TPS* is the second-best total return performing newsletter followed for the 15 years ended June 30, 1995 with a total gain of 925.3 percent, which is 16.8 percent compounded annually.

The purpose for this critique of *The Hulbert Financial Digest* is to point out that even the most ethical publications can emphasize the negative, based on concepts and calculations that do not completely capture the actual performance of a money manager or newsletter. Even as laudable a publication as *HFD* should have its biases recognized.

Reasonable Total Return Goals

There are any number of reasonable goals to strive for in terms of invested returns. Sir John Templeton's expressed goal is 15 percent compounded annually over a multiyear period. My goal is 15 to 18 percent compounded annually over a multiyear period in a cash account, but 22.5 to 24 percent compounded over a 5- to 10-year period in a heavily margined account. Barry Ziskin's goal is to obtain a 30 percent annual gain, from peak to peak or trough to trough as measured during a market cycle. Ziskin bases his goal on the premise that the corporations he selects tend to grow at 30 percent or more per year.

We know that the 69-year average for S&P 500 stocks is 10.2 percent, and for very-small-capitalization stocks is 12.2 percent, so those might be minimum goals. Given that one *should* do better than average following a systematic strategy such as this book presents, a return of 15 percent to 18 percent could be considered reasonable, handsome, and likely attainable over a multiyear period.

During various economic cycles, one might set a total return goal in terms of after-inflation returns, or after-inflation and after-tax returns. Again, we can turn to the long-term historical statistics for comparison (Tables 8–1 and 8–2). Remember,

Table 8–1. After-Inflation, After-Tax Returns, Assuming 40% Total Tax Liability

			Returns			
Inflation	**10.00%**	**12.50%**	**15.00%**	**17.50%**	**20.00%**	**25.00%**
1%	4.94	6.43	7.91	9.40	10.88	13.85
2	3.88	5.35	6.82	8.29	9.76	12.70
3	2.82	4.28	5.73	7.19	8.64	11.55
4	1.76	3.20	4.64	6.08	7.52	10.40
5	0.70	2.13	3.55	4.98	6.40	9.25
6	–0.36	1.05	2.46	3.87	5.28	8.10
7	–1.42	–0.03	1.37	2.77	4.16	6.95
8	–2.48	–1.10	0.28	1.66	3.04	5.80
9	–3.54	–2.18	–0.81	0.56	1.92	4.65
10	–4.60	–3.25	–1.90	–0.55	0.80	3.50

Table 8–2. After-Inflation, After-Tax Returns, Assuming 30% Total Tax Liability

			Returns			
Inflation	**10.00%**	**12.50%**	**15.00%**	**17.50%**	**20.00%**	**25.00%**
1%	5.93	7.66	9.40	11.13	12.86	16.33
2	4.68	6.58	8.29	10.01	11.72	15.15
3	3.79	5.49	7.19	8.88	10.58	13.98
4	2.72	4.40	6.08	7.76	9.44	12.80
5	1.65	3.31	4.98	6.64	8.30	11.63
6	0.58	2.23	3.87	5.52	7.16	10.45
7	–0.49	1.14	2.77	4.39	6.02	9.28
8	–1.56	0.05	1.66	3.27	4.88	8.10
9	–2.63	–1.04	0.56	2.15	3.74	6.93
10	–3.70	–2.13	–0.55	1.03	2.60	5.75

the effect of inflation reduces the purchasing power of the original capital investment as well as after-tax gains.

From an after-tax, after-inflation return point of view, we might consider a net 3 to 5 percent return fair or adequate. Currently, if you are in the top tax bracket and in a high-tax state, you might well be paying a 40 percent or greater income tax rate on ordinary income plus investment income and 28 percent (plus state taxes) on capital gains. Table 8–1 shows that, with 3 percent inflation, a 10 percent total return would result in a 2.82 percent after-tax (40 percent total tax liability), after-inflation gain.

Indeed, with inflation running about 5 to 6 percent during the summer of '89, you would have wanted to obtain a 15 to 17.5 percent total return in order to keep up your living standard and add incrementally to your growing capital. By mid-1995, the inflation rate was running about 3 percent, so it would take an 11 to 14 percent return to keep your buying power and increase your capital by 3 to 5 percent.

Perhaps a 30 percent (or lower) tax bracket is more appropriate for many small investors than the 40 percent assumption. If so, Table 8–2 shows that with a 5 to 6 percent inflation, a 12.5 to 15 percent gross return would provide a similar "fair" after-tax, after-inflation return. In a 3 percent inflationary environment, a 9 to 12 percent return would meet the same objective. One of the reasons that the subject of after-tax, after-inflation returns is rarely reviewed is the great variation in tax liabilities individual investors face. To cover everybody's case would require tables not unlike those in the Internal Revenue Service 1040 instruction manuals, and still there would be variations. Nevertheless, we can approximate our goals, given our situation and the two variables involved.

Being a Contrarian Is Correct but Complicated

Although I think of myself as a contrarian thinker and speculator, willing to go against the crowd, discovering and committing funds to the out-of-favor stock—assuming it is sufficiently fundamentally undervalued—I still have trouble with a contrarian rallying cry, "The majority is always wrong." For starters, always is usually inaccurate, and beyond that, it is often difficult to identify the majority or their strongly held attitude, let alone how big a majority is needed to set oneself against in a true contrarian manner.

We contrarians believe that usually at market extremes "the majority" is wrong. This is the principle of sentiment measures, when what seems an oxymoron—"Too much bullishness is bearish"—becomes both reasonable and somewhat predictive. That is, when the overwhelming majority (60 to 80 percent) is enthusiastically bullish and the market is making historic highs as registered in its major averages, most of the likely participants are in the market, with most of their capital invested; thus, there is little capital left to drive the market higher. What does not go up, at least in stock market physics, sooner or later comes down. But a substantial majority can be bullish for quite a while as the market continues advancing into overbought territory.

The reverse is true at sold-out market bottoms, where most (a majority) of the stock market participants who wanted to sell or had to sell have sold; thereafter, the line of least resistance is a market rise, in spite of the pessimistic majority. These are rationales for and descriptions of overbought and oversold markets that we've reviewed before, based on sentiment.

Still, it seems to me that many times the majority is right, and for long periods of time. As with any trend-following system, following the majority is right until the trend reverses (the market reverses) and one gets caught as part of the wrong majority. Often, the majority is a better indicator of market lows than market highs. As the market was plunging in November 1988, it looked as though the worst fears of the bearish gurus were about to be realized—the other shoe was dropping—and expectations were that soon the market would revisit and exceed the October '87 Crash lows. Bearishness was rampant, and bullishness was in small supply.

Investors Intelligence[4], edited by Michael Burke, is a publication that tracks investment newsletter (advisory) opinion and also presents its own technical and charting information, reported in its December 9, 1988 issue that only 21.1 percent of the advisory services it monitors were bullish, while 55.3 percent were bearish. As the publication pointed out: "You have to go all the way back to June 1982 to find as few bulls or as many bears as we saw 2 weeks ago, and this indicator is very bullish." In the December 8, 1988, issue of *The Prudent Speculator* we noted this condition, summarizing: "On this sentiment indicator basis, we have a screaming contrarian buy signal."

As events turned out, the market continued its strong advance until July 1990, when a combination of events, including tightening Federal Reserve action, a recession, and the Iraqi invasion of Kuwait, led to the aforementioned Selloff of '90.

Coincidentally, similar bearish majorities were registered in late 1994 and early 1995. In spite of this overwhelming negativism toward the stock market, it began to rally in November 1994 and carried through to mid-1995 in spite of the "sell signals" issued by many advisory services.

It is good to be aware of market majorities, if they can be identified, and to consider such sentiment indicators along with other technical indicators and fundamental criteria of value. It is also advisable to not try to outguess an alleged majority hoping to catch a trend reversal based only on intuitive expectations, if doing so alters one's basic approach.

---

[4] Michael Burke, *Investors Intelligence* (Chartcraft Inc., New Rochelle, NY 10801).

Over the years, I have written about the BB syndrome: The bullish-but or bearish-but psychology of individual, institutional, or stock advisory participants. The BB syndrome occurs when people report, "I'm bullish (or bearish) but I'm waiting to see how the market develops." Often that means they are not buying or selling, so their professed bullishness or bearishness is not really affecting the market's trend. This is one of the reasons why it is so difficult sometimes to get a clear picture of what a majority is and what it is doing.

By the way, a newsletter that has been a source of inspiration, comfort, and enjoyment for many years is *The Contrary Investor*, written by James L. Fraser, C.F.A. This low-key, two-page, green-tinted, biweekly generally quotes and comments upon the Contrarian's coping with the Crowd. In keeping with his New England, away-from-Wall-Street location, Fraser truly takes "the road less traveled." For instance, in the June 28, 1989 issue, as part of an essay on "What Do You Think of the Market?" Fraser writes:

> The normal person does best with a dollar averaging program that keeps emotions in the background. To be sure, the true Contrarian can do better but that means concentrating hard on your own feelings and being able to associate them with the Wall Street community. You buy when you feel bad and you sell when you feel good. That is a lot to ask from the healthy and normal thinking person. Reverence for the latest investment fashion or whoever is doing well at the moment should be set aside. The most sacred of investment duties is to be disciplined without losing your power of imagination.[5]

Shun Slogans, Minimize Maxims

Stock market slogans and *clichés* generally fall into a category of half-truths or contingent truths. That is, the kinds of slogans and maxims mentioned in previous chapters and reviewed below have elements of truth to them, but are often misleading and sometimes false. If you find yourself parroting some stock-market slogan because it makes you comfortable or rationalizes current conditions, beware that you may have been seduced by platitude, euphemism, or delusion.

"You can never go broke taking a profit" is an example of a rationalization rather than a rationale. This slogan is at best misleading and at worst false. If the profits you take are less than the after-tax, after-inflation penalties, you might not go broke, but your purchasing power and standard of living will probably decrease if you are dependent upon stock-market gains. However, there likely are people who did go broke tak-

---

[5] James L. Fraser, C.F.A., 309 South Willard St., Burlington, VT 05401. James L. Frazer, "What Do You Think of the Market?" *The Contrary Investor*, June 28, 1989, p. 1.

ing profits, especially consistently taking small profits that were more than wiped out by realized or unrealized losses. If your average realized profit is 10 to 15 percent, and your average unrealized (unsold) loss is 20 to 25 percent—and you manage about as many winners as losers, not an unheard of balance—you could go broke over time.

You must have profits that more than compensate for your losses. Many successful investors have claimed that if you are right only three or four times out of 10 you can make a fortune in the stock market. They are assuming (based on experience) that when you are right, your profits will be in the 100 to 1,000 percent or more range, while when you are wrong, your losses will tend to be less than 100 percent and perhaps only 25 percent or less, on average.

In fact, to counteract the rationalization "No one ever went broke taking a profit," we have the more widely quoted slogan, "Cut short your losses and let your profits run on." How you take profits while letting them run on is a trick I have not mastered. One strategy to reconcile these paradoxical maxims is to sell half your position after a 100 percent gain. In theory that would mean that you couldn't lose, because you recover your costs and continue playing with "house money." This "Swiss technique" violates the principle that a position is a buy, hold, or sell. Either the whole position should be sold because it is fairly valued (and the profits locked in), or the whole position should be held because it is still undervalued (letting the profits run on).

Although letting profits run on is a good idea, and cutting short losses is a good-sounding idea, the reality is that often a short-term loss could turn into a long-term gain. If you are quick to dump a stock that has a small decline, you have not only cut short your (temporary) loss in that stock, you have also cut short your potential for profit in that stock. You have "locked in your loss." As mentioned frequently in this book, many early losses or sharp declines thereafter were merely part of the pattern of market price fluctuations along the way to great gains. True, some stocks continue to lose and never recover, but the best policy is to base sells on fundamental values, accepting the occasional disaster.

Speculating by Unexamined Assertions—Don't!

"I never buy at the bottom or sell at the top; I'm content with the 60 percent in between." This self-serving assertion is a real con used by snake-oil-type salespersons. Again, any statement that has the words always or never in it is suspect if not outright false. Second, who does buy at the bottom or sell at the top? Such events are generally accidents and certainly not predictable. As for being content with only taking a large chunk out of the middle, this come-on is so illogical that it is hardly worth further comment. But I can't resist.

In Chapter 1, I wrote about some of the problems and tricks associated with performance statistics, specifically the confusion of averaged annual gains with compounded annual gains (see Table 1–2). In the merchandising of investment opportunities, there are endless examples of weak or illogical analogies or arguments.

One terrific-sounding and great-looking but absurd proposition is made when investment advisers or portfolio managers claim that they are not greedy because they never try to buy at the bottom or sell at the top: they merely capture the great gains in between. Immediately, we should be alert to the reality that no one can know the bottom or top until after the fact, and therefore no one could possibly decide in advance to trade at slightly above or below those points. If you could determine bottoms and tops, why wouldn't you trade at those points exactly, in order to maximize your gains and minimize your losses?

Some people who would normally see through charlatans claiming concurrent or advance knowledge of market tops and bottoms may become mesmerized by the attractive use of graphics, specifically a picture of a bell-shaped curve, such as the left curve in Figure 8–1. The con artist claims that if one waits for a 20 percent rise off the low, participates in the next 60 percent of the up cycle, and then gets out about 20 percent before the top, great returns with large margins of safety will be gleaned by capturing 60 percent of the move. Ah, but how do you know where 20 percent off the low is, since you have no foreknowledge of how far the apparent trend will continue? Likewise, how do you know that you are 20 percent away from the top, before the top has been made and the trend reverses?

Actually, few trends are as smooth and none is as predictable as Figure 8–1's leftmost curve would indicate, but the smooth-talking salesperson may be able to

Figure 8–1. Undisclosed Curves (I Ideal, II and III Potential)

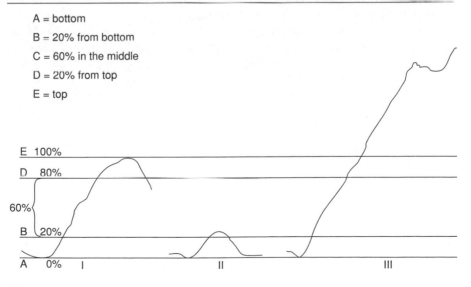

A = bottom
B = 20% from bottom
C = 60% in the middle
D = 20% from top
E = top

convince many a naive but otherwise reasonable investor that this "ungreedy" timing method is a winning strategy. And there is much that is appealing about using
an "ungreedy" method. Meanwhile, Figure 8–1's middle and right curves may be
as probable as its left one, as examples of a stock's price moving from point A to
point B and what might happen thereafter.

Over the years I have criticized and explored the consequences of the admoni-
tions "Never meet a maintenance call," "Never average down," and "It's not a loss
until you sell." One challenge—"Never confuse brains with a bull market"—might
well be an absolute guide, even though it uses the word *never*. A true bull market is
a wonderful experience to behold and participate in, as were the first seven months
of 1995, for example. Month after month, even year after year, the majority of
stocks advance in price as on a stairway to the stars. You can make many mistakes
in a bull market, but often the market will bail you out. Sooner or later almost all
industry groups participate, and while there will always be the stocks (corporations) that fail, they are so overcome by the stocks that advance that it becomes
easy to imagine that you have a special insight into the secrets of the market.

Sooner or later the day of reckoning arrives for many, and what was a brilliant
participation in the strong uptrend becomes a terrible overcommitment to the tricky
decline. The long-expected correction, which was supposed to be a minor pause to
refresh, turns into a deeper selloff than expected. After the briefest of technical
bounces up—bear market rallies—the expected resumption of the major advance
turns into a mockery as prices fall slowly or sharply. Profits are erased and it seems
too late to sell, if not too early to buy "into weakness." Losses begin to mount up,
and one quickly realizes what a good move it would have been to have sold during
the first of the setbacks or into the first "bear market rally."

Braggadocio turns to lament, gurus become ex-gurus, and oaths with the
words "never again" in them are sworn. After the down cycle, few people identify
their brains with the market at all. Who ever heard of someone saying, "Don't confuse brains with a bear market!"? And yet, in the deepest despair of a stock-market
bottom, the next bull market is being born; the darkest investment night gives rise
to the brightest investment day. At least our brains should remember the nature of
markets, not unlike the ebb and flow of nature:

> Vanity of vanities, saith the Preacher, vanity of
>   vanities; all is vanity.
> What profit hath a man of all his labor which he
>   taketh under the sun?
> One generation passeth away, and another generation
>   cometh: but the earth abideth for ever.
> The sun also ariseth.
>   *Ecclesiastes 1:2–5*

One generation of investors drops out, and another generation comes along, but the market goes on. Clearly, many investment assertions are true some of the time or under certain conditions, but often they block clear thinking. The next time you find yourself mouthing a slogan, perhaps in stentorian tones with your audience nodding in affirmative assent, try running it up the semantic flagpole—your critical, analytical flagpole—and see how it flies, in the current winds and conditions. Speculating by slogan is a great way to miss what's going on.

Using Net Asset Value to Measure Performance

I have kept much of the commentary written about the period after the Crash of '87 in this revised edition in order to show the recovery process from one of the most traumatic stock-market periods. I find it important to have a history of where I've been and where I went, speculation-wise, for perspective about what to do if or when a similar event occurs.

The Crash of '87 bottomed out during the first week of December '87. For almost two years after the dust had settled, I bought only one stock and sold seven or eight, mostly because they were sell candidates in *The Prudent Speculator*. I held onto as many shares as I could after the Crash, and continued to let them "mature." Thus, The Prudent Speculator Portfolio, which generated the performance displayed in Table 8–3, remained an almost passive investment for over 22 months. Of course, several stocks were taken away in buyouts and mergers, which provided additional funds for personal use, when needed.

I would have liked to buy more stocks with the cash received from buyouts and with the loan value developed through portfolio appreciation. Obviously, my total gains would be considerably greater if I had leveraged and pyramided the buying power generated over those 22 months. I chose rather to reduce exposure during periods when the market looked vulnerable, although the portfolio still remained fully margined.

I point out this passive speculative approach in another attempt to convince readers that long-term holding (time diversification), when combined with wide stock diversification of selected undervalued equities, can really pay off. True, there were some stocks that went bad, such as Financial Corp. of America (FIN), or did poorly, such as Equitec Financial Group (EFG) and Integrated Resources (IRE). But, as usual, the stocks that did well more than compensated for the ones that failed or have yet to approach their intrinsic values.

Displaying the performance of TPS Portfolio in the aftermath of the Crash of '87's market bottom on December 4, 1987, also gives us a chance to review net asset value (NAV), probably the best way of accounting for investment performance. NAV is the way open-end mutual funds must account for their net assets each day.

Notice in Table 8–3 that TPS Portfolio (TPSP) has a beginning equity value of $258,883. (We round up to dollars in terms of market value, debit balance, and equity.) We arbitrarily assign 258,883 "NAV shares" of TPSP with a NAV of $1 as of December 4, 1987. Thereafter, whenever cash is added, it will "buy" that amount of TPSP NAV shares at their then current value, just as you would buy shares in an open-end fund at that day's NAV. Whenever cash is withdrawn, TPSP NAV shares will be "sold" at their current value, just as you would liquidate your mutual fund shares at that day's NAV.

Although these computations are the simplest approach, and a fair, accurate representation, they may seem a bit confusing until you realize what is going on. It should be obvious that we must account for cash added to a portfolio to distinguish the portfolio's increases in value based on cash additions from those based on market appreciation. Likewise, we must account for withdrawals of cash; otherwise, the lower market value and equity amounts actually caused by cash withdrawn would look like money lost in market depreciation.

For greater accuracy, it would be better if NAV were calculated daily, as is done for mutual funds. However, mutual funds must do that in order to account for the shares that are being purchased and redeemed daily, as well as their daily withdrawal of management fees and other expenses. In a personal portfolio, where only periodic additions or withdrawals are made, monthly or even quarterly calculations could be reasonably sufficient, although provision should be made for large changes on the day they occur. We keep such figures for TPS Portfolio on a weekly basis.

Observe in Table 8–3 that after the first week (December 11, 1987), the net equity value increased $15,675, or 6.054 percent. As there was no cash added or withdrawn, there was no change in the number of TPSP NAV shares. Thus, the TPSP NAV share increased to $1.0605, a figure obtained by dividing the number of TPSP NAV shares into the net equity value.

After the second week (December 18, 1987)—which was another very big week in TPS Portfolio, with its market value jumping up $33,906 (a gain of 12.35 percent)—I withdrew $5,000 in cash, which is to say I borrowed $5,000. In doing so, I "sold" (liquidated) $5,000 worth of TPSP NAV shares. By December 18, TPSP NAV shares were worth $1.1915 each, so withdrawing $5,000 only required "selling" (an accounting transaction) 4,196.331 shares, thus reducing the TPSP NAV shares to 254,686.676, a number remain unchanged until the next time cash withdrawn on June 3, 1988. Between December 4, 1987, and June 30, 1989, no cash was added, so all the computations are to account for withdrawals, market price fluctuation, dividend income, and margin interest.

The bottom line is that TPS Portfolio appreciated 183.68 percent in NAV between December 4, 1987, and September 1, 1989, and that $173,900 in cash was withdrawn during that period. I find it particularly satisfying that the cash

Table 8–3. Net Asset Value Analysis, TPS Portfolio, 12/4/87–6/30/89

Date	Value	Debit	Equity	Add/Del	Shares	NAV
12/04/87	689205	430322	258883		258883.000	1.0000
12/11/87	704241	429683	274558		258883.000	1.0605
12/18/87	747508	439044	308464		258883.000	1.1915
12/24/87	761103	428979	332124	−5000	254686.676	1.3040
12/31/87	751794	437899	313895		254686.676	1.2325
1/08/88	768489	437208	331281		254686.676	1.3007
1/15/88	781263	436550	344713		254686.676	1.3535
1/22/88	782230	436500	345730		254686.676	1.3575
1/29/88	808779	439101	369678		254686.676	1.4515
2/05/88	802100	444257	357843		254686.676	1.4050
2/12/88	805437	440036	365401		254686.676	1.4347
2/19/88	815100	439469	375631		254686.676	1.4749
2/26/88	828787	442546	386241		254686.676	1.5165
3/04/88	865413	444522	420891		254686.676	1.6526
3/11/88	871928	443815	428113		254686.676	1.6809
3/18/88	883081	443192	439889		254686.676	1.7272
3/25/88	868731	443157	425574		254686.676	1.6710
3/31/88	866367	445928	420439		254686.676	1.6508
4/08/88	886592	445413	441179		254686.676	1.7322
4/15/88	829313	412466	416847		254686.676	1.6367
4/22/88	835299	412466	422833		254686.676	1.6602
4/29/88	847242	415398	431844		254686.676	1.6956
5/06/88	837060	407472	429588		254686.676	1.6867
5/13/88	832811	409792	423019		254686.676	1.6609
5/20/88	822250	409168	413082		254686.676	1.6219
5/27/88	828653	408186	420467		254686.676	1.6509
6/03/88	855554	442806	412748	−33000	234697.805	1.7586
6/10/88	870447	440688	429759		234697.805	1.8311
6/17/88	860594	431653	428941		234697.805	1.8276
6/24/88	858699	426895	431804		234697.805	1.8398
7/01/88	862587	429167	433420		234697.805	1.8467
7/08/88	838212	409958	428254		234697.805	1.8247
7/15/88	822128	389252	432876		234697.805	1.8444
7/22/88	811971	415007	396964	−31800	217456.401	1.8255
7/29/88	815081	407675	407406		217456.401	1.8735
8/05/88	811350	421541	389809	−14300	209823.655	1.8578
8/12/88	792287	421489	370798		209823.655	1.7672

Table 8–3. Net Asset Value Analysis, TPS Portfolio, 12/4/87–6/30/89 (cont.)

Date	Value	Debit	Equity	Add/Del	Shares	NAV
8/19/88	790010	420805	369205		209823.655	1.7596
8/26/88	779812	420435	359377		209823.655	1.7128
9/02/88	771576	411441	360135		209823.655	1.7164
9/09/88	774682	410845	363837		209823.655	1.7340
9/16/88	783586	420716	362870	−10600	203710.668	1.7813
9/23/88	787088	420800	366288		203710.668	1.7981
9/30/88	791230	424082	367148		203710.668	1.8023
10/07/88	807777	423246	384531		203710.668	1.8876
10/14/88	806898	423434	383464		203710.668	1.8824
10/21/88	823712	422395	401317		203710.668	1.9700
10/28/88	812818	422283	390535		203710.668	1.9171
11/04/88	805874	428496	377378		203710.668	1.8525
11/11/88	791196	428304	362892		203710.668	1.7814
11/18/88	769189	425878	343311		203710.668	1.6853
11/25/88	774993	424595	350398		203710.668	1.7201
12/02/88	787939	426838	361101		203710.668	1.7726
12/09/88	798432	431555	366877	−5500	200607.911	1.8288
12/16/88	802075	430413	371662		200607.911	1.8527
12/23/88	804955	430320	374635		200607.911	1.8675
12/30/88	807386	434336	373050		200607.911	1.8596
1/06/89	824328	433415	390913		200607.911	1.9486
1/13/89	831182	428615	402567		200607.911	2.0067
1/20/89	834882	427966	406916		200607.911	2.0284
1/27/89	843217	427347	415870		200607.911	2.0730
2/03/89	835816	414189	421627		200607.911	2.1017
2/10/89	817403	396075	421328	−5000	198228.937	2.1255
2/17/89	827706	398871	428835		198228.937	2.1633
2/24/89	813229	398397	414832		198228.937	2.0927
3/ 3/89	828468	420370	408098	−20000	188671.867	2.1630
3/10/89	839030	419661	419369		188671.867	2.2227
3/17/89	834490	435122	399368	−16000	181473.552	2.2007
3/23/89	827148	433122	394026		181473.552	2.1713
3/31/89	834710	437103	397607		181473.552	2.1910
4/07/89	843283	436310	406973		181473.552	2.2426
4/14/89	849301	436310	412991		181473.552	2.2758
4/21/89	857066	432882	424184		181473.552	2.3374
4/28/89	861986	441197	420789		181473.552	2.3187

Table 8–3. Net Asset Value Analysis, TPS Portfolio, 12/4/87–6/30/89 (cont.)

Date	Value	Debit	Equity	Add/Del	Shares	NAV
5/05/89	855175	433208	421967		181473.552	2.3252
5/12/89	865596	433082	432514		181473.552	2.3833
5/19/89	884961	432610	452351		181473.552	2.4927
5/26/89	892821	431162	461659		181473.552	2.5439
6/02/89	905621	440942	464679	−6800	178800.540	2.5989
6/09/89	913364	440539	472825		178800.540	2.6444
6/16/89	901935	439484	462451		178800.540	2.5864
6/23/89	919074	456580	462494	−17900	171879.743	2.6908
6/30/89	892792	462494	430298		171879.743	2.5035
7/07/89	907586	456307	451279		171879.743	2.6256
7/14/89	918446	456018	462428		171879.743	2.6904
7/20/89	917539	455392	462147		171879.743	2.6888
7/28/89	922489	449234	473255		171879.743	2.7534
8/04/89	925531	452502	473029		171879.743	2.7521
8/11/89	946203	452362	493841		171879.743	2.8732
8/18/89	938212	451752	486460		171879.743	2.8302
8/25/89	935595	451184	484411		171879.743	2.8183
9/01/89	941839	462309	479530	−8000	169041.166	2.8368
Total cash out:				−173900		

withdrawals over those 21 months amount to 67 percent of the net equity on December 4, 1987, and yet, even after these withdrawals, the net equity value was $479,503 on June 30, 1989, or 85 percent greater than that of December 4, 1987. Of course, we must not "confuse brains with a bull market" as mentioned above, especially as bull markets tend to overcome a large number of poor choices and strategic mistakes. (For the curious, TPS Portfolio as of June 30, 1995, is displayed in Appendix A.)

A superficial scan of the table above, with its handsome gain over the 21 months, might lead some to believe that it was an uninterrupted advance, just week after week of gains with nary a setback along the way. A closer inspection reveals that up to March 18, 1988, the NAV had gained 72.27 percent—a tremendous four-month appreciation—but, by November 18, 1988, the NAV was at 68.53 percent, thus indicating no gain in value for that period of eight months and one week. Even more troubling at the time, the NAV had gained 97.00 percent by October 21, 1988, only to lose $58,006 (14.45 percent) in the following four weeks, wiping out all the gains since March 11, 1988. But these kinds of fluctuations are par for the course. As a matter of fact, the October 21, 1988 to November 18, 1988 correction was relatively mild and not very damaging in the scheme of things.

Hedging with OEX Put Options

For over nine years, I have been studying the efficacy of hedging stock portfolios with OEX stock index put options. The OEX is based on the S&P 100 Index, with contracts traded on the Chicago Board Options Exchange (CBOE). A writer of a put (the option seller) agrees to buy the contract at a specified price during the life of the contract. As such, the put buyer benefits if the option falls below its cost (or premium) and strike price (index level). In short, a put option is a bet by the buyer that the index (market) will decline so the buyer will gain the difference between his or her costs and the value of the option at or before its expiration. Hedging with options is a complicated subject and a difficult enterprise, and it's too involved to explain in adequate detail in this book. All brokerages and the CBOE have free publications on the basics of OEX stock index options and other options.

Even after nine years, I have not written about hedging with OEX put options because I am still learning about market timing and option strategies. I believe hedging can be done effectively and that I am close to finding the complex keys. For now, I like to buy OEX puts 2 to 5 percent out-of-the-money (below their current OEX/S&P 100 Index level) with at least three to four weeks before expiration, paying between $1 and $2+ per put ($100 to $200 a contract of 100 puts). For example, if I believe the stock market is poised for a sharp selloff in the next few days or weeks, and the OEX is trading at 475.00, I would probably buy the 460s. Because the OEX contract at 460.00 represents $46,000 worth of stock, I would buy one contract for each multiple of that amount of stock in my portfolio. For a $100,000 stock portfolio, I would buy at least two and maybe even three contracts if my sell (correction) indicators were very strong.

The S&P 100 Index would not have to decline 3 percent before the OEX puts significantly increased in value, due to other buyers also wanting to take OEX positions (for protection), willing to pay the higher amounts (premiums) as the puts approach at-the-money or in-the-money levels. This is the tricky part. If a sharp selloff sends the market into a short-term oversold condition, we might want to liquidate the puts to capture their gains, anticipating that a bounceback rally might render them worthless. On the other hand, if the market is likely to continue to decline, then we'd want to keep the insurance hedge for even greater protection and profitability.

In the past when I have made good put buys, I have often held onto them for too long as "insurance." Because market timing is generally counterproductive for most investors, perhaps we should just forget about hedging, especially with portfolios that are not margined. I continue to work on the subject as a potentially effective technique. So the learning process goes on, even after over 20 years of market study.

The Small-Capitalization Fallacy?

I take it on faith that small-capitalization stocks (small caps) outperform large-cap stocks by a significant amount over a multiyear period. To review, the capitalization of a stock is the number of shares outstanding times the price per share. Thus, if a corporation has 10,000,000 shares outstanding that are trading for $10 per share, its market capitalization is $100 million.

It happens that there is no standard definition of a small-cap stock. Many studies use the lowest decile (10 percent) or quintile (20 percent) of capitalizations as the small-cap population. Distinctions can be made among NYSE stocks, AMEX stocks, and NASDAQ stocks. Some commentators and studies refer to a specific, if somewhat arbitrary, number, such as stocks with a market capitalization of $200 million or less.

The study that has meant the most to me comes from the Ibbotson Associates' *Stocks, Bonds, Bills, and Inflation 1995 Yearbook* (*SBBI*). When you read or hear of market statistics or performance dating back to 1926, it is probably a reference to *SBBI*. Instead of small-cap stocks as a category, *SBBI* refers to Small Company Stocks, defined as "represented by the fifth capitalization quintile of stocks on the NYSE for 1926–1981 and the performance of the Dimensional Fund Advisers (DFA) Small Company Fund thereafter." While this change in the series and the limitations of the Small Company Fund makes the performance of Small Company Stocks a bit of a mixed bag, it nevertheless is a rigorous analysis of market activity since 1926.

> A dollar invested in small company stocks at year-end 1925 grew to $2,842.77 by year-end 1994. This represents a compound annual growth rate of 12.2 percent over the past 69 years. Total annual returns ranged from a high of 142.9 percent in 1933 to a low of −58.0 percent in 1937.[6]

In contrast to small-company stocks, large-cap (S&P 500) stocks grew with dividends reinvested from $1 at year-end 1925 to $810.54 by year-end 1994, a compound annual growth rate of 10.2 percent. Fascinatingly, an average difference of just 2 percent more per year amounted to a 350 percent greater total return in 69 years. Next time somebody pooh-poohs a couple or so percent per year's difference, consider the potential of compounded annual growth over time.

---

[6] *SBBI 1995 Yearbook*, p. 51.

Of course, such statistical studies are merely quoted for background consideration. No one buys all the large-cap stocks or all the small-cap stocks in the market. One might buy an index mutual fund purporting to represent large- or small-cap stocks, but that's a different story. Still, it doesn't take too much imagination to see that if one had the choice between a portfolio full of large-cap stocks or small-cap stocks for long time periods, other things such as their equivalent undervaluedness being equal, we should choose the small-cap stocks. And, in fact, 18 years' worth of stock recommendations in *The Prudent Speculator* reveals that most are not only lower-priced stocks, but generally smaller-cap stocks, although our interest in bargain stocks (trading at 50 percent undervalued) is not limited by their capitalization.

But here comes one of my favorite market analyst/commentators, David Dreman, in his April 24, 1995, column in *Forbes*, (p. 398). Dreman points out that there is no long-term index "showing the superior performance of this group." He cites the Russell 2000 Index as the most widely used index representing small-cap stocks, but that has only been available since 1982. Since then to March 1995, according to Dreman, the Russell 2000 only returned 12.2 percent annually, compared to 15.2 percent for the S&P 500.

We know that small-cap stocks have runs of outperformance for several years (say 3 to 7) and runs of underperformance for several years, but not for the long period Dreman cites. What's going on?

According to Dreman, the small-cap studies dating from the mid-1920s were really studies of financially distressed, former large-cap stocks traded on the NYSE—not small companies that became large, "but large companies that shrank to midget size in the Great Depression." Thereafter, the surviving companies made high percentage comebacks or were never heard from again. Citing the Dimensional Fund Advisers' DFA U.S. 9–10 Fund, an index fund representing small-cap performance, Dreman writes: "Since its inception in 1982 the DFA index has been outperformed by the S&P 500 by 39 percent to the end of February 1995."

Dreman's analysis may be less than meets the eye. Index funds generally underperform their indexes because of costs associated with running the fund, commissions and shrinkage, or the bid-ask spread effect penalizing buying and selling. Over several years, the expenses of running the fund coupled with trading costs and shrinkage can amount to a significant reduction in total return compared to the index that doesn't recognize such costs and expenses.

So I went back to Ibbotson Associates *SBBI 1995 Yearbook* and worked up a table displaying small-company (small-cap) versus large-cap performances for 1982 through 1994. The results were a surprise to me. In Table 8–4, we note that large-cap stocks outperformed small-cap stocks by a significant factor of 16.10 to 12.76 percent compounded annually during the period. Thus, each $1 in small-cap stocks grew to $4.76 over the 13 years, while a $1 in large-cap stocks grew to $6.07, or some 27.52 percent greater return.

I feel lucky that my portfolio approach did not get bogged down by emphasizing small-capitalization stocks per se over undervalued large-cap stocks. I had noticed that in some years TPS Portfolio had better performance than that of small-cap stocks due to the outperformance of large-cap stocks in the portfolio. Of course, in some years, holding a majority of small-cap stocks permitted TPS Portfolio to outperform large-cap stocks. Furthermore, the big declines of 1987 and 1990 were largely due to small-cap stock selloffs.

So from now on, maybe for the next few months or years, we can discount the historical outperformance of small-cap stocks versus large-cap stocks. On the other hand, we do not select stocks mainly on the criterion of their capitalization, so we aren't giving up a cherished if dubious belief in the superior efficacy of small-cap stocks. Then too, there is always the chance that in the next several years, small-cap stocks will significantly outperform large-cap stocks.

A Technician's Nightmare

Since the stock market had a cyclical bottom on October 11, 1990, the Dow Jones Industrial Average (then 2365.10) has climbed over 2,371 points through mid-July

Table 8–4. Comparing Large- versus Small-Cap Performance 1982–1994

Year	Small-Cap	Cumulative %	Large-Cap	Cumulative %
1982	0.2801	1.2801	0.2141	1.2141
1983	0.3967	1.7879	0.2251	1.4874
1984	−0.0667	1.6687	0.0627	1.5807
1985	0.2466	2.0802	0.3216	2.0890
1986	0.0685	2.2226	0.1847	2.4748
1987	−0.0930	2.0159	0.0523	2.6043
1988	0.2287	2.4770	0.1681	3.0420
1989	0.1018	2.7291	0.3149	4.0000
1990	−0.2156	2.1407	−0.0317	3.8732
1991	0.4463	3.0961	0.3055	5.0564
1992	0.2335	3.8191	0.0767	5.4443
1993	0.2098	4.6203	0.0999	5.9881
1994	0.0311	4.7640	0.0131	6.0666
Compounded Annual Return:	0.1276		0.1610	

Source: *SBBI 1995 Yearbook*, pp. 177, 183.

1995—a gain of over 92 percent. During the same period the small-cap index Russell 2000 (then 120.02) gained over 135 percent while the OTC Composite Index (then 325.61) advanced over 186 percent. Though these percentage gains are nowhere near the record gains of other "bull markets," this market has set a record for being the longest advancing market on record since 1945 by lasting 1,712 days (through June 20, 1995) without a 10 percent correction in the S&P's 500 Index. The previous longest rally without a 10 percent correction since 1945 was 1,205 days between October 23, 1962, and February 9, 1966.[7]

In addition to the longevity of the current rally, which has frustrated bearish outlooks for years, are the terrible "technical fundamentals" of price/earnings ratios, price/book value ratios, and both DJIA and S&P 500 dividend yields. By all standard guidelines of the three fundamental criteria and time cycles, we *should* have been in a bear market in each of the past four years. And yet, during the first seven months of 1995, the stock market made all-time new highs on most of its major averages and indexes and seems to be getting stronger as it rolls along. The seven interest-rate hikes of the Federal Reserve between February 4, 1994, and February 1, 1995, while inhibiting the market through most of 1994, did not cause a 10 percent decline in the blue-chip indicators, let alone a much-called-for bear market, yet.

So what happened? Why have so many otherwise astute market commentators been so bearish? Obviously, to cut to the chase, they were fighting previous market wars and not paying sufficient attention to the sea changes that were going on all about them. They did not account enough for the billions of dollars pouring into mutual funds that felt obliged to invest them with little regard for market timing. They did not give enough weight to the secular downtrend in interest rates. They glossed over the restructuring of corporations, with massive write-offs (which nominally reduced book values while making them actually more accurate and worth a greater market multiple) and strategies of using surplus earnings to improve productivity and to buy back shares rather than pay out after-tax earnings in taxable dividends.

Many on Wall Street ignored the potential upswing in the economic cycle since the short recession of 1990. Many of them were so emotionally against President Bill Clinton—shocked at the loss of the presidency by George Bush— that they didn't count on the effects of the initial deficit-reduction legislation of the new administration coupled with its business-friendly attitude. While millions waited for a Republican to occupy the White House after the Clinton presidency, they discounted, due to their negative "attitude," the economic revival. Some looked for gold to flourish in the obvious chaos that was sure to follow. Others looked overseas, the first scoring nicely as the mini-bubble expanded, while latecomers got creamed from the overvaluations and governmental instabilities.

---

[7] Source: Ned Davis Research.

If nothing else, the past few years, especially the first seven months of 1995, have proved that there are very few magic bullets for timing stock markets. Remember, "You can be fooled by some of the indicators some of the time and some of the indicators all of the time, but you can't be fooled by all of the indicators all of the time." But which indicators and when? That's why making money in the market is not as easy as may seem, especially if one has tunnel vision and believes that the past repeats itself in clear patterns. While there are cycles and repetitive patterns that can be useful guidelines, they are not exact and they cannot be followed mechanically.

Let me admit that I did not expect the early 1995 stock market to develop as strongly as it has. I admit further that I have been lucky to have remained fully margined in relatively well-performing (on average) undervalued stocks. The facts that I have marshaled above are post hoc, after the fact, hindsight. The premise that undervalued stocks, over long periods of time, will outperform a long-term upward-trending market underscores the "good luck" of the past 56 months.

Now that some of the stocks in my portfolio are reaching fair value, I hope to be able to sell them before the next bear market begins. On April 21, 1995, I bought puts as insurance to hedge margined portfolios against a potential decline. The cost of these puts were paid for more than twice over during the first week of their existence by an advancing market, even though the OEX puts expired worthless. I expect to buy more short-term insurance hedges as the market advances farther and becomes more overbought and more fully valued, although I also expect 1995 to be a good performance year on balance.

Summary

Many individuals I meet seem to be overwhelmed at the prospect of understanding the stock market. They have been conditioned, I believe, by their early school training, that only geniuses can understand things without taking classes or courses in them. Many have been disempowered enough to believe that financial matters must be left to the experts and the highly trained.

I trust that this book will be of value to you. If you feel overwhelmed by information overload, step back and consider what is being asked of you, and what you must ask of yourself, in order to speculate successfully in the stock market. Basically, all you need to do is buy some undervalued shares of several corporations' stock. With a few hours of self-training you can select undervalued stocks as well as the next person, if not better. Spending a few more hours to understand the long-term positive nature of the market, the average upward trend of 10 percent or more for many years, within which are selloffs and rallies, you will be armed intellectually to cope with stock and market price fluctuations. This book has shown you how to recognize—and avoid—many of the pitfalls that await novices.

More difficult for many, I suspect, is controlling fear and greed. I have often confused a genial optimism with an unconscious, hidden greed. It helps to be psychologically well balanced in order to speculate effectively. On the other hand, speculating effectively may help you to become better balanced psychologically. It sure helps to earn money as easily and passively as the stock market permits with just a modicum of homework and applied effort.

Life is a trial-and-error-and-revision process. So is speculating in stocks. You do not become a brilliant person because one of your stocks brings outrageous returns, nor do you become a dummy because one of your stocks brings great losses. With my portfolio over the years as an example, I have tried to show how my stock selection can be wrong 50 percent or more of the time in a given year (ultimately 25 percent of the time over 18 years) and yet obtain handsome long-term profits. Likewise, I have shown that you can lose more than 50 percent of your equity in a few months, twice, and still come back nicely in subsequent years. Hopefully, neither you nor I shall ever again lose 50 percent of our equity. We now have experience to protect us against becoming overleveraged in overbought and overvalued markets.

You can start out small. I started with a few hundred dollars. You can build portfolios slowly and enlist the miracle of time-compounded returns and dollar-cost averaging to end up with substantial funds. You can afford to make mistakes along the way; in fact, you should recognize that you can't help but make mistakes—actually, decisions that went awry. If so-called mistakes were thoughtful, but companies and the market went against you, the next time such thoughtfully selected stocks and the markets are likely to provide handsome returns. One of our mantras is, "Winning stocks win more than losing stocks lose." That is why you can be "wrong" 30, 40, or 50 percent of the time and still make money speculating in stocks.

Happily, in the financial game even one or two clarifications or insights can be worth their weight in dollars.

9

Our Stock Analysis Printout

This is not a textbook on security analysis, yet it does involve some basic bookkeeping. I say bookkeeping because that is easier than accounting. As you may not realize, an accountant is responsible for setting up the books and accounts of an organization; a bookkeeper merely has to follow the setup, to fill in the blanks, so to speak. We have set up the accounts in our system of analyzing corporations; if you choose to become your own financial analyst using our successful methodology, you need only fill in the blanks and do a modicum of observation and comparison.

I want to impress upon you that you needn't be an accountant to develop an understanding of financial statements and the ability to systematically review corporate conditions and stock selection criteria. I said it was simple, but I didn't say it was effortless.

If you are willing to take a broad approach, based on a statistical averages, you can find undervalued stocks using seven, three, or even two criteria, as reviewed in Chapter 2. If you are a bit more concerned and less cavalier, you can make "almost final selections" from those basic criteria and go on to analyze other criteria that may be confirming, insignificant, or disconfirming.

Professionals or Chartered Financial Analysts usually go far beyond the basics reviewed in this book. They check corporate 10–K (annual) and 10–Q (quarterly) reports for items sometimes not included in the typically glossy annual reports sent to shareholders, or for items that are buried in the footnotes. For example, they check if a corporation has an underfunded pension liability, that is not reflected on the balance sheet but may impact earnings and equity in the future.

Neither stock selection nor portfolio management are sciences; they are skill-ful crafts. They might be likened to an art in the sense of working with techniques and materials. Stock selection considers corporations' valuations in relation to their stocks' market prices. Portfolio management, on the other hand, exercises patience and considers other conditions, such as stock diversification, time diversification, and risk management—which include the state of the market, economy, Federal Reserve, and the Administration's (government's) policies. Actual individual stock selection may be only a small part of the process. If so, it is nonetheless crucial, as there are few things more frustrating than to see the market advancing while your selected stocks are declining. Conversely, there are few things more satisfying than to see the market decline while your portfolio advances.

John Train, in *The Money Masters*, quotes Philip Fisher: "If the job has been correctly done when a common stock is purchased, the time to sell it is—almost never."[1] This is a wise observation. Less obvious perhaps, this observation is even more appropriate when considering when-to-sell criteria because one "knows" the corporation's fair value at the outset and can follow it over the years. Other people have pointed out that the carefully selected stock will take care of itself on the sell side. Note that, of the 11 positions in TPS Portfolio in March, 1977, nine were bought out at handsome profits and the remaining two are considered buyout or takeover candidates currently (see Chapter 7).

While statistical evidence strongly supports selecting stocks from the lowest 10 or 20 percent of the price/earnings pool and from the lowest 10 or 20 percent of market capitalization issues (despite David Dremen's argument, see Chapter 8), even among this two-criteria population one would want to guard against overindebted corporations or those showing declining trends in earnings, sales, and book value. In keeping with our responsibilities as editor and publisher of a stock advisory newsletter and as investment advisers managing other peoples' stock portfolios, we update our fundamental analysis daily, incorporating price changes and newly released financial information. This computerized updating leads to a daily buy and sell candidates' list.

Once a week or so we print out the total population (currently about 700) of closely watched stocks (see Table 9–1). This "stock analysis" was first begun with hand calculations, progressed through early personal computers (the Osborne, using SuperCalc), was converted to mainframe IBM 360s and 370s (using COBOL at a public, time share computer center), was returned to personal computers and is now run on 486 and 586 machines in-house using RBase for DOS. The results of our analyses lead to a list of currently recommended stocks published monthly in our newsletter *The Prudent Speculator*.

---

[1] John Train *The Money Masters* (New York: Penguin Books, 1981), p. 78.

Our stock analysis still could be done by hand, but working with a personal computer (PC), using any of the popular spreadsheet programs or database management programs, saves time and permits greater coverage. A relatively inexpensive PC also allows you to employ stock and market analysis programs and databases.

Still, just monitoring the *Value Line Investment Survey*, *Barron's*, *Worth*, or *Forbes* magazines, our newsletter, or corporate financial reports can be enough research to develop a buy list. Thereafter, you might want to obtain company financial reports to make your final selections. If you can visit a decent public or college library, you can find this basic public information for free. To obtain corporate reports requires only a request to the corporations' shareholder relations department, the addresses of which is printed in several publications, including our newsletter.

Stock Analysis Printout

For the previous edition of this book (*The Prudent Speculator: Al Frank on Investing*), I reproduced page 7 of our April 14, 1989 stock analysis printout and some commentary. For this revised and expanded edition, I am reproducing a stock analysis page based on a special report we issued as of December 30, 1994, "The Prudent Speculator's Favorite Stocks for 1995 and Beyond." We also include two additional stocks that are near their sell limits in June 1995.

We created this Favorite Stocks report because some readers were concerned about choosing which stock(s) to buy from among the 30 or more recommended stocks in recent issues of *The Prudent Speculator* as they could not afford to buy all of them. We often have pointed out that readers could select from our current lists of recommended stocks those that might help their portfolios to increase diversification among industry groups or that might appeal to their aggressive or conservative inclinations.

Table 9–1 compiles the fundamental information on the 12 stocks on that page. Although the Favorite Stocks have done pretty well on average so far into 1995, up 23.84 percent in market appreciation through June 31, six of them are still buy candidates and four of them are holds. We have included two other stocks, Quiksilver and Vishay, that are close to their sell prices, so we can display and review nearly fully valued stocks. Oops, Quiksilver was sold at $24.875 per share on June 5—but I am leaving the analysis unchanged for its heuristic value.

The April 14, 1989, examples I previously used were Chrysler (C), Computer Associates (CA), and Pyro Energy (BTU). Chrysler was a then-recommended corporation with an undervalued stock. Computer Associates was "the closest stock to a 'sell'," and Pyro Energy (trading at $8.375 per share) was a "hold" with a goal price of $11 to $12.

Before the previous edition could be printed, Pyro Energy was bought out for $12 per share in cash by Costain Holding Co., effective July 26, 1989. I was able

Table 9-1. Stock Analysis Printout

DATE 05/04/95 PAGE NO. 1

STOCK ANALYSIS	BGSS	BSC	CIS	F	GNA	HYDEB	LSKI	PATK	QUIK	TXHI	VSH	WDC
1 SYMBOL	BGSS	BSC	CIS	F	GNA	HYDEB	LSKI	PATK	QUIK	TXHI	VSH	WDC
2 COMPANY	BGSSystem	BearStrns	ConcordFb	FordMotor	Gainsco	HydeAthlt	Liuski	PatrickIn	Quiksilvr	THT Inc.	Vishay	WestrnDig
3 EXCHANGE	OTC	NYSE	ASE	NYSE	ASE	OTC	OTC	OTC	OTC	SmallCap	NYSE	NYSE
4 PRICE	29.37	20.87	5.93	26.00	10.00	4.25	3.75	10.87	20.75	1.56	65.00	17.00
5 DIVIDEND	1.00	0.60		1.24	0.04							
6 12-MO EARN	2.38	1.34	0.90	5.14	0.75	0.46	0.54	1.56	1.16	0.28	2.70	2.97
7 3-YR EARN	2.24	2.69	1.14	2.17	0.66	0.64	0.82	0.96	0.60	0.18	1.92	-0.50
8 PROJ EARN	2.70	2.90	1.25	6.75	0.90	0.85	0.80	1.75	1.50	0.28	3.60	2.75
9 EARNS GROWTH	12.5%	20.4%	9.0%	1.7%	22.3%	62.9%	5.1%	69.2%	-0.7%	15.4%	16.3%	8.4%
10 P/E NORM	19.0 v	12.0+	12.0+	8.5 *	21.0 v	14.0+	14.0+	17.0 v	16.0 v	12.0+	20.0 v	13.0+
11 TANG BV	4.42	14.90	11.74	16.68	4.16	7.50	6.26	7.70	5.89	-0.04	13.69	7.94
12 BOOK VALUE	4.42v	14.90	11.74*	19.03	4.16v	7.50*	6.26*	7.70	8.65v	0.71v	22.29v	8.44v
13 BV GROWTH	-2.0%	17.2%	9.9%	-5.7%	23.5%	9.2%	37.5%	11.7%	18.7%	nmf	23.4%	-9.1%
14 BV NORM	3.25	2.00	1.00	2.25	3.00	1.75	2.00	3.00	2.00	4.00	2.75	2.75
15 CASH FLOW	2.65		1.45	14.30		0.64	0.68	2.05	1.50	0.46	4.90	3.95
16 CF GROWTH	11.8%	nmf	7.0%	9.3%	nmf	27.4%	-1.0%	31.8%	3.2%	154.5%	12.6%	0.5%
17 P/CF NORM	12.0		6.0	4.0		10.0	12.0	12.0	12.0	7.0	13.0	6.0
18 REVENUES	35.4	3434.0	206.0	107137.0	96.0	108.0	365.0	341.0	136.0	17.5	1072.0	2009.0
19 REVS GROWTH	11.5%	12.3%	2.3%	0.0%	nmf	9.9%	24.6%	10.1%	10.5%	106.6%	0.6%	0.1%
20 SHARES COMM	3.10	112.80	3.60	1023.00	20.49	6.23	4.38	5.94	6.52	4.53	26.35	48.30
21 CUR ASSETS	29.3		72.0	26863.0	61.6		70.5	61.7	63.0	4.8	561.0	656.0
22 CUR LIABS	17.4		34.3	25471.0	15.7		25.5	24.3	30.3	3.1	232.0	313.0
23 L/T DEBT		3503.00	7.50	7103.00	3.50	11.90	20.00	24.40	2.60	2.80	402.00	40.50
24 TOT ASSETS	31	66842	85	219354	231	77	74	97	89	11	1334	641
25 PREF STOCK		587.00		3400.00						2.00		
26 YR-END CST	22.00	15.37	7.12	27.87	7.85	4.75	4.12	8.00	15.25	1.00	46.66	16.75
27 YEAR HIGH	30.25	23.50	10.62	35.06	11.00	8.00	13.25	15.62	22.12	1.87	65.00	20.37
28 YEAR LOW	20.50	14.75	5.75	24.75	7.14	4.25	3.62	7.75	9.75	0.93	29.76	10.87
29 HIST HIGH	43.00	24.76	10.62	33.06	15.22	12.75	13.37	13.62	30.00	3.50	34.24	19.50
30 HIST LOW	5.00	5.59	0.50	3.93	0.71	0.06	5.37	0.06	3.37	0.62	0.24	0.25
31 VL / S&P	0.5	3.0	0.6	3.4	2.0						1.4	3.6

Table 9-1. Stock Analysis Printout (cont.)

STOCK ANALYSIS		DATE			05/04/95			PAGE NO.	2		
SYMBOL	BGSS	BSC	CIS	F	GNA	HYDEB	LSKI	PATK	QUIK	TXHI	VSH	WDC
32 PROJ. ROE	51.23*	18.06*	10.10	30.93*	19.60*	10.72	12.01+	20.40*	15.95+	32.94*	14.94+	28.01*
33 CUR P/E	12.34+	15.57v	6.59+	5.05+	13.33+	9.23+	6.94*	6.97*	17.88v	5.58*	24.07v	5.72*
34 DIV YIELD %	3.40	2.87	0.00	4.76	0.40	0.00	0.00	0.00	0.00	0.00	0.00	0.00
35 PR/TANG–BV	6.64	1.40	0.50	1.55	2.40	56	0.59	1.41	3.52	–39.06	4.74	2.14
36 PRICE/BV	6.64v	1.40+	0.50*	1.36+	2.40v	0.56v	0.59*	1.41+	2.39v	2.20v	2.91v	2.01v
37 CUR RATIO	1.68v	v	2.09*	1.05v	v	3.92v	2.76*	2.53*	2.07v	1.54v	2.41*	2.09*
38 RET SALES	20.84*	4.40*	1.57v	4.90*	16.00*	2.65	0.64v	2.71	5.56*	7.24*	6.63*	7.14*
39 RET ASSETS	23.72	0.22	3.81	2.39	6.65	3.71	3.19	9.55	8.49	11.42	5.33	22.37
40 RET EQUITY	54.00*	9.00v	8.00v	27.00*	18.00+	6.00v	9.00v	20.00*	13.00+	39.00*	12.00	35.00*
41 PR/NET WKCP	7.65	-0.57	0.70	-2.91	-53.54	0.77	0.65	4.96	4.49	-2.28	-23.46	2.71
42 PRJ EN/PR	9.19	13.89	21.05	25.96	3.00	20.00	21.33	16.09	7.22	17.92	5.53	16.17
43 PRICE/REV	2.57v	0.68+	0.10*	0.24*	2.13v	0.24*	0.04*	0.18*	0.99+	0.40*	1.59	0.40*
44 PRICE/CF	11.08v	4.09+	1.81*	6.64	5.51+	5.30+	13.83v	3.39v	13.26v	4.30+		
45 MV CHANGE %	33.52	35.77	-16.66	-6.72	27.27	-10.52	-9.09	35.93	36.06	56.25	39.28	1.49
46 MKT VALUE	91.0*	2354.7	21.3*	26598.0	2C4.9	26.4*	16.4*	64.5*	135.2*	7.0*	1712.7	821.1
47 P/CF GOAL	31.80	v	8.70	57.20*	v	6.40	8.16*	24.60*	18.00v	3.22*	63.70v	23.70
48 P/E GOAL	45.22	16.08v	10.80	43.69	15.75	6.44	7.56*	26.52*	18.56v	3.36*	54.00v	38.61*
49 PROJE GOAL	51.30	34.80	15.00*	57.37*	8.90	11.90*	11.20*	29.75*	24.00	3.36*	72.00	35.75*
50 BV GOAL	14.36v	29.80	11.74	42.81	12.48	13.12*	12.52*	23.10*	17.30v	2.84	61.29v	23.21
51 2 x PRICE	58.75	41.75	11.87	52.00	20.00	8.50	7.50	21.75	41.50	3.12	130.00	34.00
52 RECOMMENDS	2A,3D	2B,	1C,2B,3E	1C,2A,3D	2A,3D	1B,2B,3B	1A,2C,3B	1A,2A,3C	2A,3D	1A,2B,3C	2A,	1B,2B,
53 LOW GOAL	35.67	26.89	11.56	50.27	15.71	9.46	9.86	25.99	19.46	3.19	62.74	30.31
54 HIGH GOAL	51.30	34.80	15.00*	57.37*	18.90	11.90*	11.20*	29.75*	24.00	3.36*	72.00	35.75*
55 APPRC POTEN %	74.63	66.70	152.63*	120.67*	89.00	180.00*	198.66*	173.56*	15.66	115.04*	10.76	110.29*
56 BALANCE SHEET	1A5	DR4	8A4	DA4	DA4	DA4	DQ4	3N5	1N5	DQ4	DA4	3V5
57 EARNINGS	15	35	25	35	35	D4	D4	35	15	D4	35	35

to note this transaction in the book, commenting that, "As Pyro's buyout price coincided with our high goal price, I think this example of a 'hold' is instructive." But that's ancient history now. Still, it shows the efficacy of the analysis.

On the April 14, 1989, analysis, Computer Associates was trading for $35.75 per share with a goal price range of $34.44 to $42.75, an example of a nearly fairly valued stock. CA split its shares two for one on June 16, 1989. In the recession of 1990, Computer Associates tumbled from a split-adjusted $16.875 to below $6. We recommended its purchase at $5.75 on September 14, 1990. CA has recovered since to trade over $77 per share in early August 1995. Our June 1995 goal price for Computer Associates is $93.50 per share.

Even as I am working on this chapter (April 18, 1995), preparing to analyze why I think Chrysler shares will probably trade in the marketplace for $80 to $90 per share over the next three to five years, an announcement is made that Tracinda Industries (Kirk Kerkorian) is making a bid to buy the 90 percent of Chrysler shares it does not own for $55 per share in cash. There is some question about the efficacy of this offer. When called by a TV station for my comment on the news, as I have been a strong advocate of Chrysler, I said I would hold my shares to see what developed, perhaps having to sell them at the current or a higher buyout price; but if the buyout fell through I would still expect to get significantly more for my Chrysler shares over the years. Chrysler was the most active stock—trading as high as $53 on the announcement—but drifted off to $47.50 during the day and closed at $48. I've already been asked if I should have sold at $52+. Prior to the buyout offer, Chrysler was a good example of a recommended corporation with an undervalued stock. Two weeks, later Chrysler shares were trading around $42. I will know in about two years if I made a mistake not jumping at this anomaly.

However, for our auto stock this time around, we will be reviewing Ford, which is one of the stocks on our Favorite Stocks report list.

In studying the stock analysis printout (Table 9–1), you will notice three marks to the right of certain figures. The asterisk (*) highlights what I consider to be a very good number, either an undervalued criterion or a superior ratio or percentage. The plus (+) is used to point out a good number, in my estimation, while the lowercase letter (v) is used to point out a bad number, either an overvalued criterion or a poor ratio or percentage. While these marks are not in themselves sufficient for determining stock selection, they aid us in quickly observing noteworthy conditions. What follows below is a systematic review of each line of our stock analysis printout of May 4, 1995 (see Table 9–1).

1. **Symbol**. Stock ticker symbols. Every issue listed on the New York Stock Exchange, the American Stock Exchange, and the National Association of Securities Dealers Automated Quotation System (NASDAQ) has a unique

Cusip number and stock "ticker" symbol. The Cusip number for Ford is 345370–10–0. You will see Cusip numbers on your stock trade confirmation slips, but normally you will only be concerned with a stock's ticker symbol. You should know your stocks' ticker symbols so as to avoid confusion in trading (buying and selling) stocks. The stock symbol or ticker for Ford Motor Company is F.

Knowing the tickers of the stocks you want to reference is also convenient when asking for current pricing information—accessing quotation machines—or recognizing trades displayed on the moving "tape" shown on daily TV programs such as CNBC or CNN, in brokerage houses, and on the various exchanges. Most companies' tickers begin with the initials of their name (F for Ford), but often you'll find a GNA, not necessarily an intuitive abbreviation for Gainsco, a small-capitalization insurance company.

2. **Company.** Abbreviated corporate names. With thousands of tickers in use, and some of them not nearly acronymic, it is easy to confuse or forget which corporation belongs to which symbol. With the capacity to use nine letters in the stock analysis printout, we can pretty much identify the names of the corporations being analyzed. At first you might not recognize that ConcordFB is Concord Fabrics or that WestrnDig is Western Digital, but soon these would be second nature for individuals following these stocks.

3. **Exchange.** Where the stock is traded. The third row displays where a stock is principally traded. You may save time in accessing information or price quotes by being able to tell your broker on which exchange or market a particular stock is traded. NYSE stands for the New York Stock Exchange; OTC shows stocks traded "over-the-counter" on the National Quotation System; ASE refers to the American Stock Exchange, and PSE represents the Pacific Stock Exchange. Some stocks are listed on more than one exchange, such as the New York and the Pacific, and there may be a benefit in trading a particular position in one place or another. With OTC stocks there likely will be more than one market maker, so it is up to your broker to shop your trade for the best execution.

Ford trades principally on the New York Stock Exchange, but it also trades on the Boston, Cincinnati, Chicago, Pacific, Philadelphia, Montreal, and Toronto exchanges. It might be of value to know that Ford or Western Digital, for example, also trade on the Pacific Exchange, which stays open for 30 minutes after the NYSE closes. Sometimes stocks can be traded in "the third market" after the regular exchanges are closed. The third market is where listed stocks are traded over-the-counter with special market makers without affecting their regular exchanges' prices. We have never traded a stock in the third market. The "fourth market" is for stocks traded among individuals without the use of a brokerage, which is rarely ever done for the small investor.

4. **Price**. That date's closing price in dollars and cents, rounded down (1/8 = 0.125, but shown here as 0.12). On our printout, this price is usually for the last trade of the day, as indicated by the date of the printout, or the last time a stock traded. During market hours prices are changing by the minute in actively traded stocks, so prices must be verified at the time the decision to trade is made. Even with all the intraday and intraweek fluctuations, some issues will close unchanged for the week as they end trading at the same price they did the preceding week. Such "unchanged" numbers can mask considerable intraweek activity and fluctuation in a stock's price and volume. In Table 9–1, we see that on May 4, 1995, Ford closed at $26 per share, while LSKI (Liuski International, a distributor of computer peripherals and products) closed at $3.75.

5. **Dividend**. Indicated annual dividend in dollars and cents. Most dividends are declared and paid quarterly, but a few represent differing time periods such as semiannual, as well as special or extra dividend declarations. Generally the annual (four-quarter) dividend rate doesn't change often, but some companies have a policy to raise dividends every year (or more frequently) if earnings warrant. During troubled times of low or no profitability, dividends may be reduced or suspended entirely, which often causes a large drop in the market price of that corporation's stock upon release of the presumed bad news. Before making any serious judgments based on the annual indicated dividend, one should check on the corporation's dividend trend, special dividends, stock splits, earnings, retained earnings, or cash flow to see if funds are adequate to support current and likely future dividends.

For many analysts and investors, dividends are a significant determinant of stock selection. Some people are dependent for their everyday needs upon the flow of funds provided by stock dividends. Such people would be more interested in a seemingly secure and handsome dividend than in a corporation's growth prospects or the potential market price appreciation of its stock. I am more interested in the total return picture, dividends plus appreciation, which results in emphasizing appreciation potentials over indicated dividends. I would be disinterested in a stock that yields about 6 percent of its market price in dividend return with a history of appreciating 4 to 6 percent per year, for a total return of 10 percent to 12 percent. I would be interested in a stock that pays no dividend but appreciates 15 to 25 percent per year on average.

If one could make consistent choices among high-dividend-paying stocks that managed a total return of 12 percent, or non-dividend-paying stocks that appreciated 15 to 25 percent on average, one would be far ahead of the game giving up dividends (which are taxed in the year they are received) in favor of strong market price appreciation. Then one could still obtain needed cash flow from capital gains sales after allowing a year or so of market price appreciation—or from margin loan withdrawals, if needed sooner. Against the more rapidly increasing value of one's "dividendless portfolio" one could borrow the equivalent 6 or 8 percent "dividend yield" until the appreciated stock was sold to repay the margin borrowings. With the additional gains from the higher returns, one could reinvest the difference and see the total portfolio grow and appreciate significantly more than its dividend-paying counterpart, even after withdrawing the equivalent of a good dividend by either borrowing it or at the lower tax rate of a capital gain proceeds.

We have seen in reviewing dividend-adjusted returns (see Table 5–4) that over the long term dividends actually are a slightly larger part of the total return than price appreciation for blue-chip stocks. An excellent and worthwhile, if highly biased, treatise supporting stock selection and portfolio management based on dividends can be found in *Dividends Don't Lie*[2], by Geraldine Weiss and Janet Lowe. Sometimes a dividend reduction, which leads to a sharp drop in the market price of a stock, can be a wonderful opportunity for an undervalued purchase, even as the dividend players dump their shares.

One such case was ITT Corp. which in July 1984 cut its $2.76 annual dividend to $1.00, causing ITT shares to drop from the low $30s to $20.625 in a few days—less than half of its January '84 high of $47.375. This dividend-reducing decision to conserve cash clearly made ITT a stronger company while driving its stock into an undervalued buy range. Eleven years later, in July 1995, ITT traded over $118 per share with a $1.98 dividend, after having spun off Rayonair (one share for each four ITT shares), which was trading at 34 3/4. ITT was still undervalued (though not a buy candidate) with a high goal price of $137 per share.

---

[2] Geraldine Weiss and Janet Lowe, *Dividends Don't Lie*, (Chicago, IL: Longmans Financial Services Services Publishing, Inc., 1988).

A more recent example is Union Carbide (UK), which lowered its annual dividend from $1.50 to $0.80 per share in May of '88. From a high of $25.875 before the cut, UK dropped to $17, after which we re-recommended it at $19 as of May 27, 1988. Seven years later, UK was trading over $39, after having spun of one share of Praxair for each share of UK. Praxair traded for over $28 per share on July 31, 1995, so the combined worth of 1988's UK plus Praxair was over $67 by mid-1995. In our June 2, 1988, newsletter we wrote: "We feel that Carbide took the right steps, inasmuch as the reduced dividend payout allows UK to retain more funds to support expansion during the current favorable industry operating conditions."

Having a preference for non-dividend- or low-dividend-paying stocks does not bring with it a complete prejudice against dividend-paying stocks, especially if they are undervalued bargains in their own right. One may have the best of both worlds, receiving a nice yield while awaiting superior appreciation and a handsome multiyear total return.

6. **12 Mo-Earn**. "Current" after-tax earnings (net income) in dollars and cents per share. Current earnings are usually reported quarterly in many sources including daily newspapers with substantial financial sections as well as the financial press, electronic data sources, and in quarterly and annual reports. We've already reviewed various definitions of earnings in Chapter 2's review of P/E criteria, and considered extraordinary earnings and earnings dilution.

    For your convenience, we can review some of the principal points about current earnings, which usually refer to trailing earnings or the most recent year's (or past four quarters', perhaps last year's) reported earnings. Even trailing earnings of the last four reported quarters are, to a degree, historical, depending upon how long it takes a corporation to close its books for the quarter and publish its financials. It might take a month or two after the end of a quarter to obtain that quarter's results, so that in the immediately preceding four to eight weeks, considerable changes, either positive or negative, could be impacting actual, real-time, current earnings. Still, these are the "current" figures with which to work.

    Timeliness of reported earnings is only one of our concerns. We must check further to see if these earnings have a significant per share dilution due to rights, warrants, or convertible issues which could increase the number of common shares outstanding. Of course, not all potential dilutions occur. Sometimes rights expire worthless and convertibles are retired without being converted, or stock is bought back on the open market and returned to the corporation's treasury, or new stock is issued at either more or less than current book value. We are also on the lookout for the effects of nonrecurring (special one-time) earnings or losses versus comparisons with continuing earnings or losses from operations.

One of the reasons that we are less concerned than many other analysts about each quarter's earnings is due to our long-term outlook and the significant variations of earnings seen over time. If a company has a down earnings quarter, its stock may sell off much more than is warranted by the temporarily lowered earnings. There is a shibboleth that one quarter's down earnings is probably a prelude to more depressed earnings. This may or may not be the case for a particular stock, and more importantly, down earnings may not matter all that much given the cyclical nature of certain corporations. For example, the auto companies' stocks' often appreciate significantly during years of losses in anticipation of large gains during the next uptrend of the auto cycle.

Quarterly, six-month, and nine-month trailing earnings are compared to like periods of the previous fiscal year. Sometimes much is made of increases or decreases from the previous quarter (or period), without realizing that the previous period, or the previous year's period, represents unusually depressed or record earnings, so that nominal comparisons distort the longer-term perspective. These distortions could lead the unwary to unreasonable euphoria or illogical disappointment. If significant, undistorted comparative earnings differences do occur, they can signal good buying or selling opportunities.

Ford's 12-month earnings (last four reported quarters' earnings) are $5.14 per share. The meanings of these "current" earnings are found in various comparisons and ratios displayed in Table 9–1 and reviewed in due course. The current earnings figures we use exclude extraordinary gains and losses and are fully diluted. This is the more conservative approach to using current earnings, but even this may sometimes mask significant changes in potential future earnings if the extraordinary items are overwhelming or the dilutive effects are mitigated by company actions (such as calling in convertible securities or buying back common shares).

7. **3-Yr Earn**. Average of past three fiscal years' earnings in dollars and cents per share per fiscal year. Three-year (or longer) averaged earnings are often more important than trailing earnings. The three-year number is generated by adding up the past three fiscal years' earnings and dividing by three. Like every fundamental item, this number can stand a bit of further analysis.

On the one hand, the three-year average earnings can represent a solid earnings trend; on the other, it can cover up highly volatile or unstable earnings over the reported 12 quarters. For example, a company may have earned $1 per share for the first year, $1.50 per share for the second year, and $2 per share for the third year. This pattern of earnings shows an average earnings of $1.50 per share for three years and a handsome growth trend (a doubling in three years, or 24 percent compounded annually). But, the same average earnings could represent the reverse pattern—$2, then $1.50, then $1—which would be a dismal trend of decreasing earnings despite amounting to the same three-year average earnings.

Still, the three-year average earnings figure is a touchstone with which to compare current earnings and projected earnings, showing flat or trending earnings. The three-year average can also give perspective to the longer term P/E ratio of the stock, a topic reviewed in greater detail below.

Ford's three-year earnings work out to $2.17 per share. We immediately see that Ford's three-year average earnings are much less than its current or projected earnings (reviewed next). As it happens, Ford had record earnings during the past two years, so it is a big positive that both current and projected earnings are above the three-year average including those record years. This earnings trend becomes a buy consideration later in our analysis.

8. **Proj Earn**. Projected or estimated earnings in dollars and cents per share, usually for the upcoming four quarters. Projected earnings are very important and very dangerous, generally representing estimated earnings for the next four quarters to be reported. However, projected earnings are not always for the next four quarters. Sometimes we "normalize" cyclical companies' earnings or sometimes we assign a number that companies may earn a few years from now after undergoing restructurings or trying times. Our estimates for projected earnings come from several public sources and sometimes our own extrapolations. We study the *Value Line Investment Survey, Standard & Poor's Earnings Guide*, and on occasion industry sources such as *Institutional Brokerage Estimates Survey (IBES)* and *Zacks Investment Research*, as well as miscellaneous brokerage and institutional publications to help us determine probable projected earnings.

We know that projected earnings are often notoriously inaccurate. Even chief financial officers of corporations have difficulties projecting earnings for 12 months in advance, given the vagaries of business. Financial analysts, at least one step removed and without as much information at their disposal, may be even more off the mark, or, because they are not so close to the trees, may come up with a better assessment of the forest than the forester.

However, estimated earnings serve at least two functions. First, they show what others believe a corporation will earn, and much stock is traded on such beliefs. Second, they are a continuing educated guess as to what might happen. It is well known that successive increases or decreases in estimated earnings tend to influence stock prices in similar directions. One can also make interpretations or adjustments based on the fact that in good times earnings estimates tend to become more and more generous, while in bad times earnings estimates tend to become pessimistic.

For several quarters in 1994 and 1995, earnings estimates had more upside adjustments and surprises than downside ones because of the bearish outlook toward the economy and corporations. These upside surprises were part of the underpinnings of the strong market rally during the first six months of 1995. A study featured in *The Wall Street Journal* (May 1, 1995, p. C1), by I/B/E/S International Inc., details these phenomena, showing that, of 559 companies monitored by I/B/E/S, 57 percent surpassed, 14 percent matched, and 29 percent fell below analysts' earnings expectations for the first quarter of 1995.

Corporations reporting earnings surprises—compared to "the Street's" consensus estimates—often see their stocks move in the direction of the unexpected difference. The April 24, 1989, *Barron's* reviewed some of the ramifications of projected earnings in "The Trader" column, written by Lauren R. Rublin. Rublin reported on quantitative research work done by Claudia Mott, who studies earnings surprises. Mott finds that earnings surprises have a 38 percent chance of being repeated in the next quarter, although there is a 15 percent probability of them going the other way. Why analysts are surprised in the first place, or surprised a second time, is likely based on disbelief and the psychological need to avoid dramatic reassessments.

The actual examples Rublin reports are instructive. Inco, the Canadian nickel producer, earned $1.90 a share in 1988's fourth quarter, compared to Street estimates of $1.67. For the first quarter of '89 analysts estimated $2.22, but Inco reported $2.44. "Seagate, the widely followed disk-drive maker, did the same trick, reporting 15 cents, versus a projected loss of 10 cents for the December quarter, and 42 cents versus a consensus 20 cents for the three months ending March."[3] Rublin gives us two negative earnings surprises, apparently not adjusted for by most analysts.

---

[3] Lauren R. Rublin, "The Trader," *Barron's*, April 24, 1989, p. 74.

On the negative side, Preston Corp., the trucker, Wednesday reported first-quarter earnings of 19 cents, compared with the 26 cents
analysts had expected. In last year's final quarter, the company net-
ted 15 cents, again considerably below the 37 cents analysts had
anticipated. And Laclede Steel recently disappointed, with earnings
of 69 cents and not the 99 cents the Street had estimated. The
guesstimators got it wrong the prior quarter, too, when the company
earned 82 cents, hardly the $1.47 the Street had in mind.[4]

While studies show the low level of confidence one should hold in estimated
earnings, that does not invalidate their potential usefulness. Better a smoky torch
than no torch at all. In a statistical sense, one might expect that the over- and
under-estimations may have a certain canceling-out effect over large numbers of
stocks and over longer periods of time. Of course, we do not depend upon estimated earnings alone, as other fundamentals must be sufficient to compensate for
potential projected earnings downgrades and disappointments.

One can select certain earnings estimates from those analysts who, or publications which, seem to have a better handle on a particular corporation's workings
based on historical accuracy. One can also note the variations of earnings estimates
and notice significant differences between the mean and modal projections. If three
estimates suggest $5 per share and one projects $1 per share (does the "contrarian"
know something the others don't, or vice versa?), then the average estimate for the
four is $4 per share. Given recent sales, earnings on revenues, cash-flow trends,
and price/sales ratios, we may have evidence in support of or against the consensus
estimated earnings. Then too, we can almost skip the whole subject of the quality
of projected earnings and merely depend upon recent trends and other current fundamental criteria.

Ford's projected earnings are displayed as $6.75 per share, about 31 percent
greater than current earnings of $5.14. Combined with the two other earnings fig-
ures, we get a picture of a company currently operating at a high earnings level.
Either this is enough information for us or we would go to Ford's annual and other
reports to try to determine if Ford's earnings have peaked as a cyclical corporation,
if it still has growth potential, or if it is an undervalued money maker at current P/E
and projected P/E levels.

9. **Earns Growth**. Five-year earnings growth rate in percentage per year. It
    is no secret that we would rather own a growing corporation than a stag-
    nant or declining one, unless perhaps the stagnant one had tremendous

---

[4] Lauren R. Rublin, "The Trader," *Barron's*, April 24, 1989, p. 74.

realizable assets—a so-called asset play. Corporations, which have the status of legal entities, have a life of their own in that they are founded, develop, grow, decline and "die" either through voluntary liquidation, bankruptcy, or merger into another corporation. Ideally, we like to find corporations that are growing nicely, perhaps at 15 percent or more per year on average, with their stock prices not yet reflecting their growth rates. If such a corporation has managed a solid growth rate over a number of years, there is some likelihood that it will continue to do so, although any number of things could go wrong.

Ford does not have a satisfactory five-year earnings growth rate because its recent earnings are not much more than its earnings six years ago. We need six years of earnings to calculate a five-year growth rate. The calculation is simple: value of growth from year one to year six. For the past six fiscal years (1989–1994), Ford's earnings per share from operations have been: $4.57, $0.93, –$2.40, –$0.73, $2.27, $4.97. Thus, its five-year earnings growth rate per share is 1.71 percent, according to our calculations.

10. **P/E Norm**. Average price/earnings ratio. The P/E norm or average multiple represents our estimation of what a stock should trade for under normal conditions (if there are such things). It is a key number for estimating present and future potential market price valuations. When we first started determining these average multiples 18 years ago, the P/E norm was calculated as an average of the previous 10 or 15 years of annual P/E ratios. The idea was that if a stock tended to trade, say, at an average 12 times earnings for long periods of time, then that would be a good criterion for estimating current, under-, over-, or fair valuation.

Over the years, this simple approach to using an average P/E ratio has been modified to take account of current and anticipated P/E levels of major indices, industry averages, and the current and anticipated returns on equity of each individual stock.

As the general stock market's P/E averages increased, and as certain companies continued to grow and improve their valuation criteria, such as their return on equity percentage, we found it fruitful to modify P/E norms upward, usually above their relatively recent and sometimes historically depressed averages. The rule of thumb that a P/E norm could reasonably equal a stock's return on equity (ROE) percentage seems to be an effective guide or starting criterion, with modification for very high ROEs that are clearly or likely unsustainable. Thus, a stock returning 15 percent on equity (a.k.a. net worth) currently and projecting an equal or greater ROE over the next four quarters could deserve and be expected to trade in the next few years at a P/E of 15, which is to say 15 times earnings.

There are cases where the current P/E ratio is absent, due to losses (no E) rather than profits, or because of sharp price changes. Though our guideline is to buy relatively low P/E stocks—hopefully at less than 30 to 50 percent of the going market or major index level, or the stock's P/E norm—there are times when I will buy stocks with much greater P/Es or having none at all. Usually these candidates are bought on the grounds of tremendous discounts from net worth (so-called asset plays), or in advance of perceived imminent turnarounds where a current short-term profit drop or loss is in the nature of a glitch, the cause of which likely has already been corrected.

I have assigned Ford a P/E norm of 8.5. I believe that in the next three to five years Ford's common stock will trade at 8.5 times its current (or projected) earnings. This is a reasonable multiple for an automotive company at its peak. *Value Line* displays an average annual P/E ratio of 7.0 in the 1998–2000 period. I believe that given a less cyclical corporate environment for the auto cycle, with its massive diversifications into financial services, aerospace, and foreign manufacturers, coupled with its 27 percent current return on equity and 30.98 percent projected ROE (both figures are reviewed below), a P/E 8.5 is appropriate if not conservative.

11. **Tang BV**. Tangible book value in dollars and cents per share. Tangible book value is essentially book value less intangible assets. Intangible (nonphysical) assets can include certain deferred charges, copyrights, franchises, goodwill, leaseholds, patents, and trademarks. Goodwill is an asset item on the balance sheet, usually representing the excess of cost basis of an asset (an acquired asset or corporation) over its own tangible book value at the time of purchase. As Peter Lynch puts it, "If you pay $450 million for a TV station worth $2.5 million on the books, the accountants call the extra $447.5 million 'goodwill'." In the bad old days decades ago, when companies overstated assets, goodwill referred to the "water" (or hot air) on a company's books, of which prudent speculators were well advised to be very wary.

While tangible book value is meant to disclose a truer picture of the hard assets-minus-liabilities value of a company than mere book value—especially if there is a big disparity between the two—we must be careful to investigate the actual values represented by goodwill and other "hidden" assets. The acquired goodwill may well represent a hidden asset bought at bargain levels, which is then written off over many years (often 20 to 40, reducing (penalizing) reported earnings (while also reducing income taxes), while the worth of these apparently opaque or intangible assets are actually increasing in value. The franchise cost in the purchase price of acquiring a business is one of these hidden "assets" as are trade names, proprietary techniques, the customer base, employees and staff, expensed research and development, and the general business franchise itself. Many companies, like some banks and savings and loans that have acquired branch offices from their competitors, carry large goodwill numbers that substantially represent tangible assets, which are growing in value in terms of replacement or duplication costs.

Our stock analysis sheet shows Ford with a tangible book value of $16.68 per share, or $3.66 per share less than its book value of $19.03. To the degree that amortizing "goodwill" reduces earnings but augments the total going value of Ford as a dynamic, growing corporation, I as a long-term speculator-investor-owner am happy. Ford is becoming more valuable as it amortizes "intangible" assets that are probably appreciating over time on balance.

12. **Book Value**. All assets less all liabilities in dollars and cents per share. Book value is essentially assets less liabilities and preferred stock (if any) at liquidating value, or what a corporation is worth from an accounting point of view. Of course, accounting points of view can get very complicated and even contentious. Not all assets or liabilities are created equal. Just as the price of a stock rarely represents the worth of its corporation fairly, so book value frequently overstates or understates the actual worth of its corporation. If you choose not to accept stated book value as an adequate reflection—I do, based on my generally statistical approach that overstated book values are compensated for by understated book values in widely diversified portfolios (a thesis that may sound idiotic to security analysts)—then you will want to look for hidden assets and hidden liabilities.

As featured in Chapter 2, we can use book value as one of the basic numbers for a quick analysis of a stock, given the historical relationships of a corporation's stock price to its book value per share. In the case of Ford, we see that its book value is $19.03 per share. This number is used in ratios of fundamental evaluation later in Table 9–1.

13. **BV Growth**. Five-year book value growth in percentage per year. Often it is instructive to see how a corporation's book value has increased over the past few years. In the case of Ford, the book value has diminished 5.7 per-

cent per year (although not shown in this analysis). It would seem that Ford's book value should increase next year, given the difference between projected after-tax reported earnings and dividends paid, perhaps $5.51 per share (barring any writedowns or writeoffs or variation in estimated earnings), which is about 28.95 percent for the year.

14. **BV Norm**. Average price/book value multiple (ratio). Just as stocks trade for a multiple of their earnings—as well as other fundamentals such as sales and cash flow—so they trade at multiples of their book values. As previously mentioned, Dow Jones Industrial stocks as an average have tended to trade between slightly below one and somewhat above two times book value, with notable exceptions. Heavy industrial corporations with large investments in plant and equipment generally trade at a smaller multiple of their book values than do service industries with smaller fixed assets. In recent years, stocks have been trading at historically high price/book value ratios given all the writeoffs taken the past few years and the increased upgrading of equipment, plant and production.

I have assigned a BV norm of 2.25 for Ford which may seem high by historical standards but which I believe to be fair and representative.

15. **Cash Flow**. Cash available with which to run business in dollars and cents per share. We have reviewed cash flow at length in Chapter 2 as one of the principal criteria for stock selection. Generally, cash flow is defined as the net income plus bookkeeping entries such as depreciation and amortization charges. Obviously, different kinds of corporations tend to have different levels of cash flow in general, which also vary in relation to the maturity of their growth cycle. Ford's indicated cash flow is $14.30 per share, more than twice its current earnings. More on Ford's cash flow later.

16. **CF Growth**. Five-year cash flow growth rate in percentage per year. We are following the five-year cash flow growth rate in a similar way as other five-year growth rates, mostly as confirmation of the overall trend, but also to see if anomalies occur which might indicate a significant change in cash flow production. This sort of monitoring can become pretty esoteric, perhaps not worth the effort, and rarely is sufficient consideration for including or excluding a stock purchase candidate.

Ford's five-year cash flow growth rate works out to about 9.3 percent, higher than its other growth rates—an encouraging sign.

17. **P/CF Norm**. Price to cash flow average multiple (ratio). As cash flow is considered by many a more important measure of a corporation's ongoing

health than earnings (net income), the price/cash flow multiple, which works like the price/earnings ratio, gives an instant picture of funds available for current business use in terms of how much "the market" is willing to pay per share for this item. Like all multiples, cash flow averages are based upon historical averages of the stock, perhaps its industry, and to a lesser degree the general market.

Cyclical stocks—corporations that traditionally have strong profit years followed by weak profit (or loss) year such as Ford— tend to trade at low multiples for P/E, P/BV, and P/CF, as investors expect these three fundamentals not to have or sustain rapid growth. We have assigned Ford a P/CF of 4.0— which sometimes seems low to me in comparison to other corporations, but then Chrysler and General Motors also carry 4.0s—because of historical precedent and the generally high dollar cash flows generated.

18. **Revenues**. Total annual sales or revenues in millions of dollars. It may be intrinsically interesting to see how a corporation is faring in terms of its annual sales (revenues). This amount figures prominently in several important ratios (such as price/revenues and return on sales, reviewed below) and is yet another measure of year-to-year growth. Ford's revenue for the past four quarters (to date, as of the printout) was approximately $107.137 billion.

19. **Revs Growth**. Five-year revenue per share (sales) growth rate in percentage per year. Just as we would like to see earnings growing at, say 15 percent per year, so we would like to see revenues increasing at an equally healthy clip. Ford shows no growth because of depressed revenues during the 1990–92 period, which included a recession.

We could have a revenue growth rate average, but that might be unduly misleading due to the volatility of revenues for most corporations over a five-year period. Still, if you are getting into analysis to this degree, you would certainly want to glance at the annual revenues for the past several years, especially happy to see them doubled in five years or less, which represents a 15 percent or greater annual growth rate. Well-managed corporations can show improved earnings per share, even while revenues remain constant, by cutting costs and improving efficiency, but static or declining sales are usually a bad sign. Sometimes improved earnings— without improved revenues—come at the expense of cutting back on maintenance, upkeep, research, and staff training, thus reducing the corporation's prospects in future years.

20. **Shares Comm**. Common shares outstanding in millions. Knowing how many shares outstanding a corporation has is a basic requirement for

calculating many ratios and per share figures. Several of these relationships are reviewed below, in the calculations portion of the stock analysis printout. Shares outstanding can change from time to time as corporations buy back shares—which then become part of their treasury shares—or sell them in the open market.

Many corporations issue shares or rights to their executives to buy shares, which may be exercised later. Sometimes warrants, convertible preferreds, or convertible bonds are converted into common shares and thus increase the pool of shares outstanding. We have mentioned the potential dilutive effect of these pending instruments in terms of book value per share and earnings per share. Ford shows approximately 1.023 billion (1,023,000,000) common shares outstanding. There are no necessary relationships among shares outstanding and revenues, for example, or earnings or price per share, although there are meaningful ratios of these and other fundamentals to the shares outstanding amount.

21. **Cur Assets**. Current assets in millions of dollars. Current assets are cash or assets that can be converted to cash usually within one year in the normal course of business, such as accounts receivable, inventories, and cash-equivalent instruments (e.g., Treasury bills, common stocks of other corporations, and certificates of deposit maturing within one year). Obviously, assets can be of higher or lower quality. Uncollectible accounts receivables, or inventories that are obsolete, slow-moving, or unsellable are of lower quality than their opposites. We would certainly want to note unusually large or growing receivables and inventories as potential signs of trouble in a corporation's operations.

Inventories should be stated at cost or market value, whichever is lower, based on first-in, first-out (FIFO) or last-in, first-out (LIFO) accounting. FIFO charges sales with the oldest inventory costs; the remaining balance sheet inventory is priced at most recent costs. LIFO charges sales with the most recent costs of inventory; the remaining balance sheet inventory is priced at older costs. During rising prices, LIFO inventory on the balance sheet is usually lower than FIFO. Inventory to sales and inventory turnover ratios may be telling in manufacturing and retail store corporations. These details can usually be gleaned from annual reports and sometimes from their footnotes.

Ford's current assets are $28.863 billion. In late 1980, accounting rule changes known as FASB 94 muddied the analytic waters by requiring corporations to include all assets of their subsidiaries. As *Value Line* put it in referring to Chrysler Corporation:

> The adoption of FASB 94 has caused the consolidation of the company's captive finance subsidiary, Chrysler Financial Corp., on the financial statements of the parent. Formerly accounted for on the equity method, CFC necessarily brings with it assets and liabilities that are huge by Chrysler's standards. As a result of the consolidation, some standard financial ratios (return on total capital, interest coverage, etc.) have ceased to be comparable either with Chrysler's historical record, or the FASB ruling. The new reporting method won't affect earnings per share or shareholder equity.[5]

22. **Cur Liabs**. Current liabilities in millions of dollars. Current liabilities, the opposite of current assets, are expenses and debts of the corporation that are due and payable within one year (or the normal operating cycle). Liabilities can also involve some esoteric and qualitative considerations, often discussed in the footnotes of annual reports (10–K reports to the Securities and Exchange Commission, which you can request from corporations).

We should be alert to liability reserves, which represent an unquestioned claim against a corporation, although the exact amount of the claim cannot be determined. Reserves for bad debts, contingent liabilities such as warranties or litigation, and insurance company loss reserves may seriously overstate or understate actual liabilities, although generally, estimates are in keeping with historical experience, accounting pronouncements, and IRS guidelines.

Ford's current liabilities are reported as $25.471 billion (under FASB 94). The ratio of current assets to current liabilities, called the current ratio, is discussed in sequence below.

23. **L/T Debt**. Long-term debt (liabilities) in millions of dollars. Those liabilities that normally need not be met within one year are called long-term debt. This is an important, basic figure used in several fundamental calculations to determine potential overindebtedness and underindebtedness or debt-to-equity trends. Ford's long-term debt is $7.103 billion (FASB 94).

---

[5] *Value Line Investment Survey*, March 24, 1989. (Copyright 1989 by *Value Line*, Inc.; used by permission.)

24. **TOT Assets**. All assets in millions of dollars. Short-term and long-term (fixed or capital) assets are combined to yield the total assets figure. Perhaps the first thing to note is to what degree a corporation's total assets are greater than its total liabilities less ownership (shareholders equity, retained earnings, etc.). Then we can see what sorts of relationships exist, such as return on assets, and how they compare to previous years. Ford's total assets are $219.354 billion (FASB 94). While the financial statement is called a balance sheet, in that assets are balanced equally by liabilities, this is accomplished by putting shareholders' equity and retained earnings on the liabilities side of the balance sheet.

25. **Pref Stock**. Preferred stock outstanding in millions of dollars at liquidating value. Preferred stocks have a prior claim over common stocks on assets in case of a corporate dissolution, and a prior claim on dividends. We common shareholders would rather the corporation had no preferred stock, because we would not like common-stock dividends suspended if the current earnings (and perhaps the retained earnings) were insufficient to meet both the required preferred-stock dividend payment and payments of the indicated common dividend, which would be "passed" (deleted) in such cases. Also, the fewer priority claims to assets the better for common shareholders in the case of liquidation or bankruptcy. Ford has $3.4 billion worth of preferred issues. Of course, Ford has many bonds outstanding, all of which have a senior claim to assets over common and preferred stock.

26. **Yr-End CST**. Price per share at December 30, 1994 in dollars and cents. This is a marginal item, only useful in referencing how the stock's price has fared since the beginning of the year.

27. **Year High**. Highest price per share for the recent four quarters in dollars and cents. Another marginal item for the convenience of checking the current price and recent four-quarter low price in relation to the stock's recent four-quarter high price. We update this number quarterly with the closing high between quarters.

28. **Year Low**. Lowest price per share for the recent four quarters in dollars and cents. Like the year high, only useful to compare recent price ranges. We update this number quarterly with the closing low price between quarters.

29. **Hist High**. Highest price per share during the past 15 to 24 years in dollars and cents. The 15- to 24-year high and low prices (which are generally 24-year highs/lows because we get these prices from Standard & Poor's, which is now reporting data back to 1971) are probably the least

valuable items in this analysis because a corporation can become a significantly or completely different enterprise over 15–24 years. This number is only updated yearly so we can see if a stock's all-time high or low was set this year. It may be almost idle curiosity to note the stock's price range over the past 15–24 years, but sometimes there is a clue to historical undervaluations and overvaluations. One must be aware of stock splits which reduce the original cost bases or prices of a stock (or reverse splits which increase said prices) and thus result in split-adjusted figures.

For example, Ford split its common shares two for one in 1994, so a share of stock bought before the first split would now be two shares and the original cost price would be divided by two to obtain the split-adjusted equivalent price. Today's market price of $26.75 per share is the equivalent of the pre-split $53.50 per share. The same process works with the pre-split yearly highs (and lows), so that *Value Line* shows a high for Ford of $35 in 1994, which means that the shares actually traded as high as $70 per share in 1994, pre-split.

30. **Hist Low**. The lowest price the stock traded during the past 15–24 years (see explanation in item 29.) All the split-adjusted considerations applying to the 15- to 24-year-high figures (reviewed above) must be applied to the 15- to 24-year-low figures, thus reducing their pre-split low prices accordingly. By the way, Ford also split its shares two for one in early 1988, three for two in 1986, and three for two in 1984, which means that one share pre-split 1984 is now nine shares. For the full 15–24 years, Ford shows a low of $3.93 on our printout. This is not to say that Ford traded for $3.93 per share in the past 15-24 years, but that is its split-adjusted low.

Probably long-term highs and lows are most interesting and useful in observing big drops or gains over the period of a few years (although you wouldn't necessarily see this in a single 15- to 24-year figure). For instance, according to one "long base" pattern theory, if a corporation's stock loses 80 percent of its price and thereafter trades in a narrow range for three years or so—say between 20 to 25 percent of its former high price—the stock has completed a "long base" and is likely to have a significant advance when it breaks out of its long-base trading range. While I do not search for this pattern, I do appreciate it when it coincides with undervalued fundamental criteria.

31. *VL / S&P*. *Value Line*'s "Timeliness" rating and Standard and Poor's "Earnings and Dividend Rankings for Common Stocks." The *Value Line Investment Survey* displays a timeliness rating "(Relative Price Performance

Next 12 Mos.)" with 1–highest, 2–above average, 3–average, 4–below average, and 5–lowest. In the early development of this analysis program, I thought it would be nice to see what *Value Line* was projecting for a stock it follows and so included this item. However, it is not without flaws. *Value Line* only follows some 1,700 stocks, usually omitting smaller-capitalization issues. From the current ranking, one cannot tell the last time it changed without leafing through several back issues. *Value Line* has demonstrated that its timeliness ranking system works most of the time, with the 1s doing better than the 2s, and so on, if timely switches are made. Note that of the 12 stocks in Table 9–1 only five have *VL* rankings and the one stock ranked "1," Vishay, is an almost-sell candidate, based on fundamental valuation, rather than a stock to be held for its (potential) performance in the year ahead.

I am not a follower of the *Value Line* timeliness rankings because they are so heavily based on relative strength and other technical considerations, whereas I am more concerned with fundamental values. I used to joke that, given the choice, I would rather buy 4s or 3s than 2s or 1s because the highest-ranked issues had already advanced so much in price. Still, it's nice to see if a recommendable stock is rated by *Value Line*, and how.

Value Line timeliness rankings at the time of the sample printout give Ford a "3," or average year-ahead price appreciation performance. By following these printouts on a weekly basis, we can tell if the stocks we are recommending have had their *Value Line* rating changed.

In a similar manner, I also have a relatively idle curiosity about Standard & Poor's rankings for common stocks, probably harking back to my desire for so-called safety criteria in stock selection. These S&P rankings are generated by "a computerized scoring system based on per-share earnings and dividend records of the most recent ten years" and are adjusted "by a set of predetermined modifiers for growth, stability within long-term trend, and cyclicality."[6]

For more details check the monthly Standard & Poor's Corporation *Stock Guide*, widely used by brokers and investors as a quick reference to more than 5,900 common and preferred stocks, with a separate section covering over 700 mutual funds. The earnings and dividend rankings for common stocks range as follows: A+, Highest; A, High; A–, Above Average; B+, Average; B, Below Average; B–, Lower; C, Lowest; D, In Reorganization. To conserve space on the printout we have attributed numerals to the letter rankings with A+ = 1, A = 2, . . . D = 8. Thus Ford, with 4 has a B+ or average ranking. Check the latest S&P *Stock Guide* for current rankings.

---

[6] Standard & Poor's Corporation, *Stock Guide*, March 1989 and October 1994, p. 5.

The *Stock Guide* prints a very important paragraph, not only relating to its ranking system but to investing in general:

> A ranking is not a forecast of future market price performance, but is basically an appraisal of past performance of earnings and dividends, and relative current standing. *These rankings must not be used as market recommendations; a high-score stock may at times be so overpriced as to justify its sale, while a low-score stock may be attractively priced for purchase.* Rankings based upon earnings and dividend records are no substitute for complete analysis. They cannot take into account potential effects of management changes, internal company policies not yet fully reflected in the earnings and dividend record, public relations standing, recent competitive shifts, and a host of other factors that may be relevant to investment status and decision.[7]

To repeat, these ratings are based on trailing earnings and dividends and do not necessarily reflect potential future stock price movements. Still, many investment counselors and money managers will only invest in common stocks with the higher ratings, even as they require similar high ratings to invest in bonds. Since we tend to deemphasize dividends as important to our stock selection process and since we find a 10-year earnings history a bit old and sometimes misleading, we do not rely on S&P earnings and dividend rankings for common stocks. Also, you will notice that five of our "Favorite 10" stocks have no S&P rankings, because their market capitalization is too small or their corporate history is not long enough.

The safety factors related to bonds are probably more significant and better reflected in various quality ratings than those applying to common stocks. It would generally be copping out to place much emphasis on either *Value Line*'s or S&P's rankings, especially in comparison with basic fundamental criteria. Non-dividend-paying stocks do not gain good S&P rankings, and the universe of *Value Line* stocks is too limited.

Analyzing Calculated Criteria from Stock Analysis Components

Up to now we have been slogging through the basic data for analyzing corporations in terms of their financial fundamentals. The rest (bottom half) of our printout deals with some of the meaningful combinations and ratios derived from the "plugged in" data on the top half. The following are the numbers that lead us toward or away from corporations, that suggest undervalued stocks to buy and fully valued to overvalued stocks to sell.

---

[7] Standard & Poor's Corporation, *Stock Guide,* October 1994, p. 5.

32. **Proj. ROE.** Projected return on equity in percent. Just as we project earnings in an effort to draw a bead on the near future prospects for a corporation's common stock, so we are interested in the probable future returns on equity. ROE, as one of the basic criteria, has been reviewed in Chapter 2. We can see at a glance that Ford has a "great" projected ROE of 30.98 percent. The formula used to obtain projected return on earnings is:

Projected ROE = Projected Earnings / (Book Value + 0.5 times
Projected Earnings – 0.5 times Dividend) × 100

33. **Cur P/E.** Current (trailing four-quarters) price/earnings ratio. By dividing the closing price per share by the current earnings per share one obtains the price/earnings ratio. The P/E ratio is frequently referred to as the price earnings' multiple (or even just the multiple), because the price of the stock is the P/E multiple times its earnings. Thus, with Ford earning $5.14 per share and trading at $26 per share, its multiple is 5.05 (5.05 times $5.14 equals $26, rounded up). Obviously, Ford's P/E is low compared both to the other stocks of Table 9–1 and to its P/E norm (row 10).

One would also compare the current P/E with the projected return on equity (row 32) and the return on equity (row 40). Comparing these germane figures can give a perspective of the appropriateness of the P/E norm and the relative value of the current P/E in relation to the other criteria and other stocks in the same industry (not shown in this sample printout).

34. **Div Yield %.** The current indicated annual dividend yield in percent. One obtains a dividend yield by dividing the indicated dividend (row 5) by the current price (row 4). Ford is currently paying an above-average dividend yield of 4.76 percent, considering the S&P 500 average dividend is 3.64 percent at this time. You might notice that eight of the displayed stocks on Table 9–1 do not pay dividends at all, in keeping with our emphasis on market appreciation versus dividend income.

For some investors who believe that Ford is undervalued, its 4.76 percent yield is a comfort while they await market price appreciation or potential future dividend increases. If we notice the year-end cost (row 26), we see that Ford is actually down $1.875 year-to-date, a drop greater than its annual indicated dividend. When we look at the current prices of most of the stocks in Table 9–1 versus their year-end prices and notice the gains— Gainsco, for example, from $7.85 (adjusted for a 5 percent stock dividend) to $10.00, a 27.39 percent gain in just over four months—we see just how trivial its 4 cent dividend (0.40 percent yield) is, even if it were yielding a whopping 6 or 8 percent.

Semi-dramatic stock price gain examples like these are why I emphasize stock price appreciation over dividend yields. Of course, one could always find a few dramatic examples, and you should understand that my bias is not based on such small samples for such short periods of time. Over very long periods of time, the S&P 500 dividends—as a proxy for large-capitalization and blue-chip stocks—actually amount to a greater compounded return than price appreciation. However, we will never be buying the S&P 500 or holding it for decades, nor will we be satisfied with its historical total returns of appreciation plus dividends.

Perhaps you can see that from my point of view I could care less about even an 8 to 10 percent dividend yield in a stock that also tends to appreciate only 4 to 5 percent per year—a total return of 12 to 15 percent—when I am searching for stocks that can appreciate over 18 to 25 percent a year, perhaps doubling in market price in four or three years.

35. **PR/TANG-BV.** Current price to current tangible book value as a ratio. I mentioned my concerns about tangible book values above and in Chapter 2, especially when compared to plain book values. We certainly like to see companies trading below their tangible book values, or at some multiple that is at least 30 percent below their average tangible book value ratios.

In the case of Ford— with a tangible book value of $16.68, somewhat below its regular book value of $19.03—we see it trading at 156 percent (1.56) of its tangible book value. We would cross-reference this with Ford's book value norm (row 14) and see that, at $19.03, Ford is trading at 137 percent (1.37) of its plain book value, so both are below a 30 percent discount from its norm of 225 percent (2.25). Of course, there is always the chance that our assigned book value norm is too high (or too low), and perhaps we should also have a specific tangible book value norm, but in reality such precision is not required as several other fundamental criteria will reinforce each other's indications. After all, these norms are all estimates and subject to dynamic revision, given the growth of corporations and support of their share prices over time by shareholders.

36. **Price/BV.** Current price to current book value per share as a ratio. This criterion is essentially the same as the one above except that it uses book value rather than tangible book value. Actually, in many cases, book value reported by corporations is also tangible book value, but we make

the distinction so as to call attention to special cases. Book value is one of the basic fundamental criteria and has been reviewed in the Chapter 2. On balance, we like stocks trading below their book values or at least 30 percent below their book value norms, and consider them potential sell candidates when they trade at or 30 percent above their book value norms, as reviewed above.

37. **Cur Ratio**. The ratio of current assets to current liabilities. For a quick check on the current health of a corporation—at least in terms of its balance sheet—we look to see if current assets are sufficiently greater than current liabilities to avoid short-term financial difficulties. For industrial companies the classic current ratio is two to one, or twice as much in current assets as current liabilities. The current ratio can be misleading if current assets represent disproportionately large accounts receivable with a poor history of collection or huge inventories that are unlikely to be sold at a profit. Very large corporations, such as auto and oil companies, rarely have anything approaching a current ratio of 2.0. You must observe company ratios and watch a corporation's current ratio over time—especially noticing deteriorations—to get a feel for this criterion.

   Ford's current ratio of 1.05 is a bit low, especially compared to its 1989 current ratio of 1.12. Lower current ratios may be an indication of leaner and more financially effective corporations which do not have unnecessary current assets on their books. Current ratios are not appropriate for financial institutions such as Bear Stearns and Gainsco. Otherwise, notice the current ratios of other stocks in Table 9–1. Experience shows that very large corporations tend to have current ratios of much less than two to one.

38. **Ret Sales**. Returns (earnings) per dollar of sales as a percent. The return on sales (revenues) percentage gives a snapshot of how much the corporation is earning per sales dollar. For large industrial corporations you like to see at least a 3 percent return on sales, but in a supermarket or other high-turnover, low-margin enterprise, you would do well with 1 percent returns. Each company has its "norm" and perhaps more important than the actual percentage are the recent and long-term trends.

   Ford's return on sales at 4.90 percent is pretty good, but looks mediocre compared to BGSS Systems' 20.84 percent, an apples and oranges comparison between a huge industrial company and a small software developer and marketer with relatively high profit margins. Figures like this can be looked at in at least two ways. Either the sales margins are high—Ford's mid-1989 return on sales was 5.81 percent—or there is room for improvement in this criterion, and Ford could conceivably increase its earnings without an increase in sales revenues by lowering manufacturing and distributing costs.

39. **Ret Assets**. Return on assets (ROA) as a percent. Return on assets is another principal criterion that was reviewed in Chapter 2. Again, absolute percentages can give a snapshot appraisal but a securities analyst—even an amateur working with pencil and paper—would want to observe the trend of this criterion (as well as others) to see if the corporation is becoming more or less effective in the profitable use of its assets.

We see that Ford's ROA is 2.39 percent compared to Bear Stearns' 0.22 percent and BGS Systems' 23.72 percent. Again, such a comparison is trying to match apples to oranges to pears. Bear Stearns had huge assets, $66.842 billion, while BGSS Systems' assets amount to a mere $31 million. These comparisons are in keeping with the kinds of corporations we are sampling. Ford with its huge investment in assets (FASB 94) in order to produce cars, trucks, and manage its financial subsidiary, is not likely to gain a much greater return on assets than an oil company or a light manufacturer/merchandising/service industry. A glance across the row at the other corporations' figures shows the variability of ROAs. Note that disk drive manufacturer Western Digital manages a ROA comparable to BGS Systems. Return on assets is an important criterion for financial companies, especially banks and savings and loans.

40. **Ret Equity**. Return on equity (ROE) as a percent. Another of the big seven criteria reviewed in Chapter 2, roe indicates how well a corporation can turn a profit on its equity or net worth. Traditionally, roes of 15 percent or better separate so-called growth stocks from other stocks, but this can be misleading, especially over short periods of time. Again, we want to watch the trend of ROE, hoping it is strong and positive. Oddly enough, if the roe of a corporation is too high or unsustainable, that condition is often represented in its stock's high, and therefore vulnerable, overvalued price.

An article in *The Wall Street Journal*[8] entitled "The '20% Club' No Longer Is Exclusive" points out that a 20 percent return on equity was once limited to a relatively small number of elite corporations like Wal-Mart Stores or Coca-Cola. According to Salomon Brothers, for the first quarter of 1995, "the average ROE of the Standard & Poor's 500 companies hit 20.1 percent. This figure represents the highest level of corporate profitability in the post-

---

[8] *The Wall Street Journal* "The'20% Club' No Longer Exclusive," May 4, 1995, p. C1 (New York, NY 10281).

war era." The article suggests that such high ROEs are unsustainable and will probably return to lower percentages in the future.

This article quotes Byron Wien of Morgan Stanley, "There have been tremendous charges taken against book value. So book is tremendously understated."[9] With lower equity (book value), only slightly improved earnings would boost return on equity percentages greatly. The article also noted that with the 1992 change in the way companies account for health benefits of future retirees, book values took a big hit in 1922. What does all this mean? Well, ROEs are at an historic high and we should not expect them to increase much more, but we should not be afraid of their high percentages because we understand how it happened. Also, as mentioned above, we must adjust price/book value ratios to account for historically low and lean book values.

Ford shows a handsome 27 percent ROE, which is supported by a projected ROE (row 32) of 30.98 percent. These are unusually high ROEs because the auto companies are near the height of their sales and profit cycle. It will be interesting to see how much of a return on equity Ford can maintain in the next business downturn or recession; that is, will Ford be able to avoid losses? Chrysler has accumulated about $7 billion as a cushion for running its business without as many problems during the next cyclic downturn as it had in past downturns. Both companies are much more efficient and apparently better managed than they were during previous business cycles.

41. **PR/NET WKCP**. Current price to net working capital as a percent. This is a filter straight out of Benjamin Graham's approach, where one looks for a stock trading for less than its net working capital. Since working capital is simply current assets minus current liabilities (net current assets), net working capital is defined as current assets minus all liabilities (current and long term). When you find a stock trading for less than its net working capital you can buy a company for less than its value, plus getting the fixed assets for nothing. Walter Schloss, a successful investor and disciple of Ben Graham, says that Graham got bored with investing when he found that buying stocks for 70 percent of net working capital was all one needed to do to make money in the stock market. These conditions are prevalent after a great market decline, such as 1969 through 1973, but quite rare in advanced and fairly valued markets, such as in 1995.

---

[9] *The Wall Street Journal* "The '20% Club' No Longer Exclusive," May 4, 1995, p. C1 (New York, NY 10281).

42. **Prj EN/PR**. Projected earnings to current price as percent. If we invert the common P/E ratio and make it an E/P ratio, then we obtain an earnings-to-price ratio, which is to say, the earnings return in relation to the price of a stock. A P/E of 5, for example (current price of $10 divided by current earnings of $2), means the stock is trading at five times earnings. But it also means that one is getting a 20 percent return on the cost of the stock, on its price (E/P, or $2 earnings divided by $10 price). This item is just a quick reference identifying the potential projected earnings return based on the current "cost basis" of a stock.

Ford, with projected earnings of $6.75 per share (row 8) turns out to have a projected P/E of 3.85 (current price $26 divided by projected earnings $6.75). The reciprocal of the projected P/E 3.85 (that is, 1 over 3.85) equals 25.97 percent, as does the projected earnings divided by the current price (that is, $6.75/$26). This tells us that we may get a 25.97 percent projected earnings return in one year on our investment of $26 per share of Ford. That is a handsome return, and if it could continue or be realized in the stock's price we would gain an even greater total return. Our initial "return on investment" could return 100 percent in slightly less than three years, not counting dividends, even without a substantial rise in the current P/E multiple.

43. **Price/Rev**. Current price per share to current revenues per share (P/R) as a ratio or percent. This is the famous price/sales ratio made popular by Kenneth Fisher, reviewed in Chapter 2 as one of the super seven selectors. Ford sports an undervalued P/R of 24 percent (0.24), which means that its stock trades for only 24 cents per dollar of sales (revenues), and could easily triple from this level when "the market" looks more favorably on the auto industry and Ford in particular.

44. **Price/CF**. Current price to cash flow (P/CF) as a ratio. P/CF is one of the super seven criteria explicated in Chapter 2. Obviously, different corporations tend toward different ratios, and the long-term trend is an important consideration. We look at a corporation's P/CF in light of its P/CF norm (row 17), which represents historical perspective, as well as its recent trend.

With Ford trading at 1.81 times cash flow we have a very undervalued reading, even though its P/CFs norm is only 4.0, currently reflecting the low esteem in which automotive companies are held and probably a tad low in relation to future norms. When I tell you that some of our norms may be too high or too low, I am expressing my intuitions or gut feelings, but that doesn't permit me to change them on a hunch. I expect that in a year or two we may be carrying Ford's P/CF norm at 4.5 to 5.

45. **MV Change %**. Market value (price) change since year-end in percent. Sometimes it's convenient to see at a glance how a stock's price has performed during the year. This row shows that Ford's stock price is down 6.72 percent for the year to date. You can see that four of our 10 favorites are down for the year, which is about par for the course. (Table 9–2, later in the chapter, displays the overall market appreciation of these 10.)

46. **Mkt Value**. Market value or capitalization in millions of dollars. An important and interesting factor is a stock's market capitalization, computed by multiplying the number of shares outstanding (row 20) by the current price per share (row 4). We have commented on market capitalization elsewhere, especially in reference to some studies which show that small-cap stocks tend to appreciate significantly more over long time periods than large-cap stocks. (A counter analysis to this thesis appears in Chapter 8.) We also use market value to consider other criteria, such as price to revenues ratios (P/R, row 44), as different sized corporations have different P/R criterion levels (see Chapter 2).

Ford is definitely a very large-cap stock with a market value over $26.598 billion—1.023 billion shares outstanding (Row 20) times $26 (row 4). The next largest market cap stock in Table 9–1 is Bear Stearns, with a market cap only 7.88 percent that of Ford's. Clearly a majority of our favorite stocks are small-cap issues.

Valuation Computations

The first 31 rows of our stock analysis printout (Table 9–1) consist of input data, some intrinsically interesting and useful individually as well as in comparison with others. Rows 32 through 46 consist of computations yielding basic ratios and percentages that indicate various levels of fundamental valuation. Now we turn to the bottom lines, rows 47 through 57, which actually give us our high and low goal prices as well as a few other convenient figures and keys. Each of these items is simple, sometimes embarrassingly so, but they add up to a fairly representative picture of an undervalued corporation's stock, especially given the limited amount of time that we want to spend on such analysis.

After wading through all these items you may feel that the whole thing is just too complicated to even begin tracking on your own. I can tell you again that once you have gained the least facility for the subject you can probably analyze a likely prospect (corporation) in an hour or less, initially, and thereafter keep up with it by spending about five minutes a week using a computer and database. Of course, you needn't follow nearly as many stocks as we do or go into such detailed analysis.

You can do computer screens rather rapidly, selecting those stocks that meet certain specified criteria to find only promising candidates and then follow up on them. If the outcome of a criterion or two for a stock, whether checked manually or by computer, doesn't satisfy your guideline, you can quit working on that stock and move on to the next one. Perhaps you will save those stocks that showed some promise in an "almost qualified file" and review them at a later date when they might have become more undervalued and thus satisfy your standards.

47. **P/CF Goal**. Price to cash flow goal in dollars. This is simply multiplying the current cash flow (row 15) by the price/cash-flow norm (row 17) to arrive at the cash flow goal. For some corporations, such as financial institutions, cash flow is not a meaningful figure, which explains the blank spaces for Bear Stearns and Gainsco in Table 9–1. Ford has a cash-flow goal of $57.20 ($14.30 × 4). These goal prices will be combined with other goal prices to arrive at a low and high goal range, reviewed below.

48. **P/E Goal**. Current price earnings goal in dollars. By multiplying the current earnings (row 6) times the P/E norm (row 10) we arrive at a normal price earnings goal. In theory, this is the price the stock should be trading at today, given its average (fair) P/E multiple and its current earnings. Thus, Ford's P/E goal is $43.69, or 68.04 percent greater than its current price. Obviously, a corporation may be worth far more than its current earnings would indicate, so while this is an important consideration it is neither necessary nor sufficient for recommending or not recommending a stock. Of course, that could be said about every criterion being reviewed.

49. **Proje Goal**. Projected earnings price goal (PEG) in dollars. By multiplying the projected earnings (row 8) times the P/E norm (row 10) we obtain the projected earnings price goal. Although it has been pointed out more than once that projected (estimated) earnings are notoriously unreliable in general, we still would like to see what a stock might reasonably trade for, given that its projected earnings were realized. Working with a large number of stocks, we can be slightly cavalier that overestimations and underestimations will tend to cancel each other out.

Ford's PEG amounts to $57.37 (note the asterisk alerting us to the good figure), more than twice its current price of $26. At this time we believe that Ford's earnings two years out could be higher than next year's projected earnings, so we are relying a lot on projected earnings in the case of Ford.

50. **BV Goal**. Book value price goal (BVG) in dollars. We have already considered that corporations trade at a multiple of their book values and thus

we derive book value norms (BV norm, row 14). By multiplying the book value norm against the book value (row 12), we obtain a book value price goal. We use book value because in takeover situations buyouts usually occur at a multiple of book value, and its easier to compare book values, both tangible and regular.

Ford's BVG is $42.81 (its book value norm of 2.25 times its book value of $19.03). Ford's BVG is only 64.68 percent greater than its current price, not as big a bargain as in the past several years. We can take some comfort noting that with projected earnings of $6.75, Ford's book value could grow by $5.50 in 1995 and perhaps a like amount in 1996.

51. **2 × Price**. Two times the current price in dollars. This item is a ready reference to show what twice the current price is, so that we can quickly see the relationships of the goal prices to twice the current market prices. Of course, the asterisks indicated when goal prices are greater than twice the current price—that is, when the current price is less than 50 percent of the goal price—since asterisks point out undervalued criteria.

We see that twice Ford's current price is $52, which is below two of our five goal price amounts.

Three Keys to Undervalued Conditions

52. **Recommends**. A quick key for noticing undervalued conditions. Every day our stock analysis database is updated with any revised fundamental information obtained, including changes in market price. We print out daily recommended buy and sell candidates, and every week the stock analysis "booklet" is printed. In order to quickly notice buy candidates or a general snapshot of a few of the more telling undervalued relationships, we use a priority system consisting of a number combined with a letter.

The first key gives an indication that a stock:

1   Is 50 percent undervalued by one or more of the following goal prices: P/E Goal (48), Low Goal (53), or High Goal (54).

A   Has three or more of these goal prices greater than twice its current price—sufficient to consider a stock undervalued.

B   Has two of these goal prices greater than twice its current price.

C   Has one of these goal price greater than twice its current price.

Thus, Ford's 1C signals a modestly undervalued buy candidate. You might note that Bear Stearns has no 1 key. That's because it has already advanced in market price beyond being 50 percent undervalued according to one of our goal prices.

The second key refers to a stock's:

2   Earnings' trend, the higher relationships among projected earnings (row 8), current earnings (row 6), and three-year average earnings (row 7).

A   Means that all three conditions are met (viz., projected earnings higher than current earnings which are higher than three-year average earnings).

B   Indicates that two conditions exist.

C   Refers to one condition being present.

These keys represent a crude "trend," given that the earnings momentum or percentage change is not indicated, nor can we tell the actual trend of the three-year average figure. Still, a positive pattern is supportive of a positive goal price ranking and other items.

With our current examples we see that Ford has a 2A because its projected earnings are greater than its current earnings, which are greater than its three-year average earnings.

The third key refers to a few miscellaneous, fundamental relationships:

3   Each stock is checked to see if its price is less than two-thirds of its book value, if its price is less than $15 per share, if it has a dividend greater than 4 percent, and if its market cap is less than $200 million.

A   Means that all four conditions of key 3 are met.

B   Indicates that three of the four conditions are satisfied.

C   Refers to two conditions being present.

D   Is assigned when any one of the four conditions exists.

These third-key parameters are neither that meaningful or critical, but they do suggest certain positives for a stock, based upon several historical market studies. These conditions were more important to me when I began fundamental analysis and many more stocks met the criterion levels. We do not pay very much attention to them in practice, unless they strongly augment a marginally undervalued set of other criteria.

Ford meets one of the third-key criteria levels as its price is not less than two-thirds of its book value and is above $15 per share, but its dividend is greater than 4 percent and its market cap is not less than $200 million. None of the stocks in Table 9–1 meets all four of key 3's criteria, but several do meet one or more.

53. **Low Goal**. The lower of an average of the four meaningful goal prices in rows 47–50 or the **Proje Goal** (row 49), in dollars. In an effort to include cash flow, earnings, projected earnings, and book value into a more encompassing goal price, we add them together (if each are present) and divide by four. In cases where cash flow is not a significant criterion, we add the remaining three goal prices together and divide by three. Clearly, this system tends to overemphasize earnings but we have not found that to

be a terrible flaw, especially when other criteria are included and reviewed. For example, inferior returns on sales, assets, and equity could be a bar to recommending an otherwise undervalued buy candidate based on its earning goal prices alone. If the current earnings are negative we eliminate earnings goal price from the average goal-price calculation.

54. **High Goal**. The higher of the projected earnings goal (row 49) or the book value goal (row 50), with consideration of other elements such as the price/cash flow goal (row 47) and the price/earnings goal (row 48). We also look at growth rates and return on equity percentages.

Ford's average (low) goal price is $50.27, not twice its current price. As a technique, we take the high and low goal prices from the calculated five— usually focusing on the low goal (average goal price, Row 53) and the projected earnings goal price (row 49)—as a suggested minimum and maximum sell limit guide. Ford's current "goal price range" is $50.27 to $57.37, and therefore it is a currently recommended stock.

55. **Apprc Poten %**. Appreciation potential from current price levels expressed in percent. This is another convenience figure showing the relationship of the average (low) goal price (row 54) to the current price (row 4). We can see that Ford's average goal price was 93.35 percent (not shown) above its current price (row 4). Ford's current price has a 120.67 percent appreciation potential to reach its high price goal.

When reviewing potential buy candidates, this figure could be used to compare how much appreciation potential these candidates have according to this system of evaluation. The appreciation potential number can also be the beginning of a search for fairly or overvalued stocks to be trimmed out. If we were convinced that we were entering an extended, severe bear market, the appreciation potential percentages could be a guide for selling short. We have never engaged in short selling.

Note that our two near-sell candidates, Quiksilver (already sold at $24.875) and Vishay, have a negative potential appreciation of their average goal price, although still a small ways to go to reach their high goal prices. If I had to raise some cash (or were extremely concerned about a market selloff), these are among the first stocks I would sell, the least undervalued in a portfolio.

56. **Balance Sheet**. Quarterly reporting times for bookkeeping purposes and to check on when the next earnings report might be expected. In the case of Ford, its DA4 abbreviation means balance sheet figures based on the

December '94 annual report. The first number is the month (1 through 9 plus O for October, N for November, and D for December). The second element is the source: Q for corporate 10Q; R for corporate quarterly report; N for news release (which sometimes includes the updated balance sheet and income statement); A for corporate annual report; or V for *Value Line*. The third number is for the year: e.g., 4 = '94, 5 = '95.

57. **Earnings**. A handy figure showing the earnings information period. This code is also used to show updated cash flow, book value, and return on equity with new earnings information. In the case of Ford's earnings, 35 means March 1995 (thus, we know that the first quarter 1995 earnings have been recorded).

x. **Inst Hold %**. Percent of shares held by institutions. While this figure is no longer displayed on our printout, we may check on it when we are considering recommending a stock. Studies show that stocks widely followed by analysts and widely held by institutions tend not to appreciate over long periods of time as much as those not widely followed or held—the so-called neglected stock effect. We like to see this criterion at a glance from other sources such as Standard & Poor's or *Value Line*.

The 10 Favorite Stocks for 1995

In order to help subscribers in their stock selection, we whittled down the 43 recommended stocks at December 30, 1994, to 10 favorite stocks, distributed in a special report. Table 9–2 displays these stocks with several of the criteria used in our selection process, and is followed by a brief commentary about each stock as published in the special report.

Note the initial P/E ratios, only two of which are over 9.6, with an overall average of 7.93. Seven of the 10 have very-small-(micro-)market capitalizations, while six of the 10 pay no dividends. Only two stocks have returns on equities of less than 13.2 percent, but these issues, Hyde Athletic "B" shares and Liuski International, were trading below their book values. Only two stocks are trading for price/sales ratios of greater than 50 percent (0.50). Perhaps this selection is overskewed toward very-small-cap stocks, yet we do not hesitate to recommend large- and mid-cap stocks when we find them undervalued.

BGS Systems (BGSS) develops and markets the Best/1® line of software products aimed at managing the performance of mainframe and distributed client/server computer systems. Despite consistent earnings growth, BGSS owns a P/E below 10, even though it pays a hefty year-end special dividend in addition to its ample $0.25 per share quarterly dividend. Because we expect at least $2.25 a

Table 9-2. The Prudent Speculator's Favorite Stocks for 1995 and Beyond

Symbol	Company	Exchange	Price	Target	YrHigh	YrLow	P/E	P/CF	P/SR	BV	ROE	Yield	MC
BGSS	BGS Systems	OTC	$22.00	$49.00	$29.00	$20.50	9.6	8.6	2.03	$5.34	43.1	4.55%	68
BSC	Bear Stearns	NYSE	15.38	34.00	23.50	14.75	6.5	nmf	0.50	14.35	16.5	3.90	1744
CIS	Concord Fabrics	ASE	7.13	18.00	10.63	6.75	4.6	3.4	0.13	11.86	13.2	nmf	26
F	Ford Motor	NYSE	27.88	55.00	35.06	25.63	6.1	2.3	0.29	15.70	29.2	3.73	28349
GNA	Gainsco	ASE	8.25	18.00	9.38	7.50	11.3	nmf	1.79	3.98	18.3	0.48	161
HYDEB	Hyde Athletic	OTC	4.75	11.00	7.38	4.25	17.0	11.9	0.30	7.23	3.9	nmf	30
LSKI	Liuski Int'l	OTC	4.13	11.00	13.63	3.88	7.6	6.3	0.05	6.43	8.4	nmf	18
PATK	Patrick Inds	OTC	8.00	27.00	15.63	7.75	6.1	4.6	0.16	6.87	19.2	nmf	49
TXHI	THT Inc	SmallCap	1.00	3.00	1.69	0.94	4.2	2.4	0.26	0.65	36.9	nmf	5
WDC	Western Digital	NYSE	16.75	35.00	20.38	8.63	6.3	4.6	0.44	7.15	36.9	nmf	752

Price = Closing Price 12/30/94

YrHigh = 52-Week High

P/E = Price to Earnings Ratio

P/SR = Price to Sales Ratio

ROE = Return on Equity

MC = Market Capitalization ($Millions)

Target = 3- to 5-Year Potential Goal Price

YrLow = 52-Week Low

P/CF = Price to Cash Flow Ratio

BV = Per Share Book Value

Yield = Dividend Yield

nmf = Not a Meaningful Figure

share in dividends in '95, BGSS now actually yields over 10 percent, making it an immense bargain up to $24.625.

Bear Stearns (BSC) is a leader, worldwide, in investment banking, securities trading, and brokerage services. Although earnings per share are expected to decline in the near term from the record $2.89 tallied in fiscal '94 (ended June 1994) due to weakness in the stock and bond markets, we think BSC shares are approaching bottom after tumbling 26 percent in value during '94. Because we expect it to earn as much as $5 per share by 1998, we view BSC as a fine long-term holding. Trading near book value and yielding 4 percent, we deem BSC a buy below $17.

Concord Fabrics (CIS) develops, designs, styles, produces, and markets woven and knitted fabrics of natural and synthetic fibers in a wide variety of colors and patterns for sale to manufacturers (primarily of women's apparel) and to retailers for resale to the home sewing market. Greater customer demand and better margins have boosted current operating earnings per share to $1.56, giving CIS a P/E of less than five. Because it also trades below book value and for just 12 percent of sales, we find CIS to be a very cheap stock below $9.

Ford Motor (F) is the second-largest U.S. automobile manufacturer. F has registered red-hot, record results of late as automobile demand remains extremely strong. Earnings per share are expected to climb above $5 in '95, despite rising interest rates. Yet F now trades for under six times the '95 estimate. Because we think it will trade for more than $55 before the current boom in auto sales ends, we would acquire decent-yielding (3.73 percent) F up to $30, as it owns a P/CF ratio of just two.

Gainsco (GNA) is a small, A.M. Best-rated "A+" (Superior) property and casualty insurer specializing in underwriting excess and surplus lines. Despite posting record earnings in each of the last nine years and achieving a better than 22 percent return on beginning stockholders equity in each of those years, GNA now trades for less than 10 times our '95 earnings estimate while owning a clean, conservatively managed balance sheet. GNA is among our favorite stocks up to $9.375.

Hyde Athletic "B" (HYDEB) designs, produces, and markets a broad line of performance-oriented athletic shoes for adults and outdoor recreational products for children and young adults. Brand names include Saucony and Brookfield. Despite recently announcing good news—it began shipping orders for its Disney licensed *Lion King* roller skates and accessories and unveiled a stock buyback plan for up to 8 percent of its shares—HYDEB still languishes below book value. We rate it a buy up to $5.95.

Liuski International (LSKI) is a wholesale distributor of 1,500+ brand-name micro-computer peripherals, components, and accessories through 11 sales locations in the United States, Canada, and Hong Kong. Although a $1 to $1.5 million inventory writedown will cause Liuski to post its first ever loss in the fourth quarter (ended December 1994), it has become extremely undervalued, thanks to a 63 percent share price plunge during '94. Now trading below book value with a P/SR of just 5 percent, we like LSKI below $5.875.

Patrick Industries (PATK) is a distributor and manufacturer of building products to the manufactured housing and recreational vehicle industries. Business is booming in PATK's markets, propelling ahead '94 nine-month revenues and net income of 31 percent and 57 percent, respectively, compared to '93. The stock market has overlooked this strong showing, however, as PATK now trades for just 15 percent of sales, less than five times cash flow and only six times earnings. Because it appears quite inexpensive, we would add PATK to portfolios below $13.50.

Tiny **THT Inc. (TXHI)**, through two wholly owned subsidiaries, is a manufacturer of rolled paper sticks used primarily in confection and sanitary health-related products and a manufacturer of various fabricated steel products used on gas stoves and as pail handles, strap hooks, and door anchors. TXHI earned $0.24 a share in fiscal '94 (ended September 1994) and management claims that $0.30, or higher is possible in '95, yet the stock price languishes around $1. We think thinly traded and market-neglected TXHI is a diamond in the rough. Buy up to $1.50.

Western Digital (WDC) is a designer and manufacturer of computer hard disk drives, integrated circuits, and graphics-controller board-level products. After recording red ink for three straight years, WDC posted record net income in fiscal '94 (ended June 1994) while transforming its balance sheet into one of the industry's strongest. With earnings per share expected to hit $2.70 in fiscal '95, we find WDC a bargain, now trading for just six times that estimate. We would buy WDC up to $17.50.

In Conclusion

I wish I could summarize with a simple analogy—for instance, water runs downhill seeking its lowest level, or something equally profound but not so basic. That would be a neat conclusion, but we wouldn't have to go through all the steps above to agree on water's tendencies. In one sense, this chapter means that corporations can be evaluated, and appraised—as an appraiser might value your house or private business—and their stocks selected for purchase or sale based on the outcomes of their analyzed fundamentals.

It means that although a corporation's stock (such as Ford's) is somewhat out of favor today, it nevertheless has a sufficient configuration of undervalued fundamental criteria that there is a good chance that its stock is trading for less than half its probable market price in the next three to five years. It means that we should hold stocks like Ford and Western Digital (for quite a while at least) and be prepared to sell Quiksilver and Vishay, according to the analyses in Table 9–1 and recognized economic and market conditions.

Additionally, by slowly becoming familiar with such numbers and relation-ships as presented in this chapter, we can build our knowledge and expertise and develop intuition about stock selection in general, based on the limited number of stocks that have come to our attention. As the quarters and years go by, we can see how Ford and others (as just a few of many possible examples) develop as corpora-tions and how their stocks fare in relation to that development and to stock market conditions. Perhaps Ford will continue to disappoint and Vishay will continue to advance beyond our "reasonable" fundamental analysis and selling price. Still, over the years and with a large number of stocks, my experience has shown that such analysis leads to a considerable majority of winners, which far overcome the sizeable number of inevitable losers.

10

What's Wrong with Mutual Funds?

I don't like most open-end stock mutual funds. For me, they are a lesser form of investing. I am told that 70 percent of all equity mutual funds do not perform as well as the major market averages. Still, well selected mutual funds with or with-out a modicum of effective market timing may be a good way for some investors to participate in the stock market.

One way to cope with the average underperformance of the majority of mutual funds is to use so-called index funds. Indexed mutual funds are composed of the same stocks and in the same proportion—or a bundle of stocks selected to match those—of a stock group index such as the Standard & Poor's 500, *Value Line*, or the Major Market Index (MMI). The MMI is composed of 20 stocks selected to echo the performance of the Dow Jones Industrial Average, as Dow Jones has declined to allow their indexes to be used as the basis for mutual funds. The realization that one is unlikely to do as well as the market by using mutual funds and thus should be will-ing to settle for at least obtaining about average market returns is not my idea of investing/speculating. As mentioned throughout this book, we expect to do at least 50 percent better than the market without the use of leverage or dramatic efforts.

There are two types of stock mutual funds: *open-end* mutual funds sell and redeem their fund shares at each day's net asset value—often effectuated by writing checks against one's account; *closed-end* mutual funds, are traded like individual shares of stock. A closed-end mutual fund begins with an initial capital position and thereafter its fund shares are traded independently of its net asset value. Such shares are not sold or redeemed by the fund, although from time to time there may be a pro-vision to sell additional shares, terminate and liquidate the closed-end fund, or convert to an open-end mutual fund. Investors should understand that mutual funds are not issued or guaranteed by any government agency. While this chapter is not about closed-end mutual funds, we will briefly review the subject later on.

All stock mutual funds—as well as bond and money market mutual funds—are established for the purpose of making money for their underlying management companies. There is nothing necessarily wrong or unethical with establishing and selling mutual fund shares to the public based upon their track records or professed strategies. Their basic premise is to provide professional management and wide diversification. These are services for the investor who has neither the time, inclination, nor skill to manage his or her own stock, bond, or mixed (including money market funds) portfolio, nor the sufficient funds required for sufficient diversification with individual stocks. There may be something wrong with the merchandising of such funds, especially with the expressed or implied promises of minimal or reduced risk with optimal or superior performance, in spite of the required disclaimer that past performance is no guarantee of future performance.

A great variety of mutual funds are offered, pegged to various strategies. In addition to various indexed funds there are growth funds, value funds, mixed growth and value, income funds, mixed growth and income funds, small-capitalization funds, foreign market funds, and sector funds that specialize in stock selection based on technology, energy, banks, and other specific groups. The Investment Company Institute, which represents the mutual fund industry, classifies 21 major categories of investment objectives.

Each must offer a prospectus to potential investors that "sets forth concise information about the Fund that a prospective investor should know before investing." Said information includes an introduction, description of the fund's investment adviser, objectives and policies, special considerations such as borrowing by the fund, the use of options, foreign issues, investment restrictions, and so forth. There are details about the management of the fund, the computation of its net asset value, how to purchase and redeem shares, the distribution of investment income and capital gains, shareholder services, and additional miscellaneous information.

Most information in a fund's prospectus is written in legalese and boilerplate in order to meet the requirements of Securities and Exchange laws and dicta. Sometimes the prospectus will contain within the same paragraph one sentence that negates another. For example, in The Prudent Speculator Fund, a fund I know something about (but in which, since June 1989, I have had no say in management—to be reviewed later), one paragraph begins: "The Fund does not engage in short-term trading of investments," while the last sentence of that same paragraph reads, "However, the turnover rate is not a limiting factor when the Investment Adviser deems it appropriate to buy or sell portfolio securities."

When Edwin Bernstein and I started the Prudent Speculator Leveraged Fund in June 1987 (its name since changed to eliminate both that "terrible word" and the use of *leverage*), the overriding principle of our fund was long-term investing. Since my departure, the caveat of unlimited buying and selling has been the fund manager's *modus operandum*. I mention this example of a prospectus—not particularly unique in my opinion—which states an overall basic principle while containing a caveat that may eviscerate said principle at the discretion of the fund's management.

It is well known that many people who invest in funds do not read their prospectuses, and even if they do read them, do not understand much of them and are not really clear on the discretionary powers of the fund's management. I am not saying that mutual funds are managed willy-nilly without regard to their prospectuses; usually they are not. I would like to suggest that one fund adviser may manage it to the letter of the prospectus, while another (perhaps his or her successor) may manage it in the spirit of the fund, modified by some idiosyncratic pragmatism that might be shocking to fund owners if they but understood what is actually taking place.

There is an effort afoot in early 1995, sponsored by Arthur Levitt, Chairman of the Securities & Exchange Commission, to simplify the writing of prospectuses, especially in the clarity of their language. This can only be a positive for mutual fund purchasers, if they but read and consider the message of the prospectus and if fund advisers do not deviate from the fund's stated principles.

What's a Fund Worth?—Net Asset Value

To understand open-end stock mutual funds you need to understand the practice of determining *net asset value* (NAV). Ostensibly, funds are marked to the market each day to determine their net worth. This is done by adding the total value of each position in the fund plus any cash or cash equivalents (perhaps 91-day Treasury bills or cash on deposit) and dividing the sum by the number of fund shares outstanding. Thus, if a fund's portfolio and cash was worth $100 million and it had 10 million fund shares outstanding on a given day's close, its NAV would be $10 per share and that is the price shares would be sold for or redeemed that day. The SEC is very strict about accurate reporting of NAV and has taken strong action against funds that it finds to be in violation.

So far, so simple. The NAV, however, is reduced tiny amounts each day as the fund management subtracts its management fees, distribution fees (if any), and miscellaneous other expenses, which when combined are called the *annual expense ratio*. Generally, the smaller the fund's total assets under management, the larger its expense ratio. Expense ratios can vary from under 0.50 percent for indexed funds—which require no advisers to select stocks—to several percent.

Every fund owner should be aware of the funds' annual expense ratios. If the expense ratio is high, between 1.5 and 4.0+ percent per year, you can see that the fund must appreciate by 1.5 to 4.0+ percent each year before breaking even. Considering the long-term average compounded annual total return of larger capitalization stocks to be about 10.2 percent per year, even if the fund did manage with its stocks and dividends (and interest on cash equivalents) to appreciate 10.2 percent in market price a year, its NAV could be up only 8.7 to 6.2 percent, depending upon its annual expense ratio.

Other considerations are probably beyond the scope or interest of most mutual fund investors, such as how the fund is marked to the market. Generally, stocks traded every day are marked at their closing prices, which doesn't take into consideration the bid-ask spread existing for each stock. Over long periods of time the bid-ask spread probably doesn't matter so much. Its effect may be minimized by patiently and successful selling of highly appreciated stocks into market advances. Otherwise, its negative effect may be exacerbated when selling depreciated stocks into market declines. On any given day's market opening and transactions, it is clear that the fund redeemer might not receive the previous day's closing prices of its stocks (usually a bid if the last transaction was a sell or an ask if the last transaction was a buy). In a rapidly declining market, a fund's previous day's NAV compared to the actual value of its portfolio, if it had to sell shares in order to meet redemptions or become defensive, could vary by several percent.

In the case of stocks that do not trade every day or securities regularly traded in the over-the-counter market, marking to the market may be accomplished by valuing them at the mean between the latest bid and ask prices. If these stocks had to be sold, the fund would likely only obtain the lower bid price, perhaps 5 to 10 percent below their mean value. Happily, recent criticism of the over-the-counter market's self-serving, wide bid-ask spreads has led to a noticeable reduction of these spreads, although there are many spreads of over $1 between the bid and the ask.

Then there is the case of "Securities for which market quotations are not readily available and all other assets of the Fund are valued at fair value as our Trustees may determine in good faith."[1] Sure. I doubt that most (or even few) of the fund's trustees meet every day to value not readily marketable securities, or even meet at all for such purposes, at least for the smaller funds' more esoteric holdings, which may be vulnerable to such needs.

So NAVs—which are such nice, neat figures, available everyday for most funds in the pages of *The Wall Street Journal* and every week in the pages of *Barron's* and elsewhere—are not always so neat in their computations and mask the incremental daily percentage decreases of their prorated cost ratios.

---

[1] The Prudent Speculator Fund, Prospectus, February 28, 1994, p. 9. (P.O. Box 75231, Los Angeles, CA 90075).

The Potential for Disaster

Another reason I do not like investing in stock mutual funds is their potential for disaster. I do not mean the risk one takes that a fund will be mismanaged and lose a large percentage of its net asset value or go for years without making a significant gain in value, which is bad enough. I am thinking about the next true bear market, when stocks may decline 25 to 75 percent of their market prices and mutual funds do the same or worse, given the mechanics of public buying and redemption of mutual fund shares.

Most mutual funds keep at least a small amount of cash available for redemptions of their shares, which may be requested at any time and are supposed to be paid promptly. As redemptions or the threat of redemptions overwhelm new sales of the fund, this cash reserve is usually increased. The cash reserve also may be increased as a defensive maneuver if the fund manager is concerned that the market will soon decline or continue to decline.

Here's the rub. If there is a general market decline greater than the tolerance of many fund shareholders to remain invested, redemptions will increase rapidly and new sales will diminish or even dry up. As this mutually reinforcing process begins, the fund must sell enough stock to meet redemptions without the luxury of waiting for stock prices to increase. At first, such sales will probably be orderly and the decline in NAV will more or less mirror the decline in the market or its specific indexes and groups, unless the fund's portfolio contains many stocks that are weaker than the average stock.

As the down market cycle continues and fund redemptions continue at lower and lower prices, the NAV will continue to decline in line with the market and be only as alarming to the fund holders' stalwarts as the market's selloff. Meanwhile, the funds' assets under management will be decreasing as redemptions exceed new sales and the value of their stock portfolios declines. This vicious cycle can become devastating to fund shareholders, even as it would be to individual stock portfolios that remain fully or mostly invested for the whole decline. At the bottom of the next great bear market, most funds will have relatively little cash and far fewer assets with which to participate in the next up cycle because they were forced to liquidate much of their portfolios and pay for redemptions. Some funds, probably many, will go out of business or may be slow in paying their redemptions.

After the carnage, relatively few individuals or institutions will want to buy shares in the surviving mutual funds, given their recent devastating experience. It will take years for a new generation of investors to "discover" the efficacy of mutual funds, as some of the remaining funds show good performance, albeit from a smaller base, in the subsequent bull market advance.

You may ask, "What's the difference in losing 50 percent or more of one's equity in a mutual fund or portfolio of mutual funds versus in one's own stock portfolio?" To answer this question, we have to review certain, individual stock-portfolio strategies and our personalities as investors and speculators.

As mutual fund investing is generally a much more passive activity than individual stock investing there is a tendency for many mutual fund shareholders to stay in their funds through thick and thin. Happily, for example, during the selloffs of '87 and '90 there were relatively few mutual fund redemptions, shareholders having been conditioned to a buy-and-hold forever strategy. Unhappily, most mutual fund shareholders have no idea what their funds are worth on a fundamental analytical basis, and thus are unaware if their fund shares are egregiously overvalued in toto because most of the stocks in the fund are overvalued. That makes fund shareholders more vulnerable to a large market decline than individual shareholders who are aware of the fundamental value of each of their positions and tend to take profits or small losses during vulnerable market periods rather than remain passively holding an overvalued set of stocks in an overvalued fund until it becomes severely undervalued.

The Rise of Mutual Funds

The stock market is changing all the time. Day to day, we might not realize how much change is taking place. With a few years of hindsight and observation, we can easily see that the magnitude or quantity of change can make a significant difference in the quality of the market.

When we peruse the Investment Company Institute's *1995 Mutual Fund Fact Book* we see some startling (to me) figures. For example:

> The mutual fund industry's presence as a major force on the U.S. economic landscape is undeniable. Over the past dozen years, it has grown into the nation's second largest financial intermediary, with $2.16 trillion in assets.[2]

The growth of mutual funds has changed the face of capital markets, affecting borrowing and often decreasing its costs for small- and middle-sized businesses:

> Over the past 10 years, both short- and long-term mutual funds maintained high-asset levels in open-market paper (i.e., commercial paper and banker's acceptances). By year-end 1994, mutual funds owned $268.8 billion worth of open-market paper, which represents 43.1 percent of the market.[3]

---

[2] *Mutual Fund Fact Book 1995*, p.9.

[3] *Mutual Fund Fact Book 1995*, p.10.

Mutual funds have become more important to individuals in recent years. By 1994, household discretionary assets were 15 percent invested in mutual funds, up from 12 percent in 1990. The past 55 years have seen an astounding growth in mutual funds, accelerating in recent years:

> From $448 million in assets under management and 296,00 share-holder accounts in 1940, the industry quickly reached $1 billion in assets in 1945 and one million accounts by 1951. By the early 1970s, the industry was already composed of nearly 400 funds with more than $50 billion in assets. At the end of 1994, the industry had grown to more than 5,300 funds with more than $2.1 trillion in assets.[4]

The skyrocketing growth of mutual fund assets occurred in the past decade, from $292.9 billion at the end of 1983 to over $1 trillion in 1990, past $2 trillion in 1993, ending that year at $2.1 trillion. At the end of 1994, equity funds stood at $866.4 billion. This acceleration has continued throughout 1994 and into 1995. As you probably know, there are more mutual funds than stocks listed on both the New York and the American stock exchanges combined, with a net increase since 1980 of some 4,800 funds. In 1993, nearly 800 funds were started. The total number reached 5,357.

The mutual fund industry is obviously here to stay and probably will continue growing, at least until the next big, bad bear market. The purchasing power and decisions of a large equity mutual fund manager can exert a crucial influence on individual stocks and the stock market. Some analysts are concerned that the mutual fund phenomenon is a financial "bubble" that will one day burst, causing havoc in the financial community. I do not take such a dramatic and pessimistic view; however, I have expressed my concern about the possibility of mutual funds exacerbating the next bear market. To whom will they sell their huge positions?

Are Mutual Funds for You?

The fact that I don't like investing in mutual funds, that I believe each person should develop his or her own portfolio (a personal mutual fund of 30 or more positions), doesn't mean that well-selected mutual funds (like well-selected stocks) are inappropriate for everyone. Their original, valid premises still hold: If you need professional management and wide diversification and do not want to spend the time and energy to do it yourself—even though you likely could outperform most mutual funds—then mutual funds may be the way for you to invest/speculate.

---

[4] *Mutual Fund Fact Book 1995*, p.23.

If you are willing to settle for the gains from indexed funds, perhaps trying some market-timing switching among equity and money market funds or just trying to select funds that perform better than average, good luck. As in building individual portfolios with *Patience And Selection And Diversification And Risk Management* (PASADARM), these principles can be applied toward building a portfolio of mutual funds. The keys are still "Investigate before you invest," and "Understand the risk/reward ratios of your strategy." Need I mention the qualities of eternal vigilance coupled with noncompulsive behavior?

Instead of individual stock selection, you will be working with individual fund selection. It would be nice to do fundamental analysis on each of the stocks in each fund, but that is unreasonable to expect, especially as the reason for buying funds is to avoid such detailed effort.

Many sources describe and analyze funds and can aid your selection. I particularly like the mutual fund newsletters *Mutual Fund Forecaster* and *Mutual Fund Buyer's Guide*[5], two of the several fund-oriented publications of The Institute for Econometric Research (3471 N. Federal, Fort Lauderdale, FL 33306, 800–442–9000). Although not a constant subscriber (because I don't do funds), I have enjoyed and been enlightened by reading some write-ups of funds in the Morningstar Service. I can also suggest *The Donoghue Strategies*[6] by William E. Donoghue with Robert Chapman Wood (New York: Bantam Books, 1989).

If you live near a good library or university business school, you might spend a few hours browsing through their selections. As usual, it is important that a newsletter, book, or service makes sense to you. Alleged performance returns from some service are of little value to you if you can't comprehend them. Many regular stock newsletters also review and recommend mutual funds, although we at *The Prudent Speculator* do not because we have all we can do to keep up with our buy, sell, and hold stock recommendations.

Selecting Mutual Funds

Just as diversification in stocks, industries, and over time is so important to prudent speculation in the stock market, so too is diversification among mutual funds. Some people may think that since a given mutual fund is already diversified, having 30 to several hundred stocks in its portfolio, they need not be concerned for

---

[5] This and the following quotes are Reprinted by permission from the March 1995 edition of Mutual Find Buyer's Guide ($39 per year by the Institute for Econometric Research, 3471 North Federal, Fort Lauderdale, FL 33306; telephone 800–442–9000).

[6] William E. Donoghue with Robert Chapman Wood, *The Donoghue Strategies*, (New York: Bantam Books, 1989).

diversification. However, each mutual fund attempts to carve out a niche with its own particular strategy in the stock market. Some funds are always almost fully invested, the managers believing that, "I'm not being paid to time the market, which is a fool's game anyway." Other fund advisers fancy themselves market timers and may have as much as 50 percent or more in cash when they believe the market is going to take a tumble. Still other funds hedge their portfolios with considerable short selling.

We have already mentioned sector funds, which invest only in specific industry groups of companies. We have not mentioned overseas specialty funds that invest in particular regions of the world, particular countries, or any country (including America) where they can find the biggest apparent stock bargains available. Often, such specialized funds do spectacularly well when the market for their investment concentration is in favor, only to do spectacularly poorly when problems arise and interest in their sector subsides as "hot money" moves on to another area.

As I am not a fund expert, I can only pass on some ideas that make sense to me, that you may not have considered. My knowledge comes from being a fund's portfolio sub-adviser for two years, several newsletters, books, commentaries, lectures I've heard, and, (I hope) some common sense.

Let us begin with the *load* versus *no-load* controversy. As you probably know, when mutual funds got started they traditionally involved a sales fee or load, limited by law to 9.3 percent, although 8.5 percent became a common high load. Most funds in the old days had provisions for reducing the load in proportion to the dollar amount of fund shares purchased at the time or within one year. So, for example, the first few thousands dollars of the fund might carry the 8.5 percent load, which was deducted from the total cash paid, while amounts over certain "break points" such as $10,000, $25,000, $50,000, or $100,000 would lower the load. The relatively small investor could count on suffering the 8.5 percent load, which meant that for each $1,000 invested, only $915 worth of fund shares were issued.

Having to give up 8.5 percent at the outset is quite a burden to bear. It means that the fund will have to appreciate 9.3 percent for the new small investor just to break even in theory, although in practice that 9.3 percent appreciation actually could be taxable. Thus, ironically, *even if the fund had an average year and gained 9.3 to 12 percent in net asset value, you would be right where you started net after tax*. Successful load funds, which over a multiyear period can show, say, 12 percent or better compounded annual returns, claim that the initial load is not important because fund owners are delighted that their investment doubled in seven years or less (instead of six years or less without a load) and thereafter redoubled in the next six years or less, and so on.

Happily, the world of mutual funds has changed, due to the strong competition among and widespread marketing of no-load funds, the best of which match or surpass the best of the load funds in multiyear performance. I strongly urge you to search for no-load funds and forget about load funds, despite their venerable names and decent long-term performances. A motto of the mutual fund industry is, "Funds are sold, not bought." In other words, either a salesperson or a great sales effort is needed to get shares distributed (sold) to potential clients. I suggest that you be skeptical of sales pitches and literature, that if you use funds, become a prudent selector of no-load mutual funds.

Your search may be somewhat compromised by the so-called low-load funds, with up-front loads that vary from 4 to 6 percent, or back-end loads, say of 5 percent, which are reduced 1 percent for each year the fund is held. Such loads may be paid to sellers of the funds and deducted over the years as distribution costs, so that in effect you have paid them but not realized it in the initial nominal dollars invested and the funds' NAV gains.

If mutual funds became my investment vehicle of choice, I would choose them based on the research done in the *Mutual Fund Buyer's Guide* and the *Mutual Fund Forecaster*, coupled with a market-timing, switching technique such as presented in *The Donoghue Strategies*, or using technical market sell signals (reviewed below).

What I like about the *Mutual Fund Buyer's Guide*, for starters, is its "All-Star Fund of the Month" feature (which for March 1995 was Longleaf Partners), its "This Month's Top All-Star Funds" listing, its market ratings in up and down markets, and its "Your Guide to the Buyer's Guide" explication of the various ratings, rankings, and considerations in choosing mutual funds.

It happens that:

> Less than one out of 40 *Buyer's Guide* funds rates above average ("A") or ("B") for performance in *both* up and down markets. Only one out of every 85 funds rates above average in both up and down markets and has a top All-Star Rating of Five Stars for risk-adjusted performance. One of these privileged few is Longleaf Partners.[7]

Right away I see that my population of mutual funds from which to choose probably should be made up of the 28 Top Five-Star Common Stock Funds listed on pages 1 and 2 of the *Buyer's Guide*. In reviewing Longleaf Partners (which I am not recommending, as I have not done due diligence on this fund), many of the considerations and criteria appropriate to superior fund performance and selection are mentioned:

> Strong performance in up markets, a safety net in down markets, and a top Star Rating are not the only attributes of this $960-million

---

[7] This and the following quotes are Reprinted by permission from the March 1995 edition of *Mutual Find Buyer's Guide* ($39 per year by The Institute for Econometric Research, 3471 North Federal, Fort Lauderdale, FL 33306; telephone 800–442–9000).

stock fund. Through the end of February, Longleaf was in the top 10% of all funds for one-month, three-month, one-year, three-year, and five-year return. Its 117% gain over the last five years is nearly twice the 61% average of all stock funds. Its 60% return through three years ended February is *more* than twice the performance of all stock funds. Its one-year gain of +16% is vastly superior to the average 2% loss recorded by the average fund.[8]

Not only do we get the shorter-term and longer-term performance of Longleaf, but we are told of these relationships to the average stock fund. For example, we can deduce that the three-year average stock fund's performance ended February 1995 was something less than 30 percent, and we note that the average fund lost 2 percent during the 12 months ended February 1995. The report continues with performance and baseline averages:

Other favorable points: (1) Longleaf is completely no-load, (2) its Annual Expense Ratio of 1.26% is below the average 1.40% for all stock funds, (3) its Safety Rating of 7.7 is above the 7.1 average of all stock funds, and (4) its Annual Turnover Ratio of 27 percent is one third that of the average stock fund; this means lower trading costs in the portfolio and smaller taxable capital gains distributions to shareholders.[9]

All may not be perfect about Longleaf for every investor; its minimum initial investment is $10,000, and its current yield is a very small 0.9 percent. Thus, from my point of view, you would need about $50,000 in order to put Longleaf in your mutual fund portfolio, because you would want to have at least five funds of roughly even dollar amounts in your account for minimum fund diversification. Perhaps $30,000 would be enough; you could buy $5,000 worth of four other mutual funds, taking an overweighted "double position" in Longleaf without being significantly imprudent. On the other hand, if you only had $15,000 or so to invest, it would be easy to find five or six other superior performing funds that had initial minimums of $2,500 or less. The Longleaf review continues with information that could be gleaned from its prospectus or a conversation with its portfolio manager:

Formerly Southeastern Management Value, Longleaf focuses on companies with market capitalization of more than a half-billion dollars. Portfolio manager O. Mason Hawkins views stocks strictly

---

[8] *Mutual Fund Buyer's Guide*, March 1995, p. 1.

[9] *Mutual Fund Buyer's Guide*, March 1995, p. 1.

as ownership interests in business enterprises. That means he tries to calculate the intrinsic value of a stock based on its value as an operating business by estimating (1) the real economic value of the company's assets, and (2) its ability to generate future cash flow. To qualify for purchase, a stock must be priced at least 40% below Hawkins' estimate of intrinsic value. To aid in the analysis, Hawkins maintains a database of actual sales of businesses and corporations.[10]

From the above information, I can see that Mr. Hawkins adheres to several of the important principles we at Al Frank Asset Management, Inc., employ, and a few we eschew. I am pleased to learn that Mr. Hawkins views stocks strictly as ownership interests in business enterprises. This coincides with our view that our emphasis is on buying corporations rather than just stocks. Hawkins is also concerned with the intrinsic (read fundamental) value of a stock based on its company's assets and ability to generate future cash flow, as are we. While our criterion purchase level is 50 percent of our estimate of fundamental value, Hawkins' guide that "a stock must be priced at least 40 percent" of its intrinsic value is consistent with our approach. Furthermore:

> The fund also gives favored status to companies whose management's [sic] own (or have incentives to buy) shares of their firm's business, that have sound financial statements, and that have the capacity to produce meaningful earnings gains within three to five years.[11]

Wow, we couldn't agree more, especially with Hawkins' three- to five-year timeframe. Finishing up:

> The approach generally produces a concentrated portfolio. At the end of last year, Longleaf owned just 31 stocks, albeit diversified among 19 industries. Ten stocks accounted for approximately 5% of the portfolio, the largest Knight-Ridder at 5.6%.[12]

It's almost eerie to compare our management principles with Hawkins' management when one also considers that our minimum diversification guideline is 25 to 35 stocks apportioned among 16 to 18 industries. We find no major fault for a mutual fund of Longleaf's size (and performance record) with its relatively small number of diversified stocks, although I would rather see 100 or more stocks in such a large portfolio. Lastly:

---

[10] *Mutual Fund Buyer's Guide*, March 1995, p. 2.

[11] *Mutual Fund Buyer's Guide*, March 1995, p. 2.

[12] *Mutual Fund Buyer's Guide*, March 1995, p. 2.

Since year-end, Longleaf has brought in $200 million from new shareholders and cash holdings have increased from less than 2% of the portfolio to 10 percent. For a prospectus, call 800–445–9469.[13]

This final paragraph raises a couple of potential yellow flags. A $900-million-dollar fund that has grown by $200 million or some 29 percent in two months may have a bit of a digestion problem. Have its cash holdings increased from 2 percent to 10 percent because it couldn't find enough stocks that meet its criteria in which to invest or is the portfolio manager holding a larger cash position because he thinks the market is about to tank and he would rather be 90 percent (or less) invested than 98 percent? A telephone call to Mr. Hawkins might answer this question.

The Prudent Speculator Fund

As mentioned before, I started The Prudent Speculator Leveraged Fund with Mr. Edwin Bernstein in June 1987. Here's how it happened. In 1984 a friend of mine introduced Mr. Bernstein to me socially at a Saturday morning breakfast, a routine that had developed among a few individuals interested in the stock market. He was very complimentary to me and took a subscription to *The Prudent Speculator*. Later, Mr. Bernstein became a client. He had made a lot of money buying and managing apartment buildings, but he had a passion for investing, especially in very-small-capitalization, little-known stocks. He would show me quarterly earnings reports cut from newspapers. As time went on he said that, with my performance record and reputation, I should run a mutual fund. He was not the first to make such a suggestion.

My response to running a mutual fund was that things were going so well with my money management and newsletter that I didn't have the time or interest to undertake such an enterprise. I did not know much about running a mutual fund, but I had discussed such a business with Charles Allmon and others and learned that it would involve a lot of legal and compliance work as well as a substantial staff in order to answer questions about the fund, mail prospectuses, and service customers' accounts.

Mr. Bernstein insisted that he would be happy to organize the management company and take care of the "back office" work if I would agree to manage the portfolio. Although I had reservations about this arrangement and working with Mr. Bernstein (I have an ingrained distrust of landlords from my family's experience in the '30s and the '40s), I could not resist the apparent opportunity to expand, make more money, and use my speculative strategy in a larger venue.

---

[13] *Mutual Fund Buyer's Guide*, March 1995, p. 2.

It took a couple years for Ed to get the fund organized, developed as a Massachusetts Trust. Had we started in 1985 or 1986, we would have had two wonderful years based on the performance of The Prudent Speculator Portfolio, our recommended stocks, and the markets' strong advance. We finally got going in June 1987, as it happened, just in time to get creamed in the Crash of '87. The Prudent Speculator Leveraged Fund (TPSLF) began with a net asset value of $10 per share and after two months had risen to $10.60 or so per share. We were able to obtain some $10 million dollars without much advertising, mostly through TPS subscribers and clients of my money management company.

In the Crash of '87 the NAV of TPSLF declined to $6.02 and many shareholders redeemed, though not as many as expected. By June 1989, TPSLF had "recovered" to a NAV of $8.65. It might have done better if Ed had been willing to let me buy more stocks in late '87 or early '88, after the market had bottomed and turned around into a strong rally, but he wanted to keep a substantial amount of cash available for redemptions. This is one of the problems that all mutual funds, but especially smaller ones, face under such conditions.

By May 1989, Ed said he could no longer tolerate my managing TPSLF and took control himself. We had had arguments about my holding undervalued stocks, especially those that had declined or failed to advance much. He did not like the auto stocks and said they were "dead." Unfortunately, our original arrangement called for me to be sub-adviser to TPSLF in the employ of The Prudent Speculator Group. I had signed a document that permitted Ed to organize the management company using the name The Prudent Speculator as a California corporation.

My three-year tenure as sub-adviser was subject to reappointment by the Trustees of TPSLF. Most of the shareholders of The Prudent Speculator Group, the fund's adviser, were friends and business associates of Mr. Bernstein and all of the Trustees were his appointments. Although I was paid as sub-adviser for the year's balance of my three-year contract, I had nothing to do with the management of TPSLF. Ed Bernstein, as president of The Prudent Speculator Group, was able to take control of the fund against my protestations to the Group's board of directors and the Fund's trustees. I was bitter that Ed continued to use my photograph on the prospectus and my name as sub-adviser, especially as his management of TPSLF was not in keeping with my prudent speculator principles. He got rid of most large capitalization stocks and replaced them with very-small-capitalization, often highly-illiquid issues. The turnover rate of stocks in TPSLF ran over 100 percent for the next couple years.

The Prudent Speculator Leveraged Fund did not do well after my departure as its sub-adviser. Although I attended a few annual and board meetings as a 17 percent owner of The Prudent Speculator Group, to voice my criticism of Ed's changes in management objectives, most of his cronies continued to support him.

For a year, Ed blamed the poor performance of TPSLF on the stocks I had put into the portfolio, saying that it was taking a long time to liquidate them. For me, this excuse was patently absurd in that most if not all the stocks I had purchased for TPSLF were highly liquid, especially in the rising market between the summers of 1989 and 1990, before the selloff that began in mid-July 1990.

At subsequent periods, after TPSLF had a nice bounce upwards but thereafter declined, Ed blamed the Fund's poor performance on hot money that rushed into it during its strong rise but then rushed out as it stalled or began to decline in its NAV. Finally, Ed blamed TPSLF's poor performance on the fact that it used leverage. He arbitrarily eliminated the use of leverage and changed the name of the fund to The Prudent Speculator Fund (TPSF).

A couple of the board members urged Mr. Bernstein to change the name of the fund. Clearly, he was not managing it according to The Prudent Speculator's original principles and I was no longer associated with TPSF. Even though I hired attorneys and put pressure on him and The Prudent Speculator Group, Ed refused to change the name. Of course, letting him have use of the name without recourse to recapturing it if I were no longer associated with the fund was my fault. Though we had talked of a document to said effect, I never saw to its existence.

Finally, in 1994, after much disappointment by board members and shareholders of the management company, TPS Group offered to buy back its shares at their then book value, about 31 cents on the dollar. I leapt at the chance, selling all but a very few shares, so that I would continue to receive annual reports and follow the progress of TPS Group and TPS Fund.

I have mixed feelings in reporting that The Prudent Speculator Fund had a net asset value of $7.62 on June 22, 1995. Its NAV has never reached its initial $10.00 per share since the Crash of '87, let alone its $8.65 NAV in June 1989 when I was relieved of managing its portfolio. I believe TPSF has been called the second-worst performing fund over the years of its existence. The net effect is that after eight years, its NAV is still down some 24 percent from its initial value. There have been some very small distributions.

When I check out TPSF in the February *1995 Mutual Fund Guide*, I see Market Rankings of "D" in up markets and "E" (worst) in down markets. Its Worst-Ever Loss was –64 percent between August 1987 and November 1990. Its Annual Expense Ratio is a whopping 4.41 percent, with a Portfolio Turnover of 89 percent and only $3 million in assets.

At almost every investment seminar where I give workshops and speak, I am asked, "Your fund isn't doing very well, is it?" Ironically and irritatingly, six years after I no longer manage its portfolio, I am still associated with TPSF in the minds of many investors. A couple years ago I changed the name of my corporation from The Prudent Speculator, Inc., to Al Frank Asset Management, Inc., to minimize being confused with TPSF, but I guess I always will be, as my reputation was made as The Prudent Speculator.

Things could be worse. According to the July 21, 1995 edition of *The Hulbert Financial Digest*, *The Prudent Speculator* as of June 30, 1995 was the second-best-performing newsletter monitored with a total return of 925.3 percent or 16.8 percent compounded annually for 15 years. Our actual total return is significantly better than that, but Hulbert starts us as 50 percent equity each year, deducts higher commission fees than we pay, and counts our trades when he receives our letter (which is fair). (For additional commentary on Hulbert, see Chapter 8.)

Market Timing for Stocks versus Mutual Funds

Market timers believe they can enhance total returns by being out of markets that are declining and in markets that are advancing. Who could argue with this claim? Unfortunately, many studies have shown that most stock market investors do better with a buy-and-hold approach rather than by trying to outguess the market's or a stock's direction and change in trend. Most of a market's gain is made in a relatively few days and weeks, so that if one is not invested during those days, one will not do well overall. Obviously, you might think that the same buy-and-hold considerations apply to mutual funds as they do to stocks. Not quite.

There is a significant difference between speculating with individual stocks and with mutual funds. Even in a buy-and-hold stock strategy, stocks are bought when they are undervalued and sold when they are fully valued, mostly independent of stock market action. But who knows if a mutual fund is fundamentally undervalued or overvalued unless one does a tremendous amount of analysis? Thus, the diversified mutual fund tends to follow market ups and downs more than an active personal portfolio of fundamentally selected individual stocks, wherein many stocks may trend contrary to the market's general trend. No shareholder can sell specific stocks in a mutual fund, although they can sell shares of the whole fund.

Of course, individual sector funds and individual stocks have their traditional periods of favor and disfavor. They can be bought and sold based on their tendencies and hot or cold periods. Many stocks tend to advance during a down market and begin to decline during an uptrending market. The auto stocks, for example are called early cyclicals. The general reason for this variation in trend—their contra-trend tendency—is that, at market lows, perhaps during recessions, investors begin to anticipate the large profits auto companies usually earn as the economy begins to improve. And during market highs, these same investors (mostly institutions) believe that when auto companies' earnings are peaking, it is time to sell these stocks as their earnings will only decline on balance for several years from then on.

Sometimes, such as in 1994–95, there is a big question as to whether the auto stocks' earnings have peaked and, given the very undervaluedness of their stocks, should be held or bought for more reasonable market-price valuations.

So, market timing for mutual funds is an all-or-none shotgun approach, while for individual stocks it is more like picking off targets one at a time with a rifle. A popular way of investing in mutual funds is to take advantage of the ability to switch from one fund to another in a family of funds, especially between a stock equity fund and a money market fund, which may be thought of as a cash equivalent situation. Thus, when you believe the market is about to decline significantly you would want to get into cash and out of your indexed or general equity fund, which would certainly decline with its index, or out of other stock mutual funds which would probably decline with the market.

One of the benefits of mutual funds is that you can liquidate them with a phone call (although sometimes it requires a letter) either for no cost or only a nominal switch charge, but without paying commissions on each of the many stock issues involved. The proceeds from this liquidation can be transferred immediately into a money market fund that pays the going interest rates. Of course, such a switch triggers a tax consequence, a realized profit or loss (if 31 days elapse before reentering the fund) which must be reported on your income tax return.

How can you tell if the market is going to advance or decline significantly? The best answer is you can't, for sure. However, certain technical indicators are a big help in generally signaling a significant change in market direction. Probably the most commonly used single technical indicator is the 39-week or 200-day moving average. When the index or average (or more than one of them) closes below its (their) 200-day (some prefer a 150-day) moving average, it is often a sign that the market is in a declining trend and likely to decline further. This doesn't always work, and from time to time you will be whipsawed as the index or average reverses and advances, closing above its criterion moving average.

The exclusive use of a moving average—one that has daily closes above and below a long-term average—can involve other inefficiencies. A market or sector may top out several percent above its 200-day moving average. Then, you must wait for a large decline before the daily close drops below its moving average, finally issuing a sell signal.

Then too, the signal to switch out of the money fund and back into the equity fund would be when the daily close (of the index you are monitoring) closes above its 200-day moving average. Again, you might have to wait for a rise of several percent in the index before it closes above its long-term moving average providing a buy signal. Also, you may be whipsawed as the index closes above its long-term moving average for a day or two before it begins to decline again. Still, following consistently such a system is said to produce better results for total returns in mutual funds than the buy-and-hold-until-fairly-valued strategy which is more appropriate for well-selected, individual, undervalued stocks.

There are many methods for timing the market short term, intermediate term, and long term, some of which are reviewed in Chapter 4 on technical analysis. Yet another system that is interesting, sounds good, and is particularly appropriate for mutual funds uses "The Donoghue Signals" reviewed in Chapter 2 of *The Donoghue Strategies*.

A general principle is that higher interest rates lead to lower stock prices, although it might take several months for this relationship to take effect. The rationale behind this ultimate truism is that, with higher interest rates, the bond and money markets become more attractive to some investors than the stock market. Additionally, higher interest rates raise the cost of doing business and tend to lower the profits of corporations, especially if interest rates rise rapidly to high levels. Often, however, the stock market continues to rise as interest rates rise because these rising interest rates are stimulated by the strongly uptrending business cycle and corporate profits, at least for a while. The trick is to anticipate when rising interest rates will cause the market or certain stock sectors to sell off. Donoghue's premise is, "Do not invest in the stock or bond markets when interest rates are rising."[14]

Donoghue points out that interest rate trends typically become established first in the money market, "where people make *short-term* loans at market-determined interest rates on which repayment is guaranteed by *highly reliable borrowers*" such as the U.S. Treasury, large banks, and major corporations. Money market mutual funds account for 10 to 15 percent of money market cash. Over 500 money market mutual funds with over $330 billion report weekly to the Donoghue Organization their net assets, 7- and 30-day yields, the average maturity of their portfolios, and how much is invested in Treasury bills, government securities, repurchase agreements, certificates of deposit, and the like.

Donoghue distributes his Money Market Funds table in a newsletter, *Donoghue's Money Fund Report* (Holliston, MA 01746), and to over 60 major newspapers including *Barron's*. Donoghue has "found the *average maturity* of taxable money funds to be an extremely useful *warning signal of higher rates ahead*." He points out that generally the average maturity is 46 days or higher:

> If the average maturity is *46 days or higher* and there is no sign of a declining trend—that is, the average maturity has not declined during the past three weeks—Wall Street's 'smart money' definitely believes that interest rates are stable or falling.

---

[14] *The Donoghue Strategies*, p. 11. (New York: Bantam Books, 1989)

If the average maturity of all taxable money funds is *39 days or less*, however, that's a danger signal.[15]

For stock and bond market investors, Donoghue notes that "when the average maturity falls to the 39- to 35-day range, trouble is brewing and you had better be on your guard." He mentions that for the two weeks before the October 19, 1987 Crash, the average maturity had shortened to 38 days. Donoghue states that you can make safe returns in the 8 to 13 percent range with long-term bonds or bond mutual funds, but you must learn when to sell them:

> If you want to earn returns of 20 percent or more, with risk only slightly greater than you would face in the bond market, you must learn to invest in the stock market. You need to select the right stock market mutual funds to buy and also learn the right time to sell.[16]

Donoghue tried several approaches, including moving averages that didn't perform as well as hoped for. Finally, the Donoghue Interest Rate Signal was derived using Donoghue's Money Fund Average 7-day uncompounded yields in a 25-week exponential moving average. Back-tested over the eight-year period from January 1, 1980 through December 31, 1987—which contained two stock and bond market crashes, a period of high inflation, and a great bull market— Donoghue claims:

- The signal generated only 17 switch signals in eight years.
- Only four of those were false, resulting in trivial losses.
- The 'buy' and 'sell' signals would have improved your return in each of the 46 stock market funds in the Donoghue fund universe that had an eight-year record.
- The average improvement was 124.41 percent.
- The average fund returned about 14.52 percent a year using a buy-and-hold strategy, with some returning only 8.35 percent, but every fund averaged at least 18 percent a year using the switching signal, with an average performance of 23.69 percent.

Donoghue admits that these are "backcasted" results and can't be guaranteed to predict the future.

You need only two pieces of information to calculate the Donoghue Interest Rate Signal: The current Donoghue's 7-day average (uncompounded) yield of taxable money market funds and the previous week's 25-week moving average.

---

[15] *The Donoghue Strategies*, p. 8.

[16] *The Donoghue Strategies*, p. 8.

Actually it's even easier than that:

> *To calculate this week's Donoghue Signal Number, you just multi-*
> *ply last week's Donoghue's Signal Number by .925 and this week's*
> *7-day average (uncompounded) yield for taxable money market*
> *funds by .075. Then add up the two numbers you get.* That gives you
> this week's exponentially smoothed moving averages, the
> Donoghue Signal Number.[17]

I checked with Donoghue's office (1–800–445–5900, in Massachusetts, 508–429–5930) on April 7, 1995, and found out that the Donoghue Signal Number was 5.05, a sell signal because it was below the seven-day average of 5.58. As chance would have it, many people were on a sell signal for the market for a variety of reasons, but not by the analysis of most moving averages. I must admit that I read Donoghue's book *The Donoghue Strategies* because of writing this chapter, but I have found useful information and ideas in it which apply to stock-market timing as well as mutual-fund timing.

On the other hand, I have not followed Donoghue's methods and cannot verify that they are as effective as he claims. For me, the sell signal of April 7, 1995, was false. In general, I am concerned that as the stock, bond, and money markets change over time, previously successful techniques may become less so. I particularly question whether or not it would be better to take a few relatively minor drops in well-selected mutual funds and avoid tax consequences and churning decisions than slavishly following certain mathematical-mechanical systems. It would take some time to real-time test Donoghue's system and confirm its efficacy, although in the absence of some other proven system I would do so if I were a mutual fund investor.

Closed-End Funds

As pointed out, a closed-end fund begins with the money put up by its initial shareholders. Thereafter, it trades on various exchanges and over-the-counter the same as common stock issues. Obviously, some closed-end funds have better track records than others and have periods of outperformance and underperformance depending upon their professed style of investing and market fluctuations.

A classic technique of investing in closed-end funds is to watch for discounts or premiums in market price compared to their underlying net asset value. From time to time, a closed-end fund's shares will trade in the markets at a double-digit percent difference from its underlying NAV. The main idea is to buy an otherwise "good" (based on its long-term performance record or the likeliness of it outper-

---

[17] *The Donoghue Strategies*, p. 8.

forming the next market cycle) closed-end fund when it's trading at a 15 percent or greater discount to its net asset value, thereafter selling it when it trades at only a 5 percent discount, at par, or for a premium. When you sell the closed-end fund after it advances to a smaller discount, you will likely gain a profit greater than the percentage of shrinkage in the discount, because in the process the net asset value also will probably have grown appreciably.

Again, I do not find this a personally satisfying way of investing, especially as there are long periods when most closed-end funds do not sell at a significant discount. To explore this investment technique, you should consult a book or newsletter dedicated to the strategy.

Summary

Obviously, though I am not a mutual fund speculator and am concerned for others getting trapped in their mutual funds in the next bear market, I can see that a prudent speculator's approach to mutual funds could be relatively successful, probably outperforming the market averages. Now that mutual funds can be easily bought on margin at several brokerage houses, one might even consider developing a margined mutual fund portfolio, not unlike a margined stock portfolio. Just using well managed no-load indexed mutual funds, one might expect to outperform the index by 50 percent or so, after the expenses of the margin interest. Then too, one might be able to enhance total returns in either an unmargined or sometimes margined open-end mutual fund portfolio through the use of market timing, although this is more dubious.

Sector and market cycle analysis is probably more important for mutual fund investing than "bottom up" individual stock selection based on corporate fundamentals. We see in 1995 how high-tech stocks continued to advance in spite of extreme negativity about the stock market. We see how the auto stocks peaked out in early 1994, after the Federal Reserve began raising interest rates, losing some 30 percent of their high market prices before recovering only slightly. With the weaker dollar, attention is focused on multinational corporations' stocks, such as Coca-Cola, that make much of their profits from overseas sales, which are enhanced by currency exchange rates.

Finally, although my experience with Ed Bernstein (and The Prudent Speculator Group and Fund) has helped to sour me on the mutual fund industry, I have considered starting an "Al Frank" fund, of which I would have complete portfolio control. Conceivably, I could get lucky with its timing, launching it after the next major correction.

A

Appendix

TPS Portfolio at June 30, 1995 (Positions of less than $50 omitted.)

Shrs	Symbol	Security	Original Cost/Shr	Total Cost	6/30/95 Price	Market Value	Percent Equity
600	ASTA	AST Research	14.50	8,702.50	15.50	9,300.00	2.0
500	APFC	American Pacific	10.59	5,295.00	4.75	2,375.00	0.5
500	ARTG	Artistic Greetings	5.31	2,654.00	3.50	1,750.00	0.4
200	BGSS	BGS Systems	21.89	4,379.00	32.75	6,550.00	1.4
176	BAC	Bank of America	25.20	4,435.00	52.62	9,262.00	2.0
400	BK	Bank of New York	10.04	4,015.83	40.37	16,150.00	3.5
500	RGB	Barry, R.G.	10.17	5,087.50	17.87	8,937.50	2.0
1,000	BELF	Bel Fuse	7.31	7,313.00	11.50	11,500.00	2.5
350	BOAT	Boatmen's Bancorp	7.85	2,747.50	35.25	12,337.50	2.7
200	BA	Boeing Company	36.91	7,382.00	62.62	12,525.00	2.7
200	SBOS	Boston Bancorp	34.14	6,829.00	42.50	8,500.00	1.9
144	CAL	California Federal	11.35	1,634.00	13.12	1,890.00	0.4
1,000	CBEX	Cambex Corp.	3.80	3,804.00	10.62	10,625.00	2.3
375	CATA	Capitol Transamerica	8.14	3,053.00	19.25	7,218.75	1.6
500	C	Chrysler Corp.	19.03	9,512.67	47.87	23,937.50	5.2
500	CLE	Claire's Stores	11.31	5,654.00	18.12	9,062.50	2.0
387	COL	Columbia/HCA Health	10.78	4,170.12	43.25	16,737.75	3.7
300	CPQ	Compaq Computer	11.93	3,578.00	45.25	13,575.00	3.0
1,000	CIS	Concord Fabrics	5.78	5,783.00	6.06	6,063.00	1.3
200	CNR	Conner Peripherals	24.26	4,853.00	12.37	2,475.00	0.5

329

Shrs	Symbol	Security	Original Cost/Shr	Total Cost	6/30/95 Price	Market Value	Percent Equity
200	CUB	Cubic Corp.	18.15	3,631.00	22.50	4,500.00	1.0
1,100	DHTK	DH Technology	5.29	5,818.48	27.50	30,250.00	6.6
2,000	DSPT	DSP Technology	1.41	2,815.00	6.25	12,500.00	2.7
50	DRM	Diamond Sham R&M	15.78	788.77	25.75	1,287.50	0.3
200	DEC	Digital Equipm't	21.64	4,329.00	40.75	8,150.00	1.8
225	DSL	Downey S&L	12.53	2,818.50	18.25	4,106.25	0.9
500	DYPR	Drypers Corp.	6.55	3,275.00	7.50	3,750.00	0.8
500	EMPI	Empi, Inc.	10.06	5,029.00	15.00	7,500.00	1.6
600	FNM	Fed Nat'l Mortgage	9.02	5,409.80	94.50	56,700.00	12.4
200	FNB	First Chicago	22.64	4,528.12	59.87	11,975.00	2.6
250	FED	First Fed'l Fin'l	15.62	3,905.00	14.62	3,656.25	0.8
3,520	FFHC	First Fin'l Corp.	2.21	7,762.06	17.50	61,600.00	13.5
450	FFOM	FirstFed Michigan	10.71	4,818.50	28.00	12,600.00	2.8
400	FSR	Firstar Corp.	4.93	1,972.50	33.62	13,450.00	2.9
200	FLT	Fleet Fin'l Group	12.79	2,558.85	37.12	7,425.00	1.6
800	F	Ford Motor Company	6.32	5,057.14	29.75	23,800.00	5.2
578	GNA	Gainsco	7.39	4,272.99	9.94	5,744.16	1.3
300	GM	General Motors	33.28	9,983.38	46.87	14,062.50	3.1
20	GMH	General Motors H	35.18	703.51	39.50	790.00	0.2
172	GLN	Glendale Federal	9.04	1,555.50	12.50	2,150.00	0.5
200	GDW	Golden West Fin'l	18.50	3,700.00	47.12	9,425.00	2.1
600	GWF	Great Western	16.87	10,119.47	20.62	12,375.00	2.7
150	HGIC	Harleysville Group	14.68	2,202.00	25.00	3,750.00	0.8
761	HIB	Hibernia Corp."A"	9.80	7,454.44	8.87	6,753.87	1.5
1,000	HYDEB	Hyde Athletic "B"	5.55	5,554.00	4.37	4,375.00	1.0
500	IPLSA	IPL Systems	10.31	5,154.00	6.31	3,156.50	0.7
100	ITT	ITT Corp.	31.13	3,113.37	117.50	11,750.00	2.6
400	INTC	Intel Corp.	29.71	11,883.00	63.37	25,350.00	5.5
200	IFG	Inter-Regional	25.27	5,054.00	29.50	5,900.00	1.3
100	KT	Katy Industries	17.24	1,723.82	7.87	787.50	0.2
403	KBH	K'fman & Broad Home	11.75	4,737.23	14.50	5,843.50	1.3
400	KZ	Kysor Industries	9.61	3,845.24	20.75	8,300.00	1.8
2,000	LSKI	Liuski International	5.93	11,863.00	4.62	9,250.00	2.0
200	MXM	MAXXAM Inc.	12.99	2,597.76	35.75	7,150.00	1.6
800	MCU	Magma Copper Co.	6.09	4,875.00	16.25	13,000.00	2.8
201	MYG	Maytag	9.45	1,900.45	16.00	3,216.00	0.7
1,000	MRI.A	McRae Ind's CL "A"	5.21	5,215.00	6.19	6,188.00	1.4
1,000	MCH	MedChem Products	5.68	5,679.00	8.62	8,625.00	1.9

Shrs	Symbol	Security	Original Cost/Shr	Total Cost	6/30/95 Price	Market Value	Percent Equity
200	MRK	Merck Corp.	29.89	5,979.00	49.12	9,825.00	2.1
300	NBD	NBD Bancorp	2.92	877.29	32.00	9,600.00	2.1
200	NWLIA	National Western	39.91	7,983.00	43.25	8,650.00	1.9
2,000	PFINA	P & F Ind's CL "A"	1.54	3,074.00	2.31	4,626.00	1.0
600	PRN	Puerto Rican Cement	2.25	1,350.00	30.50	18,300.00	4.0
600	PVFC	PVF Capital	11.38	6,829.00	14.37	8,625.00	1.9
1,000	PATK	Patrick Industries	10.09	10,089.00	11.25	11,250.00	2.5
200	PD	Phelps Dodge	32.45	6,490.50	59.00	11,800.00	2.6
100	MO	Philip Morris	49.79	4,979.00	74.37	7,437.50	1.6
400	POLK	Polk Audio Inc.	8.34	3,338.00	12.50	5,000.00	1.1
300	QNTM	Quantum Corp.	11.97	3,590.50	22.87	6,862.50	1.5
400	RJF	Raymond James	15.20	6,079.00	19.37	7,750.00	1.7
25	RYN	Rayonier Inc.	11.40	285.01	35.50	887.50	0.2
400	SB	Salomon Inc.	32.78	13,110.24	40.12	16,050.00	3.5
600	SCR.A	Sea Containers	11.17	6,700.80	16.75	10,050.00	2.2
200	SEG	Seagate Technology	19.14	3,829.00	39.50	7,900.00	1.7
400	AOS	Smith (A.O.)	6.38	2,553.00	23.50	9,400.00	2.1
1,000	SPCO	Software Publishing	5.93	5,929.00	3.50	3,500.00	0.8
200	STJM	St. Jude Medical	25.89	5,179.00	50.12	10,025.00	2.2
204	STO	Stone Container	11.77	2,402.00	21.25	4,335.00	0.9
300	SAI	SunAmerica	8.91	2,671.62	51.00	15,300.00	3.3
440	SFY	Swift Energy	8.99	3,955.00	9.12	4,015.00	0.9
200	TX	Texaco Inc.	36.21	7,241.52	65.62	13,125.00	2.9
1,000	THMP	Thermal Industries	3.92	3,923.00	9.62	9,625.00	2.1
700	UTMD	Utah Medical	7.31	5,114.00	12.37	8,662.50	1.9
200	VAT	Varity Corp.	27.34	5,469.00	44.00	8,800.00	1.9
8	WMX	WMX Technologies	37.26	298.11	28.37	227.00	0.0
100	WFC	Wells Fargo	77.15	7,715.50	180.25	18,025.00	3.9
1,000	WDC	Western Digital	4.93	4,929.00	17.50	17,500.00	3.8
200	WX	Westinghouse Elec.	12.76	2,553.00	14.62	2,925.00	0.6
		TOTAL:		423,101.09		892,041.54	

B

Appendix

All Formerly Recommended Stocks That Have Not Been Closed Out

	Date 1st Recommend	TPS#	Symbol	Common Stock	1st Rec. Price	Price 6/30/95	Percent Change
1	10/05/90	279	AAPL	Apple Computer	28.000	46.500	66.071
2	9/08/78	40	ABC	Ambase Corp	18.375	0.190	–98.966
3	10/09/87	227	ABIG	Amer Bankers Ins	11.875	31.750	167.368
4	1/29/93	316	ACN	Acuson	13.875	12.125	–12.613
5	8/11/78	38	ACT	Actava Group	3.063	13.125	328.501
6	6/05/87	221	AEPI	AEP Industries	3.444	21.250	516.935
7	2/19/82	128	AFG	American Fin'l Group	5.246	26.000	395.663
8	3/07/80	79	AFL	AFLAC Inc.	1.364	43.750	3107.478
9	9/26/86	209	AHM	Ahmanson (H F)	20.750	22.000	6.024
10	12/30/94	339	AKLM	Acclaim Entertainmt	14.375	18.438	28.261
11	11/11/88	246	AL	Alcan Aluminum	19.500	30.375	55.769
12	2/19/82	128	ALD	Allied–Signal	9.700	44.500	358.739
13	6/30/89	257	ALEX	Alexander & Baldwin	35.250	22.250	–36.879
14	8/11/89	259	AMH	Amdahl	15.000	11.125	–25.833
15	7/09/82	136	AMN	Ameron Inc	10.188	36.250	255.811
16	7/29/94	334	AMRC	Amer Rec Centers	6.750	7.250	7.407
17	7/29/94	334	AMSWA	American Software	4.750	5.125	7.895
18	2/24/89	251	AMX	Alumax	10.660	31.125	191.992
19	12/28/84	179	ANT	Anthony Industries	4.603	18.500	301.955
20	1/13/78	23	AOS	Smith (A.O.)	4.958	23.500	373.934

	Date 1st Recommend	TPS#	Symbol	Common Stock	1st Rec. Price	Price 6/30/95	Percent Change
21	10/26/90	280	APFC	American Pacific	7.875	4.750	−39.683
22	9/11/78	40	APGI	Green, A P Inds	2.461	19.750	702.628
23	10/09/81	120	APS	Am President Cos	6.000	23.750	295.833
24	4/03/87	218	ARB	Amer Realty Trust	29.250	13.125	−55.128
25	2/07/86	198	ARC	Atlantic Richfield	52.125	109.750	110.552
26	1/26/90	267	ARI	ARI Holdings	11.500	8.000	−30.435
27	6/30/93	321	ARTG	Artistic Greetings	7.000	3.500	−50.000
28	10/30/87	228	ARX	Aeroflex Inc.	6.591	4.750	−27.932
29	11/29/91	299	ASTA	AST Research	16.000	15.500	−3.125
30	6/30/92	309	ATVC	American Travelers	8.375	17.625	110.448
31	11/16/93	326	AU	Amax Gold	7.500	5.500	−26.667
32	12/11/87	230	AXP	American Express	17.750	35.250	98.592
33	4/11/86	201	AZE.A	A American Maize "A"	9.500	33.875	256.579
34	6/30/92	309	BA	Boeing Co	39.875	62.625	57.053
35	12/12/80	99	BAC	BankAmer(CBK merger)	53.547	52.625	−1.722
36	6/15/84	170	BAC	Bank of America	15.625	52.625	236.800
37	7/09/82	136	BAC	BankAmer(SPC Merger)	12.192	52.625	331.634
38	10/30/87	228	BANC	BankAtlantic S&L	10.870	17.500	61.000
39	11/11/88	246	BCO	Blessings Corp	3.667	12.500	240.909
40	5/28/93	320	BELF	Bel Fuse	12.500	11.500	−8.000
41	10/31/94	337	BGSS	BGS Systems	22.250	32.750	47.191
42	3/26/82	130	BK	Bank of New York	6.396	40.375	531.254
43	6/30/94	333	BMCS	BMC Software	43.750	77.250	76.571
44	5/29/81	111	BOAT	Boatmen's Banc	5.214	35.250	576.000
45	10/26/90	280	BOSA	Boston Acoustics	8.125	19.000	133.846
46	5/27/88	238	BS	Bethlehem Steel	19.125	16.250	−15.033
47	10/30/87	228	BSC	Bear Stearns	6.682	21.375	219.887
48	5/27/88	238	BVFS	Bay View Capital	17.000	27.250	60.294
49	12/30/83	162	C	Chrysler Corp	12.278	47.875	289.925
50	9/14/90	278	CA	Computer Associates	5.750	67.500	1073.913
51	5/25/84	169	CAL	Calif. Fed Bank	63.125	13.125	−79.208
52	3/17/89	252	CANXA	Cannon Express "A"	2.550	13.250	419.608
53	3/17/89	252	CANXB	Cannon Express "B"	2.550	11.625	355.882
54	10/05/90	279	CATA	Capitol TransAmer	8.133	19.250	136.680
55	5/31/95	344	CAV	Cavalier Homes	11.125	11.750	5.618
56	5/15/92	307	CBEX	Cambex Corp.	12.000	10.625	−11.458
57	10/30/87	228	CCI	Citicorp	20.250	57.875	185.802
58	10/30/87	228	CDO	Comdisco	16.071	30.375	89.000
59	2/19/82	128	CDX	Catellus Develop.	9.839	6.375	−35.207
60	8/28/87	225	CHCR	Chancellor Corp	7.750	0.063	−99.194

	Date 1st Recommend	TPS#	Symbol	Common Stock	1st Rec. Price	Price 6/30/95	Percent Change
61	10/19/84	176	CHRZ	Computer Horizons	1.704	16.000	839.131
62	3/26/82	130	CI	CIGNA Corp	50.375	77.625	54.094
63	11/20/87	229	CIS	Concord Fabrics	3.750	6.063	61.667
64	11/20/87	229	CIS.B	Concord Fabrics "B"	3.750	6.000	60.000
65	12/07/90	282	CLE	Claire's Stores	9.125	18.125	98.630
66	8/24/90	277	CLF	Cleveland Cliffs	23.000	38.500	67.391
67	1/31/95	340	CMB	Chase Manhattan	33.125	47.000	41.887
68	8/24/90	277	CMIC	California Microwave	6.875	25.063	264.545
69	8/31/92	311	CMY	Community Psych	9.500	11.250	18.421
70	3/22/91	287	CNR	Conner Peripherals	24.500	12.375	−49.490
71	9/08/78	40	CNV	City Investing	0.875	nmf	
72	10/09/87	227	COFD	Collective Bancorp	5.438	20.250	272.414
73	6/13/86	204	COL	Columbia/HCA Health	13.685	43.250	216.034
74	1/13/78	23	CP	Canadian Pacific	5.000	17.375	247.500
75	5/03/91	289	CPQ	Compaq Computer	16.792	45.250	169.479
76	6/30/94	333	CRFT	Craftmade Int'l	8.938	8.000	−10.490
77	2/26/93	317	CRH	Coram Healthcare	27.778	14.125	−49.150
78	9/18/87	226	CSA	Coast Savings	18.375	20.625	12.245
79	7/29/94	334	CSYI	Circuit Systems	5.750	3.375	−41.304
80	8/17/84	173	CUB	Cubic Corp	17.250	22.500	30.435
81	11/29/91	299	CVB	CVB Financial	6.574	12.750	93.946
82	2/28/95	341	CVCO	Cavco Industries	10.000	10.000	0.000
83	2/24/89	251	CYM	Cyprus Amax Minerals	14.840	28.500	92.043
84	1/12/79	49	DAL	Delta Air Lines	24.092	73.750	206.118
85	8/27/82	139	DBRSY	DeBeers Consol	4.125	25.875	527.273
86	5/27/88	238	DEC	Digital Equipment	100.125	40.750	−59.301
87	6/30/93	321	DELL	Dell Computer	18.750	60.125	220.667
88	5/24/91	290	DFLX	Dataflex	11.500	7.625	−33.696
89	1/09/87	214	DHTK	DH Technology	5.000	27.500	450.000
90	11/11/88	246	DRM	Diamond Sham R&M	15.000	25.750	71.667
91	8/07/87	224	DSL	Downey Financial	12.833	18.250	42.208
92	12/07/90	282	DSPT	DSP Technology	1.063	6.250	488.235
93	9/30/94	336	DTM	Dataram Corp	4.625	5.375	16.216
94	11/20/87	229	DWD	Dean Witter Discover	24.051	47.000	95.420
95	6/14/85	187	DXYN	Dixie Yarns	4.784	6.750	41.092
96	1/31/95	340	DYPR	Drypers	10.625	7.500	−29.412
97	10/30/87	228	DYTC	Dynatech	8.500	18.750	120.588
98	12/11/87	230	ECOL	American Ecology	6.500	5.000	−23.077
99	9/26/86	209	ELCN	Elco Industries	9.500	18.688	96.711
100	4/28/95	343	ELY	Callaway Golf	12.375	15.000	21.212

Date 1st Recommend	TPS#	Symbol	Common Stock	1st Rec. Price	Price 6/30/95	Percent Change
101 3/31/94	330	EMPI	Empi, Inc	11.500	15.000	30.435
102 1/17/86	197	ESCA	Escalade Corp	2.595	4.250	63.760
103 9/30/92	312	EXBT	Exabyte	14.375	13.875	−3.478
104 3/22/85	183	EXC	Excel Industries	5.867	14.500	147.134
105 12/09/83	161	F	Ford Motor Corp	6.917	29.750	330.131
106 10/21/88	245	FBO	Fed'l Paper Board	19.500	35.375	81.410
107 7/31/92	310	FCA	Fabri–Centers	12.125	20.750	71.134
108 8/28/87	225	FED	FirstFed Fin'l	10.880	14.625	34.421
109 9/28/84	175	FFHC	First Financial Cp	1.875	17.500	833.333
110 2/08/85	181	FFOM	FirstFed Michigan	7.333	28.000	281.818
111 12/11/87	230	FG	USF&G Corp	29.500	16.250	−44.915
112 2/22/80	78	FIGI	Figgie Int'l "B"	3.833	7.563	97.283
113 2/22/80	78	FIGIA	Figgie Int'l "A"	3.833	8.625	125.000
114 3/21/80	80	FLD	Fieldcrest–Cannon	12.000	21.625	80.208
115 10/03/80	94	FLT	Fleet Financial Grp.	2.406	37.125	1443.018
116 3/23/84	166	FNB	First Chicago Corp.	24.250	59.875	146.907
117 8/16/85	190	FNM	Fed'l Nat'l Mort	6.750	94.500	1300.000
118 8/08/80	90	FSR	Firstar Corp	3.157	33.625	965.262
119 8/24/90	277	FTR	Frontier Insurance	8.527	26.875	215.181
120 8/24/90	277	FVB	First Virginia Banks	14.000	37.500	167.857
121 10/26/90	280	GAN	Garan, Inc.	9.875	16.750	69.620
122 4/24/87	219	GD	General Dynamics	8.313	44.375	433.835
123 5/05/78	31	GDW	Golden West Fin'l	2.139	47.125	2103.132
124 10/30/87	228	GDYN	Geodynamics	8.250	11.000	33.333
125 2/10/84	164	GLN	Glendale Fed'l Bank	225.000	12.500	−94.444
126 2/08/85	181	GM	General Motors	38.803	46.875	20.803
127 2/08/85	181	GMH	General Motors "H"	1.072	39.500	3584.701
128 11/16/90	281	GNA	Gainsco	2.172	9.938	357.627
129 8/07/87	224	GNT	Green Tree Fin'l	6.406	44.375	592.683
130 5/05/78	31	GWF	Great Wstern Fin'l	6.233	20.625	230.900
131 10/05/90	279	GY	GenCorp	5.875	10.750	82.979
132 9/18/87	226	HEI	HEICO Corp	18.750	17.375	−7.333
133 10/30/87	228	HELE	Helen of Troy	3.667	21.000	472.727
134 10/30/92	313	HF	House of Fabrics	10.250	1.125	−89.024
135 8/19/88	242	HGIC	Harleysville Group	9.921	25.000	152.000
136 8/24/90	277	HI	Household Int'l	15.563	49.500	218.072
137 2/28/86	199	HIB	Hibernia Corp	10.326	8.875	−14.055
138 12/11/87	230	HIL	Hillhaven	8.750	28.250	222.857
139 1/13/78	23	HMX	Hartmarx Inc	4.945	5.000	1.112
140 12/30/88	248	HOC	Holly Corp	9.500	23.125	143.421

	Date 1st Recommend	TPS#	Symbol	Common Stock	1st Rec. Price	Price 6/30/95	Percent Change
141	9/14/90	278	HRS	Harris Corp.	23.688	51.625	117.942
142	10/26/90	280	HST	C.H. Heist	4.833	8.125	68.103
143	5/24/85	186	HYDEA	Hyde Athletic "A"	2.625	4.000	52.381
144	5/24/85	186	HYDEB	Hyde Athletic "B"	2.625	4.375	66.667
145	10/23/81	121	IAD	Inland Steel	23.250	30.500	31.183
146	9/30/92	312	IASG	Intl Airline Sup.	5.250	0.438	–91.667
147	9/05/86	208	IFG	Inter–Reg Fin'l	13.750	29.500	114.545
148	12/02/88	247	INDB	Indep Bank Corp	11.250	6.938	–38.333
149	4/29/94	331	INTC	Intel Corp.	30.500	63.375	107.787
150	8/24/90	277	IPLSA	IPL Systems	7.500	6.313	–15.833
151	8/11/89	259	IRDVE	Intl Rsrch & Devel	7.625	0.750	–90.164
152	8/03/84	172	ITT	ITT Corp	22.903	117.500	413.025
153	1/17/86	197	JII	Johnston Inds	2.815	7.875	179.770
154	11/20/87	229	JPM	Morgan (J P)	34.375	70.125	104.000
155	3/07/80	79	KBH	Kaufman&Broad Home	2.754	14.500	426.507
156	9/18/87	226	KLM	KLM Royal Dutch	25.625	32.625	27.317
157	3/21/80	80	KM	K–Mart Inc	6.250	14.625	134.000
158	2/19/82	128	KREG	Koll Real Estate	19.625	0.344	–98.248
159	3/31/95	342	KSWS	K–Swiss	15.000	13.000	–13.333
160	12/28/79	74	KZ	Kysor Industrial	5.813	20.750	256.959
161	12/11/87	230	LEH	Lehman Brothers	20.000	21.875	9.375
162	10/30/87	228	LMS	Lamson & Sessions	5.375	5.750	6.977
163	10/02/86	209	LMT	Lockheed–Martin	27.991	63.125	125.521
164	10/30/87	228	LNDL	Lindal Cedar Homes	2.732	3.750	37.259
165	11/30/93	326	LSKI	Liuski Int'l	10.750	4.625	–56.977
166	4/15/88	236	LUR	Luria(L) & Son	10.125	7.250	–28.395
167	10/29/93	325	MCH	MedChem Products	6.625	8.625	30.189
168	4/07/89	253	MCU	Magma Copper	5.875	16.250	176.596
169	10/30/87	228	MDBK	Medford Savings	5.625	18.500	228.889
170	2/28/94	329	MKC	Marion Merrell Dow	16.500	25.500	54.545
171	1/26/90	267	MLE	Martin Lawrence	7.500	0.688	–90.833
172	7/08/88	240	MO	Philip Morris	21.344	74.375	248.463
173	5/24/91	290	MRCY	Mercury General	14.250	34.375	141.228
174	7/17/87	223	MRI.A	A McRae Inds "A"	6.250	6.188	–1.000
175	7/30/93	322	MRK	Merck & Co.	30.625	49.125	60.408
176	11/30/94	338	MRLL	Merrill Corp	13.750	19.000	38.182
177	10/19/84	176	MXM	MAXXAM Inc	15.000	35.750	138.333
178	3/31/93	318	MXTR	Maxtor Corp.	7.750	6.375	–17.742
179	12/02/77	20	MYG	Maytag Corp	2.880	16.000	455.556
180	4/09/82	131	NBD	NBD Bancorp	3.204	32.000	898.890

Date 1st Recommend	TPS#	Symbol	Common Stock	1st Rec. Price	Price 6/30/95	Percent Change
181 9/14/90	278	NHWK	Harris Computer Sys	8.750	13.750	57.143
182 10/05/90	279	NKE	Nike Inc. Cl "B"	31.000	84.000	170.968
183 8/24/90	277	NRES	Nichols Research	5.625	17.125	204.444
184 8/21/81	117	NSH	Nashua Corp	9.500	19.000	100.000
185 9/28/84	175	NTK	Nortek Corp	10.500	8.625	−17.857
186 10/29/93	325	NWLIA	Nat'l Western Life	54.500	43.250	−20.642
187 10/30/87	228	NYN	NYNEX Corp	15.524	40.250	159.268
188 2/19/82	128	OLN	Olin Corp	19.875	51.500	159.119
189 1/31/95	340	OXM	Oxford Industries	18.000	18.250	1.389
190 12/30/94	339	PAR	CoastCast	11.750	10.875	−7.447
191 10/29/93	325	PATK	Patrick Industries	10.375	11.250	8.434
192 2/03/89	250	PD	Phelps Dodge	23.938	59.000	146.475
193 12/19/86	213	PFINA	P&F Industries	3.125	2.313	−26.000
194 10/30/92	313	PFS	Pioneer Fin'l	4.000	14.750	268.750
195 10/30/87	228	PGI	Ply–Gem Inds	10.375	17.750	71.084
196 12/20/91	300	PNRL	Penril Datacomm	6.000	4.500	−25.000
197 5/11/90	272	POLK	Polk Audio	9.000	12.500	38.889
198 10/30/87	228	POP	Pope & Talbot	12.750	16.250	27.451
199 1/12/79	49	PRN	Puerto Rican Cement	1.542	30.500	1878.378
200 12/11/87	230	PSX	Pacific Scientific	5.000	18.000	260.000
201 2/28/94	329	PVFC	PVF Capital	10.833	14.375	32.692
202 11/28/80	98	PVN	Providian Corp	4.469	36.250	711.143
203 10/30/87	228	PWJ	Paine Webber	7.556	18.875	149.816
204 3/22/91	287	QNTM	Quantum Corp	15.667	22.875	46.011
205 8/24/90	277	RAVN	Raven Industries	7.333	19.750	169.318
206 11/07/86	211	RAY	Raytech Corp	5.000	3.000	−40.000
207 6/05/92	308	RBK	Reebok International	23.500	34.000	44.681
208 10/30/87	228	RDRT	Read–Rite Corp	33.078	26.750	−19.131
209 10/09/87	227	RGB	Barry (R G)	6.000	17.875	197.917
210 10/13/89	262	RGR	Sturm, Ruger & Co	13.750	32.375	135.455
211 5/15/92	307	RJF	Raymond James	14.083	19.375	37.574
212 10/09/87	227	RLI	RLI Corp	10.000	22.750	127.500
213 9/28/84	175	RLM	Reynolds Metals	14.375	51.750	260.000
214 11/20/87	229	ROK	Rockwell	18.500	45.750	147.297
215 10/30/87	228	RTN	Raytheon	34.625	77.625	124.188
216 3/02/94	329	RYN	Rayonier Inc.	8.387	35.500	323.299
217 11/20/87	229	S	Sears	26.113	59.500	127.858
218 3/07/80	79	SAI	Sun America	1.702	51.000	2896.475
219 4/18/80	82	SB	Salomon Inc.	10.138	40.125	295.788
220 10/30/87	228	SBIG	Seibels Bruce	11.750	1.000	−91.489

	Date 1st Recommend	TPS#	Symbol	Common Stock	1st Rec. Price	Price 6/30/95	Percent Change
221	10/30/87	228	SBOS	Boston Bancorp	14.250	42.500	198.246
222	11/06/81	122	SCR.A	A Sea Containers	7.393	16.750	126.566
223	10/30/87	228	SEG	Seagate	13.000	39.500	203.846
224	2/28/86	199	SEQP	Supreme Equipment	7.750	0.080	−98.968
225	7/26/91	293	SEVN	Sevenson Environ.	11.000	18.250	65.909
226	9/14/90	278	SFH	San Francisco Co.	105.000	4.500	−95.714
227	9/22/89	261	SFY	Swift Energy	10.227	9.125	−10.778
228	9/13/85	191	SG	Samuel Goldwyn	0.000	7.125	nmf
229	8/24/90	277	SIF	SIFCO Industries	8.000	4.375	−45.313
230	8/03/90	276	SIVB	Silicon Valley Banc	9.070	18.000	98.450
231	10/30/87	228	SP	Spelling Ent. Group	5.500	9.750	77.273
232	10/05/90	279	SPCO	Software Publishing	15.000	3.500	−76.667
233	8/07/87	224	SPF	Standard Pacific	12.125	6.875	−43.299
234	9/08/78	40	SQA.A	Sequa Corp "A"	57.721	29.250	−49.325
235	10/05/90	279	SRCE	1st Source	6.796	29.250	330.430
236	4/29/94	331	SSPE	Software Spectrum	13.750	20.750	50.909
237	10/29/93	325	STJM	St. Jude Medical	28.000	50.125	79.018
238	3/31/95	342	STK	Storage Technology	19.625	24.625	25.478
239	11/20/87	229	STO	Stone Container	20.017	21.250	6.162
240	10/05/90	279	SUNW	Sun Microsystems	18.250	48.500	165.753
241	7/17/87	223	SUPD	Supradur Cos.	9.750	.750	−92.308
242	10/26/90	280	TBCC	TBC Corp.	3.722	10.750	188.806
243	12/11/87	230	THC	Tenet Healthcare	8.313	14.375	72.932
244	10/30/87	228	TIIMP	Thermal Inds	4.750	9.625	102.632
245	10/26/90	280	TJX	TJX Companies	9.250	13.250	43.243
246	12/11/87	230	TMK	Torchmark Corp	15.083	37.750	150.276
247	11/15/85	194	TNI	Transcisco	3.466	1.563	−54.919
248	4/13/84	167	TOD	Todd Shipyards	32.125	6.000	−81.323
249	10/29/82	142	TOS	Tosco	75.000	31.875	−57.500
250	10/30/87	228	TRV	Travelers Inc.	9.223	43.750	374.383
251	12/30/94	339	TSNG	Tseng Labs	5.875	8.750	48.936
252	10/30/87	228	TT	TransTechnology	15.000	13.500	−10.000
253	10/05/90	279	TTI	Tyco Toys	6.250	6.875	10.000
254	12/27/85	196	TUR	Turner Corporation	25.750	10.000	−61.165
255	10/26/90	280	TW	Twentieth Century	9.625	12.500	29.870
256	4/17/81	108	TX	Texaco Inc	28.875	65.625	127.273
257	6/30/94	333	TXHI	THT Inc.	1.188	1.438	21.053
258	3/09/90	269	UFF	Union Fed Financial	115.000	0.047	−99.959
259	11/03/89	263	UFI	Unifi, Inc	6.933	24.000	246.154
260	1/26/90	267	UIC	United Industrial	9.875	7.125	−27.848

	Date 1st Recommend	TPS#	Symbol	Common Stock	1st Rec. Price	Price 6/30/95	Percent Change
261	2/26/93	317	UPJ	Upjohn Co.	28.500	37.625	32.018
262	10/09/87	227	USCG	U.S. Capital Group	33.000	2.500	–92.424
263	12/31/87	231	USH	USLIFE Corp	19.000	40.250	111.842
264	10/19/84	176	USO	US 1 Industries	10.000	0.750	–92.500
265	7/30/93	322	USS	U.S. Surgical	22.875	20.750	–9.290
266	12/31/93	327	UTMD	Utah Medical	7.875	12.375	57.143
267	11/14/80	97	VAT	Varity Corp	51.250	44.000	–14.146
268	5/25/84	169	VFC	VF Corporation	11.938	53.750	350.243
269	10/09/81	120	VO	Seagram Co	4.208	34.625	722.789
270	8/03/90	276	VSH	Vishay	6.268	36.125	476.320
271	4/30/93	319	WBN	Waban Inc.	12.250	14.875	21.429
272	5/16/80	84	WCN	WorldWay Corp	3.813	9.500	149.148
273	10/30/87	228	WDC	Western Digital	16.500	17.500	6.061
274	4/23/82	132	WFC	Wells Fargo Bank	11.313	180.250	1493.300
275	10/30/87	228	WLD	Weldotron	4.750	0.750	–84.211
276	8/03/90	276	WLM	Wellman	20.500	27.375	33.537
277	11/24/89	264	WND	Windmere Corp	12.375	8.250	–33.333
278	6/16/78	34	WNT	Washington Natl	16.500	20.625	25.000
279	11/29/91	299	WX	Westinghouse	15.750	14.625	–7.143
280	5/19/78	32	Z	Woolworth Co	5.063	15.125	198.765
281	4/29/94	331	ZOOM	Zoom Telephonics	10.625	7.125	–32.941
				AVERAGES:	15.073	24.588	180.745

C

Appendix

All Formerly Recommended Stocks That Have Been Closed Out

	Date 1st Recommend	TPS#	Symbol	Common Stock	1st Rec. Price	Price 6/30/95	Percent Change	Closed
1	7/11/80	88	AAE	Amerace Corp.	20.375	47.500	133.13	10/84
2	2/19/82	128	AAG	American Annuity	1.801	8.375	365.02	1/93
3	2/19/82	128	ABE	Abex Inc.	0.000	7.875	nmf	6/94
4	12/04/81	124	ABZ	Arkansas Best	4.000	26.000	550.00	7/88
5	2/21/92	303	ACAD	Autodesk	12.687	38.500	203.46	11/94
6	7/05/85	188	ACF	ACI Holdings	9.875	15.000	51.90	4/87
7	10/05/90	279	ADBE	Adobe Systems	19.625	62.000	215.92	4/91
8	10/30/87	228	ADVN	Advanta Corp.	7.250	9.500	31.03	5/89
9	3/12/82	129	AGM	Amalgamated Sugar	42.500	66.000	55.29	11/82
10	10/21/77	17	AH	Allis-Chalmers	23.625	3.625	-84.66	12/85
11	4/24/87	219	AIIC	American Integrity	5.875	0.000	-100.00	11/93
12	3/22/85	183	AINC	American Income Life	10.375	19.000	83.13	5/89
13	3/01/85	182	AM	AM International	4.750	0.000	-100.00	11/93
14	9/25/81	119	AMA	Amfac Corp.	20.250	32.250	59.26	6/87
15	4/22/77	4	AMI	Amer. Medical Int'l	9.636	39.500	309.92	6/80
16	12/11/87	230	AMSWA	Amer Software "A"	3.278	16.375	399.58	2/91
17	9/21/79	67	AMT	Acme–Cleveland	22.250	12.875	-42.13	6/87
18	11/06/81	122	AMZ	Amer. Seating	11.875	29.250	146.32	1/83
19	10/30/87	228	APK	Apple Bancorp	21.875	38.000	73.71	10/90
20	12/05/79	72	AR	Asarco	28.250	20.750	-26.55	3/86

	Date 1st Recommend	TPS#	Symbol	Common Stock	1st Rec. Price	Price 6/30/95	Percent Change	Closed
21	1/17/86	197	ARAI	Allied Research	5.125	2.375	−53.66	11/90
22	2/07/86	198	ARC	Atlantic Richfield	52.125	86.000	64.99	4/87
23	8/19/88	242	ARDNA	Arden Group A	44.000	49.250	11.93	10/93
24	9/23/77	15	ARM	Armtek	6.532	46.000	604.23	10/88
25	7/13/90	275	ARTG	Artistic Greetings	3.417	14.375	320.73	9/91
26	2/19/82	128	ARV	Arvin Industries	6.500	26.125	301.92	6/91
27	9/11/81	118	ASR	Amstar Corp.	21.875	47.000	114.86	2/84
28	10/05/90	279	ATM	Anthem Electronics	17.000	40.375	137.50	1/92
29	9/23/77	15	AV	Avco Corp.	15.000	50.000	233.33	1/85
30	12/02/88	247	AVX	AVX Corp.	15.250	34.750	127.87	1/90
31	11/20/87	229	AWCSA	AW Computer	1.375	0.750	−45.45	6/88
32	11/20/87	229	BC	Brunswick Corp	15.250	17.625	15.57	11/93
33	4/18/80	82	BCH	Bache Group	7.875	32.000	306.35	6/81
34	2/19/82	128	BE	Benguet	3.750	5.500	46.67	3/85
35	11/18/77	19	BF	Budd Corp.	23.625	34.000	43.92	4/78
36	7/28/78	37	BG	Brown Group	8.583	43.625	408.27	6/87
37	4/06/79	55	BHW	Bell & Howell	8.063	53.750	566.63	6/87
38	9/28/84	175	BIRD	Bird Inc.	5.500	10.500	90.91	4/86
39	12/04/81	124	BNK	Bangor Punta	19.875	27.500	38.36	2/84
40	8/24/79	65	BRF	Borman's Inc.	5.875	27.000	359.57	1/89
41	10/05/90	279	BSD	BSD Bancorp	6.500	0.000	−100.00	8/94
42	2/28/94	329	BSX	Boston Scientific	10.395	28.750	176.58	4/95
43	3/22/85	183	BTU	Pyro Energy	8.625	12.000	39.13	7/89
44	6/02/78	33	CAL	Continental Airlines	13.875	6.125	−55.86	?/82
45	3/28/80	81	CAN	Cannon Mills	21.375	50.000	133.92	3/82
46	1/26/90	267	CARL	Karcher, Carl Ent	10.000	10.000	0.00	12/93
47	5/25/84	169	CBU	Commodore Int'l	27.250	0.000	−100.00	5/94
48	1/13/78	23	CCF	Cook United	2.519	1.250	−50.38	3/85
49	9/25/81	119	CCX	CCX Inc	5.625	0.500	−91.11	5/93
50	2/09/79	51	CEN	Ceridian	16.438	15.250	−7.23	7/92
51	7/21/89	258	CFA	Computer Factory	10.000	4.400	−56.00	5/91
52	10/09/87	227	CFG	Copelco Fin Svc.	8.000	8.750	9.38	11/88
53	1/12/79	49	CHD	Chelsea Industries	9.318	29.500	216.59	10/89
54	10/05/90	279	CHPS	Chips&Technologies	7.250	4.250	−41.38	7/93
55	12/12/80	99	CIH	Cont'l Illinois Hld	17.170	0.125	−99.27	3/88
56	5/05/78	31	CKE	Castle & Cooke	6.200	18.750	202.42	11/86
57	9/08/78	40	CKH.P	Collins&Aikman Prfd	180.489	26.488	−85.32	11/86
58	12/27/85	196	CLG.P	Clabir Pfd.	11.375	7.625	−32.97	3/88
59	12/27/85	196	CLG.X	Clabir "B" Wt.	1.500	0.063	−95.83	3/88
60	11/30/79	72	CNK	Crompton & Knowles	1.240	37.500	2925.21	10/91

	Date 1st Recommend	TPS#	Symbol	Common Stock	1st Rec. Price	Price 6/30/95	Percent Change	Closed
61	3/07/80	79	CPG	Colonial Penn Gp.	17.250	35.000	102.90	1/86
62	7/28/78	37	CPS	Columbia Pictures	22.125	73.000	229.94	6/82
63	9/28/84	175	CSA	Caressa Inc.	10.500	15.750	50.00	11/84
64	1/05/90	266	CSTL	Constellation	25.750	8.375	−67.48	6/93
65	5/05/78	31	CSX	CSX Inc	7.710	46.750	506.36	6/91
66	10/21/77	17	CTB	Cooper Tire	0.773	32.750	4134.34	8/91
67	3/21/80	80	CTR	Constar Int'l	6.500	35.250	442.31	1/92
68	12/16/77	21	CUM	Cummins Engine	38.375	49.250	28.34	4/90
69	4/12/85	184	CVRS	Converse Inc.	16.250	28.000	72.31	9/86
70	10/30/87	228	CWCC	Capital Wire	7.500	13.750	83.33	7/88
71	10/09/81	120	D	Dominion Resources	16.313	56.500	246.35	12/91
72	3/26/77	2	DML	Dan River	8.625	22.500	160.87	6/83
73	10/31/80	96	DNA	Diana Corp	5.227	3.750	−28.26	10/90
74	9/18/87	226	DPT	Datapoint	8.000	1.500	−81.25	10/90
75	9/08/78	40	DSO	DeSoto Inc.	15.250	38.875	154.92	11/89
76	2/28/86	199	DTM	Dataram Corp	11.625	24.500	110.75	1/92
77	12/28/84	179	DUCK	Duckwall–Alco	13.500	17.750	31.48	9/85
78	8/12/77	12	DWR	Dean Witter	10.000	50.000	400.00	1/82
79	11/20/81	123	DYN	DynCorp.				
80	12/02/77	20	EAL	Eastern Air	6.250	0.000	−100.00	11/93
81	4/18/80	82	EC	Englehard Corp.	19.107	37.500	96.26	2/87
82	11/30/84	178	ECOL	American Ecology	7.125	22.625	217.54	6/87
83	11/09/84	177	EFG	Equitec Financial	10.625	3.000	−71.76	11/88
84	9/28/84	175	ELK	Elcor Corp	5.625	7.000	24.44	2/91
85	11/09/84	177	EMLX	Emulex Corp.	7.125	9.750	36.84	4/86
86	12/11/87	230	ENVR	Envirodyne Indus.	15.750	40.000	153.97	5/89
87	2/07/86	198	EQUI	Equion Corp.	7.500	9.750	30.00	4/89
88	10/19/79	69	ETN	Eaton Corp.	17.250	64.000	271.01	7/91
89	11/30/84	178	ETX	Entex Inc.	20.250	22.500	11.11	2/88
90	9/13/85	191	EXCG	Exchange Bancorp	3.667	24.000	554.45	2/90
91	12/16/77	21	EXR	Elixir Industries	4.875	10.000	105.13	2/82
92	2/19/82	128	EY	Ethyl Corp.	2.406	30.500	1167.66	4/87
93	10/30/87	228	FBC	First Boston	25.375	52.500	106.90	1/89
94	6/17/77	8	FBG	Faberge Inc.	8.625	32.000	271.01	3/84
95	12/28/84	179	FBT	Fst City Banc Tex	1462.500	22.250	−98.48	8/88
96	11/30/79	72	FCA	Fabri–Centers	2.111	19.500	823.73	2/91
97	3/12/82	129	FEN	Fairchild	12.125	9.125	−24.74	3/86
98	2/12/88	233	FEXC	First Executive	10.582	0.000	−100.00	12/91
99	7/29/88	241	FFA	First Fed America	14.625	38.500	163.25	7/90
100	3/23/84	166	FIN	Financial Corp Amer.	17.000	0.875	−94.85	8/88

	Date 1st Recommend	TPS#	Symbol	Common Stock	1st Rec. Price	Price 6/30/95	Percent Change	Closed
101	7/15/77	10	FM	Franklin Mint	11.125	27.000	142.70	3/81
102	7/28/78	37	FMC	FMC Corp.	24.000	112.750	369.79	2/87
103	11/30/84	178	FRA	Farah Mfg	17.500	10.250	−41.43	8/93
104	3/07/80	79	FS	Fisher Scientific	15.625	55.000	252.00	8/81
105	8/28/87	225	FWES	First Western Fin'l	11.250	9.812	−12.78	11/94
106	1/27/78	24	FWF	Far West Financial	2.958	1.750	−40.84	7/90
107	10/05/90	279	GB	Guardian Bancorp	7.600	0.000	−100.00	4/95
108	12/27/85	196	GDV	Gen'l Development	15.500	0.000	−100.00	12/90
109	7/28/78	37	GDV	GDV Inc.	9.875	20.000	102.53	10/81
110	7/25/86	206	GEMH	Gemcraft Inc.	9.000	0.875	−90.28	8/88
111	2/19/82	128	GENC	General Cable	1.563	6.000	284.00	8/9?
112	7/01/77	9	GFC	Gibraltar Financial	6.917	2.875	−58.44	8/88
113	3/12/82	129	GH	General Host	6.960	17.625	153.23	12/84
114	3/26/82	130	GLM	Global Marine	12.250	1.125	−90.82	6/88
115	8/21/81	117	GNO	Gino's Inc.	7.875	18.000	128.57	5/82
116	10/05/90	279	GO	Collins Indus	2.400	6.500	170.83	3/92
117	9/08/78	40	GORA	Gordon Jewelry	10.188	36.750	260.72	6/89
118	7/24/81	115	GOTLF	Gotaas Larsen	6.000	48.000	700.00	12/88
119	1/13/78	23	GR	Goodrich	19.750	51.000	158.23	2/87
120	11/09/84	177	GRR	GRI Group	5.375	0.000	−100.00	5/92
121	10/31/80	96	GRX	Gen'l Refract	7.750	22.500	190.32	8/88
122	3/22/85	183	GST	Genstar Corp.	21.500	41.823	94.53	5/86
123	3/28/80	81	GT	Goodyear Tire	11.875	48.000	304.21	11/86
124	10/30/87	228	GT	Goodyear Tire	47.875	69.000	44.13	4/92
125	9/28/84	175	GTA	Great Amer Savings	7.083	3.000	−57.65	7/90
126	12/31/90	283	GVF	GoldenValleyMicrowav	10.000	24.625	146.25	6/91
127	8/11/78	38	GW	Gulf + Western	12.800	65.625	412.70	8/86
128	7/09/82	136	GX	GEO International	10.000	5.500	−45.00	6/87
129	10/30/87	228	GXY	Galaxy Carpet	12.750	14.000	9.80	6/89
130	10/ 4/85	192	HASR	Hauserman Inc.	14.750	5.000	−66.10	11/88
131	7/09/82	136	HC	Helene Curtis	3.000	24.250	708.33	11/90
132	3/23/84	166	HFD	HomeFed Corp.	13.750	0.000	−100.00	5/92
133	4/08/77	3	HGH	Hughes & Hatcher	7.000	11.730	67.57	11/77
134	9/25/81	119	HLY	Holly Sugar	30.125	121.875	304.56	5/86
135	11/28/80	98	HML	Hammermill Paper	17.667	64.500	265.09	10/86
136	2/26/93	317	HNSI	Home Nutritional	6.250	7.850	25.60	4/94
137	10/30/87	228	HOF	Hofmann Inds.	2.125	8.250	288.24	1/90
138	8/07/87	224	HTHR	Hawthorne Fin'l	26.000	13.000	−50.00	11/90
139	6/13/86	204	HUM	Humana Inc.	6.311	16.125	155.52	11/93
140	7/05/85	188	HWG	Hallwood Group	19.250	7.750	−59.74	3/92

Date 1st Recommend		TPS#	Symbol	Common Stock	1st Rec. Price	Price 6/30/95	Percent Change	Closed
141	6/14/85	187	HYO	Husky Oil, Ltd.	7.250	8.750	20.69	4/87
142	1/13/78	23	HZ	Hazeltine	3.417	18.000	426.78	8/86
143	1/13/78	23	ICA	Imperial Corp	8.173	0.000	−100.00	12/90
144	8/28/87	225	ICH	I C H Corp	13.125	5.000	−61.90	4/91
145	3/26/82	130	ICX	IC Industries	7.407	34.000	359.03	6/87
146	6/11/82	135	ID	Ideal Toy	11.000	14.850	35.00	8/82
147	8/16/85	190	IDCC	Intek Diversified	2.375	2.500	5.26	12/92
148	10/26/90	280	IFSIA	Interface, Inc.	8.250	16.875	104.55	2/94
149	10/26/90	280	IGT	Intl Game Technology	5.625	29.625	426.67	10/91
150	10/31/80	96	INA	INA Corp.	38.625	45.375	17.48	4/82
151	5/02/80	83	INR	Insilco Corp.	7.817	31.750	306.17	10/88
152	9/18/87	226	IRE	Integ. Resources	29.375	4.000	−86.38	7/89
153	9/08/78	40	IU	IU International	12.000	16.375	36.46	12/84
154	11/20/87	229	IV	Mark IV Inds	3.748	21.625	476.99	6/93
155	10/30/87	228	JAC	Johnstown Amer.	2.500	0.313	−87.50	8/88
156	1/12/79	49	JAN	Jantzen Inc.	17.250	30.000	73.91	1/80
157	10/30/87	228	JMY	Jamesway Corp	6.625	0.375	−94.34	8/94
158	1/13/78	23	JOL	Jonathan Logan	7.417	28.000	277.51	10/84
159	3/12/82	129	KAB	Kaneb Services	13.750	2.250	−83.64	11/88
160	1/12/79	49	KCC	Kaiser Cement	22.750	27.500	20.88	12/86
161	7/09/82	136	KEN	Kenai Corp.	6.625	0.090	−98.64	4/86
162	5/05/78	31	KES	Keystone Corp.	7.083	18.000	154.13	6/87
163	3/12/82	129	KGM	Kerr Group	10.750	9.000	−16.28	4/93
164	9/11/81	118	KML	Kane Miller	10.750	21.000	95.35	2/84
165	4/20/79	56	KOE	Koehring	17.125	37.000	116.06	9/80
166	8/11/89	259	KOSM	Cascade Intl	3.004	0.000	−100.00	12/91
167	3/07/80	79	KT	Katy Industries	12.000	18.500	54.17	4/86
168	10/05/90	279	KWD	Kellwood	8.375	26.125	211.94	10/91
169	11/20/87	229	LADF	LADD Furniture	12.375	13.500	9.09	1/93
170	2/09/79	51	LEN	Lennar Corp.	2.958	36.875	1146.48	12/91
171	11/30/79	72	LES	Leslie Fay	6.875	16.000	132.73	6/82
172	7/28/78	37	LEV	Levitz Furniture	9.813	39.000	297.43	4/85
173	8/24/90	277	LOTS	Lotus Development	18.000	42.250	134.72	9/93
174	5/04/79	57	LST	Lowenstein M.	11.200	63.000	462.50	10/85
175	9/11/81	118	LTV	LTV Corp.	17.875	9.125	−48.95	4/86
176	8/24/90	277	LUC	Lukens Inc	19.083	41.500	117.47	12/92
177	5/25/84	169	LZB	La–Z–Boy	7.000	26.250	275.00	1/92
178	2/03/89	250	MASX	Masco Inds	9.375	9.250	−1.33	3/92
179	4/21/78	30	MCC	Mesta Machinery	21.500	2.875	−86.63	12/84
180	7/30/82	137	MCN	Midcon Corp.	21.000	80.039	281.14	6/87

Date 1st Recommend	TPS#	Symbol	Common Stock	1st Rec. Price	Price 6/30/95	Percent Change	Closed
181 11/20/87	229	MCN	MCN Corp	13.973	30.875	120.96	1/93
182 7/09/82	136	MDR	McDermott Int'l	17.875	25.125	40.56	7/89
183 1/13/78	23	MG	Monogram Ind.	14.000	57.750	312.50	8/83
184 9/11/81	118	MGU	Michigan Sugar	14.125	43.500	207.96	5/84
185 5/04/79	57	MHT	Manhattan Ind.	9.557	18.000	88.34	2/88
186 9/25/81	119	MM	Marine Midland	17.875	83.510	367.19	10/87
187 5/06/77	5	MME	McNeil Corp.	12.125	39.000	221.65	8/86
188 11/30/79	72	MMO	Monarch Mach. Tool	10.063	20.000	98.75	6/87
189 10/09/81	120	MOB	Mobil Corp	27.375	70.750	158.45	10/91
190 10/19/84	176	MODI	Modine Mfg	6.850	27.500	301.46	11/91
191 1/12/79	49	MOH	Mohasco Corp.	5.111	35.000	584.80	6/88
192 9/11/81	118	MRO	USX–Marathon	25.062	28.875	15.22	8/91
193 7/29/77	11	MRS	Morse Shoe	7.800	30.500	291.03	4/86
194 1/13/78	23	MRX	Memorex Corp.	27.375	14.000	–48.86	12/81
195 5/06/77	5	MTM	Marathon Mfg.	8.125	47.250	481.54	12/79
196 10/19/84	176	MTN	Mountain Medical	3.750	6.000	60.00	6/88
197 10/03/80	94	MWK	Mohawk Rubber	13.875	40.000	188.29	1/84
198 10/09/81	120	MXS	Maxus Energy Corp.	3.125	7.625	144.00	8/88
199 10/21/88	245	N	Inco Ltd	20.125	32.000	59.01	6/92
200 11/28/80	98	NAC	National Can	23.250	42.000	80.65	4/85
201 11/18/77	19	NAV	Navistar Int'l	29.125	3.875	–86.70	3/91
202 11/30/84	178	NIN	NI Industries	15.500	22.000	41.94	2/85
203 3/24/78	28	NPH	North Amer. Phillips	12.563	56.000	345.75	10/87
204 11/30/79	72	NSD	National Standard	14.125	9.375	–33.63	5/93
205 11/09/84	177	NSO	New American Shoe	11.500	1.375	–88.04	11/88
206 6/27/80	87	NTY	National Tea	4.125	8.000	93.94	1/82
207 10/30/87	228	NUVI	NUVision	7.750	7.600	–1.94	6/95
208 10/13/89	262	NX	Quanex	15.000	22.875	52.50	1/92
209 2/08/80	77	OI	Owens–Illinois	12.063	60.500	401.53	3/87
210 9/25/81	119	OM	Outboard Marine	6.563	18.875	187.60	8/93
211 12/11/87	230	OMM	OMI Corp	3.250	11.125	242.31	1/90
212 1/11/80	75	OPKM	Opelika Ind.	39.000	8.250	–78.85	12/84
213 10/09/81	120	OSG	Overseas Shipping	13.929	23.500	68.72	12/93
214 11/04/77	18	OXM	Oxford Industries	2.406	47.500	1874.23	4/92
215 4/17/81	108	OXY	Occidental Petroleum	29.625	38.250	29.11	6/87
216 10/23/81	121	P	Phillips Petroleum	12.875	16.625	29.13	4/87
217 8/22/80	91	PCF	PennCorp Financial	8.125	14.000	72.31	1/83
218 4/01/83	149	PCG	Pacific G&E	9.602	26.875	179.89	4/91
219 10/09/81	120	PET	Pacific Enterprises	22.149	44.625	101.48	7/89
220 1/12/79	49	PHL	Philips Industries	2.500	35.250	1310.00	4/86

	Date 1st Recommend	TPS#	Symbol	Common Stock	1st Rec. Price	Price 6/30/95	Percent Change	Closed
221	8/19/88	242	PICN	Pic'n'Save	12.875	11.625	−9.71	2/91
222	6/27/80	87	PII	Pueblo International	3.000	26.000	766.67	6/88
223	8/24/90	277	PIOG	Pioneer Group	18.875	44.875	137.75	7/93
224	10/07/77	16	PIR	Pier One	6.125	16.500	169.39	11/79
225	9/25/81	119	PLA	Playboy Enterprises	8.500	11.250	32.35	12/84
226	10/05/90	279	PLAB	Photronics, Inc.	6.250	35.750	472.00	3/95
227	11/20/87	229	PMK	Primark	3.750	13.875	270.00	9/91
228	10/30/87	228	PMSI	Prime Medical	2.000	3.000	50.00	7/92
229	9/08/78	40	PN	Pan American	10.375	1.625	−84.34	10/90
230	12/27/85	196	PNW	Pinnacle West Cap.	27.250	5.125	−81.19	11/89
231	9/25/81	119	POR	Portec Inc.	11.375	18.250	60.44	12/84
232	3/12/82	129	PSG	PS Group	22.750	36.000	58.24	10/89
233	3/25/77	2	PVH	Phillips Vn–Heusen	1.038	28.750	2671.08	2/93
234	10/05/90	279	QUIK	Quiksilver Inc.	11.375	24.875	118.68	6/95
235	11/20/81	123	R	Uniroyal	7.375	22.000	198.31	9/85
236	5/05/78	31	R	Ryder Systems	6.708	31.875	375.18	7/93
237	1/13/78	23	RAY	Raymark	24.382	9.375	−61.55	12/85
238	11/09/84	177	RBSNE	Robeson Inds	6.364	0.000	−100.00	4/95
239	9/25/81	119	RC	Research–Cottrell	10.750	43.000	300.00	7/87
240	10/23/81	121	RCI	Reichold Chemicals	12.500	33.625	169.00	4/86
241	7/24/81	115	RD	Royal Dutch Petro	16.688	80.000	379.40	10/90
242	1/12/79	49	REP	Republic Corp.	14.479	43.000	196.98	2/85
243	7/30/82	137	RHH	Robertson (H.H.)	23.875	38.750	62.30	12/84
244	4/11/86	201	RHT	Richton Int'l	6.250	1.313	−79.00	12/92
245	9/28/84	175	RI	Radice	8.875	0.750	−91.55	6/88
246	10/07/77	16	ROC	Rockower Bros.	11.500	21.000	82.61	12/80
247	3/07/80	79	ROP	Roper Corp.	2.375	54.000	2173.68	4/88
248	3/12/82	129	RSR	Riser Foods	11.375	8.000	−29.67	10/89
249	7/11/80	88	RVB	Revere Copper	13.500	22.500	66.67	12/86
250	4/08/77	3	RYR	Rymer Corp.	10.593	19.375	82.90	11/86
251	4/13/84	167	SA	Safeway Stores	23.750	67.044	182.29	11/86
252	9/23/77	15	SBI	Sterchi Bros.	9.125	33.000	261.64	2/86
253	8/03/84	172	SC	Shell Transport	15.750	53.875	242.06	10/90
254	3/21/80	80	SCM	SCM Corp.	20.875	75.000	259.28	4/86
255	2/28/86	199	SFDS	Smithfield Foods	5.625	14.000	148.89	9/89
256	2/19/82	128	SFR	Santa Fe Energy	19.607	10.250	−47.72	6/95
257	2/19/82	128	SFX	Santa Fe Pacific	7.130	12.000	68.31	12/91
258	1/12/79	49	SGIB	Slattery Group	16.125	30.000	86.05	6/90
259	6/02/78	33	SHA	Shapell Industries	24.625	65.000	163.96	7/84
260	11/16/79	71	SHC	Shaklee Corp.	6.813	18.375	169.70	4/86

Date 1st Recommend		TPS#	Symbol	Common Stock	1st Rec. Price	Price 6/30/95	Percent Change	Closed
261	5/25/84	169	SHG	Sheller–Globe	n/a	81.500	n/a	11/89
262	6/02/78	33	SHP	Stop & Shop	3.000	39.000	1200.00	2/88
263	10/23/81	121	SHW	Sherwin Williams	1.156	25.500	2104.93	6/91
264	12/04/81	124	SIA	Signal Apparel	4.563	9.000	97.24	10/90
265	7/09/82	136	SII	Smith International	22.375	8.125	–63.69	6/87
266	4/21/78	30	SKC	Skil Corp.	13.000	30.000	130.77	4/79
267	1/12/79	49	SLE	Sara Lee	3.463	42.375	1123.83	7/91
268	6/17/77	8	SLT	Salant Corp.	7.125	12.000	68.42	6/87
269	9/08/78	40	SMB	Sunbeam Corp.	22.500	27.750	23.33	1/82
270	7/01/77	9	SMI	Springs Industries	6.125	34.500	463.27	6/87
271	3/28/80	81	SMP	Standard Mtr. Prod.	2.000	16.750	737.50	4/86
272	4/13/84	167	SMRK	Southmark Corp	6.324	0.000	–100.00	12/90
273	3/01/85	182	SNY	Snyder Oil Partner	29.630	17.625	–40.52	4/93
274	7/21/89	258	SSI	Safecard Services	5.000	18.500	270.00	1/95
275	8/19/88	242	SSMPV	SSMC Inc Preferred	22.875	30.500	33.33	10/90
276	1/18/85	180	SSSI	Servamatic Systems	1.875	0.020	–98.93	8/86
277	9/14/90	278	SSW	Sterling Software	7.000	18.250	160.71	10/91
278	6/30/89	257	STK	Storage Technology	14.000	37.625	168.75	4/91
279	2/10/78	25	SVN	Sav–On–Drugs	7.125	18.750	163.16	11/80
280	9/25/81	119	SVS	Sav–A–Stop	7.875	16.000	103.17	3/82
281	3/23/79	54	SWS	Sargent–Welch Sci.	13.375	33.000	146.73	12/84
282	2/26/93	317	SYN	Syntex Corp.	18.875	24.000	27.15	9/94
283	7/14/78	36	TA	Transamerica	15.750	37.125	135.71	4/86
284	5/18/79	58	TAN	Tandy Corp.	19.750	42.500	115.19	6/80
285	10/20/78	43	TF	20th Century Fox	23.910	68.000	184.40	6/81
286	9/25/81	119	TK	Technicolor	16.625	23.000	38.35	11/82
287	12/27/85	196	TKA	Tonka Corp.	18.333	12.000	–34.54	8/88
288	5/05/78	31	TKA	Tonka Corp.	9.875	14.625	48.10	3/85
289	2/26/93	317	TRCR	TriCare Inc.	2.438	4.000	64.10	3/95
290	5/20/77	6	TRI	Triangle Industries	2.375	32.625	1273.68	7/88
291	9/25/81	119	TSO	Tesoro Petroleum	14.625	7.250	–50.43	8/93
292	4/13/84	167	TWA	Trans World Airlines	8.750	26.750	205.71	3/88
293	12/31/81	126	TYC	Tyco Laboratories	3.094	47.375	1431.19	11/93
294	9/28/84	175	U	USAir Group	28.000	6.375	–77.23	3/95
295	7/26/85	189	UAC	Unicorp–American	11.125	0.313	–97.19	4/91
296	11/11/88	246	UCC	Union Camp	32.000	46.250	44.53	6/91
297	12/24/81	125	UER	United Energy Res.	40.500	41.000	1.23	9/85
298	4/22/77	4	UFL	United Financial	11.700	33.600	187.18	1/80
299	9/27/91	296	UFN	Unicare Financial	10.500	29.000	176.19	1/94
300	11/28/80	98	UK	Union Carbide	5.683	47.500	735.83	4/92

Date 1st Recommend		TPS#	Symbol	Common Stock	1st Rec. Price	Price 6/30/95	Percent Change	Closed
251	4/13/84	167	SA	Safeway Stores	23.750	67.044	182.29	11/86
301	9/08/78	40	USG	USG Corp.	7.657	48.000	526.88	7/88
302	3/07/80	79	USI	US Industries	7.875	23.000	192.06	5/84
303	6/02/78	33	USL	US Leasing Int'l	15.000	68.000	353.33	11/87
304	11/20/87	229	UTD	Utd Investors Mgt	6.750	30.500	351.85	11/87
305	4/13/84	167	VRO	Varo Inc.	10.250	15.750	53.66	4/86
306	10/30/87	228	WGO	Winnebago	8.000	5.750	−28.13	3/91
307	8/10/79	64	WHMCG	White Motor	6.750	1.900	−71.85	4/80
308	2/09/79	51	WHX	Wheeling–Pittsburgh	15.750	22.000	39.68	8/88
309	6/13/86	204	WILF	Wilson Foods	9.250	14.500	56.76	3/89
310	12/27/85	196	WLC	Wellco Enterprises	7.938	28.750	262.18	9/93
311	4/01/83	149	WMS	Williams Electronic	11.750	7.125	−39.36	6/87
312	2/19/82	128	WMX	Waste Management	37.438	40.875	9.18	2/91
313	5/28/82	134	WN	Wynn's International	13.000	25.750	98.08	9/89
314	8/12/77	12	WPI	Western Pac. Ind.	20.750	186.000	796.39	11/86
315	3/21/80	80	WPM	West Point–Pepperell	5.908	58.000	881.72	5/89
316	1/12/79	49	WRC	Warnaco Ind.	5.188	46.500	796.30	5/86
317	7/30/82	137	WSN	Western Co. No. Amer	9.000	0.500	−94.44	6/88
318	2/19/82	128	WTI	Wheelabrator Tech	29.987	50.500	68.41	3/91
319	5/20/77	6	WUR	Wurlitzer Co.	8.750	3.125	−64.29	12/85
320	1/27/78	24	WWW	Wolverine WorldWide	3.250	15.125	365.38	1/93
321	9/11/81	118	X	USX–U.S. Steel	20.942	38.000	81.46	2/93
322	1/13/78	23	YES	Yates Industries	5.250	40.000	661.90	7/80
323	10/19/84	176	YNK	Yankee Companies	6.750	0.750	−88.89	6/88
324	7/29/77	11	ZAL	Zale Corp.	14.750	50.000	238.98	12/86
325	7/09/82	136	ZOS	Zapata Corp.	15.250	2.750	−81.97	6/88
326	6/26/87	222	ZSEV	Z–Seven Fund	23.000	16.750	−27.17	1/95
327	11/04/77	18	ZY	Zayre Corp.	0.959	24.000	2402.61	4/88
				AVERAGES:	17.430	25.889	204.30	

Index

About the Author

Al Frank, a child of the Great Depression, considers himself lucky. He spent his formative years learning a wide variety of jobs. Among them, IBM operator for the Prudential Insurance Company, associate editor of *The UCLA Daily Bruin* newspaper, copy boy at the *New York Times*, linotypist, typographer, and print shop owner. He was also a Las Vegas shill at the old Flamingo Hotel, a university professor, and, in his latest incarnation, a notable investment advisor and editor of the highly rated financial newsletter, *The Prudent Speculator*.

Frank, holds an undergraduate degree from U.C. Berkeley in General Curriculum and two master degrees, one in American Studies and the other in Vocational Rehabilitation Counseling, from Cal State University, Los Angeles. He became a Ph.D. candidate in Philosophy of Education at UCLA, with a dissertation on "The Concept of Consciousness in Higher Education." In the middle of writing his dissertation, the stock market captured his attention, and he made the decision to study in earnest the machinations of the market. This decision resulted in his becoming an avid devotee of Benjamin Graham and Warren Buffett.

In March 1977, Frank began managing money and publishing *The Prudent Speculator*, now in its 22nd year. He is President of Al Frank Asset Management, Inc., and is registered with the SEC and several states as an investment advisor, managing stock portfolios for individuals and businesses.

His diverse, practical, and professional pursuits have made him an unlikely candidate for Wall Street, yet his style has always been to avidly follow his interests and become expert at them. His success in the stock market substantiates that expertise with high ratings over the years from *The Hulbert Financial Digest*.

Al Frank lives with his wife, Victoria Baldwin, in Santa Fe, New Mexico, and his office, Al Frank Asset Management, Inc., is located in Laguna Beach, California. It is managed by his associate, John Buckingham.

Special 15% Discount Subscription to *The Prudent Speculator*

According to *The Hulbert Financial Digest* (*HFD*), *The Prudent Speculator* was the 1st best performing newsletter followed by *HFD* for the past 15 years, with an 18.3% compounded annual total return. These returns were gained in TPS Portfolio, Al Frank's actual margined portfolio.

21 Year Perfomance of TPS Portfolio

Since the inception of *The Prudent Speculator* on March 10, 1977, our model TPS Portfolio, which is Al Frank's actual *margined* portfolio, has managed a compounded annual total return of 26.23% per year, as audited and attested to by three CPA firms.

While past performance is no guarnantee of future performance or profitability, this long-term record includes two years of greater than 50% declines (1987 and 1990), and shows the potentiality for recovery after such setbacks. Our two big declines were largely due to overleverage, a condition we have taken steps to avoid in the future.

Other books of interest to you from McGraw-Hill . . .

SOROS
The Life, Times, and Trading Secrets of the World's Greatest Investor
Robert Slater

On George Soros:
"No other investor has produced better results for such a long period—not Peter Lynch, not Warren E. Buffett."

— Business Week

He has been called **"THE WORLD'S MOST SUCCESSFUL INVESTOR."** Enter the world of George Soros, and discover his 31 most closely guarded trading secrets. This fascinating story of the remarkable life, stunning accomplishments, and unique personal vision of George Soros, the world's premier investor, probes the unique investment philosophies, strategies, methods, and tactics that have given Soros enormous influence over world financial markets. (300 pages)
0–7863–0361–1

STOCKS FOR THE LONG RUN
A Guide to Selecting Markets for Long–Term Growth
Jeremy J. Siegel

"One of the Best Business Books of 1994. The book belongs on every investor's shelf."

— Business Week

Financial expert, Jeremy Siegel of the Wharton School of the University of Pennsylvania offers solid strategies for long–term investment success, showing investors how to understand and interpret the movements of the market over time. *Stocks for the Long Run* includes a detailed description of market performances since 1802—including nearly one hundred original charts and graphs. It also provides a unique perspective on returns and market fluctuations, and examines the economic, political, and fiscal changes that affect the stock market, such as deficits, taxes, and inflation. (250 pages)
1–55623–804–5

THE MUTUAL FUND MASTERS
A Revealing Look into the Minds & Strategies of Wall Street's Best & Brightest
Bill Griffeth

"An invaluable addition to any investor's library. There is no wiser or surer way to become a successful investor than to learn from the masters themselves."

— Don Phillips, Publisher
Morningstar Mutual Funds

In a series of revealing interviews, Bill Griffeth elicits the philosophies, strategies, and formative experiences of 20 of today's most popular fund managers. Some of the top managers featured in this book include Peter Lynch, J. Mark Mobius, William Gross, John Neff, Mario Gabelli, and James Benham. (350 pages)
1–55738–582–3

SHAREHOLDER REBELLION
How Investors Are Changing the Way America's Companies Are Run
George P. Schwartz, CFA

"A must read for anyone who owns or has ever owned a single share of stock in a corporation."

— Michael F. Price
President, Mutual Series Fund, Inc.

This book takes you behind the scenes and details the battles and personalities that led to the ousting of corporate executives of such blue–chip companies as General Motors, Sears, and Goodyear. With keen insight and an engaging, colorful style, professional investment manager George P. Schwartz describes how shareholders across America are asserting their rightful authority to influence the management of the companies they own. (207 pages)
1–55738–883–0